A COMPANION TO THE
FALKLANDS WAR

GREGORY FREMONT-BARNES

FOREWORD BY MAJOR GENERAL JULIAN THOMPSON

First published 2017

The History Press
The Mill, Brimscombe Port
Stroud, Gloucestershire, GL5 2QG
www.thehistorypress.co.uk

British Library Cataloguing in Publication Data.
A catalogue record for this book is available from the British Library.

ISBN 978 0 7509 8177 4

Typesetting and origination by The History Press
Printed and bound in Great Britain by TJ International Ltd

CONTENTS

FOREWORD

Gregory Fremont-Barnes' latest work is a tour de force. He has brought his considerable skill and knowledge as a military and naval historian, a senior lecturer at the Royal Military Academy Sandhurst, and battlefield guide to writing *A Companion to the Falklands War*. The weaving together of fact and narrative is masterly and the end result is a book that will be an invaluable reference and research tool for writers and scholars. But it is also an accessible guide for members of the public seeking answers to questions they may have about the Falklands War of 1982. Readers will find every ship and unit that participated on the British side in the Falklands War listed in this book with relevant technical detail as well as an account of the actions in which that ship or unit participated.

With the exception of the British landings in Madagascar in 1942, the Falklands War involved an amphibious operation carried out at greater distance from home base to intermediate base to objective than any other amphibious enterprise in history, including the Pacific campaigns of the Second World War. A Ministry of Defence Study in 1981 had concluded that retaking the Falklands, in the event of their seizure by Argentina, was impossible; mainly, although not exclusively, because of the distances involved. So not only was the Task Force invited to carry out 'mission impossible', but also, in the opinion of some in the British Foreign and Commonwealth Office (FCO), 'mission undesireable' since it ran counter to the aspirations of elements within the FCO who hoped to hand over the Falkland Islands to Argentina regardless of the desire of the Islanders to remain British. While these views within the FCO did not impinge on the conduct of the campaign, geography is immutable, and distance was to present a massive challenge, especially logistically, hence due regard being accorded in this book to merchant Ships Taken Up From Trade, or STUFT for short.

Anyone contemplating just the array and variety of ships in particular listed in this *Companion* might question whether such an operation would be possible today; just one fact: twenty-three British frigates and destroyers took part in the Falklands War. This was less than half the total number of such vessels in the Royal Navy at that time. Now the frigates and destroyers in the navy total a mere nineteen. As well as providing food for thought, Gregory Fremont-Barnes' book fills a gap that has existed for thirty-five years in the profusion of works on the Falklands War. He is to be congratulated.

Major General Julian Thompson CB OBE RM
CO 3 Commando Brigade during the Falklands War
January 2017

PREFACE

With no single volume reference work on the Falklands War hitherto existing, a gap worthy of filling presented itself, with this humble offering seeking to fulfil the needs of those who desire a single accessible book to guide them in their understanding of this short but fascinating conflict.

Owing to limitations of space, this work confines itself to the British aspects of the campaign, and within that context it focuses on military and naval affairs rather than matters political and diplomatic. While additional space self-evidently provides the opportunity for the inclusion of more detail, every work must retain manageable limits; thus, where readers require further information, they should find the lengthy 'Further Reading' section more than ample.

Many books on the Falklands suffer from discrepancies in timings, either owing to the perpetuation of errors committed in one work and unfortunately repeated in another, or through neglect by the author to identify the classification of time employed by the author, i.e. Falkland Islands local time, British Summer Time, or Zulu Time (Greenwich Mean Time or GMT) – the last employed by UK Headquarters at Northwood to ensure clarity and uniformity for individuals, troops, ships, aircraft and the like both in and out of theatre. In April to June 1982, Zulu Time, identified by the suffix 'Z', was one hour ahead of British Summer Time and four hours ahead of the Falklands, where during the campaign dawn occurred at about 1030Z (i.e. 0630 hrs local) and dusk at about 2015.

Where the text appears in **bold**, this indicates an available cross-reference to which readers may refer for additional information.

In most instances distances are indicated in feet, yards and miles, as consistent with Imperial measurements used in the UK.

In light of the particular interest shown by readers in the events at Goose Green, considerable space has been devoted to this subject, although this is not to imply that this action necessarily carried greater importance than those ground engagements that followed.

Only ships present in the theatre of operations before 14 June 1982 receive coverage here; this therefore excludes treatment of the handful of vessels (e.g. HMS *Ledbury*, MV *Laertes*, MV *G A Walker* and RMS *St Helena*) that arrived at Ascension or the Total Exclusion Zone after that date and therefore – notwithstanding their important post-war service – did not serve during the actual period of hostilities.

For reasons of space, separate entries on the commanding officers of Army battalions and Royal Marines Commandos are not included, nor for ships' captains.

Any errors contained herein remain my own, but are subject to correction in later editions. Readers are therefore encouraged to advise the author where these may arise, as accuracy must stand paramount in any reference work.

Finally, I wish to express very special thanks to Major General Julian Thompson CB OBE RM for kindly offering suggestions for changes, helpfully identifying various errors requiring correction, and for preparing so fulsome a foreword.

Gregory Fremont-Barnes, DPhil FRHistSoc
Department of War Studies, Royal Military Academy, Sandhurst
January 2017

INTRODUCTION

A Synopsis of Operation Corporate, April–June 1982

When Argentine forces descended on the Falkland Islands on 2 April 1982, Britain faced a daunting challenge: repossessing a territory geographically extremely remote from the United Kingdom at a time when most of her resources were not immediately deployable owing first to the country's NATO commitment to the defence of Western Europe and the North Atlantic, and second to its ongoing struggle against the nationalist insurgency in Northern Ireland. Margaret Thatcher's government laboured under the further disadvantage that the Argentine invasion caught it completely by surprise and lacking any contingency plan for repossessing the islands, which lay 8,000 miles away in the South Atlantic. Nor could the armed forces call upon any recent operational experience, for one had to look back to the failed Suez Crisis of 1956 for the most recent example of a major expeditionary operation launched from British shores. In the event, the forces assembled to liberate the Falklands represented the UK's largest military and naval endeavour since the Second World War.

This response the Argentines certainly did not anticipate, and indeed confidently launched their invasion on the basis of various signals from London of waning interest in the South Atlantic – above all, in light of the withdrawal of the Royal Navy's last patrol vessel, HMS *Endurance* – and on the mistaken assumption that Britain would not resort to force once occupation became a *fait accompli*. Britain had moreover yet to carry out its extensive, planned defence cuts stipulated by the Nott Review of the previous year. Yet if Britain found herself caught unprepared, poor planning characterised the Argentine position from the very start, for by invading in early April the Argentines inadvertently furnished their opponents with a very narrow – yet in the event a sufficiently large – window of opportunity in which to retake the islands before the Southern Hemisphere winter reached its height. Such miscalculations – above all the failure of Argentina's military *junta* accurately to gauge Thatcher's, not to mention the British public's, exasperation and resolve – obliged Buenos Aires to mount a poorly devised defence of a bleak and inhospitable possession 400 miles east of its southern coast, leaving many of its best troops behind to protect its long border with Chile, with whom, like Britain, Argentina also maintained a long-running territorial dispute.

The speed with which Britain launched the first elements of the Task Force mark out its efforts at mounting an expeditionary operation on this scale as both remarkable and impressive, particularly in light of the absence of any plans for operations in such a remote part of the globe. In very short order the Royal Navy deployed two aircraft carriers, *Hermes* and *Invincible*, which sailed from Portsmouth on 5 April, only three days after the Argentine landings, while further departures swiftly followed with the requisitioned P&O liner *Canberra* conveying 40 and 42 Commando Royal Marines and 3 Para, accounting for much of 3 Commando Brigade. By the middle of April many of the warships and supply vessels of the Task Force had reached Ascension Island, 4,000 miles to the south – although still only halfway to the Falklands. Wideawake Airfield on Ascension Island would prove itself an absolutely essential element in the success of the campaign, providing a secure base of operations that would assist decisively in maintaining an exceptionally long logistics and command chain.

In fact, while the logistics chain remained vulnerable yet intact throughout the war, its command counterpart proved one of the weaker elements of the operation as a whole, for the campaign involved no overall theatre commander *in situ*. Owing to the essential maritime nature of the operation, the Royal Navy took precedence, with the Task Force Commander drawn from that arm in the person of the Commander-in-Chief Fleet, based at Northwood, Admiral Sir John Fieldhouse RN, who reported to Admiral Sir Terence Lewin RN, Chief of the Defence Staff. Beneath them served the land forces commander, Major General Jeremy Moore, plus several operational commanders, including Rear Admiral 'Sandy' Woodward RN, who commanded the Carrier Battle Group; Commodore Michael Clapp RN, who commanded the Amphibious Task Group plus escorts; and Brigadier Julian Thompson RM, commanding the Landing Task Group, which consisted principally of 3 Commando Brigade, the first of the two major ground formations dispatched to the South Atlantic.

British strategists well understood that success in so distant an area of operations hinged upon an efficiently managed logistics chain. Indeed, nothing less than a gargantuan effort undertaken by the Royal Navy, the Royal Fleet Auxiliary and the Royal Air Force could transport troops and supplies such a prodigious distance, thus sustaining the fighting capabilities of British forces so remote from home shores. To facilitate supply, large numbers of C-130 Hercules, VC10s, strategic freighters and Boeing 707s would be required to convey tens of thousands of tons of freight and thousands of personnel, supported by heavy-lift helicopters to cross-deck supplies and move troops once in theatre. At sea, the Royal Fleet Auxiliary and dozens of Ships Taken Up From Trade (STUFT) transported vital supplies of oil and vast amounts of other supplies in cargo vessels, while the Ministry of Defence requisitioned many other types of vessels, including the previously mentioned *Canberra*, the North Sea ferry *Norland*, which transported the whole of 2 Para, and the luxury liner *Queen Elizabeth 2*, which carried most of 5 Infantry Brigade.

This array of vessels, numbering more than eighty, supported the largest force of warships deployed by Britain on active operations since 1945, including two aircraft carriers (carrying between them twenty Sea Harriers), eight destroyers, fifteen frigates and three nuclear submarines. The critical importance of this naval force – not least its logistic element – cannot be overstated. The Argentines need only have disrupted it by sinking a few key vessels – either high-profile warships such as a carrier or a heavily laden troopship, or several cargo vessels holding essential equipment such as helicopters, spare parts for aircraft, or oil – to put the entire operation in jeopardy. Even without doing so, if the Argentines could simply maintain a lengthy occupation of the capital, Port Stanley, deteriorating weather conditions would bring their opponents' logistic system to a halt and oblige the Task Force to withdraw at least as far as Ascension – thus rendering the renewal of operations after winter a very remote possibility. For with the initiative lost and the mood of public opinion almost certainly dampened by the failure of British forces to achieve a quick, decisive victory at minimal cost in lives, there could remain no appetite for renewed hostilities by the time the skies finally cleared and the seas calmed. In short, an expeditionary operation conducted at such great distance from home waters faced the very pressing constraint of time, for with winter approaching, operations intended to secure repossession of the Falklands could not extend much beyond mid-June before snow, high winds, poor visibility and heavy seas rendered impossible operational sorties conducted by fighter aircraft as well as heli-borne resupply and troop transport.

The objective of the Task Force was to establish an air and sea blockade of the islands in order to prepare the way for an amphibious landing, first by 3 Commando Brigade and later by 5 Infantry Brigade, with the expedition's ultimate goal the capture of Port Stanley, the site of the majority of the islands' 1,800 inhabitants and the location of the principal airfield and port. The Argentines garrisoned the islands with 13,000 troops, artillery and anti-aircraft guns, against which Britain could deploy 8,000 ground troops plus supporting naval and air elements. Yet if the British could not match the Argentines numerically, they benefited enormously from the fact that the airstrips on the Falklands were not substantial enough to enable the Argentines to employ their best aircraft, thus obliging them to launch their Skyhawks, Super Etendards, Mirages and Daggers from bases on the South American mainland about 400 miles west of Stanley. This marked the practical limit of their range, which left pilots only a few minutes of flight time over the Falklands – a serious disadvantage for aircraft such as the Skyhawk and Dagger, which closely matched the capabilities of the British Harrier. In addition to fighters, the Argentines operated a number of Pucara ground attack aircraft that could operate throughout the islands, supplemented by helicopters that, like their opponents, they possessed in insufficient numbers.

From the British point of view, recapturing the islands would require a strategy based on stages: first, imposing a sea blockade around the Falklands and retaking South Georgia (which lies 800 miles to the south-east) to make use of it as a secure base and transit area; second, establishing air and naval supremacy around the Falklands; and finally, defeating the Argentine garrison on the Falklands and reoccupying the islands. Strategists intensively studied the characteristics of the islands to determine the best site for a landing, a task made considerably easier by the expert, first-hand knowledge of the coastline provided by Major Ewen Southby-Tailyour RM, who had sailed around and mapped the islands' periphery a few years earlier. Although the Falklands cover about 4,600 square miles, once the landings occurred ground forces would focus their attention on the Argentines in and around Stanley, at the eastern end of East Falkland.

British strategists appreciated that they could largely ignore West Falkland, for although the Argentines deployed about 1,700 men on that island, the garrison there possessed no amphibious capability to facilitate a crossing of Falkland Sound, the narrow body of water that separated it from its far more strategically important counterpart to the east. Moreover, no jet aircraft could operate from this very sparsely inhabited area owing to the absence of a suitable airfield and ground facilities. In short, Argentine forces on West Falkland stood isolated and static, unable to affect operations to the east. On East Falkland, conversely, about 1,000 Argentines occupied the twin settlements of Darwin and Goose Green, towards the western end of the island, while the bulk of their remaining forces garrisoned in Stanley and the mountains immediately west of the town. There infantry and marines had established prepared positions among the rocky crags of Mount Harriet, Two Sisters, Mount Tumbledown, Mount Longdon and Wireless Ridge, the last of these less than 2 miles from the capital and the final point of the Argentine defensive ring. The island boasted very few roads, a few isolated settlements involved in sheep-farming, and large stretches of open, wind-swept, treeless, water-logged ground made all the more difficult to traverse by the ubiquitous presence of substantial tufts of grass known as 'babies' heads' – the bane of the soldiers' knees and ankles.

The first phase of operations took place in late April when a small force of Royal Marines landed on South Georgia and forced the surrender of the token Argentine garrison there. Shortly thereafter, in order to tighten the ring around the Falklands themselves, the British government declared a Total Exclusion Zone of 200 nautical miles around the islands, a course intended to alert the Argentine navy that all vessels operating within this area now stood subject to attack – though it should be stressed that Britain retained its right to attack vessels operating outside these designated limits.

The first strike against the Argentines on the Falklands themselves came on 1 May when an RAF Vulcan bomber, flown in history's longest sortie (from Britain to Ascension and thence to East Falkland – all made possible by regular in-flight refuelling), targeted Stanley airfield with 1,000lb bombs. Due to incorrect mapping, however, the Vulcan inflicted relatively little damage. Further attacks by carrier-borne aircraft caused more substantial harm, particularly on Argentine aircraft both at Stanley and at Goose Green. The following day, the Task Force struck a mortal blow on the naval front when the nuclear-powered submarine HMS *Conqueror* sank the cruiser *General Belgrano*, taking 368 lives, and constituting a loss of sufficient magnitude to persuade the Argentines to recall their entire fleet, including their single aircraft carrier, to home waters. Yet if their naval assets were no longer to play a role in the conflict, this certainly did not apply to the impressive air power the Argentines could bring to bear from the mainland. Three days after the sinking of the *Belgrano*, an Exocet missile fired from a Super Etendard launched from Tierra del Fuego struck HMS *Sheffield*, setting the ship ablaze, killing more than a dozen, injuring twice as many more, and leaving the stricken vessel a useless hulk.

Nevertheless, the Argentines failed to achieve air supremacy over the islands, as a consequence of which amphibious commanders adhered to their schedule for landings on 21 May in San Carlos Water, an inlet on the west coast of East Falkland. Chosen from among many potential landing sites, the beaches there proved suitable for landing craft, the surrounding hills offered good cover from air attack and the narrow passages provided a sheltered anchorage for supply vessels. The Argentines maintained only a small observing force in the area that Special Forces could easily drive off. The only disadvantage lay in its distance from Stanley: almost 60 miles of entirely exposed, boggy ground over which helicopters could theoretically convey large amounts of supplies and equipment and a substantial body of troops – but only if three conditions were satisfied. First, a successful offensive required the availability of sufficient numbers of helicopters and fuel; second, the inability of the Argentines to mount an effective counter-attack against San Carlos or any main forward supply base that the British might establish closer to Stanley; and third, the availability of sufficient air assets to keep the Argentines' Pucaras or jet aircraft at bay while helicopters flew the many dozens of sorties required to convey ground forces and artillery forward – not to mention keeping them supplied with rations, water and ammunition thereafter.

The landings proceeded unopposed in the early hours of 21 May, but even as the Marines and Paras established a firm presence on the ground, over the course of the next four days a series of determined air attacks struck British warships in Falkland Sound, now dubbed 'Bomb Alley'. More than ten warships fell victim to Argentine bombs and Exocets, including the frigate *Ardent* and the destroyer *Coventry*, which sank, and the frigate *Antelope*, which blew up. Fortunately for the British, many Argentine bombs failed to explode and ten Argentine aircraft were shot down, mostly by Sea Harriers. Although the Argentines had inflicted serious damage on their opponents' shipping, they failed to concentrate on the Task Force's most vulnerable elements: the supply ships, the heavy loss of which, as noted earlier, might have put paid to the entire British effort in a matter of days. Indeed, one loss struck the Task Force particularly hard: that of the container ship *Atlantic Conveyor*, the destruction of which during an Exocet attack on 25 May denied the British forces ten helicopters and vital supplies, thus posing a very serious blow to the Task Force in terms of its ability to move and resupply its ground forces. Still, just enough helicopters remained at the disposal of Brigadier Thompson to enable him to formulate plans for conveying a portion of his troops eastwards; the remaining Marines and Paras he ordered to 'yomp' and 'tab', respectively.

At the same time, on 28 May, 2 Para attacked the Argentine garrison at Darwin and Goose Green where the battalion, despite lacking proper fire support, overran a composite force enjoying a clear numerical superiority and a trench-lined front stretching across a narrow, easily defensible isthmus. The British captured the entire garrison – more than 1,000 troops – for a loss of eighteen dead, including the CO, and several dozen wounded. Meanwhile, as 40 Commando remained behind to protect the supply base and medical facility at San Carlos, helicopters conveyed 42 Commando to a forward position at Mount Kent, 10 miles east of Stanley, while 3 Para and 45 Commando proceeded on foot bearing kit in excess of 100lb – a remarkable feat that only troops enjoying the highest degree of fitness and endurance could possibly hope to achieve.

A few days later, on 2 June, 5 Infantry Brigade landed at San Carlos, now making the entire ground force available to Major General Jeremy Moore, on whom devolved command of all ground forces, enabling Brigadier Thompson to resume his normal role as commander of 3 Commando Brigade. All now seemed to bode well for the British; but if poor intelligence and an inability to fly reliably in darkness denied the Argentines the opportunity to slow the British advance, on 8 June they offered a graphic reminder that the skies did not go uncontested everywhere. Over Fitzroy, bombs dropped by Skyhawks struck the landing ship *Sir Galahad*, carrying Welsh Guardsmen awaiting orders to disembark, killing almost fifty and injuring or burning twice as many.

If the sinking of *Sir Galahad* (*Sir Tristram* had also been struck, but less severely) put the Welsh Guards out of action, Moore nevertheless enjoyed a commanding position: 3 Commando now stood poised within 10 miles of Stanley at the outer ring of Argentine defences, with elements from 5 Infantry Brigade, including the Scots Guards and a battalion of Gurkhas deployed to play an equal part in the assaults that now followed in short order. They consisted of a series of well-conducted, comprehensively successful night attacks executed on 11–12 June against Mount Harriet, Two Sisters and Mount Longdon conducted by 42 Commando, 45 Commando and 3 Para, respectively, and, on the following evening, against Wireless Ridge and Mount Tumbledown, led by 2 Para and the Scots Guards, respectively. In each case the survivors fled east into Stanley where, on the morning of 14 June, the Argentine commander, General Mario Menéndez, surrendered all his forces on the Falklands. The entire ground phase of the campaign thus concluded after a mere three weeks – 21 May to 14 June – a remarkable achievement considering the fact that not only did the Argentines enjoy a clear numerical superiority over the British, but possessed ample time with which to prepare their defences and establish stockpiles of supplies during the nearly seven-week period between their own invasion of 2 April and the British landings on 21 May.

Total British losses in the conflict amounted to 253 military personnel and civilians serving in all capacities with the Task Force, three civilians in Stanley and 777 wounded across all services. The Task Force lost four warships and a landing craft, one fleet auxiliary vessel and one merchantman. Helicopter losses amounted to twenty-three from the Royal Navy, seven from the RAF, three from the Royal Marines and one from the Army. Argentine fatalities amounted to about 750, plus 1,100 personnel wounded or ill. The entire garrison of approximately 13,000 men fell into British hands, plus numerous armoured vehicles, aircraft and artillery, rendering this one of the most successful expeditionary operations in British military history.

In analysing the factors behind British success, several stand out particularly prominently: the assembly of the Task Force with extraordinary rapidity, including the acquisition and fitting out of requisitioned vessels to supplement the existing resources of the Royal Navy and Royal Fleet Auxiliary within days of the Argentine invasion; the formulation of a clearly laid-out and effective strategy for retaking the islands; the dispatch of naval and air assets – all trained and equipped to a high standard – in sufficient numbers to drive off the Argentine navy as well as to confine air attacks to an acceptable, albeit expensive, level; the deployment of first-rate ground forces boasting superb levels of fitness, training, motivation and junior officer and NCO leadership; the skilful use of Special Forces (both SAS and SBS) for reconnaissance and raiding; and the acquisition, via diplomatic channels, of clandestine, non-operational American logistic support in the form of vast quantities of aviation fuel based at Ascension Island, as well as critical satellite intelligence.

No proper explanation of British victory must rest alone on the successes attributed to the Task Force and to strategists in Northwood and Whitehall. Rather, a balanced approach must consider some of the principal errors committed by the Argentines. Among many of their shortcomings, they failed to concentrate their air attacks against the British logistic chain – a far more important element of the Task Force in terms of maintaining the operational longevity of ground forces than high-profile naval assets; they neglected to concentrate their efforts against the two opposing aircraft carriers, the loss of either of which might alone have caused a setback of sufficient magnitude as to jeopardise the entire British effort; they made the short-sighted and fatal decision to deploy to the Falklands and South Georgia predominantly inexperienced recruits as opposed to marginally better-prepared reservists or, above all, marines and Special Forces, both composed of full-time professional personnel; and they failed to recognise that light armour could operate across most of the islands despite the boggy nature of the ground, giving them an incalculable advantage over the British, who brought only small numbers of such vehicles. Additionally, although they were incapable – quite understandably – of protecting the entire coastline of East Falkland in anticipation of the British landing, they failed once it materialised to mount a counter-attack against the beachhead at San Carlos, thus enabling 3 Commando Brigade to advance simultaneously south against Goose

Green and east towards enemy defences immediately west of Stanley; they maintained an inflexible, static defence throughout the campaign, thus abandoning the initiative to the British from the moment they effected their landing on 21 May; they operated an appallingly poor logistic system within Stanley, such that while the garrison there received adequate provisions and rest, their comrades only a few miles away in the mountains suffered from food shortages owing to faulty administration, pilfering by their own commissariat, and an almost total absence of supply vehicles capable of negotiating trackless ground; they failed to hold out in the defence of Stanley even after the collapse of their defensive ring just west of the town, neglecting the supreme advantage still remaining to them: deteriorating weather conditions, for with the steady decline in visibility and temperature no British forces – whether on land, at sea and in the air – could sustain themselves, much less fight, for long after mid-June.

CHRONOLOGY OF EVENTS

Friday, 19 March	Scrap metal workers arrive at the derelict whaling station at Leith on South Georgia and raise the flag of Argentina.
Sunday, 21 March	*Endurance*, at Stanley, sails for South Georgia with two helicopters and a Royal Marines detachment.
Monday, 22 March	The *Bahia Buen Suceso* leaves Leith harbour; forty-eight scrap metal workers remain behind.
Wednesday, 24 March	Royal Marines detachment from *Endurance* lands to monitor Argentine activity at Leith.
Thursday, 25 March	Argentine marines land at Leith from *Bahia Paraíso*.
Monday, 29 March	Replacement for Naval Party 8901 arrives in Stanley.
Wednesday, 31 March	Royal Marines detachment disembarks from *Endurance* at Grytviken, South Georgia.
Thursday, 1 April	Naval Party 8901 for the 1981–82 deployment passed operational command to the new Royal Marines detachment; both take up defensive positions in and around Stanley; submarine *Splendid* leaves from Faslane; orders given for the SBS to mobilise.
Friday, 2 April	Argentine invasion of the Falklands begins; after brief resistance Governor Rex Hunt surrenders; the UN condemns the act with Resolution 502; Task Force begins to assemble.
Saturday, 3 April	Royal Marines at Grytviken, outnumbered and outgunned, surrender; NP 8901 is flown to Montevideo for repatriation.
Sunday, 4 April	Brigadier Thompson briefs his commanding officers at Plymouth; submarine *Conqueror* leaves Faslane.
Monday, 5 April	Task Force sails from Portsmouth with HQ 3 Commando Brigade and elements of 40 and 42 Commando; Naval Party 8901 arrives back in the UK.
Tuesday, 6 April	Naval Party 1222, intended for the island's defence, arrives at Ascension.
Thursday, 8 April	*Broadsword* and *Yarmouth* depart from Gibraltar.
Friday, 9 April	*Canberra* departs from Portsmouth carrying 3 Para and most of 40 and 42 Commando.
Saturday, 10 April	Antrim Group arrives at Ascension.
Sunday, 11 April	Antrim Group sails for South Georgia from Ascension with M Company 42 Commando aboard.
Monday, 12 April	UK imposes 200-mile Maritime Exclusion Zone around the Falklands.

Wednesday, 14 April	Brilliant Group leaves Ascension; Rear Admiral Woodward departs from Ascension aboard *Glamorgan*, with *Alacrity*, *Broadsword* and *Yarmouth*.
Friday, 16 April	Task Force sails from Ascension; *Hermes* arrives at Ascension; *Invincible* leaves Ascension; Woodward discusses campaign strategy with Commodore Clapp and Thompson aboard *Fearless*.
Saturday, 17 April	Admiral Fieldhouse, C-in-C Fleet and Major General Moore, Land Forces Commander, fly to Ascension to meet Woodward, Thompson and Clapp aboard *Hermes*.
Sunday, 18 April	Carrier Battle Group leaves Ascension: *Hermes*, *Invincible*, *Glamorgan*, *Broadsword*, *Yarmouth*, *Alacrity* and RFA *Olmeda* and *Resource*.
Tuesday, 20 April	*Canberra* and *Elk* arrive at Ascension; Royal Marines captured at South Georgia arrive in the UK.
Wednesday, 21 April	SBS and SAS teams inserted by helicopter on to South Georgia.
Thursday, 22 April	SAS team rescued from Fortuna Glacier; two Wessex helicopters crash.
Friday, 23 April	M Company 42 Commando lands on South Georgia.
Sunday, 25 April	*Intrepid*, *Atlantic Conveyor*, and *Europic Ferry* depart from the UK; Carrier Battle Group joins with Sheffield Group.
Monday, 26 April	Argentine forces on South Georgia surrender.
Tuesday, 27 April	Cabinet in London gives approval for Operation Sutton; *Norland* and *Sir Bedivere* depart from the UK.
Wednesday, 28 April	UK declares 200-mile Total Exclusion Zone, now including aircraft and ships of all nations; hospital ship *Uganda* arrives at Ascension.
Thursday, 29 April	*Uganda* departs from Ascension.
Friday, 30 April	UK begins enforcing the Total Exclusion Zone; main Task Group arrives in TEZ.
Saturday, 1 May	Vulcan bomber attacks Stanley airport; Sea Harriers also conduct attacks; naval bombardments commence of the same area; SAS and SBS patrols inserted on East and West Falklands; UK government requisitions RMS *Queen Elizabeth 2*.
Sunday, 2 May	*Conqueror* sinks the cruiser *General Belgrano*.
Tuesday, 4 May	Black Buck 2 raid against Stanley airport; *Sheffield* struck by Exocet missile; Sea Harrier shot down over Goose Green.
Wednesday, 5 May	Eight RAF Harriers arrive at Ascension.
Thursday, 6 May	Argonaut Group leaves Ascension; 2 Para arrives at Ascension.
Friday, 7 May	*Norland* arrives at Ascension; most of Amphibious Task Group departs.

Saturday, 8 May	First of refuelled air drops flown to the Task Force.
Monday, 10 May	*Sheffield*, heavily damaged six days previously, sinks while under tow; Bristol Group leaves UK; Nimrods begin work in support of the Task Force.
Wednesday, 12 May	*Queen Elizabeth 2* departs from Southampton with most of 5 Infantry Brigade aboard; *Glasgow* damaged by Argentine aircraft; *Cardiff* leaves Gibraltar; 3 Commando Brigade HQ issues Operational Order for the landings in San Carlos Water.
Friday, 14–Saturday 15 May	SAS raid against airstrip at Pebble Island.
Wednesday, 19 May	Cabinet gives approval for amphibious landings; Sea King carrying SAS crashes into the sea during cross-decking.
Thursday, 20 May	Sea King lands in Chile; crew turn themselves in to authorities and are repatriated.
Friday, 21 May	3 Commando Brigade executes landings in San Carlos Water; *Ardent* sunk.
Saturday, 22 May	3 Commando Brigade all ashore; Brigade Maintenance Area established at Ajax Bay.
Sunday, 23 May	*Antelope* sunk.
Monday, 24 May	*Sir Galahad*, *Sir Lancelot* and *Sir Tristram* are bombed in San Carlos Water, but the bombs fail to explode in all cases.
Tuesday, 25 May	*Coventry* and *Atlantic Conveyor* hit by Exocet missiles, the former sinking.
Wednesday, 26 May	2 Para leaves Sussex Mountain for advance on Goose Green.
Thursday, 27 May	3 Para and 45 Commando tab and yomp, respectively, from San Carlos Water; SAS patrol flies to Mount Kent; *Queen Elizabeth 2*, *Canberra* and *Norland* rendezvous at South Georgia; 5 Infantry Brigade begins cross-decking on to troopships.
Friday, 28 May	2 Para engages Argentine defenders at Darwin and Goose Green.
Saturday, 29 May	Major Keeble accepts Argentine surrender of 1,100 troops at Goose Green; *Atlantic Conveyor* sinks under tow.
Sunday, 30 May	Major General Moore arrives off the Falklands.
Monday, 31 May	42 Commando move by air to Mount Kent; Mountain and Arctic Warfare Cadre defeat Argentine troops at Top Malo House; 3 Para arrives at Douglas settlement; 45 Commando arrives at Teal Inlet settlement; Black Buck 5 raid strikes radar position in Stanley.
Tuesday, 1 June	5 Infantry Brigade begin disembarking in San Carlos Water; 3 Commando Brigade forward base established at Teal Inlet in preparation for major engagements; 3 Para and 42 and

	45 Commando begin patrolling areas in vicinity of planned objectives.
Wednesday, 2 June	2 Para fly to Bluff Cove.
Thursday, 3 June	Black Buck 6 raid conducted against runway at Stanley.
Saturday, 5 June	Scots Guards embark in *Sir Tristram* for Bluff Cove.
Sunday, 6 June	Welsh Guards embark in *Fearless* for Fitzroy but the ship is ordered not to sail; Scots Guards land at Bluff Cove; 5 Infantry Brigade establishes forward base there.
Tuesday, 8 June	*Sir Galahad* and *Sir Tristram* hit by bombs in Port Pleasant; LCU Foxtrot Four sunk by Argentine aircraft in Choiseul Sound; *Plymouth* damaged by unexploded bomb; Moore explains plans for offensive against Stanley.
Friday, 11 June	Major assaults on the outer ring of Argentine defences around Stanley: 42 Commando at Mount Harriet, 3 Para at Mount Longdon, and 45 Commando at Two Sisters.
Saturday, 12 June	By sunrise all attacks have succeeded; *Glamorgan* struck by land-based Exocet missile; Black Buck 7 raid conducted against radar installation at Stanley.
Sunday, 13 June	2 Para attack Wireless Ridge; Scots Guards attack Mount Longdon; Gurkhas occupy Mount William.
Monday, 14 June	By early morning all assaults successful; Argentine forces surrender.

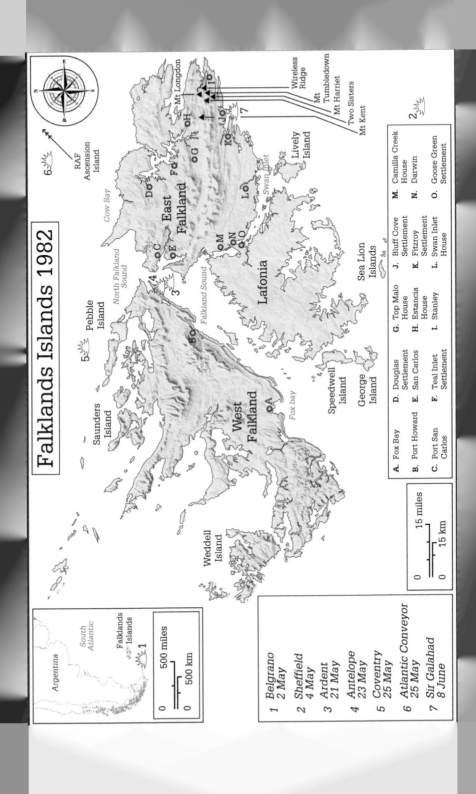

Falklands Islands 1982

Argentina

South Atlantic

Falklands Islands

0 500 miles

0 500 km

1 Belgrano 2 May
2 Sheffield 4 May
3 Ardent 21 May
4 Antelope 23 May
5 Coventry 25 May
6 Atlantic Conveyor 25 May
7 Sir Galahad 8 June

RAF Ascension Island

Cow Bay

North Falkland Sound

Saunders Island

Pebble Island

Weddell Island

West Falkland

Fox bay

Falkland Sound

East Falkland

Speedwell Island

George Island

Lafonia

Sea Lion Islands

Lively Island

Swan Inlet

Mt Longdon

Wireless Ridge
Mt Tumbledown
Mt Harrier
Two Sisters
Mt Kent

A. Fox Bay
B. Port Howard
C. Port San Carlos
D. Douglas Settlement
E. San Carlos
F. Teal Inlet Settlement
G. Top Malo House
H. Estancia House
I. Stanley
J. Bluff Cove Settlement
K. Fitzroy Settlement
L. Swan Inlet House
M. Camilla Creek House
N. Darwin
O. Goose Green Settlement

0 15 miles
0 15 km

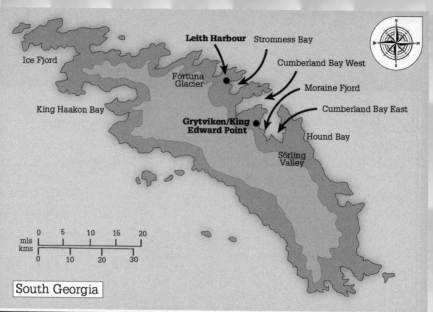

Ice Fjord

King Haakon Bay

Fortuna Glacier

Leith Harbour — Stromness Bay

Cumberland Bay West

Moraine Fjord

Cumberland Bay East

Grytviken/King Edward Point

Hound Bay

Sörling Valley

| 0 | 5 | 10 | 15 | 20 |
mls
kms
| 0 | 10 | 20 | 30 |

South Georgia

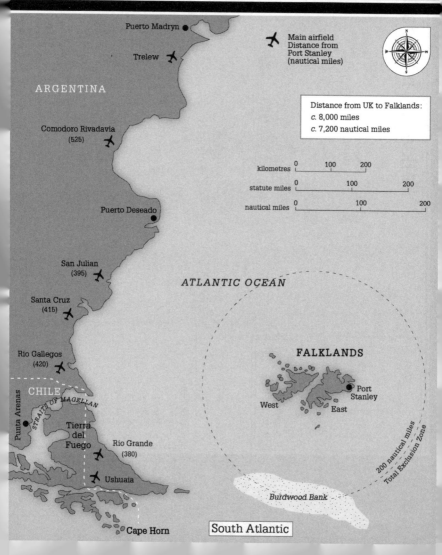

Puerto Madryn

Trelew

ARGENTINA

Comodoro Rivadavia
(525)

Puerto Deseado

San Julian
(395)

Santa Cruz
(415)

Rio Gallegos
(420)

CHILE

Punta Arenas

STRAITS OF MAGELLAN

Tierra del Fuego

Rio Grande
(380)

Ushuaia

Cape Horn

✈ Main airfield
Distance from
Port Stanley
(nautical miles)

Distance from UK to Falklands:
c. 8,000 miles
c. 7,200 nautical miles

kilometres	0	100	200
statute miles	0	100	200
nautical miles	0	100	200

ATLANTIC OCEAN

FALKLANDS

West   East

Port Stanley

200 nautical miles
Total Exclusion Zone

Burdwood Bank

South Atlantic

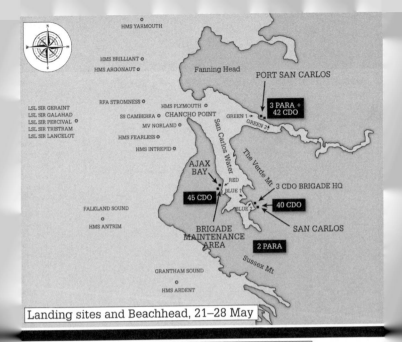

Landing sites and Beachhead, 21–28 May

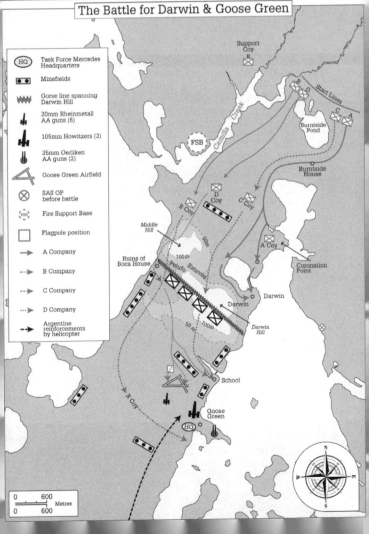

The Battle for Darwin & Goose Green

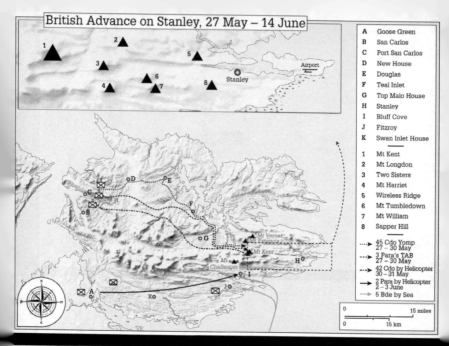

British Advance on Stanley, 27 May – 14 June

A	Goose Green
B	San Carlos
C	Port San Carlos
D	New House
E	Douglas
F	Teal Inlet
G	Top Malo House
H	Stanley
I	Bluff Cove
J	Fitzroy
K	Swan Inlet House
1	Mt Kent
2	Mt Longdon
3	Two Sisters
4	Mt Harriet
5	Wireless Ridge
6	Mt Tumbledown
7	Mt William
8	Sapper Hill

.... 45 Cdo Yomp 27 – 30 May
– – – 3 Para's TAB 27 – 30 May
– ▪ – 42 Cdo by Helicopter 30 – 31 May
——▶ 2 Para by Helicopter 2 – 3 June
——▶ 5 Bde by Sea

0 ————— 15 miles
0 ————— 15 km

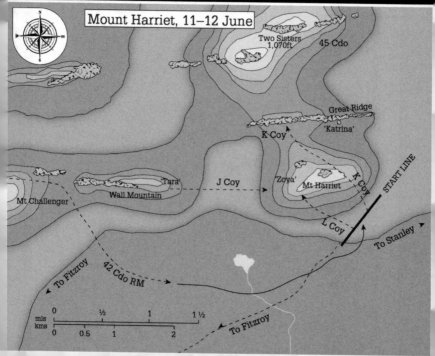

Mount Harriet, 11–12 June

Two Sisters 1,070ft   45 Cdo

Great Ridge
'Katrina'

K Coy

Mt Challenger

Wall Mountain   'Tara'   J Coy   'Zoya'   Mt Harriet   K Coy   START LINE

L Coy

To Stanley

To Fitzroy   42 Cdo RM

To Fitzroy

mls
0   ½   1   1½
kms
0   0.5   1   2

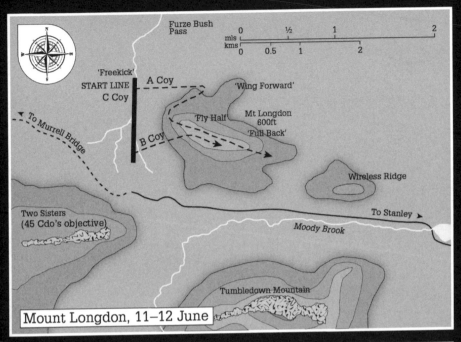

Mount Longdon, 11–12 June

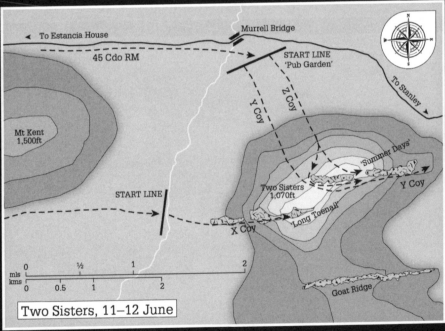

Two Sisters, 11–12 June

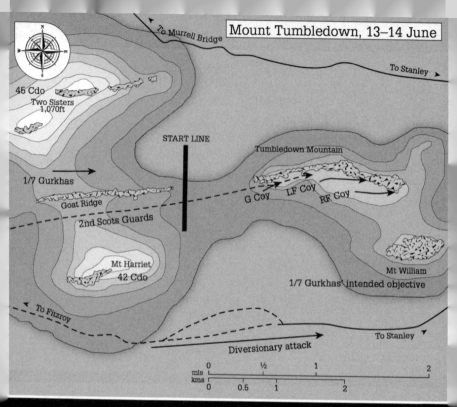

Mount Tumbledown, 13–14 June

To Murrell Bridge

To Stanley ▸

45 Cdo
Two Sisters
1,070ft

START LINE

Tumbledown Mountain

1/7 Gurkhas

Goat Ridge

G Coy   LF Coy   RF Coy

2nd Scots Guards

Mt Harriet
42 Cdo

Mt William

1/7 Gurkhas' intended objective

To Fitzroy

To Stanley ▸

Diversionary attack

mls 0   ½   1   2
kms 0   0.5   1   2

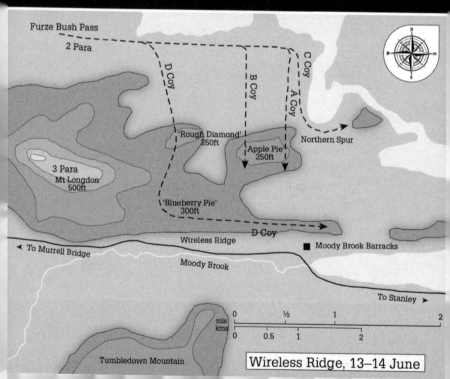

Wireless Ridge, 13–14 June

Furze Bush Pass

2 Para

D Coy

B Coy

C Coy

A Coy

'Rough Diamond'
250ft

'Apple Pie'
250ft

Northern Spur

3 Para
Mt Longdon
500ft

'Blueberry Pie'
300ft

D Coy

Wireless Ridge

◂ To Murrell Bridge

Moody Brook

■ Moody Brook Barracks

To Stanley ▸

Tumbledown Mountain

mls 0   ½   1   2
kms 0   0.5   1   2

Active, HMS

A

Of the fifteen **frigates** in the South Atlantic, *Active* numbered among seven of the Type 21 Amazon class, the others being *Alacrity, Ambuscade, Antelope, Ardent, Arrow,* and *Avenger.* She departed Devonport on 10 May and arrived in Falklands waters on 25 May. Three days later, she left **San Carlos Water** and sailed to the Tug, Repair and Logistic Area (TRALA) for repairs, setting off back for San Carlos Water on the 30th. On 3 June, *Active* issued fire against **Fitzroy** settlement. *Active* was originally meant to support the attack on **Stanley** that Admiral **Woodward** expected to take place on the night of 5–6 June, but when Major General **Moore** postponed the attack to the 9th, Woodward recalled *Active* and *Arrow* from this mission. In the event, she did not come into action until the night of the 13th when, together with *Avenger*, she fired eight star shell and 220 high-explosive rounds against Argentine defenders on **Mount Tumbledown** in support of the **Scots Guards** attack. She arrived back in Devonport on 3 August.

Commander:	Commander P.C.B. Canter	
Builders:	Vosper Thornycroft	
Launched:	23 November 1972	
Commissioned:	17 June 1977	
Displacement (tons):	2,750 Standard	3,250 Full load
Dimensions: length × beam; feet (metres):	384 × 42 (117.0 × 12.8)	
Draught:	6.8m	
Propulsion:	2 × Olympus gas turbines	50,000shp = 31+ knots
	2 × Tyne gas turbines	8,500shp = 18 knots (cruising)
Armament:	1 × 4.5in Mark 8 gun	
	2 × 20mm AA guns	
	1 × **Seacat** system (GWS 24)	
	4 × MM.38 **Exocet**	
Aircraft:	1 × **Wasp HAS1**	

Aden 30mm Cannon

Aden 30mm cannon were deployed aboard **Sea Harrier** FRS1s and **Harrier** GR3s and used in both air-to-air and air-to-ground roles. Although not as deadly in the Falklands as the **Sidewinder** missile, this heavy-calibre weapon accounted for a number of kills, destroying four helicopters on the ground and downing one Pucara, a Hercules already disabled by a Sidewinder, and two A-4 Skyhawks.

Aircraft Carriers

As a result of continuous reductions in the budget of the **Royal Navy** since the end of the Second World War, only three aircraft carriers remained in service in 1982, two of which were deployed to the South Atlantic. The carriers had fixed-wing aircraft, of course, but there were no further plans to build more vessels for this purpose and long-range air cover for the fleet and responsibility for air strikes against enemy vessels would become the responsibility of the **Royal Air Force**. Increasingly, the Navy required deployment of anti-submarine helicopters, resulting in acquisition of the through deck carrier for vertical and/or short take-off and landing (V/STOL) aircraft, particularly the **Sea Harrier**, which could perform several important roles: provide local air defence for the fleet, strike surface vessels in the area, and operate in a ground-attack role in support of operations on land in tandem with, or independently of, RAF assets.

Hermes and *Invincible* played a vital – indeed, indispensable – role in the campaign, for without them the **Task Force** could neither defend itself with its integral aircraft, nor provide the necessary strike capability in support of ground forces or provide platforms for essential **logistics**. **Helicopters** aboard the two carriers provided continual anti-submarine patrols and the Sea Harriers played an important role in diminishing the effectiveness of Argentine air attacks, particularly those over **San Carlos Water**. In short, without these two carriers Britain would simply have been incapable of deploying forces to the South Atlantic.

As defence of the aircraft carriers stood supremely important, after the loss of *Sheffield* on 4 May, Admiral **Woodward** shifted them – and obviously the rest of the **Carrier Battle Group** at the same time – well to the east of the Falklands to offer them greater protection from air attack, though this of course impinged upon the range of the Sea Harriers as a result.

Ajax Bay

When the decision was reached to land **3 Commando Brigade** in **San Carlos Water**, Ajax Bay was chosen as one of the three sites. In the event, on 21 May, **45 Commando** landed there on **Red Beach**, together with Brigade HQ. Ajax Bay also served as the site of the **Brigade Maintenance Area** (BMA) – a massive stores dump situated around the derelict refrigeration plant, which held the principal land-based **medical services** in the form of the Land Forces Main Dressing Station under Surgeon Commander Rick Jolly. This medical facility came under air attack by two Skyhawks on 27 May, the Argentines apparently as yet unaware that this was a field hospital, although because of its proximity to the BMA Brigadier **Thompson** chose not to identify it with a red cross.

Two bombs penetrated the roof of the field hospital, lodging themselves but failing to explode. An RAF bomb disposal expert found them too difficult to diffuse, but considered them not to have armed, as a consequence of which they remained in place throughout the war. The raid on the 27th cost the lives of eight British personnel and twenty-six were wounded, with damage to the stores dump and the loss of some ammunition due to fire. **Sea King** HC4s ferried the casualties to the hospital ship *Uganda* for treatment.

The field hospital experienced a surge in cases on 8–9 June when helicopters continually ferried in casualties after the attacks on the *Sir Tristram* and *Sir Galahad* in **Port Pleasant**. Once stabilised, the patients were flown out to the *Uganda*.

Alacrity, HMS

Of the fifteen **frigates** in the South Atlantic, *Alacrity* numbered among seven of the Type 21 variety, the others being *Active, Ambuscade, Antelope, Ardent, Arrow,* and *Avenger*.

Departing from Devonport on 5 April, *Alacrity* arrived at **Ascension** on the 16th and in the **Total Exclusion Zone** (TEZ) on the 30th. On 1 May, while positioned off Cape Pembroke with *Glamorgan* and *Arrow* and firing briefly on **Stanley** airfield, *Alacrity* was attacked by a Dagger A that her radar failed to detect. The aircraft dropped two 500lb parachute-retarded bombs but failed to hit its target, though *Alacrity*, which managed to loose off a few rounds of ineffective 20mm cannon fire in response, nevertheless received minor damage below the waterline due to the explosion of bombs in the vicinity.

On 8 May, *Alacrity* fired approximately ninety shells at an Argentine position on Stanley Common, partly as a diversion to allow *Yarmouth* to proceed to the position of the burned out *Sheffield* in order to tow her away for possible salvaging.

On the night of 10–11 May, *Alacrity* proceeded along the coasts of both main islands before sailing up through the Sound between them, marking this as the first instance during the war when a British vessel made this journey. She discovered no mines and enjoyed a certain degree of protection from air attack, owing to poor weather grounding Argentine aircraft. On the night of the 11th, while sailing near Swan Island, *Alacrity* encountered an Argentine navy transport ship, the 2,684-ton *Isla de los Estados*, which *Alacrity* hit with several 4.5in shells, detonating her target's cargo of aviation fuel and ammunition and killing twenty out of the twenty-two-man crew.

As part of the **Carrier Battle Group** north of Stanley, *Alacrity* was not directly involved in the landings in **San Carlos Water** on 21 May. When *Atlantic Conveyor* was hit by an **Exocet** missile on 25 May, *Alacrity* helped to rescue survivors of that disaster. On the night of 27–28 May, in company with *Glamorgan* and *Avenger*, *Alacrity* took part in a heavy shore bombardment of Argentine positions around Stanley, the three vessels unleashing 250 rounds. She left the TEZ on 2 June for Ascension to undergo repairs to her main engine and did not return to South Atlantic waters, instead proceeding back to Devonport, arriving on 24 June.

Commander:	Commander C.J.S. Craig	
Builders:	Yarrow (Scotstoun)	
Launched:	18 September 1974	
Commissioned:	2 April 1977	
Displacement (tons):	2,750 Standard	3,250 Full load
Dimensions: length × beam; feet (metres):	384 × 42 (117.0 × 12.8)	
Draught:	12.8m	
Propulsion:	2 × Olympus gas turbines	50,000shp = 31 + knots
	2 × Tyne gas turbines	8,500shp = 18 knots (cruising)
Armament:	1 × 4.5in Mark 8 gun	
	2 × 20mm AA guns	
	1 × **Seacat** system (GWS 24)	
	4 × MM.38 **Exocet**	
Aircraft:	1 × **Lynx** HAS2	

Alvega, MV

One of the large number of **Ships Taken Up From Trade** (STUFT), *Alvega* was a motor tanker chartered from Silver Line on 1 May and departed Portsmouth four days later for **Ascension**, where she served as a base storage tanker for fleet refuelling both there and off the Falklands. She did not arrive back in Rosyth until 21 March 1984.

Commander:	Captain A. Lazenby	
Launched:	1977	
Tonnage:	33,329 Gross Register	57,372 Deadweight
Dimensions: length × beam; feet (metres):	690 × 108 (210 × 32.9)	
Propulsion:	1 diesel engine	17,400bhp = 16 knots

Ambulance Vessels

Three survey vessels served in this capacity: *Hecla*, *Herald* and *Hydra*.

Ambuscade, HMS

Of the fifteen **frigates** in the South Atlantic, *Ambuscade* numbered among seven of the Type 21 (Amazon class), the others being *Active*, *Alacrity*, *Antelope*, *Ardent*, *Arrow* and *Avenger*.

She departed Gibraltar on 3 May and arrived at **Ascension** eight days later. Entering the **Total Exclusion Zone** on 22 May, on the afternoon of the 25th *Ambuscade* was with the **Carrier Battle Group** about 60 miles north-east of **Stanley** when two Super Etendards fired their **Exocet** missiles, the intended targets probably being the **aircraft carriers** *Hermes* and *Invincible*. *Ambuscade* fired chaff rockets as a decoy, which may have successfully diverted the Exocets, but at least one of them reacquired a target in the form of *Atlantic Conveyor*. *Ambuscade*, together with *Yarmouth*, supported **2 Para's** attack on **Wireless Ridge** on 13–14 June. She arrived back at Devonport on 24 July.

Commander:	Commander P.J. Mosse	
Builders:	Yarrow (Scotstoun)	
Launched:	18 January 1973	
Commissioned:	5 September 1975	
Displacement (tons):	2,750 Standard	3,250 Full load
Dimensions: length × beam; feet (metres):	384 × 42 (117.0 × 12.8)	
Draught:	6.8m	
Propulsion:	2 × Olympus gas turbines	50,000shp = 31 + knots
	2 × Tyne gas turbines	8,500shp = 18 knots (cruising)
Armament:	1 × 4.5in Mark 8 gun	
	2 × 20mm AA guns	
	1 × **Seacat** system (GWS 24)	
	2 × triple ASW torpedo tubes (STWS)	
Aircraft:	1 × **Lynx** HAS2	

Amphibious Assault Ships

Also known as Landing Platform (Docks) or LPDs, the only two possessed by the **Royal Navy**, *Fearless* and *Intrepid*, served on Operation **Corporate**, together playing a vital role in the conflict. With a displacement of more than 12,000 tons and a speed of 21 knots, both could operate **landing craft**, **helicopters** and function as command ships. An amphibious assault ship carried a crew of 480, including its complement of ninety **Royal Marines**, with accommodation for 700 embarked troops. To launch its landing craft or LCUs, an LPD flooded its docking area at the stern, a process known as 'docking down', allowing in 3,000 tons of ballast, after which the troops could embark directly from their mess decks into the four craft, which then sailed out of the stern. She also carried four LCVPs slung from davits on the upper deck. The landing craft themselves belonged to a Royal Marines Assault Squadron consisting of approximately eighty Royal Marines and Royal Navy personnel, including an Amphibious Beach Unit. LPDs carried sophisticated Command and Control communications facilities.

Facilities for aircraft included a flight deck from which two **Wessex** helicopters could operate at any one time, with space for more parked rotary wing aircraft if required. **Sea Harriers** could also operate from LPDs if circumstances demanded. For close range air defence, LPDs carried four **Seacat** systems and two 40mm Bofors.

Amphibious Task Group

Commanded by Commodore Michael Clapp RN, who held the post of Commander Amphibious Warfare at Plymouth, this force was responsible for planning the amphibious landing, directing inshore operations and supporting ground operations in pursuit of Argentine defeat. *Fearless* served as HQ ship of the Amphibious Task Group. While the Commander Amphibious Task Group neither controlled operations on shore nor laid down the design for battle for the landing force, he did make the ultimate decision in respect of whether or not a landing should proceed on the basis that he furnished the transport for the landing force, and other assets such as ship-to-shore movement craft and **helicopters, naval gunfire support**, and control of fixed-wing support.

For Operation **Sutton**, the amphibious landings executed on 21 May in **San Carlos Water** (officially designated the Amphibious Operating Area or AOA), the Amphibious Task Group and its escorts consisted of the destroyer *Antrim*, the **frigates** *Ardent, Argonaut, Brilliant, Broadsword, Plymouth* and *Yarmouth*, the **amphibious assault ships** *Fearless* and *Intrepid*, seven **Royal Fleet Auxiliaries** and three **Ships Taken Up From Trade**. The total number of **helicopters** aboard these vessels amounted to one **Wessex**, five **Lynx HAS2s**, two **Wasp HAS1s**, twelve **Sea King HC4s**, four **Sea King HAS5s**, nine **Gazelle AH1s**, and nine **Scout** AH1s.

Anco Charger, MV

A motor tanker forming part of the large number of **Ships Taken Up From Trade** for the campaign, *Anco Charger* was chartered from Panocean on 18 April for refuelling duties and departed from Fawley on 24 April with a Naval Party supplied by the **Royal Fleet Auxiliary**, reaching **Ascension** on 5 May. At the end of the fighting she served off the Falklands from 27 June and arrived at Portsmouth on 16 August.

Commander:	Captain B. Hatton	
Launched:	1973	
Tonnage:	15,568 Gross Register	25,300 Deadweight
Dimensions: length × beam; feet (metres):	541 × 82 (165.1 × 25)	
Propulsion:	1 diesel engine	12,000bhp = 15.5 knots

Andromeda, HMS

One of fifteen **frigates** deployed to the South Atlantic, but the only one of the ageing Batch 3 (Broadbeam) Leander class. She departed Devonport on 10 May, reached

Ascension eight days later and arrived in theatre with other ships of the **Bristol Group** on the 25th, spending the majority of her time as 'goalkeeper' (or anti-aircraft 'screen') for the **aircraft carriers** in tandem with *Brilliant* and *Broadsword*. She did not reach Devonport until 10 September.

Commander:	Captain J.L. Weatherall	
Builders:	HM Dockyard, Portsmouth	
Launched:	24 May 1967	
Commissioned:	2 December 1968	
Displacement (tons):	2,640 Standard	3,100 Full load
Dimensions: length x beam; feet (metres):	372 × 43 (113.4 × 13.1)	
Draught:	5.5m	
Propulsion:	2 sets geared steam turbines	30,000shp = 28 knots
Armament:	2 × 40mm Bofors AA guns	
	1 × **Sea Wolf** system (GWS 25)	
	4 × MM.38 **Exocet**	
	2 × triple ASW torpedo tubes	
Aircraft:	1 × **Lynx** HAS2	

Antelope, HMS

Of the fifteen **frigates** deployed to the South Atlantic, *Antelope* numbered among seven Type 21s (Amazon class), the others being *Active*, *Alacrity*, *Ambuscade*, *Ardent*, *Arrow* and *Avenger*.

Departing from Devonport on 5 April, she reached **Ascension** on the 21st. Having only just arrived in the **Total Exclusion Zone** the day before, *Antelope* came under

HMS *Antelope* in her death throes, 24 May. (AirSeaLand Photos)

attack at 1650Z on 23 May, when four A-4B Skyhawks encountered her close to **Fanning Head** in **San Carlos Water**. One of the aircraft dropped its 1,000lb bomb on the starboard side of the ship's stern, but it failed to explode. Two of the aircraft left the area, one damaged by a surface-to-air missile, while the remaining two continued their attack, hitting *Antelope* again with another 1,000lb bomb, which also failed to explode but inflicted serious damage on the port side of the vessel below the bridge. Her mainmast was also damaged by a low-flying Skyhawk. One sailor was killed in the attack.

Antelope proceeded to **Ajax Bay**, where an Explosive Ordnance Disposal team tried to defuse the two bombs; one exploded, instantly killing Staff Sergeant James Prescott of the **Royal Engineers** and severely injuring Warrant Officer John Phillips. After the explosion the crew of 175 evacuated the ship without injury, transferring to other vessels nearby as fires quickly consumed the ship. These continued through the night until a second explosion, almost certainly the other bomb, broke the frigate's back at about 1100Z on the 24th.

Commander:	Commander N.J. Tobin	
Builders:	Vosper Thornycroft	
Launched:	16 March 1972	
Commissioned:	19 July 1975	
Displacement (tons):	2,750 Standard	3,250 Full load
Dimensions: length × beam; feet (metres):	384 × 42 (117.0 × 12.8)	
Draught:	6.8m	
Propulsion:	2 × Olympus gas turbines	50,000 shp = 31 + knots
	2 × Tyne gas turbines	8,500 shp = 18 knots (cruising)
Armament:	1 × 4.5in Mark 8 gun	
	2 × 20mm AA guns	
	1 × **Seacat** system (GWS 24)	
	2 × triple ASW torpedo tubes (STWS)	
Aircraft:	1 × **Lynx** HAS2	

Anti-Ship Missiles

The **Royal Navy** employed three types of anti-ship missiles on Operation **Corporate**: the **AS.12**, the MM.38 **Exocet** and the **Sea Skua**.

Antrim, HMS

One of two County class guided missile **destroyers** on Operation **Corporate**, the other being *Glamorgan*. In late March she was engaged in Exercise **Springtrain** off Gibraltar as flagship to Admiral **Woodward**, together with four other destroyers. After cross-decking stores and transferring personnel and aircraft in Gibraltar, *Antrim* formed part of the initial **Task Force**. During the voyage south she was, however, detached for service on Operation **Paraquet**, the recapture of **South Georgia**, off which she arrived on 21 April. In providing **naval gunfire support** to the ground forces there, she and *Plymouth* played a decisive part in persuading the Argentine garrison to surrender without resistance.

Antrim arrived off the Falklands on 20 May and the following morning, at approximately 0200Z, she entered Falkland Sound from the north to insert an **Special Boat Squadron** (SBS) team to monitor Argentine positions on **Fanning Head**. She then assumed a post, together with *Argonaut* and *Broadsword*, at the mouth of **San Carlos Water** for the remainder of the day to provide an air defence screen to protect the amphibious ships unloading troops and supplies further south. At 0452Z she opened fire with her 4.5in gun, shelling Argentine positions on Fanning Head ahead of the SBS assault.

At 1325Z, while still off Fanning Head, *Antrim* was surprised by two Dagger As and hit by several rounds of cannon fire, but the aircrafts' bombs missed their target. Shortly thereafter, a second group of Daggers appeared, one striking *Antrim* with a 1,000lb bomb, which bounced off the flight deck, smashed through various compartments including the magazine containing **Seaslug** surface-to-air missiles, before finally settling in one of the vessel's heads. Miraculously, the bomb failed to detonate an armed missile that it passed close to and did not itself explode. Minor fires were extinguished, but some damage was caused by bomb splinters to one of the ship's **helicopters**. A bomb disposal team defused the device later that day. Owing to damage sustained by her **Seacat** system, *Antrim* joined the **Carrier Battle Group** to the east of the Falklands, where she performed escort duties in the replenishment area for the remainder of the conflict. *Antrim*'s service in the war ended with her arrival in Plymouth on 17 July.

Commander:	Capt B.G. Young	
Builders:	Fairfield (Govan)	
Launched:	19 October 1967	
Commissioned:	14 July 1970	
Displacement (tons):	5,440 Standard	6,200 Full load
Dimensions: length × beam; feet (metres):	520 × 54 (158.5 × 16.5)	
Draught:	6.3m	
Propulsion:	2 sets geared steam turbines, 2 G6 gas turbines	30,000shp + 15,000shp = 32.5 knots
Armament:	2 × 4.5in (114mm) Mark 6 dual purpose guns (surface/AA)	
	2 × 20mm Oerlikon AA guns	
	1 × **Seaslug** 2 system (GWS 10)	
	2 **Seacat** systems (GWS 22)	
	4 × MM.38 **Exocet**	
Aircraft:	1 × **Wessex** HAS3	
	1 × **Wessex** HU5	

Antrim Group

Those vessels constituting the first flotilla to leave on operations in the South Atlantic. They headed from Exercise **Springtrain** for **Ascension** on 2 April, the day of the invasion of the Falklands, led by Rear Admiral **Woodward** in his flagship, the County class destroyer *Antrim*, her sister ship *Glamorgan*, Type 42 **destroyers** *Coventry*, *Glasgow* and *Sheffield*, the **frigates** *Arrow*, *Brilliant* and *Plymouth*, and the RFA fleet tankers *Appleleaf* and *Tidespring*. They arrived at Ascension on 10 April.

Appleleaf, RFA

One of five Leaf class support tankers chartered to the Ministry of Defence, together with *Pearleaf*, *Plumleaf*, *Bayleaf* and *Brambleleaf*. *Appleleaf* departed Exercise **Springtrain** on 2 April and served as a refuelling ship in the South Atlantic for ships transiting to and from the Falklands. She did not take part in the amphibious landings in **San Carlos Water** on 21 May and arrived back at Rosyth 9 August.

Commander:	Captain G.P.A. MacDougall	
Builders:	Cammell Laird	
Launched:	24 July 1975	
Commissioned:	November 1979	
Tonnage:	12,549 Gross Register	19,200 Deadweight
Dimensions: length × beam; feet (metres):	560 × 72 (170.7 × 21.9)	
Draught:	11.9m	
Propulsion:	2 diesel engines (one propeller)	9,500bhp = 15 knots
Fuel capacity:	2,498 tons	

Ardent, HMS

Of the fifteen **frigates** in the South Atlantic, *Ardent* numbered among seven of the Type 21 Amazon class, the others being *Active*, *Alacrity*, *Ambuscade*, *Antelope*, *Arrow*, and *Avenger*. *Ardent* departed from Devonport on 19 April and arrived at **Ascension** ten days later.

At midnight (Zulu) on 19–20 May she entered Falkland Sound from the north as the lead vessel of the **Amphibious Task Group** approaching **San Carlos Water** for the initial amphibious landings, then carried on to Grantham Sound, part of Falkland Sound, 12.5 miles from **Goose Green**, to support an **Special Air Service** (SAS) diversionary attack on Goose Green and **Darwin** timed to coincide with the landings.

Accordingly, at around 1130Z on D-Day, 21 May, she bombarded the grass airstrip there with 4.5in shells, hoping to hit the handful of Pucaras there, though these all withdrew to **Stanley** in the course of the day.

The Type 21 HMS *Ardent*, which sank on the evening of 22 May, after being struck by multiple bombs the previous evening. (AirSeaLand Photos)

At 1555Z a 1,000lb bomb dropped by a Skyhawk narrowly missed the frigate, inflicting no damage apart from bending the ship's radar antenna 30 degrees out of alignment. Later, three Dagger As appeared over Grantham Sound and at 1744Z attacked *Ardent*, which not only could not rotate its 4.5in gun to fire at aircraft approaching from behind but was unable to engage its **Seacat** system owing to a malfunction of its missile control, leaving the ship's defence to its Oerlikon 20mm guns and light machine guns. One 1,000lb bomb struck the sea, bounced and penetrated the ship's hull without exploding. A second bomb, however, landed on the hangar deck and detonated, killing or injuring several members of the crew, destroying the ship's hangar and Seacat launcher, rendering the ship's gun inoperable by severing power cables and causing several fires. A third Dagger missed *Ardent* with its bomb, but the ship was already in serious distress and slowly proceeded to the protection offered by friendly vessels at the mouth of San Carlos Water.

While proceeding northwards off North West Island at 1806Z, two A-4Q Skyhawks attacked *Ardent* from her rear quarter, both aircraft dropping their respective loads of four 500lb Snakeye bombs, an uncertain number of which struck her stern, adding to her already stricken state and setting new fires. A third Skyhawk also released its bombs, but apparently missed.

Having been struck by nine bombs, two of which failed to explode, bereft of her steering, her lower decks flooding, causing the ship to list, Commander West ordered the crew to abandon her, whereupon the survivors transferred to *Yarmouth* and then to *Canberra*, while **helicopters** flew her wounded directly to the latter vessel. She had lost twenty-two killed and more than thirty wounded. *Yarmouth* towed the frigate but on the evening of the 22nd *Ardent* exploded and sank off North West Island.

Commander:	Commander A.W.J. West	
Builders:	Yarrow (Scotstoun)	
Launched:	9 May 1975	
Commissioned:	13 October 1977	
Displacement (tons):	2,750 Standard	3,250 Full load
Dimensions: length × beam; feet (metres):	384 × 42 (117.0 × 12.8)	
Draught:	6.8m	
Propulsion:	2 × Olympus gas turbines	50,000shp = 31 + knots
	2 × Tyne gas turbines	8,500 shp = 18 knots (cruising)
Armament:	1 × 4.5in Mark 8 gun	
	2 × 20mm Oerlikon AA guns	
	1 × **Seacat** system (GWS 24)	
	4 × MM.38 **Exocet**	
Aircraft:	1 × **Lynx** HAS2	

Argonaut, HMS

One of fifteen **frigates** in the South Atlantic, but only one of three of the Batch 2 Leander class of this type of vessel, the others being *Minerva* and *Penelope*. *Argonaut* departed Devonport on 19 April and reached Ascension nine days later, finally reaching Falklands waters on 19 May.

On D-Day, 21 May, *Argonaut*, together with *Antrim* and *Broadsword*, was stationed off the mouth of **San Carlos Water** to form a screen against air attack, so offering at least limited protection to ships unloading troops and stores to the south. At 1315Z, as *Argonaut* lay off **Fanning Head**, an Argentine MB-339A attacked the frigate as a target of opportunity, firing rockets and 30mm cannon, causing minor damage to the **Seacat** missile deck and wounding three sailors.

Arriving over San Carlos Water about fifteen minutes later, some of a group of six Dagger As strafed *Argonaut* with cannon fire, causing only minor damage. However, at 1330Z six Skyhawk A-4Bs, each carrying a single 1,000lb bomb, concentrated against *Argonaut*, which was sailing close to the coast to derive the best protection possible from air attack. Two bombs hit their mark, one crashing through to the boiler room, where a boiler exploded, and the second reaching the forward magazine containing **Seacat** missiles, two of which partially exploded, causing serious flooding and a fire. Although neither bomb detonated, *Argonaut*'s extensive damage left her crippled, her engines out of action and her steering disabled. The various fires started were eventually controlled, but the ship struggled for Fanning Head and only avoided becoming grounded when the crew dropped her spare anchor. Two sailors in the Seacat magazine were killed in the attack.

Plymouth later towed her to a safe anchorage within San Carlos Water so she could be repaired and the bombs defused and disposed of, a process that took eight days in all, requiring holes to be cut into two decks through which the bombs were carefully extracted before being lowered into the sea. *Argonaut* was declared operational on the 26th and resumed air defence duties in San Carlos Water, but on the 29th the newly arrived *Minerva* relieved her so the ***Stena Seaspread*** could undertake repairs in the Tug, Repair and Logistic Area (TRALA). However, *Argonaut's* extensive damage could not be repaired at sea, so she departed from the **Total Exclusion Zone** for the UK on 5 June, to be overflown two days later 400 miles north of the TRALA by what was probably the last Argentine Air Force Boeing 707 to perform this form of reconnaissance over a British vessel during the conflict. *Argonaut* reached Devonport on 26 June.

Commander:	Captain C.H. Layman LVO	
Builders:	Hawthorn Leslie	
Launched:	8 February 1966	
Commissioned:	17 August 1967	
Displacement (tons):	2,650 Standard	3,200 Full load
Dimensions: length × beam; feet (metres):	372 × 41 (113.4 × 12.5)	
Draught:	5.8m	
Propulsion:	2 sets geared steam turbines	30,000shp = 28 knots
Armament:	2 × 40mm Bofors AA guns	
	3 × **Seacat** systems (GWS 22)	
	4 × MM.38 **Exocet**	
	2 × triple ASW torpedo tubes (STWS)	
Aircraft:	1 × **Lynx** HAS2	

Army Air Corps

The Army Air Corps supplied 658 Squadron to **5 Infantry Brigade** operations, consisting of six **Gazelle AH1** and seven **Scout AH1 helicopters**, stored aboard *Nordic Ferry* and *Baltic Ferry*, while most of its personnel sailed in the *Queen Elizabeth 2*. 656 Squadron came ashore in **San Carlos Water** on 2 June with the rest of 5 Infantry Brigade, with its helicopters operating throughout in forward areas, providing a continuous stream of resupplied ammunition while returning to field hospitals with casualties. Forward ammunition and refuelling points enabled these light helicopters to operate well beyond their peacetime hours and ordinary load limits to meet the pressures of operational requirements.

Arrow, HMS

Of the fifteen **frigates** in the South Atlantic, *Arrow* numbered among seven of the Type 21 (Antelope class), the others being *Active*, *Alacrity*, *Ambuscade*, *Antelope*, *Ardent* and *Avenger*.

She departed from Exercise **Springtrain** on 2 April and reached **Ascension** on the 11th. On the first day she arrived off the Falklands, 1 May, *Arrow* positioned herself off Cape Pembroke and briefly shelled **Stanley** airfield, in company with *Alacrity* and *Glamorgan*, when a Dagger A fighter-bomber came close to hitting her with two 500lb parachute-retarded bombs. These missed their target, but *Arrow* was hit by a few rounds of cannon fire from one of the three Daggers that attacked the formation. When her radar failed to detect the approach of the aircraft, *Arrow* only had time to unleash a few rounds of 20mm cannon fire in response, but to no effect.

Three days later, on 4 May, *Arrow* came alongside the blazing *Sheffield* and rescued most of her survivors, breaking away, however, when she erroneously detected the presence of a torpedo fired at her.

On the evening of 11 May, while in the company of *Alacrity* near the northern mouth of Falkland Sound, the two vessels came under attack by the Argentine submarine *San Luis*, whose torpedo missed both vessels but appeared to have damaged *Arrow*'s towed torpedo decoy. Five days later, *Arrow*'s **Lynx HAS2** inserted three Special Forces teams on to the north coast of East Falkland to gather intelligence in aid of the impending amphibious landings in **San Carlos Water**.

As part of the **Carrier Battle Group**, *Arrow* was not directly involved in the landings in San Carlos Water on 21 May, but she was later detached to provide **naval gunfire support** to **2 Para** during the Battle of **Goose Green**. At 0700Z on 28 May, the frigate began firing high-explosive rounds with her 4.5in gun – 135 in all – before the gun jammed, leaving the infantry with no further naval gunfire support. Thereafter, she spent the next fortnight in Falkland Sound and San Carlos Water, rejoining the Carrier Battle Group largely unscathed on 7 June.

Originally meant to support the attack of **3 Commando Brigade** on Stanley, which Admiral **Woodward** hoped would take place on the night of 5–6 June, *Arrow* did not become engaged at that time, since Major General **Moore** pushed back the operation to the 9th, as a result of which he recalled both *Arrow* and *Active*. In the event, her last aggressive act occurred on 13 June when, in support of ground operations, she fired 103 4.5in shells on **Sapper Hill** and along Moody Brook. In total, since entering the **Total Exclusion Zone**, *Arrow* had fired 902 shells in various bombardments. She reached Devonport on 7 July.

Commander:	Commander P.J. Bootherstone	
Builders:	Yarrow (Scotstoun)	
Launched:	5 February 1974	
Commissioned:	29 July 1976	
Displacement (tons):	2,750 Standard	3,250 Full load
Dimensions: length × beam; feet (metres):	384 × 42 (117.0 × 12.8)	
Draught:	6.8m	
Propulsion:	2 × Olympus gas turbines	50,000shp = 31 + knots
	2 × Tyne gas turbines	8,500 shp = 18 knots (cruising)

A

Armament:	1 × 4.5in Mark 8 gun
	2 × 20mm AA guns
	1 × **Seacat** system (GWS 24)
	4 × MM.38 **Exocet**
Aircraft:	1 × **Lynx** HAS2

Artillery

See Royal Artillery

AS.12 Anti-ship Missile

Manufactured by the French firm, Aerospatiale, the AS.12 was launched by helicopter and wire-guided, its 6ft (1.87m), 165lb (75kg) missile propelled by a solid fuel rocket capable of carrying it to a range of approximately 7,500yd (7km).

Ascension

Located in the South Atlantic at position 7.56 degrees south, 14.22 degrees west, 4,200 miles (3,700 nautical) from the UK and 3,800 miles (3,300 nautical) from the Falklands, Ascension served as the only viable forward operating base for British forces operating in the South Atlantic. Its isolated position offered a number of advantages: good security from attack; a fine anchorage; Wideawake Airfield; and no access to the media. The British Support Unit established on the island had the task of being the forward logistic support for Operation **Corporate**. This involved first, supporting ships in the South Atlantic engaged in trans-shipping men, stores, ammunition and **helicopters** from the island; second, supporting **Royal Air Force** operations launched from the island; third, providing facilities for

A Wessex at Ascension with Nimrods and a Victor tanker in the background. (AirSeaLand Photos)

fitness and weapon training for troops arriving by air or sea en route to the Falklands; and fourth, securing the defence of the island, which at the outset of the campaign had a population of some 1,100 inhabitants, of whom only 250 comprised the permanent staff of the British Forces Support Unit.

The 10,000ft airstrip on Ascension, built by the United States during the Second World War and operated by Pan American Airways, normally handled about forty movements a month; yet in astonishingly short order became a fully fledged airport – a veritable unsinkable aircraft carrier – handling close to 400 movements every day, and on 18 April achieved, by virtue of facilitating 500 air movements, the dubious honour of being the busiest airport in the world. The runway could accommodate aircraft of any size, but could only park about two dozen aircraft at a time including **Hercules** C1/C3, **Phantom** FGR2, **Nimrod** MR1/MR2, **Vulcan** B2, **Victor** K2, and **Sea King** HAR3. Ascension also posed particular engineering problems for aircraft, with fine particles of volcanic ash clogging air filters and damaging engines.

During the course of the campaign the island's two Pan Am air traffic controllers managed 2,500 fixed-wing flights and 10,600 helicopter rotations, all with a single runway at their disposal. RAF personnel on Ascension would move 5,800 personnel and 6,600 tons of stores with a combination of aircraft: Hercules, Belfast transports decommissioned from military service but chartered from a civilian firm, and **VC10** passenger and medical aircraft.

In order to cope with the tremendous need for aircraft fuel, **Royal Engineers** laid a 4-mile fuel pipeline between the storage facility, topped up by tankers offshore, and Wideawake. Sappers also constructed additional hardstanding to expand the airfield capacity for parking aircraft. Fuel *in situ* was also provided by the United States, amounting to 1.2 million gallons plus a small reserve.

Measures were taken to enlarge the island's limited water supply through the introduction of desalinators, to rapidly increase the supply of aviation fuel, to provide additional sanitation facilities, expand local transport, and to erect tented accommodation at English Bay to supplement existing housing – adequate hitherto, but now utterly insufficient for the new requirement. By the assiduous efforts of the Royal Engineers and civilian staff from Cable and Wireless, by the middle of April the island could accommodate 1,500 personnel and facilities had been organised for the stowage of vast amounts of equipment and stores.

On 6 April, the first stores arrived by RAF transport aircraft and were distributed into dumps to the south and east of the airfield by a combination of Army and **Royal Navy** personnel. Ascension was to form the hub for most of the **logistics** connected with operations, which would eventually involve some impressive statistics.

Helicopters had a particularly busy time while ships of the **Task Force** were using Ascension Island as a staging post. Two Royal Navy **Wessex** based at Wideawake soon became overwhelmed with work in HDS and CERTREP tasks, but were assisted by passing ships' helicopters as available. Thus, when for instance *Atlantic*

Conveyor reached Ascension on 5 May, one of her **Chinooks** stayed behind until 3 June, offering a heavy-lift capability unmatched by other machines.

As an Argentine air attack or commando assault remained a possibility, albeit remote, plans were made for the island's defence. The RAF deployed three **Harrier GR3s** of 1 Squadron on air defence duties in the first week of May, accompanied by **Rapier** batteries, and an early warning **radar** system established on Green Mountain. When the Harriers joined the Task Force on 24 May, two Phantom FGR2s from RAF Coningsby replaced them, and a third two days later, all flown down with in-flight refuelling provided by Victors and taking nine and a half hours. Ascension hosted Naval Party 1222, which arrived on 6 April, formed as a Naval Aircraft Servicing Unit and varying in size between ninety and 120 personnel.

3 Commando Brigade spent three weeks off Ascension from 20 April, remaining on their ships throughout and going ashore for physical and weapons training, as well as carrying out helicopter and **landing craft** practice drills from the assortment of ships, including merchant ships, which happened to be at hand – though these were not designed as amphibious ships. This period also offered the brigade the opportunity to restow its equipment in a more efficient manner. Admiral **Fieldhouse** arrived at Ascension on 17 April to plan the landings with Brigadier **Thompson**, Commodore Clapp and Admiral **Woodward**.

On 6 May, a detachment from 2 Wing, RAF Regiment, arrived on the island both to contribute to air defence and to provide security to the airfield. Shortly thereafter, a small body from 15 Field Squadron, RAF Regiment, joined them. Within days they had established an air surveillance radar system on Green Mountain, the island's highest point, to assist with other early warning features. In the same month, authorities established a 200-mile Terminal Control Area that required all air traffic entering and leaving to register their movements with radar controllers at Wideawake, barring which a Harrier would be scrambled for interception.

The first of sixteen Nimrods refitted for in-flight refuelling began to arrive at Ascension on 7 May, from where they would fly extended surveillance and search-and-rescue missions in the South Atlantic. The first extended-range Hercules reached Wideawake on 5 May and flew operationally for the first time two days later. Ascension also served as the base from which the **Black Buck** raids were launched on the night of 30 April/1 May and on subsequent occasions.

Wideawake nearly reached its capacity on 27 May when it hosted two Vulcan B2s, seventeen Victor tankers, two Harriers, three Nimrods, three Hercules, three Phantoms, one Chinook, one Sea King and two Wessex.

Astronomer, MV

A roll-on/roll-off motor container ship, *Astronomer* was requisitioned from the Harrison Line on 28 May as a helicopter carrier and repair ship, one of numerous

Ships Taken Up From Trade, but did not depart from Devonport until 8 June, arriving at **Ascension** eight days later, and in Falklands waters on 26 June, twelve days after the end of the fighting. Nevertheless, her cargo of **helicopters** was much needed to replace those airframes fatigued from intensive activity during Operation **Corporate**. She carried in her Naval Party 2140 under Lieutenant Commander R. Gainsford RN and did not arrive back in Devonport until 3 December.

Commander:	Captain H.S. Braden	
Launched:	1977	
Tonnage:	27,870 Gross Register	23,120 Deadweight
Dimensions: length × beam; feet (metres):	670 × 102 (204.2 × 31)	
Propulsion:	1 diesel engine	26,100bhp = 20 knots
Armament:	2 × 20mm AA guns	
Aircraft cargo:	6 × **Wessex** HU5	
	3 × **Scout** AH1	
	3 × **Chinook** HC1	

Atlantic Causeway, SS

One of the many **Ships Taken Up From Trade**, *Atlantic Causeway* was a steam ro-ro container ship requisitioned from Cunard/ACL on 3 May for use in the helicopter support role. She carried aboard her Naval Party 1990 under Commander R.P. Seymour RN.

Departing from Devonport on 14 May with the bulk of the support equipment, vehicles and stores for **5 Infantry Brigade**, and reaching **Ascension** on the 22nd, her cargo included eight **Rapier** fire units of 63 Squadron, RAF Regiment, and twenty-eight **helicopters**, which became particularly precious when she arrived in the **Total Exclusion Zone** on 29 May, four days after the loss of the *Atlantic Conveyor*. The first of her helicopters flew ashore to a Forward Operating Base (FOB) at **San Carlos** before dawn on 1 June; on the same day she also unloaded special vertical and/or short take-off and landing (V/STOL) pads designed as hardstandings for the temporary aluminium airstrip being constructed near **Port San Carlos** for use by **Harriers** and **Sea Harriers**. With eight remaining **Wessex** HU5s of 847 NAS, she sailed on 2 June to the Tug, Repair and Logistic Area (TRALA) to serve as a floating reserve, arriving back in Devonport on 27 July.

Commander:	Captain M.H.C. Twomey	
Launched:	1969	
Tonnage:	14,950 Gross Register	18,150 Deadweight
Dimensions: length × beam; feet (metres):	696 × 92 (212.1 × 28.1)	
Propulsion:	2 sets of geared steam turbines	38,500shp = 23 knots
Aircraft cargo:	8 × **Sea King** HAS2A	
	20 × **Wessex** HU5	

Atlantic Conveyor, SS

One of many **Ships Taken Up From Trade**, a steam ro-ro container ship, requisitioned from Cunard/ACL at Devonport on 14 April for use in the aircraft and helicopter support role. Her large flat deck area proved ideal as a secondary temporary **aircraft carrier** in the event of the loss of *Hermes*. Work began immediately in clearing all objects from her deck that could inhibit stowage of aircraft and supplies and the take-off and landing of **helicopters** and **Sea Harriers**. Her decks were strengthened, and aircraft refuelling facilities and additional accommodation added. She also carried Naval Party 1840 under Captain M.G. Layard.

All the Sea Harriers and **Harriers** carried south by *Atlantic Conveyor* had been transferred before she was sunk; before then, one 809 Naval Air Squadron Sea Harrier FRS1 remained permanently armed and ready on deck in the event of a hostile aircraft or ship falling within its range.

On the afternoon of 25 May, radar aboard *Exeter* and *Ambuscade*, both with the **Carrier Battle Group** approximately 60 miles north-east of **Stanley**, detected the approach of two Super Etendards. *Atlantic Conveyor* was in the vicinity and expected later that night in **San Carlos Water** to unload its valuable cargo of **Wessex HU5** and **Chinook HC1 helicopters** to be used to convey troops during the coming ground offensive. As many Sea Harriers as could be spared immediately left *Hermes*'s and *Invincible*'s decks to intercept the **Exocet**-armed aircraft while

Atlantic Conveyor burning after an Exocet missile strike on 25 May. (AirSeaLand Photos)

all **Lynx** helicopters aboard both aircraft carriers took to the air to employ their countermeasures, including chaff rockets, many of which were fired. By this time the Exocets had already been launched, however, and at 1841Z one of them struck the *Atlantic Conveyor* 10ft above the waterline. As she lay only 2 miles from *Hermes* and 8 more from *Invincible*, either of these vessels may in fact have been the intended target, with chaff fired by *Ambuscade* possibly having decoyed the missile away from the carriers to the next available target, the unfortunate *Atlantic Conveyor*. It is possible that she was hit by both Exocets, but it appears the second missile was deflected by chaff and jamming, although possibly hit by one of six **Sea Darts** fired by *Invincible*.

The Exocet smashed its way through her starboard hull and exploded in an open deck containing fully fuelled trucks, which immediately caught fire. This initiated a rescue operation, with Wessex and **Sea Kings** responding from *Hermes* and *Invincible*, which proceeded to collect a small number of crew members trapped on the forward deck of the ship. *Alacrity* and *Brilliant* rescued many others who had taken to life rafts, with 133 personnel rescued in all. Twelve men died, including Captain Ian North, who drowned before he could reach a lifeboat. Many of the survivors arrived at Brize Norton on 7 June via a **VC10 C1** flown from **Ascension**.

The loss of *Atlantic Conveyor* left the ground forces without vital helicopters and stores, including vast quantities of aircraft spare parts, aircraft refuelling equipment, cluster bombs and 1,000lb bombs, tents, food, ammunition, cooking and laundry equipment, and material to construct a temporary Harrier airstrip. In all, ten helicopters were lost: three Chinook HC1s, six Wessex, and one Lynx. This loss would leave **3 Commando Brigade** to depend on whatever stores remained unloaded and supplies already in possession of the troops. The loss of the ten helicopters had a profound effect on the campaign, as it delayed the advance on **Stanley** since many troops were obliged to advance on foot rather than by air.

By extraordinary good fortune, the only remaining Chinook HC1 with the **Task Force** (ZA718 of 18 Squadron) and stored on the deck of *Atlantic Conveyor*, was aloft at the time of the attack, piloted by Flight Lieutenant John Kennedy, engaged in resupply sorties to other ships. It took refuge aboard *Hermes* until transferring the following day to the Eagle Base near **San Carlos**. A Wessex in temporary use onboard but belonging to *Fort Austin*, happened to be airborne at the time of the attack and, after assisting in the rescue operation, it landed on *Hermes*.

Three days after the attack a party from the tug *Irishman* boarded the badly burned hulk of the *Atlantic Conveyor* for purposes of ascertaining what cargo could still be salvaged. Damage, however, proved so extensive, that the ship's back broke during a storm on the 30th, the forward section sinking while the aft section refused to go under. To avoid the risk of leaving this derelict section afloat as a potential hazard to other shipping, naval gunfire put paid to the last of the cargo vessel.

Commander:	Captain I. North	
Launched:	1970	
Tonnage:	14,950 Gross Register	18,150 Deadweight
Dimensions: length × beam; feet (metres):	696 × 92 (212.1 × 28.1)	
Propulsion:	2 sets of geared steam turbines	38,500shp = 23 knots
Aircraft Cargo:	8 × **Sea King** HAS2A	
	20 × **Wessex** HU5	

Avelona Star, MV

Motor refrigerated cargo ship, this **Ships Taken Up From Trade** was chartered from Blue Star Line on 28 May for transporting refrigerated food and provisions. The Royal Navy Supply and Transport Service supplied her Naval Party. She departed from Portsmouth on 10 June and arrived nine days later in **Ascension**, five days after the end of the war. She served off the Falklands from 1 July and arrived in Portsmouth on 29 November, though her period of requisition did not cease until May 1984.

Commander:	Captain H. Dyer	
Tonnage:	9,784 Gross Register	11,092 Deadweight
Dimensions: length × beam; feet (metres):	511 × 70.5 (155.8 × 21.5)	
Propulsion:	1 diesel engine	17,400bhp = 24 knots
Helicopter platform – no embarked aircraft		

Avenger, HMS

Of the fifteen **frigates** in the South Atlantic, *Avenger* numbered among seven of the Type 21 variety, the others being *Active, Alacrity, Ambuscade, Antelope, Ardent* and *Arrow*.

She departed Devonport 10 May, reaching **Ascension** in eight days. Having arrived off the Falklands on 25 May, a **Special Boat Squadron** (SBS) team went ashore at Volunteer Bay just north of **Berkeley Sound** care of a **Lynx** flown from *Avenger* on 29 May. The following day, a Super Etendard fired the last air-launched **Exocet** missile available to the Argentines during the conflict. Probably deflected off course by chaff, this fell into the sea between *Avenger* and *Exeter*, which were 10 miles apart, without causing any harm.

On 3 June *Avenger* issued fire against **Pebble Island** off **West Falkland**. About the same time it bombarded **Fox Bay** before examining Albermarle harbour as a possible refuge for ships carrying troops from **5 Infantry Brigade** bound for the **Port Pleasant** area. On 7 June at about 1930Z she entered Falkland Sound, together with *Fearless* and *Penelope*, and inserted a SBS patrol to search for a suspected radar station on Sea Lion Island. For part of her journey to the south coast of East Falkland, *Avenger* escorted the two *Fearless* **landing craft** conveying two companies of the **Welsh Guards**, which landed at **Bluff Cove** in the early hours of 8 June. Thereafter, throughout most of the 11th, when she returned to **San Carlos Water**, *Avenger* patrolled off the coast of West Falkland searching for Argentine ships and aircraft seeking to bring in supplies.

On the night of 11–12 June, in company with *Glamorgan* and *Yarmouth*, she stood on the southern gunline to bombard Argentine positions in support of the ground operations under way that evening against **Mount Longdon**, against which she fired 156 rounds, and **Two Sisters**. Together with *Active*, she fired a total of 856 rounds against Argentine positions on **Mount Tumbledown** in support of the **Scots Guards** assault on the evening of 13–14 June. On 15 June a Lynx from *Avenger* flew a small party to Fox Bay on West Falkland to accept the surrender of the 8th Regiment. *Avenger* arrived back in Devonport on 10 September.

Commander:	Captain H.M. White	
Builders:	Yarrow (Scotstoun)	
Launched:	20 November 1975	
Commissioned:	15 April 1978	
Displacement (tons):	2,750 Standard	3,250 Full load
Dimensions: length × beam; feet (metres):	384 × 42 (117.0 × 12.8)	
Draught:	6.8m	
Propulsion:	2 × Olympus gas turbines	50,000shp = 31 + knots
	2 × Tyne gas turbines	8,500shp = 18 knots (cruising)
Armament:	1 × 4.5in Mark 8 gun	
	2 × 20mm Oerlikon AA guns (increased to 3 in June)	
	1 × **Seacat** system (GWS 24)	
	4 × MM.38 **Exocet**	
	2 × triple ASW Mark 46 torpedo tubes (STWS)	
Aircraft:	1 × **Lynx** HAS2	

Balder London, MV

B

One of many **Ships Taken Up From Trade**, *Balder London* was a motor tanker chartered on 12 May from Lloyds Industrial Leasing for fleet refuelling duties and carried a Naval Party supplied by the **Royal Fleet Auxiliary**. She departed Portsmouth on 12 May, arriving off the Falklands about the time of the end of fighting, and back in Portsmouth on 15 August.

Commander:	Captain K.J. Wallace	
Launched:	1979	
Tonnage:	19,975 Gross Register	
Dimensions: length × beam; feet (metres):	560 × 72 (170.7 × 21.9)	33,750 Deadweight
Propulsion:	2 diesel engines (1 propeller)	14,000bhp = 16 knots

Baltic Ferry, MV

A roll-on/roll-off vehicle ferry built for Stena Cargo Line and requisitioned from Townsend Thoresen on 1 May for troop and helicopter transport. She constituted one of the many **Ships Taken Up From Trade** requisitioned during the conflict, with Naval Party 1960 aboard under Lieutenant Commander G.B. Webb.

Together with *Nordic Ferry*, she sailed from Southampton on 12 May in company with *Queen Elizabeth 2*, and carried part of **5 Infantry Brigade's** vehicles and stores to the South Atlantic. After troops from *QE2* cross-decked on to *Canberra* and *Norland* off **South Georgia** on 27 May, *Baltic Ferry* accompanied them into Falklands waters, arriving there on 1 June and proceeding into **San Carlos Water**, where she anchored near the **Blue Beaches**. She remained in the South Atlantic until finally reaching Felixstowe on 12 April 1983.

Commander:	Captain E. Harrison	
Built:	1978	
Tonnage:	6,455 Gross Register	8,704 Deadweight
Dimensions: length × beam; feet (metres)	495 × 71 (151 × 21.7)	
Propulsion:	2 diesel engines	15,600bhp = 17 knots
Aircraft cargo (UK to San Carlos):	3 × **Scout** AH1	

Bayleaf, RFA

One of five Leaf class support tankers chartered to the Ministry of Defence, together with *Pearleaf*, *Plumleaf*, *Appleleaf* and *Brambleleaf*. *Bayleaf* was of such a recent design that she was still under construction when the **Task Force** sailed. During her conversion she was fitted with replenishment at sea and helicopter facilities. She departed from Devonport on 26 April, reached **Ascension** on 8 May and the **Total Exclusion Zone** on the 25th, arriving back at Devonport on 31 August.

Commander:	Captain A.E.T. Hunter	
Builders:	Cammell Laird	
Launched:	27 October 1981	
Commissioned:	26 March 1982	
Tonnage:	12,549 Gross Register	19,200 Deadweight
Dimensions: length × beam; feet (metres):	560 × 72 (170.7 × 21.9)	
Draught:	11.9m	
Propulsion:	2 diesel engines (1 propeller)	9,500bhp = 15 knots
Fuel capacity:	2,498 tons	

Beagle Ridge

A desolate, elevated position overlooking **Stanley** from the north, which the **Special Boat Squadron** used as an observation post.

Berkeley Sound

During the course of their journey to **Ascension**, Commodore Clapp and Brigadier **Thompson** chose three possible beaches on which to effect a landing, including Berkeley Sound, a few miles north of **Stanley**.

Black Buck Raids

The Black Buck raids involved strikes executed by a single **Vulcan** B2 bomber mounted from **Ascension** to **Stanley** airfield for the purpose of rendering it operationally useless, at least temporarily; they would also test the impressive ground-based air defences around the capital. Each sortie lasted at least fifteen hours in the air – an unprecedented feat on operations – and required at least eighteen air-to-air refuellings carried out by a minimum of fifteen **Victor** K2 tankers, the whole effort requiring precise timings and careful execution. As in each case the Vulcan would be travelling from Ascension, no opposition was anticipated from air assets, but a **Sea Harrier combat air patrol** operated in the area as a precautionary measure.

A successful bomb run would render the runway at Stanley airfield non-operational, so confining the Argentines' fast jets – Mirages, Super Etendards and Skyhawks – to missions flown from the mainland 400 miles to the west. This would reduce their loiter time over the Falklands to a few minutes, thus decreasing their options for targeting and providing more time to detect their approach. The raid was also designed to open the air campaign in a dramatic fashion, so signifying Britain's determination to press through its offensive to retake the islands.

An RAF Vulcan at Wideawake Airfield, Ascension. (AirSeaLand Photos)

Two Vulcans, each loaded with twenty-one 1,000lb high-explosive bombs, took off just after midnight on 30 April/1 May, but owing to a defect in the window seal of the primary aircraft resulting in its inability to pressurise the aircraft at high altitude, the reserve aircraft (Squadron Leader R.J. Reeve and Flight Lieutenant W.F.M. Withers in XM607) had to replace it, refuelling six times on the journey and proceeding in the company of ten Victors, each returning to Ascension after progressively refuelling Withers' aircraft and two Victors that accompanied it to the extremity of its mission south. To preserve secrecy the aircraft flew without navigation lights and in complete radio silence, at a height of 8,000ft and a ground speed of 300 knots.

To avoid detection by Argentine **radar**, the Vulcan descended to 250ft when approximately 300 miles from Stanley, which was to be hit from 10,000ft and thus required XM607 to climb again when about 40 miles from its target. The Vulcan's electronic countermeasures jammed the radar detecting it and at 0738Z, catching the Argentines completely by surprise, it released its bomb load in a diagonal run across the runway, at approximately 48yd spacings, effectively guaranteeing at least one direct hit. One bomb struck the runway while the others extended away, and by the time Argentine anti-aircraft guns responded the Vulcan was considerably beyond their range.

Owing to complications connected to refuelling on the journey south, the Vulcan became short of fuel and another Victor had to be dispatched from Ascension to assist her. This occurred with little time to spare, allowing Withers to reach Wideawake

Airfield safely at 1452Z on 1 May after a sixteen-hour flight which had covered a total of 7,860 miles.

The success of the Black Buck 1 mission may be assessed as mixed, for while it planted a bomb on target, it only denied the Argentines its use for two days while damage was repaired. Other damage to the control tower and facilities around the airport contributed to degrading the Argentines' capacity, but the facility was not crippled. On the other hand, the raid represented a triumph of signalling and planning, with sixteen Victor sorties (two sorties flown by five aircraft each) and eighteen refuellings carried out. Psychologically, too, the raid drove home to the Argentines not only the resolve of British forces to carry through their declared intention to repossess the islands by force, but demonstrated the potential for a British attack against mainland airbases and possibly even Buenos Aires itself, as a result of which the Argentine Air Force moved some of its Mirages to protect bases hitherto thought invulnerable to attack.

A second raid on Stanley airfield, designated as Black Buck 2, took place on 4 May. Taking off just before midnight on the 3rd, Squadron Leader Reeve in XM607, accompanied by a reserve Vulcan (XM598) and Victor tankers, dropped his bombs at 0830Z from 16,000ft – 6,000ft higher than in Black Buck 1 – in order to provide greater protection from air defences on the ground. The ordnance failed to hit the runway, though it did cause damage to the area around it. The Vulcan had spent approximately fifteen hours in the air by the time it returned safely to Ascension.

In preparation for Black Buck 3, Vulcan B2 XM612 flew from RAF Waddington to Ascension on 14 May, arriving the following day, as did XM607, with the sortie to Stanley airport due for the 16th. The mission was cancelled owing to strong winds carrying the potential of requiring expenditure of too much reserve fuel and to the ground crews' removal at Waddington of the port underwing pylon in the mistaken belief that it was responsible for excessive drag. The two aircraft consequently returned to Waddington, one on the 20th and the other three days later.

As part of the preparation for Black Buck 4, XM598 flew from Waddington to Ascension on 26 May. The mission was to destroy sophisticated radar in Stanley that was providing Argentine aircraft with early warning of Sea Harrier CAPs, thus enabling them to avoid interception. With these radar facilities sited with civilian houses close by conventional bombs could not be risked for fear of inflicting collateral damage; instead, a precision-guided weapon – the US-built AGM-45A Shrike anti-radar missile that was too large for the Sea Harrier and **Harrier** – would be deployed by an adapted Vulcan. Two Vulcans were duly converted, XM598 and XM597 arriving at Wideawake on 26 and 27 May, respectively. Owing to a fault aboard one of the Victors in the early hours of 29 May that required its return to Ascension, Black Buck 4 was cancelled.

Black Buck 5 was launched a few minutes before midnight on 30 May, with the same objective as before: the radar installation at Stanley. Two toss-bomb missions against the airfield by two sets of Sea Harriers prior to the Vulcan strike were flown to divert the attention of Argentine radar to other aircraft while the Vulcan approached. After some initial difficulty identifying the Argentine radar signal, XM597 launched its two Shrikes at 0845Z on the 31st, one of which struck the ground nearby and only caused enough damage to put the radar out of action for twenty-four hours.

Black Buck 6 sought out the same target as the previous mission – the TPS-43F surveillance radar system somewhere in Stanley. Vulcan XM597 left Ascension on the night of 2 June, but after arriving over Stanley on the 3rd it found that, as before, Argentine operators reduced their signal strength to confound detection, thus obliging the Vulcan to spend forty minutes looking for a radar signal on which to lock. In the event, a Skyguard anti-aircraft gun-control radar illuminated the Vulcan rather than the TPS-43F surveillance radar that was the intended target. With fuel low, no more time available to maintain the search, and now coming under anti-aircraft fire, the Vulcan launched two of its four Shrikes and destroyed the Skyguard radar and its crew.

XM597 took on additional fuel from a Victor tanker about 2,000 miles south of Ascension, but when the probe broke the Vulcan found itself unable to reach Wideawake. The only alternative was to land at the closest available airfield, at Rio de Janeiro in Brazil. By increasing elevation from 20,000 to 40,000ft the navigator burned less fuel. To avoid the security and diplomatic problems associated with landing in a neutral country with a fully armed aircraft, the crew tried to fire off the two remaining Shrikes, but one failed to launch, though they did manage to throw classified documents and maps into the sea in a weighted bag. The Foreign Office frantically organised the aircraft's unscheduled reception in Rio, where the authorities gave clearance for landing, with the Vulcan having so little fuel left as to deny it a second approach to the airport. The Brazilian authorities impounded the Vulcan, but the crew remained with the aircraft and flew to Ascension on 10 June.

Black Buck 7, the last of its kind, took place on 12 June, directed against the airfield facilities at Stanley as opposed to the runway, as in the past. At this advanced stage of the campaign there was a requirement for the runway to be captured largely intact to enable British air transport on to the islands as part of the maintenance and recovery period. In the event, the mission did not inflict significant damage.

If the results of the Black Buck missions fell well short of expectation, they nevertheless represented a remarkable logistic and technological achievement. The runway at Stanley was not put out of use; on the other hand, the Argentines were aware from 1 May of the British capacity to bomb the mainland airfields, and thus the psychological impact of the missions should not be underestimated.

Blowpipe

Carried by 43 Battery, 32nd Guided Weapons Regiment, this cumbersome, 42lb shoulder-borne anti-aircraft missile system had a range of 3,000yd, was optically aimed and operated with a radio guidance system. Blowpipe appears only to have scored one hit against Argentine aircraft during the conflict – the MB-339A downed at **Goose Green** on 28 May by Marine Strange of **3 Commando Brigade** Air Defence Troop. The fact that ninety-five missiles were fired, of which almost half failed to deploy, is testament to the weapon's poor performance. For instance, a Blowpipe missile was fired at one of five Skyhawks that attacked *Sir Galahad* and *Sir Tristram* near **Fitzroy** on 8 June, but missed its target.

Blue Beaches

Designated 'One' and 'Two', they formed the landing sites near **San Carlos** settlement for **2 Para** and **40 Commando**, respectively, on 21 May. At the end of May, *Norland* and *Canberra*, accompanied by *Baltic Ferry*, anchored off the Blue Beaches, where the troops went ashore by **landing craft** and ships' boats.

'Blue on Blue'

The NATO term, also known as 'friendly fire', for an unwitting discharge against, or exchange of fire with, friendly units. Numerous 'Blue on Blue' incidents occurred during the conflict, on land, at sea and in the air.

While **3 Para** was clearing the Argentine withdrawal from **Port San Carlos** on 21 May, the day of the landings, a clash occurred between A and C Companies. The mortar platoon became involved, and two **Scimitars** fired on C Company. A helicopter evacuating two wounded Paras was also damaged.

The presence of a large number of friendly vessels in, and aircraft over, the confined spaces of Falkland Sound and particularly **San Carlos Water** from 21 May greatly increased the potential for friendly fire incidents. **Rapier** missile crews were particularly wary of inadvertently firing on friendly aircraft amidst the extremely confined and busy airspace.

On 22 May, with the build-up of stores around San Carlos Water in full swing and a great deal of air activity under way, a **Sea King** from *Fearless* was almost fired at after *Intrepid* reported it as hostile.

When at 1820Z on 25 May two **Sea Harriers** spotted two Skyhawks over **West Falkland** within 3 miles of them and poised to launch their **Sidewinders**, they were ordered to break off for fear that the **Sea Dart** system aboard *Coventry*, which had tracked the Argentine jets, would inadvertently lock on to the Sea Harriers.

On 1 June, owing to being inserted in the wrong area near **Mount Kent**, a sergeant in the **Special Boat Squadron** was killed when his patrol was ambushed by an **Special Air Service** counterpart.

A potentially disastrous 'Blue on Blue' incident was narrowly averted when on 2 June the sole surviving **Chinook** in theatre transported elements of **2 Para** to the **Fitzroy** area without any prior notice being given to HQ 3 **Commando Brigade** or HQ Land Forces Falkland Islands. A team from the **Mountain and Arctic Warfare Cadre** (M&AWC) spotted the helicopter and some of the troops landing, but in heavy mist and low visibility it could not make positive identification. Cadre HQ at **Teal Inlet**, co-located with HQ 3 Commando Brigade, confirmed that no friendly troops were in the area – a situation made more unclear by the fact that the Argentines also flew the Chinook – as a result of which M&AWC called in a fire mission, tasked to 7 (Sphinx) Commando Battery, 8 miles north of the target. Just before this was initiated, the mist cleared long enough for the patrol to identify a **Scout** helicopter with British markings and the fire mission was cancelled.

On the night of 5 June, while part of **5 Infantry Brigade** was en route by sea to **Bluff Cove**, a **Gazelle** (XX377) piloted by Staff Sergeant C.A. Griffin and Lance Corporal S.K. Cockton of 656 Squadron took off from **Goose Green** at 2030Z carrying Signals Squadron personnel to Mount Pleasant Peak to establish a broadcast relay station. Having completed this task, they returned to Goose Green. When several hours later, however, the station ceased to function, another sortie was sent, at 0350Z on the 6th. However, HQ 5 Infantry Brigade did not advise other units and vessels of this movement, and so when at approximately 0350Z the destroyer *Cardiff* detected its presence near Mount Pleasant Peak – over an area considered hostile – she fired a **Sea Dart** in the belief that the contact was an Argentine C-130 en route to **Stanley**. The missile destroyed the helicopter, killing all aboard, including the Signals Squadron commanding officer, Major M. Forge, and Staff Sergeant J.I. Baker. A post-war Ministry of Defence investigation determined that the Gazelle was not brought down by a Sea Dart; but at the insistence of Lance Corporal Cockton's family, an independent enquiry was undertaken and when parts of a Sea Dart were discovered in the wreckage the MoD admitted that *Cardiff* had in fact brought the aircraft down.

Nevertheless, the fact remained that XX377 executed a flight over an area still considered hostile, flying higher and more quickly than the established limit for friendly **helicopters**: not above 100ft or above 100 knots. Helicopters exceeding these limits were assumed to be hostile and could be fired upon under the existing rules of engagement.

In the early hours of 6 June, *Cardiff*, still close inshore off Fitzroy in order to provide **naval gunfire support** to troops advancing in the areas of **Mount William**, **Moody Brook** and **Mount Tumbledown**, and unaware that *Intrepid* had retracted four **landing craft** off Lively Island as part of the **Scots Guards** move to Bluff Cove, fired six star shells over the craft before signalling them to 'heave to' and identifying them as friendly. As a consequence, disaster facing 600 men was narrowly averted.

On the night of 9–10 June, poor weather and poor communications resulted in a **45 Commando** patrol firing on their own mortar platoon, killing four **Royal Marines** and wounding four more.

On 10 June, when D Company 1/7th **Gurkhas** advanced to **Mount Challenger**, poor unit co-ordination and faulty **radio communication** nearly resulted in an exchange of fire with the **Welsh Guards**.

On the morning 11 June, when two **Harrier** GR3s sought to attack targets in Stanley they aborted the mission only twenty minutes after take-off when one of the aircraft's IFF (Identification, Friend or Foe) systems malfunctioned, rendering the pair vulnerable to both sides' surface-to-air capabilities – and hence at serious risk of falling victim to a 'Blue on Blue' incident.

On the afternoon of 13 June, a Harrier returning to *Hermes* from a cluster bomb sortie against Mount Tumbledown came under small arms fire from troops of the Scots Guards, but the aircraft escaped unscathed.

One of the last incidents occurred on 14 June, the last day of the war, when a British artillery shell hit a house in Stanley, killing three female civilians, and at **Wireless Ridge**, British artillery killed two soldiers from 2 Para.

Blue Rover, RFA

A Rover class fleet tanker with a capacity of about 6,000 tons of fuel and fitted with a helicopter deck, but with no embarked aircraft, *Blue Rover* left Portsmouth on 16 April, arrived off **Ascension** ten days later and, from 9 May, supported the operation to retake **South Georgia**. Arriving off the Falklands at the end of May, she supplied AVCAT (aviation fuel) and MOGAS (gasoline) for aircraft and vehicles, respectively, leaving the area of operations to refuel herself from requisitioned merchant tankers before returning to **San Carlos Water**. *Blue Rover* arrived back in Portsmouth on 17 July.

Commander:	Captain J.D. Roddis			
Builders:	Swan Hunter			
Launched:	11 November 1969			
Commissioned:	15 July 1970			
Tonnage:	4,700 Light Displacement	11,520 Full Load	7,510 Gross Register	6,800 Deadweight
Dimensions: length × beam; feet (metres):	461 × 63 (140.5 × 19.2)			
Propulsion:	2 diesel engines (1 propeller)	16,000shp = 19 knots		
Capacity:	6,600 tons FFO1 stores and dry provisions			
Armament:	Improvised – machine guns and rifles			

Blues and Royals

Today part of the Household Cavalry along with the Life Guards, in peacetime the unit supplied mounted squadrons for ceremonial duties in London. Deployed to the Falklands in its **Scorpion** and **Scimitar** light tanks, known as **CVR(T)s** – Combat Vehicle Reconnaissance (Tracked) – for purposes of armoured reconnaissance, its service proved extremely useful in the Falklands in support of infantry in the attack, substantially increasing their firepower, as well as carrying out en route reconnaissance, route clearance and in the evacuation of casualties.

Given scepticism over the CVR(T)s' dubious anticipated performance over the rough Falklands terrain and the almost total absence of paved roads, only two troops (Nos 3 and 4) of B Squadron served in the campaign, each equipped with two Scorpions and two Scimitars, the former mounting a 76mm L23 gun and the latter a 30mm Rarden cannon, as well as a GPMG on both vehicles. A Samson Armoured Recovery Vehicle, manned by Royal Electrical and Mechanical Engineers personnel, served to extract vehicles bogged down, disabled or otherwise inoperable, with a rear winch designed to pull 11.5 tons.

The rough Falklands terrain at first appeared to pose considerable obstacles even to tracked, much less wheeled, vehicles, but the CVR(T)s proved themselves very

A Scimitar of the Blues and Royals dug in for protection from air attack, probably at San Carlos, where they came ashore on 21 May. (AirSeaLand Photos)

versatile and manoeuvrable, capable of traversing both boggy and stony ground, although the larger rock runs and hills proved genuine obstacles to these vehicles.

The two troops left Southampton aboard the *Elk* on 9 April, and during the amphibious landings on 21 May the CVR(T)s were carried in the bow of the **landing craft** of the first wave, so enabling their guns to offer covering fire on the beaches if necessary.

On the night of 31 May, they escorted the overland movement of HQ **3 Commando Brigade** from **San Carlos** to **Teal Inlet**, as well as the **BV 202E** oversnow vehicles, known as 'band-wagons', in the course of which journey the CVR(T)s picked up stragglers and those suffering from trench foot and injured ankles and knees. One troop remained with 3 Commando Brigade while the other was tasked to join **5 Infantry Brigade** to the south – a cross-country trek expected to take two days but which in the event only took six hours. This troop then provided mobile fire support to the attack of the **Scots Guards** on **Mount Tumbledown** on 13–14 June. The troop remaining with 3 Commando Brigade supported **2 Para** at **Wireless Ridge**, using its highly effective night vision capability to lay down accurate fire against the defenders. The need for more CVR(T)s figured as one of the many lessons learned from the campaign.

Bluff Cove

After **Goose Green**, as part of a plan to move **2 Para** forward to Bluff Cove, Major Crosland, OC B Company, 2 Para, telephoned Bluff Cove settlement from **Swan Inlet House** on 2 June to enquire into the level of Argentine presence in the **Fitzroy**/Bluff Cove area, discovering from Ron Binney, the settlement manager, that they were clear. Bluff Cove therefore became the first destination for 2 Para's (and therefore **5 Infantry Brigade's**) movement east. This consisted of A Company HQ and two platoons, B Company HQ and a platoon, as well as Mortar and Anti-Tank Platoons detachments, all flown by **Chinook** in two groups: 81 and 74. Other elements of 2 Para followed.

Thereafter, with respect to Bluff Cove in the plan devised by Brigadier **Wilson**, the **Welsh Guards** would replace 2 Para and guard Bluff Cove, while the **Scots Guards** were to take over from D Company, 2 Para, east of Bluff Cove Inlet. On the morning of 3 June, C (Patrol) Company, 2 Para was meant to be flown to Bluff Cove, but instead was delivered to Fitzroy. D Company, 2 Para, was put down on the eastern shores of Bluff Cove creek, 2 miles from where they were supposed to be landed and in easy sight of **Mount Harriet**, under Argentine control.

With the entire battalion now in the Bluff Cove/Fitzroy area, those elements of 2 Para closest to Bluff Cove were A, C and D Companies. B Company and Battalion HQ were at Fitzroy. Much in the way of hospitality for the troops in Bluff Cove was provided by the Kilmartins, who offered food, shelter and transport to move

B

Scots Guards at Bluff Cove with a 50-calibre machine gun. (AirSeaLand Photos)

equipment. Nine Polish seamen who had defected in February were conscripted as labourers in the settlement.

As part of the southern thrust to **Stanley**, Commodore Clapp advocated shifting the Scots Guards and Welsh Guards to the Bluff Cove area in stages, starting on 6 June, with *Intrepid* carrying all the Scots Guards and half the Welsh Guards. The remainder of the Welsh Guards and the rest of the required units would be landed at Fitzroy.

On 5 June, 29 (Corunna) Battery was flown by **Chinook** to Bluff Cove and on the same day **Special Boat Squadron** and **Royal Engineers** beach recce teams reported the absence of obstacles and identified two beaches, Yellow Beaches One and Two, suitable for **landing craft** operations. Major Davies RE disagreed, citing the poor supply of freshwater for large numbers of men, insufficient cover from Argentine fire that could be directed from the clear view offered by high ground overlooking the area, and the advantages of the more substantial buildings at Fitzroy offering protection from the cold and constant wind. **Brigadier Wilson** concurred.

The plan called for *Intrepid* to land the Scots Guards at Bluff Cove on the night of 6–7 June, with LCUs left at a forward operating base there in order to transport them to shore. The plan was altered, however, with *Intrepid* ordered not to proceed beyond Lively Island, thereby condemning the Scots Guards to move by four LCUs. The troops consequently arrived in a freezing, wet and exhausted state to Bluff Cove in the early hours of 7 June to be met by Lieutenant Colonel Chaundler, CO 2 Para, who ordered them to move north and dig in. Shortly thereafter, Chaundler ordered those elements of 2 Para at Bluff Cove to move via LCU to Fitzroy to join up with the remainder of the battalion, but faulty **radar**, extensive kelp and poor visibility forced their return after two hours on the water.

In the pre-dawn hours of 8 June, two companies of Welsh Guards and some supporting elements landed at Bluff Cove, the remainder having returned to **San Carlos** due to insufficient numbers of landing craft to effect the passage.

Despite popular reference to the so-called 'Bluff Cove disaster' in connection with the Skyhawk attacks on *Sir Galahad* and *Sir Tristram* on 8 June, the vessels were actually anchored in **Port Pleasant**, the next inlet south of Bluff Cove, but actually closer to Fitzroy.

'Bomb Alley'

The nickname applied by the British press to Falkland Sound during the period of incessant low-level Argentine air attacks commencing on the first day of the amphibious landings in **San Carlos Water** on 21 May and culminating on the evening of the 25th, also known as the 'Battle for **San Carlos**'. The Argentine Air Force and Naval Air Command tended to launch raids consisting of two to four aircraft each, which by way of protection from British air defences used high ground to shield their approach.

On the 21st, with clear weather conditions once the fog lifted, Argentine aircraft subjected the ships of the **Task Force** to six hours of attacks, opposed by the vessels' air defence assets and a small number of **Sea Harriers**. At about 1330Z six Dagger As arrived over San Carlos Water and caused minor damage to *Broadsword* and *Argonaut* with cannon fire. *Antrim* narrowly escaped disaster a few minutes later when struck by a bomb dropped by a Dagger that failed to explode.

At 1806Z *Ardent* was struck again, this time by Skyhawks, several of whose 500lb bombs struck her stern, adding to her damage and causing fires. When the ship began to list due to flooding, the captain ordered her abandoned, the fires eventually spreading and causing her to explode and sink the following evening. She had lost twenty-two killed and more than thirty wounded.

Despite the attacks of the 21st, the landings had been achieved without a single loss to those landed and the air defence screen established in Falkland Sound had greatly aided operations in putting troops ashore unharmed. The Argentines made a cardinal error in focusing their attention on the warships instead of the troop transports, particularly vulnerable and vital to the success of the day as they were.

By the end of 21 May, ten Argentine Air Force aircraft had been shot down, while the Navy lost three, for a total of thirteen aircraft destroyed, of which **Sea Harriers** accounted for ten. Only one Argentine aircraft fell victim to a surface-to-air missile.

Poor weather conditions on the mainland grounded most Argentine aircraft on the 22nd, resulting in only one bombing raid at dusk by two Skyhawks which failed to hit their targets. Improved weather conditions on the 23rd enabled the resumption of air attacks on ships in San Carlos Water and Falkland Sound from midday.

Two bombs struck *Antelope* on the 23rd; both failed to explode until an Explosive Ordnance Disposal officer attempted to defuse one, which exploded, causing raging fires and obliging the crew to abandon ship. A second explosion on the 24th, probably the unexploded bomb, broke the ship's back.

At about 1400Z on 24 May, with the skies again clear enough for air operations, four Daggers arrived over San Carlos Water, but their bombs fell harmlessly. Shortly thereafter, two more Daggers unsuccessfully attacked ships in San Carlos Water, this time with parachute-retarded bombs. Another attack, completely without warning by aircraft approaching from the direction of the **Sussex Mountains**, occurred at about 1500Z involving five Skyhawks, all of which again failed to strike their targets. Just over an hour later, a further six Skyhawks appeared, half of them being shot down by ships' crews. Nevertheless, both *Sir Lancelot* and *Sir Galahad* were hit by bombs, none of which exploded.

By the end of the 24th, two LSLs had been damaged, though not fatally, while the Argentines had lost four aircraft. British vessels had offered a withering level of anti-aircraft fire from both ship and shore that, when combined with the **combat air patrols** flown by the Sea Harriers, offered a formidable defence to the ships in San Carlos Water, blunting the Argentine air offensive and enabling the build-up to continue at pace.

The 25th witnessed the last concerted efforts by the Argentines to disrupt the landings in San Carlos Water, with numerous air attacks, all them unsuccessful against vessels there, with sixty-three sorties carried out by twenty-four Sea Harriers, the highest number that was to be reached in the course of the campaign.

On the 25th, *Coventry* was lost off **West Falkland**, marking the end of the five-day period for which 'Bomb Alley' is known. *Ardent* and *Antelope* had also been sunk, but ground forces had been put ashore in large numbers, albeit at fairly heavy cost to the **Royal Navy**. However, during the same period the Argentines had lost nine Daggers, seven Air Force Skyhawks and three Navy Skyhawks, a rate of attrition they could not afford to sustain for any lengthy period.

Brambleleaf, RFA

One of five new Leaf class support tankers chartered to the Ministry of Defence, together with *Pearleaf, Plumleaf, Appleleaf* and *Bayleaf*. In east African waters at the start of the conflict, she departed from Mombasa on 5 April and arrived off **South Georgia** around the 23rd.

Commander:	Captain M.S.J. Farley	
Builders:	Cammell Laird	
Launched:	22 January 1976	
Commissioned:	3 March 1980	
Tonnage:	19,975 Gross Register	33,750 Deadweight
Dimensions: length × beam; feet (metres):	560 × 72 (170.7 × 21.9)	
Draught:	11.9m	
Propulsion:	2 diesel engines (1 propeller)	14,000bhp = 16 knots
Fuel capacity:	2,498 tons	

Brigade Maintenance Area

See Ajax Bay

Brilliant, HMS

Of the fifteen **frigates** in the South Atlantic, *Brilliant* numbered among two of the Type 22 variety (Broadsword class Batch 1), the other being *Broadsword*.

Called away from Exercise **Springtrain** on 2 April, she reached **Ascension** on 11 April, and **South Georgia** waters on the 22nd – where she took part in the recapture of that island – before reaching Falklands waters on the 29th. On 1 May, *Brilliant* and *Yarmouth*, together with three **Sea Kings**, patrolled the coastal waters north of East Falkland in search of an Argentine submarine suspected of being present, although they discovered nothing. A week later, *Brilliant* entered Falkland Sound, using her **helicopters** to make an Electronic Support Measures (ESM) sweep in search of Argentine shipping north of the sound before strafing Argentine troop positions at **Port Howard** with machine-gun fire. On the 10th, together with the destroyer *Glasgow*, *Brilliant* relieved *Broadsword* and *Coventry* from their duties bombarding **Stanley** and serving on radar picket.

At 1644Z on 12 May, two A-4B Skyhawks attacked *Brilliant*, on that day in the company of *Glasgow* while the two ships were withdrawing from their positions of bombardment approximately 15 miles south of Stanley. Two other aircraft attacked *Glasgow*. With *Glasgow*'s 4.5in gun out of action and her **Sea Dart** launcher also suffering a fault, *Brilliant* found herself obliged to look to rely on her own means of defence, launching two **Sea Wolf** missiles, both of which struck their targets, while the third Skyhawk crashed into the sea in an attempt to evade a third Sea Wolf which missed its target but produced the desired outcome nonetheless. The fourth pilot escaped, but his two 500lb bombs had failed to hit either of the ships, although one bounced off the surface of the sea and passed over *Glasgow*'s stern. Four more Skyhawks attacked *Brilliant* and *Glasgow* at 1715Z, with damage inflicted against the latter, but the former remained unscathed despite her computer's failure

The Type 22 frigate HMS *Brilliant*. (AirSeaLand Photos)

to launch any Sea Wolf missiles owing to its confusion over the rapid movements of the attacking aircraft.

On the night of 17 May, *Brilliant* landed a **Special Boat Squadron** patrol at Middle Bay and confirmed the presence of a small Argentine force at **Fanning Head**, off which the frigate continued to lay for the next several days. In the early afternoon of 21 May, the first day of the landings, several Daggers As attacked *Brilliant* and two other vessels, but inflicted very little damage. Later, at about 1750Z, two Daggers reached **San Carlos Water** and attacked *Brilliant*, causing minor damage and wounding several of her crew. She remained on station on the 22nd, but with her Sea Wolf launcher unserviceable.

On the 25th she was with the **Carrier Battle Group** north of Stanley and helped rescue survivors from the stricken *Atlantic Conveyor*. Two days later *Brilliant* sailed to the Tug, Repair and Logistic Area (TRALA) in order for *Stena Seaspread* to repair the damage to the frigate's Sea Wolf system. She reached Devonport on 13 July.

Commander:	Captain J.F. Coward	
Builders:	Yarrow (Scotstoun)	
Launched:	15 December 1978	
Commissioned:	15 May 1981	
Displacement (tons):	3,500 Standard	4,400 Full load
Dimensions: length × beam; feet (metres):	430 × 48.5 (131.2 × 14.8)	
Draught:	4.3m	

Propulsion:	2 R-R Olympus gas turbines	54,400shp = 30 knots
	2 R-R Tyne gas turbines	8,200shp = 18 knots (cruising)
Armament:	2 × 40mm Bofors AA guns	
	2 × **Sea Wolf** SAM systems (GWS 25)	
	4 × MM.38 **Exocet**	
	2 × triple ASW Mark 46 torpedo tubes (STWS)	
Aircraft:	2 × **Lynx** HAS2	

Bristol, HMS

One of eight guided missile **destroyers** serving in the South Atlantic, although the only Type 82, of which there were originally to have been eight. As a result of a major refit after serving as a **Sea Dart** trials ship, she was equipped in 1976–78 as a Command and Control ship, and thus fitted with a Satellite Communication Onboard Terminal (SCOT) Link 11 automated action data communications system, which was compatible with the American NTDS and French SENIT systems. She was armed with the Sea Dart (GWS 30), an anti-missile or anti-aircraft missile system deployed for medium range area defence. Unique within the **Task Force**, *Bristol* also carried the Ikara anti-submarine torpedo. Capable of operating as a platform for **helicopters**, she nonetheless possessed no hangar nor repair facilities. Two years before the war she was fitted with the American SATCOMM WSC-3, together with a new navigation system.

Bristol sailed later than the initial Task Force, leading the **Bristol Group's** three Type 21 **frigates** south from Portsmouth on 10 May and reaching **Ascension** on the 18th. She arrived off the Falklands on 25 May and was responsible for defending and managing the vessels of the **Royal Fleet Auxiliary** and **Ships Taken Up From Trade** in the Logistics and Loitering Area (LOLA), ensuring the availability of vessels for service in the Battle Group or the Area of Operations. She reached Portsmouth on 17 September.

Commander:	Captain A. Grose	
Launched:	30 June 1969	
Commissioned:	31 March 1973	
Displacement (tons):	6,100 Standard	7,100 Full load
Dimensions: length × beam; feet (metres):	507 × 55 (154.6 × 16.8)	
Draught:	5.2m	
Propulsion:	2 sets geared steam turbines, 2 Rolls-Royce Olympus gas turbines	30,000shp + 44,600shp = 28 + knots
Armament:	1 × 4.5in Mark 8 dual purpose gun	
	4 × 20mm AA guns	
	1 × **Sea Dart** system (GWS 30)	
	1 × Ikara ASW missile system	
	1 × three-barrelled ASW Mortar Mark 10	

HMS *Bristol*, with her 4.5 main armament clearly visible. (AirSeaLand Photos)

Bristol Group

On 10 May the Bristol Group of ships, the last major component of the **Task Force** to disembark from the UK, left Devonport and Portsmouth bound for the South Atlantic. This element initially consisted of eight vessels: the destroyer *Bristol*, the **frigates** *Active*, *Andromeda*, *Avenger*, *Minerva* and *Penelope*, the helicopter support ship *Engadine*, and the tanker *Olna*. All these, apart from *Minerva*, arrived in the **Total Exclusion Zone** on 25 May, with *Minerva* arriving a day later, together with *Cardiff* and *Bayleaf*, both of which had left Gibraltar and Devonport, respectively, at different dates than the rest of the Bristol Group. The Bristol Group's arrival in theatre helped compensate for the loss of the **destroyers** *Coventry* and *Sheffield*, and the frigates *Antelope* and *Ardent*.

British Avon, MV

A motor tanker chartered from British Petroleum on 20 April for fleet refuelling duties and numbering among the large fleet of **Ships Taken Up From Trade** deployed on Operation **Corporate**. Departing from Devonport on 26 April with a **Royal Fleet Auxiliary** (RFA) Naval Party aboard, *British Avon* was employed to refuel the RFAs in the South Atlantic, but also carried back to Britain the Argentine naval officer, Lieutenant Commander Alfredo Astiz, captured on **South Georgia**. Arriving in Portsmouth on 5 June, she returned to South Atlantic waters on 14 June, the last day of the war, and to Rosyth on 28 December.

Commander:	Captain J.M.W. Guy	
Launched:	1972	
Tonnage:	12,973 Gross Register	25,620 Deadweight
Dimensions: length × beam; feet (metres):	562 × 82 (171.2 × 25.05)	
Propulsion:	1 diesel engine	9,000bhp = 15.5 knots

British Dart, MV

A motor tanker chartered from British Petroleum on 6 April for fleet refuelling duties in the South Atlantic, one of many **Ships Taken Up From Trade** and carrying a Naval Party supplied by the **Royal Fleet Auxiliary**. *British Dart* departed Loch Striven on 22 April, reaching **Ascension** on 4 May. She arrived back in Plymouth on 2 July.

Commander:	Captain J.A.N. Taylor	
Launched:	1972	
Tonnage:	15,650 Gross Register	25–26,000 Deadweight
Dimensions: length × beam; feet (metres):	562.5 × 82 (171.5 × 25)	
Propulsion:	1 diesel engine	9,000bhp = 15.5 knots

British Enterprise III, MV

A **Ship Taken Up From Trade**, this motor offshore vessel requisitioned from British Underwater Engineering served as a dispatch vessel and the mother ship for submersibles. She had a helicopter platform fitted but embarked no aircraft. Requisitioned on 18 May and manned with Naval Party 2090 under Lieutenant Commander B.E.M. Reynell RN, she departed Rosyth on 26 May and arrived off the Falklands in late June, completing her service when she reached Portsmouth on 29 August.

Commander:	Captain D. Grant	
Builders:	British Underwater Engineering	
Launched:	1965	
Tonnage:	1,595 Gross Register	1,197 Deadweight
Dimensions: length × beam; feet (metres):	249 × 42 (75.9 × 12.9)	
Propulsion:	1 diesel engine	2,140bhp = 14 knots

British Esk, MV

A motor tanker chartered from British Petroleum on 6 April to conduct fleet refuelling duties, she carried a Naval Party supplied by the **Royal Fleet Auxiliary** like nearly all **Ships Taken Up From Trade**. Leaving Portland on 11 April, she arrived off the Falklands on 14 May. In the wake of the disaster befalling *Sheffield*, *British Esk* carried 262 survivors from the destroyer back to **Ascension**. She returned to home waters before the end of the war, reaching Portsmouth on 8 June.

Commander:	Captain G. Barber	
Launched:	1973	
Tonnage:	15,650 Gross Register	25–26,000 Deadweight
Dimensions: length × beam; feet (metres):	562.5 × 82 (171.5 × 25)	
Propulsion:	1 diesel engine	9,000bhp = 14.75 knots

British Tamar, MV

A motor tanker chartered from British Petroleum on 6 April for fleet refuelling duties, this **Ships Taken Up From Trade** was employed to refuel ships en route to and from the Falklands. Manned by a Naval Party supplied by the **Royal Fleet Auxiliary**, she left Milford Haven on 14 April, reaching Ascension on the 28th. She arrived back in Portsmouth on 20 June 1983.

Commander:	Captain W.H. Hare	
Launched:	1973	
Tonnage:	15,650 Gross Register	25–26,000 Deadweight
Dimensions: length × beam; feet (metres):	562.5 × 82 (171.5 × 25)	
Propulsion:	1 diesel engine	9,000bhp = 15.5 knots

British Tay, MV

A motor tanker chartered from British Petroleum on 6 April to refuel ships moving to and from the Falklands, she departed Devonport on 9 April and arrived off **Ascension** after eleven days at sea. Some 133 survivors of *Atlantic Conveyor* sailed in *British Tay* to Ascension, from where they were flown home by a **VC10**. Her status as one of dozens of **Ships Taken Up From Trade** did not cease until she arrived back in Portsmouth on 24 January 1983.

Commander:	Captain T. Morris	
Launched:	1973	
Tonnage:	15,650 Gross Register	25–26,000 Deadweight
Dimensions: length × beam; feet (metres):	562.5 × 82 (171.5 × 25)	
Propulsion:	1 diesel engine	9,000bhp = 14.75 knots

British Test, MV

A motor tanker chartered from British Petroleum on 6 April for fleet refuelling duties, specifically in supplying ships en route to and from the Falklands. Supplied with a Naval Party by the **Royal Fleet Auxiliary** and one of numerous **Ships Taken Up From Trade**, she left Gibraltar on 18 April and reached **Ascension** nine days later. Together with other vessels, she was also used as an ambulance ship to ferry casualties from *Uganda* to Montevideo for onward aeromedic **VC10** flights to naval and military hospitals in Britain. Her duties connected with the conflict ceased when she arrived in Portsmouth on 4 July.

Commander:	Captain T.A. Oliphant	
Launched:	1973	
Tonnage:	15,650 Gross Register	25–26,000 Deadweight
Dimensions: length × beam; feet (metres):	562.5 × 82 (171.5 × 25)	
Propulsion:	1 diesel engine	9,000bhp = 14.75 knots

British Trent, MV

One of many **Ships Taken Up From Trade**, the motor tanker *British Trent* served as a fleet refuelling vessel for ships sailing to and from the Falklands. Chartered from British Petroleum on 12 April, she left the Isle of Grain five days later with a Naval Party furnished by the **Royal Fleet Auxiliary** and arrived at **Ascension** on the 29th.

British Trent, together with other vessels, was used as an ambulance ship to ferry casualties from *Uganda* to Montevideo for onward aeromedic **VC10** flights to naval and military hospitals in Britain. She arrived at Portland on 5 July.

Commander:	Captain P.R. Walker	
Launched:	1973	
Tonnage:	15,650 Gross Register	25–26,000 Deadweight
Dimensions: length × beam; feet (metres):	562.5 × 82 (171.5 × 25)	
Propulsion:	1 diesel engine	9,000bhp = 14.75 knots

British Wye, MV

One of dozens of **Ships Taken Up From Trade**, *British Wye* was a motor tanker chartered from British Petroleum on 20 April for the purpose of refuelling ships in the South Atlantic. She departed from Devonport on 25 April and arrived at **Ascension** on 5 May. Arriving off the Falklands in mid-May, on the 29th of that month, while about 700 miles east of the Islands, *British Wye* came under one of the most unusual forms of air attack of the war when an Argentine C-130H cargo aircraft dropped eight 500lb bombs from 150ft from its open rear ramp. Four of the bombs hit the sea and failed to explode, three exploded off *Wye*'s port side and one struck the ship's foredeck without exploding, bounced off and plunged into the water, causing no serious damage. She arrived back at Portland on 11 July.

B

Commander:	Captain D.M. Rundell	
Launched:	1974	
Tonnage:	15,650 Gross Register	25–26,000 Deadweight
Dimensions: length × beam; feet (metres):	562.5 × 82 (171.5 × 25)	
Propulsion:	1 diesel engine	9,000bhp = 14.75 knots

Broadsword, HMS

Of the fifteen **frigates** in the South Atlantic, *Broadsword* numbered among two of the Type 22 variety (Broadsword class Batch 1), the other being *Brilliant*.

She departed from Gibraltar on 8 April, reaching **Ascension** eight days later. *Broadsword* appeared off the Falklands on 1 May and on the 9th, in company with *Coventry*, lay about 12 miles to the east of **Stanley** for the purpose of firing on any Argentine aircraft seeking to make use of the airfield there. She was relieved on the 10th by the frigate *Brilliant* and the destroyer *Glasgow*.

In company with *Glamorgan* and *Hermes*, *Broadsword* sailed close to **Pebble Island** on the night of 14–15 May to support the **Special Air Service** raid on the airstrip there. Following this operation she then sailed away north-east at high speed so as to avoid being caught by Argentine aircraft near land at dawn.

In the early hours of 18 May, *Broadsword* escorted *Invincible* west of the Falklands to enable a helicopter from the latter bearing an SAS team to proceed on a mission to Rio Grande air base. The two ships then returned to the **Task Force**.

On the day of the landings, 21 May, *Broadsword*, in company with *Antrim* and *Argonaut*, stood on station off the mouth of **San Carlos Water** as part of a protective screen against possible air attacks directed against vessels further south engaged in unloading troops and supplies. Argentine Dagger As strafed *Broadsword* with cannon fire at about 1330Z on the 21st, but inflicted no serious damage. One Dagger, hit by a surface-to-air missile, was probably brought down by a **Sea Wolf** fired by *Broadsword*.

On the following day, in company with *Coventry*, *Broadsword* lay to the north of Pebble Island on radar picket duty, providing a missile screen against Argentine aircraft approaching from the north that could threaten the **Amphibious Task Group** that, with its escorts, consisted of the destroyer *Antrim*; the frigates *Ardent*, *Argonaut*, *Brilliant*, *Broadsword*, *Plymouth*, and *Yarmouth*; the **Landing Ships Logistic** *Fearless* and *Intrepid*; the **Royal Fleet Auxiliaries** *Sir Galahad*, *Sir Geraint*, *Sir Lancelot*, *Sir Percivale*, *Sir Tristram*, *Fort Austin* and *Stromness*; and three **Ships Taken Up From Trade**: *Norland*, *Europic Ferry* and *Canberra*.

On the 23rd, two Daggers failed to strike her with their bombs, while *Broadsword's* Sea Wolf also missed its mark in the ship's defence. On the following day she stood on radar picket duty north of Pebble Island, together with *Coventry*.

At about 1820Z on 25 May, two Skyhawks attacked *Broadsword*, hitting her with only a single bomb, which bounced off the sea and into her hull on the starboard side and exited through the flight deck, severely damaging a **Lynx** on loan from *Brilliant*, before finally disappearing into the water, all without exploding. A second flight of Skyhawks appeared only minutes later, but these concentrated instead on *Coventry*. *Broadsword* tried to engage her Sea Wolf system and fire her missiles at the attackers, but when *Coventry* interposed herself between *Broadsword* and the approaching aircraft, she disrupted the radar lock achieved on the Skyhawks and no missile was launched. As a consequence, three bombs struck *Coventry*.

On the 26th, *Broadsword* returned to the **Carrier Battle Group**, following which she underwent repairs conducted by *Stena Seaspread*, before being assigned to protect *Hermes*. She arrived in Devonport on 23 July.

Commander:	Captain W.R. Canning	
Builders:	Yarrow (Scotstoun)	
Launched:	12 May 1976	
Commissioned:	3 May 1979	
Displacement (tons):	3,500 Standard	4,400 Full load
Dimensions: length × beam; feet (metres):	430 × 48.5 (131.2 × 14.8)	
Draught:	4.3m	
Propulsion:	2 R-R Olympus gas turbines	54,400shp = 30 knots
	2 R-R Tyne gas turbines	8,200shp = 18 knots (cruising)
Armament:	2 × 40mm Oerlikon AA guns	
	2 × Sea Wolf systems (GWS 25)	
	4 × MM.38 **Exocet**	
	2 × triple ASW torpedo tubes (STWS)	
Aircraft:	2 × **Lynx** HAS2	

BV 202E

Seven BV 202E oversnow vehicles, normally deployed in north Norway, accompanied **45 Commando** on its **yomp** from **Port San Carlos** to **Mount Kent**. Three carried radios for Headquarters 3 **Commando Brigade** and four carried ammunition.

Camilla Creek House

See Goose Green

Canberra, SS

C

A passenger liner and flagship of the P&O fleet, *Canberra* was requisitioned on 5 April while sailing homeward from the Mediterranean with 1,650 passengers on board. She docked at Gibraltar two days later and disembarked her passengers in preparation for an immediate refit, undergoing a remarkable four-day transformation into a troop transport beginning in Gibraltar and continuing at Southampton from 6 to 9 April. Modifications by Vosper Thornycroft included the fitting of improved communications systems and helicopter pads over the two swimming pools, which were designed to support the weight of at least 70 tons of water and therefore easily capable of sustaining a crash-landing by a fully laden helicopter. Her newly strengthened decks could accept tons of stores and featured rail-mounted General Purpose Machine Guns, and her colour soon prompted journalists to nickname her 'the Great White Whale'.

With most of her crew choosing to remain aboard for the campaign, *Canberra* embarked more than 3,000 men, including **40 Commando**, **42 Commando**, **3 Para** and various ancillary units before sailing from Southampton on 9 April, with modifications continuing all the way to **Freetown**, which she reached on the 17th. Despite concerns that mixing red (Para) and green (Commando) berets might lead to trouble, no serious incidents occurred during the journey south.

The requisitioned SS *Canberra*, which served a vital role throughout the conflict as a troopship. (AirSeaLand Photos)

Canberra arrived at **Ascension** on 20 April and remained there for a fortnight, landing all her troops for training on the island and rearranging and replenishing her stores. As with **2 Para** aboard *Norland*, the troops on *Canberra* made good use of their time at sea with physical training – running around the Promenade deck, enhancing existing medical training, studying Argentine aircraft recognition, practising live firing at targets thrown out to sea, and other skills.

Reaching Falklands waters on 18 May, on the following day 40 Commando and 3 Para were cross-decked by **landing craft** to the **Landing Ships Logistic** *Fearless* and *Intrepid*, respectively, leaving 42 Commando aboard as a floating reserve. On D-Day, 21 May, *Canberra* left the more exposed area of Falkland Sound and positioned herself due west of Chancho Point, at the opening of **San Carlos Water**, while the troops landed at first light and the Argentine air response arrived hours later.

In the absence of the hospital ship *Uganda*, casualties were flown to *Canberra* for initial medical treatment, with more than thirty alone from the stricken frigate *Ardent*, *Canberra* having converted one of her larger lounges into a hospital ward. Considering the virulence of Argentine air attacks near and within San Carlos Water on 21 May, it is almost miraculous that the extremely conspicuous *Canberra* survived the day unscathed. In the course of the conflict she would receive 174 patients, eighty-two British and ninety-two Argentine, all of whom survived. The bodies of three **Royal Marines** aircrew killed on D-Day were brought on board and committed to the deep from her deck.

The original intention to retain *Canberra* – a conspicuous and vulnerable ship – in San Carlos Water as an *ad hoc* hospital ship was altered in light of the ferocity of air attacks the day before. She left Falklands waters for **South Georgia** before dawn on 22 May, in company with *Norland*, to collect troops of **5 Infantry Brigade** aboard **Queen Elizabeth 2**, the transfer timed for five days hence. Accordingly, while anchored off Grytviken on 27 May, **Scots Guards** and **Welsh Guards** from 5 Infantry Brigade cross-decked on to *Canberra*, as well as *Norland*, from QE2, a process that took more than twenty-four hours.

Arriving in San Carlos Water on 1 June, on the following day she disembarked the Welsh and Scots Guards while protected by **Sea Harrier combat air patrols**, the anti-aircraft defences of warships and by **Rapier**. The following day saw more than 100 helicopter loads of stores taken ashore from *Canberra* before she left San Carlos Water, to which she was not to return until the 15th, the day following the Argentine surrender, when she took aboard 1,121 **prisoners of war**, plus another 3,046 two days later. These she landed at Puerto Madryn on the 19th. *Canberra* then proceeded to a position off **San Carlos**, collecting 40 Commando, before sailing for Stanley, where 42 Commando embarked on 25 June. At Ascension **45 Commando** joined its colleagues aboard *Canberra*, which reached Southampton on 11 July to a rapturous welcome.

Commander:	Captain W. Scott-Masson	
Launched:	1961	
Naval Party 1710	Capt C.P.O. Burne RN	
Tonnage:	44,807 Gross Register	9,910 Deadweight
Dimensions: length × beam; feet (metres):	818.5 × 102.5 (249.5 × 31.3)	
Propulsion:	2 sets geared steam turbines	88,200shp = 27.5 knots
Aircraft:	1 × **Sea King** HC4 (Ascension to San Carlos)	
	2 × Sea King HAS2A (South Georgia to San Carlos)	

Cardiff, HMS

One of eight **destroyers** that served in the South Atlantic, *Cardiff* belonged to the Type 42, Sheffield class laid down in the 1970s and designed for area air defence. She was powered by a dual set of engines, both designed by Rolls-Royce: the gas turbine Tyne for cruising, and the Olympus for full power, which could be achieved after approximately thirty seconds. With her **Sea Dart** system, *Cardiff* could force Argentine aircraft down to sea level.

At the outbreak of hostilities she had just completed patrolling in the Persian Gulf and was en route to the UK via the Mediterranean, reaching Gibraltar on 7 May. Northwood duly diverted her south and she sailed on the 12th, reaching **Ascension** six days later. Arriving off the Falklands on 26 May, the following day she relieved *Brilliant*, which sailed to the Tug, Repair and Logistic Area (TRALA) for repairs. *Cardiff* was meant to support the attack on **Stanley** by **3 Commando Brigade**, which Admiral **Woodward** hoped to launch on the night of 5–6 June, but when Major General **Moore** postponed it, *Cardiff*, together with *Yarmouth*, was instead tasked with ambushing aircraft en route to Stanley. On the evening of 5 June, while off **Fitzroy** providing **naval gunfire support** in the area around **Mount Tumbledown**, **Moody Brook** and **Mount William**, and in the absence of knowledge from HQ **5 Infantry Brigade** of the presence of a friendly helicopter en route to Pleasant Peak, *Cardiff* shot it down with a Sea Dart, killing four.

Miscommunication nearly led to a second **'Blue on Blue'** incident when, before dawn on the following morning, after her **radar** detected the presence of four **landing craft** from *Intrepid* while unaware of a friendly presence in the waters near East Island, *Cardiff* fired six star shells before withdrawing after discovering the vessels to be carrying friendly troops from the **Scots Guards**. She arrived back in Portsmouth on 28 July.

Commander:	Captain M.G.T. Harris	
Builders:	Vickers (Barrow)	
Launched:	22 February 1974	
Commissioned:	24 September 1979	
Displacement (tons):	3,150 Standard	4,100 Full Load
Dimensions: length × beam; feet (metres):	410 × 47 (125 × 13.3)	
Draught:	5.8m	
Propulsion:	2 Rolls-Royce Olympus gas turbines	54,400shp = 30 knots
	2 Rolls-Royce Tyne gas turbines	8,200shp = 18 knots (cruising)
Armament:	1 × 4.5in Mark 8 gun	
	2 × 20mm Oerlikon AA guns	
	1 × Sea Dart system (GWS 30)	
	2 × triple Mark 46 ASW torpedo tubes	
Aircraft:	1 × **Lynx** HAS2	

Carrier Battle Group (CBG)

The Carrier Battle Group, designated as CTG 317.8, consisted of the surface naval vessels of the **Task Force**, commanded by Rear Admiral 'Sandy' **Woodward** RN, whose task it was to establish a naval and air blockade of the Falklands, defeat Argentine naval forces, achieve air superiority, and protect the **Landing Force Group** (LFG) through to its destination. The CBG and the LFG rendezvoused for the first time early on the morning of 20 May, or D –1.

The CBG entered the **Total Exclusion Zone** (TEZ) at about 0530Z on 1 May and positioned itself about 100 miles north-east of the Falklands. Led by the three Type 42 **destroyers** *Glasgow*, *Coventry* and *Sheffield*, these vessels served as an advanced air defence screen for the protection of the **aircraft carriers** *Hermes* and *Invincible*, from which vessels air operations were soon to begin against Argentine positions on the islands.

As a result of the loss of *Sheffield* on 4 May, Woodward shifted the CBG considerably east of the Falklands and maintained it there with few exceptions for the remainder of the campaign. While this offered further protection to the carriers – the loss of even one might have imperiled Operation **Corporate** altogether – this decision necessarily shortened the time available for **Sea Harriers** to remain aloft on their **combat air patrol** (CAP) stations by lengthening the distance between the CBG and the islands.

At the time of the landings, code-named Operation **Sutton**, on 21 May, the Carrier Battle Group consisted of *Hermes*, *Invincible*, *Coventry*, *Glamorgan*, *Glasgow*, *Alacrity* and *Arrow*, these vessels positioning themselves to the south of East Falkland to divert Argentine attention from the **Amphibious Task Group** as it approached Falkland Sound from the north.

On the 25th, Woodward moved the CBG to within 80 miles east of **Stanley**, in so doing bringing his Sea Harriers to within 130 miles of Falkland Sound, and thus enabling them to fly longer CAPs. This reduction in transit time to and from the carriers thereby increased the availability of these vital aircraft to protect Woodward's force. Remarkably, during the course of the day the distance narrowed to just 60 miles north-east of Stanley.

Following the loss of *Atlantic Conveyor* on 25 May, the Carrier Battle Group shifted to a position approximately 200 miles east of the Falklands, on the edge of the TEZ.

Casualties

Total fatal casualties during the war amounted to eighty-five for the **Royal Navy**, twenty-six for the **Royal Marines**, fifty-eight for the Army, one for the **Royal Air Force**, and eighteen civilians operating aboard vessels in the **Total Exclusion Zone**, for a total of 253. To these should be added the three civilians living in **Stanley** killed accidentally by an artillery shell. Breaking with long tradition, the Ministry of Defence offered to repatriate the bodies of service personnel killed and buried in

Burial of British dead by their comrades. (AirSeaLand Photos)

the Falklands. In the event, all but sixteen were returned to the UK, with fourteen buried at the **Blue Beach** Military Cemetery at **San Carlos**, and two others buried in **Goose Green** and **Port Howard**, respectively. Some naval personnel were buried at sea, while a few bodies were never recovered, lost with their ships or aircraft at sea.

Chinook HC1

A twin-rotor, heavy-lift helicopter operated by the RAF, it shifted stores, troops, prisoners, ammunition, and the wounded. A Chinook was capable of carrying 192 palletted rounds of 105mm artillery ammunition. Alternatively, it could lift two 105mm guns at the same time.

Four Boeing-Vertol Chinook HC1s, each when fully laden weighing 46,000lb, were dispatched to the Falklands, of which three were lost when the *Atlantic Conveyor* was hit on 25 May. The survivor was aloft at the time and managed to land on another vessel. This left just one Chinook (ZA718 of 18 Squadron, popularly known as 'Bravo November' after its code letters 'BN') available for operations, and only one other machine arrived in theatre – but not until 14 June,

A Chinook collecting stores – part of the vast logistic effort in the absence of whose effectiveness British troops simply could not have succeeded. (AirSeaLand Photos)

the last day of the war. Bravo November worked tirelessly, flying 109 hours from 27 May to the Argentine surrender, carrying 2,150 troops – among these ninety-five casualties and 550 **prisoners of war** – and conveying 550 tons of supplies. On 28 May, for instance, the day of the engagement at **Goose Green**, ZA718 flew to the hospital ship *Uganda* some of those wounded during the air attack on **Ajax Bay** the previous day.

The sole-surviving Chinook brought K Company **42 Commando** to **Mount Kent** on 29 May, but on its return to **San Carlos** experienced difficulty with its navigation in a snowstorm and suffered minor damage when it hit a stream about halfway between Mount Kent and **Teal Inlet**. It returned to Mount Kent with L Company, artillery ammunition and other personnel. It also airlifted three 105mm field guns to the same position on 30 May, two carried internally and one underslung – a testament to the remarkable capability of these machines.

On 2 June Bravo November transported **2 Para** from Goose Green to Fitzroy Ridge, the first in groups of eighty-one and seventy-four fully armed and kitted men – well above the recommended limit of forty men.

From 5 June ZA718 performed up to fifteen return journeys each day from Teal Inlet, airlifting artillery shells for the batteries on Mount Kent.

On 7 June, it recovered two unserviceable **helicopters**, a **Sea King** from **Fanning Head** damaged by accident on 23 May, and another Sea King, in this case from Lookout Hill, where it had been damaged while landing on 4 June. Both machines were airlifted to Forward Operating Bases around **San Carlos Water**.

The Chinook played its part along with many other helicopters after the disaster at **Port Pleasant** on 8 June, flying sixty-four wounded from **Fitzroy** to *Uganda* in a single flight.

On 11 June it moved fuel in air-portable fuel cells from San Carlos to Fitzroy and elsewhere, thereby enabling **helicopters** based there or operating in support of the southern advance on **Stanley** to refuel locally rather than flying all the way back to Goose Green or San Carlos.

The fact that only a single Chinook bore such a large share of the heavy lift burden of the conflict underlines the critical value of these impressive workhorses to an efficient system of supply and transport.

Clansman

See Radio communication

Combat Air Patrol (CAP)

Flown by **Sea Harriers** (and to a lesser extent, **Harriers**) to provide air defence of the fleet against Argentine aircraft, ground-to-air and air-to-air missiles, CAPs also served to cover other aircraft delivering air strikes. The first CAP flown over the Falklands occurred on 1 May, connected with the first **Black Buck raids**.

Combined Task Force 317

Designated as CTF 317 and led by Admiral Sir John **Fieldhouse**, this umbrella organisation contained all the elements for Operation **Corporate**, with a structure consisting of the **Amphibious Task Group** (CTG 317.0); **Landing Force Group** (CTG 317.1); **Carrier Battle Group** (CTG 317.8); a force of **submarines** designated as CTG 324.3; and 18 Group **Royal Air Force**.

Commando Logistic Regiment

Commanded by Lieutenant Colonel Ivar Hellberg, **Royal Corps of Transport**, it was based around the disused refrigeration plant at **Ajax Bay** in **San Carlos Water** and provided the **logistics** for **3 Commando Brigade**, with Hellberg being informed as early as 0400Z on 2 April – the day of the invasion – that the brigade was to be sent to the Falklands. Within three hours he had dispatched the first trucks to collect ammunition. This corps differed from similar formations in the Army by virtue of it being ready for immediate service in the Arctic or tropics, and it was designed to be transported by sea. All its logistic sub-units fell under a single command consisting of five squadrons: headquarters, workshop, medical, transport and ordnance. The Commando Logistic Regiment worked hard in terms of supplying not merely units under Brigadier **Thompson**, but those of Brigadier **Wilson**, commander of **5 Infantry Brigade**. This stretched it to the limit, but through Hellberg's immense force of will and the dedication of his personnel this workload never broke his unit.

Command Structure

From the outset, the command structure for British forces created difficulties, for Admiral **Fieldhouse** neglected to appoint an overall theatre commander. Thus, although Admiral **Woodward** was appointed Commander, **Carrier Battle Group**, which included all surface vessels and ground and air forces, it left Brigadier **Thompson** and Commodore Clapp confused about the chain of command; specifically, as one-star officers, they were unsure whether they reported to Woodward, a two-star officer, or if they held equal rank with one another and reported directly to Fieldhouse. This uncertainty was to cause confusion and tension on a number of occasions over the course of the campaign.

According to amphibious doctrine of the time, the amphibious force commander was the 'lead', in this case Clapp, Commander **Amphibious Task Group** (CATG). Despite this principle being laid down in NATO Allied Tactical Publication No. 8

(ATP 8), which had guided **3 Commando Brigade** for years, Northwood did not understand it. The CATG remained the lead commander until he devolved command to the landing force commander when the latter was satisfied that his forces were established ashore. Clapp and Thompson operated on this basis, with the failure of both Northwood and Woodward to understand this relationship leading to many misconceptions.

For instance, in early June, when Clapp ordered *Avenger* to investigate the possibility of ships using Albermarle harbour on **West Falkland** as a refuge from air attack if necessary while ferrying troops from **5 Infantry Brigade** to the **Port Pleasant** area, Woodward countermanded it without consulting Clapp, who ignored the signal, believing his own decision the correct one.

Clapp argued that, although his rank as commander of amphibious operations gave him the equivalent Army rank of brigadier, his role suggested he held the same status as Jeremy **Moore**, Commander Land Forces and a major general, with the title of Chief of Staff (Navy) to Moore, so facilitating, in Clapp's view, co-operation between land and naval units. Woodward declined the suggestion, observing that in his role as commander of the Amphibious Task Group, Clapp needed to retain authority to command ships. In the event, although Woodward presumed himself overall commander of operations in the South Atlantic, in fact no separate overall commander existed; the failure by Northwood at the outset of Operation **Corporate** to make this explicitly clear – and with that appointment made to someone not serving as one of the task group commanders – left various senior commanders to make decisions either unilaterally or via direct communication with military and civilian authorities back in the UK.

Conqueror, HMS

Six **submarines** served in the South Atlantic, of which *Conqueror* numbered among three of the Fleet, all nuclear-powered Valiant class, the others being *Courageous* and *Valiant*.

Conqueror left Faslane on the west coast of Scotland on 4 April and arrived in the South Atlantic on the 11th. She took part briefly in the operation to retake **South Georgia** before proceeding on patrol between the Falklands and the Argentine coast. Positioned just over 200 miles south of the Falklands and 35 miles outside the **Total Exclusion Zone**, at 1858Z on 2 May she attacked the cruiser *General Belgrano* from a range of 1,400yd, observing two hits, although three explosions were heard. The stricken vessel sank within fifteen minutes with the loss of 321 sailors. As a result, the Argentines returned virtually all their vessels to home ports, surrendering naval supremacy in the South Atlantic to the **Royal Navy**. This constituted the only overtly hostile act perpetrated by submarines during the war. *Conqueror* also embarked 6 **Special Boat Squadron**, conveying them to South Georgia, where they

were transferred to a surface vessel and eventually taken to the Falklands, carrying
out operations in Port Salvador and elsewhere. *Conqueror* arrived back in Faslane on
3 July.

Commander:	Commander C.L. Wreford-Brown	
Builders:	Vickers (Barrow)	
Launched:	28 August 1969	
Commissioned:	9 November 1971	
Displacement (tons):	3,500 Standard	4,000 Full Load, Surface 4,900 Submerged
Dimensions: length × beam; feet (metres):	285 × 33.0 (86.9 × 10.1)	
Draught:	8.2m	
Propulsion:	1 nuclear reactor = 2 geared steam turbines	20,000shp = approximately 25 knots submerged
Armament:	6 × 21in (533mm) bow torpedo tubes; Mark 8 and 21in Tigerfish torpedoes	
Complement:	13 officers, 96 ratings	

Contender Bezant, MV

A motor ro-ro container ship, one of dozens of **Ships Taken Up From Trade**,
chartered from Sea Containers on 12 May for fixed-wing aircraft and helicopter
transport. She carried Naval Party 2050 under Lieutenant Commander D.H.N.
Yates RN.

She left Devonport on 21 May with vital aircraft reinforcements: three **Chinook**
HC1s, two **Wasp** HAS1s and a **Sea King** HAS2A. By the time she left **Ascension**
on 31 May her cargo of precious rotary and fixed-wing aircraft had increased
by four **Harrier** GR3s that had flown over from the UK, two **Gazelle** AH1s,
and another Chinook HC1. She arrived in Falklands waters on 10 June but as
it happened, none of these aircraft were offloaded; instead they remained aboard
as replacements when required and in any event took no part in the war owing
to poor weather conditions delaying the assembly of the Chinooks on deck and
to mechanical problems that plagued the ship. She arrived at Southampton on
1 August.

Commander:	Capt A. Mackinnon	
Built:	Harland & Wolff	
Launched:	1981	
Tonnage:	11,445 Gross Register	17,993 Deadweight
Dimensions: length × beam; feet (metres):	568 × 100.5 (173 × 30.6)	
Propulsion:	2 diesel engines	23,400bhp = 19 knots

Aircraft Cargo:	1 × Sea King HAS5
	2 × Wasp HAS1
	4 × Harrier GR3
	4 × Chinook HC1
	2 × Gazelle AH1

Cordella, HMS

A motor freezer trawler commissioned into the **Royal Navy** on 26 April and converted to a minesweeper. She left Portland on 27 April and arrived at **Ascension** on 11 May, from there proceeding to **South Georgia**, which she reached on the 27th. She did not serve in Falklands waters until 21 June, a week after the conflict ended, and arrived in Rosyth on 11 August.

Commander:	Lt M.C.G. Holloway	
Builders:	J. Marr & Son (Hull)	
Launched:	1973	
Tonnage:	1,238 Gross Register	
Dimensions: length × beam; feet (metres):	230 × 42 (70.2 × 12.7)	
Propulsion:	1 diesel engine	3,250bhp = 16.5 knots

Courageous, HMS

Six **submarines** served in the South Atlantic, of which *Courageous* numbered among three of the Fleet Valiant class, all nuclear powered, the others being *Conqueror* and *Valiant*. *Courageous* left Faslane on 4 April and arrived in Falklands waters around the 19th, thereafter patrolling between those islands and Argentina. She arrived back in Faslane on 13 August.

Commander:	Commander R.T.N. Best	
Builders:	Vickers (Barrow)	
Launched:	7 March 1970	
Commissioned:	16 October 1971	
Displacement (tons):	3,500 Standard	4,000 Full Load, Surface 4,900 Submerged
Dimensions: length × beam; feet (metres):	Length: 285 × 33.0 (86.9 × 10.1)	
Draught:	8.2m	
Propulsion:	1 nuclear reactor = 2 geared steam turbines	20,000shp = approximately 25 knots submerged
Armament:	6 × 21in (533mm) bow torpedo tubes; Mark 8 and 21in Tigerfish torpedoes	
Complement:	13 officers, 96 ratings	

Coventry, HMS

One of eight **destroyers** that served in the South Atlantic, the others being *Antrim*, *Bristol*, *Cardiff*, *Exeter*, *Glamorgan*, *Glasgow* and *Sheffield*. She belonged to the Type 42, 'Sheffield' class laid down in the 1970s and designed for area air defence. She was powered with a dual set of engines, both designed by Rolls-Royce: the gas turbine Tyne for cruising, and the Olympus for full power, which could be achieved after approximately thirty seconds. Armed with the **Sea Dart** system, with its medium level capability, she could keep Argentine aircraft flying at extremely low altitude, though this did not in the event prevent calamity when she was struck by bombs that overwhelmed her inadequate damage control systems.

In late March 1982, *Coventry* was on Exercise **Springtrain** together with four other destroyers off Gibraltar where, having transferred personnel and aircraft and cross-decked supplies, she sailed on 2 April with the initial **Task Force** and reached **Ascension** on the 11th.

Coventry entered Falklands waters on 1 May and, two days later, while off the north coast of East Falkland, she launched her **Lynx** (XZ242) against a radar contact that turned out to be the patrol vessel *Alferez Sobral*, which was struck and damaged by two **Sea Skua** missiles, as well as two more from the Lynx carried by *Glasgow*.

On 9 May, *Coventry*, in the company of *Broadsword*, lay 12 miles off **Stanley**, positioned so as to intercept Argentine aircraft making use of **Stanley** airfield. She also shelled shore positions with her main armament, although it eventually jammed. Both vessels were relieved the following day by *Brilliant* and *Glasgow*.

As part of the **Carrier Battle Group**, *Coventry* was not directly involved in the landings in **San Carlos Water** on 21 May, being instead, in company with *Broadsword*, on **radar** picket duty to the north of **Pebble Island** to intercept with its missiles Argentine aircraft approaching on a northerly route.

She was still patrolling north of **West Falkland** when on 25 May at about 1820Z she tried to engage two Skyhawks when her Sea Dart system failed, enabling a Skyhawk to hit *Broadsword* with a bomb that, however, failed to explode. A second flight of Skyhawks soon appeared, but *Coventry*'s Sea Dart defences again failed to acquire the targets. Her missile operator launched one without the benefit of radar guidance, but the attackers found no trouble outmanoeuvring it; one Skyhawk hit *Coventry* with all three of its 1,000lb bombs, all of which penetrated deep into the ship, exploding and causing mortal damage. Ablaze and rapidly taking on water, the ship rotated on to her side within fifteen minutes of the attack and inverted completely shortly thereafter. The crew abandoned her at 1848Z, with the vessel finally disappearing beneath the waves at 1922Z.

Helicopters responded immediately to distress calls and began to winch up uninjured survivors and transfer them to *Broadsword* or *Fort Austin*, while those in need of medical attention went straight to the hospital ship *Uganda* or the field hospital at

Ajax Bay. In total, 234 men were rescued from *Coventry*, but eighteen naval personnel and one civilian had been killed and many others were seriously injured.

Commander:	Captain D. Hart-Dyke	
Builders:	Cammell Laird	
Launched:	21 June 1974	
Commissioned:	20 October 1978	
Displacement (tons):	3,150 Standard	4,100 Full Load
Dimension: length × beam; feet (metres):	410 × 47 (125m × 13.3)	
Draught:	5.8m	
Propulsion:	2 Rolls-Royce Olympus gas turbines	54,400shp = 30 knots
	2 Roll-Royce Tyne gas turbines	8,200shp = 18 knots (cruising)
Armament:	1 × 4.5in Mark 8 gun	
	2 × 20mm Oerlikons	
	1 × Sea Dart system (GWS 30)	
	2 × triple Mark 46 BASW torpedo tubes	
Aircraft:	1 × Lynx HAS2	

CVR(T)

Acronym for Combat Vehicle Reconnaissance (Tracked), consisting of **Scorpions** and **Scimitars** from the two Troops of B Squadron, the **Blues and Royals**. Although it was initially believed that the vehicles could not negotiate the soft, boggy ground of the Falklands, this was soon discovered to be false. The CVR(T)s escorted HQ **3 Commando Brigade** on its overland movement from **San Carlos** to **Teal Inlet** on the night of 31 May and fought at **Wireless Ridge** and **Mount Tumbledown**.

Darwin

A small sheep farming settlement of about twenty-five inhabitants situated on the eastern shore of the isthmus that bears its name and about 5 miles north of **Goose Green**, during the battle for which on 28 May Darwin formed the objective for A Company, **2 Para**. In the event, no fighting took place there.

Destroyers

Eight guided missile destroyers of three different classes served in the South Atlantic during Operation **Corporate**: *Antrim*, *Glamorgan*, *Bristol*, *Cardiff*, *Coventry*, *Exeter*, *Glasgow* and *Sheffield*.

The County class *Antrim* and *Glamorgan* and the Type 82 *Bristol* were of 1960s vintage and designed as escorts providing area air defence, although as with other destroyers they also operated in an anti-submarine role and could be deployed to bombard land-based targets. Owing to their size, *Antrim* and *Glamorgan* qualified more as light cruisers than destroyers, and were armed with **Seacat** and **Seaslug** missile systems. In the mid-1970s they were fitted with the French-designed and built **Exocet** missile. The other five destroyers, laid down in the 1970s and also designed for area defence, were Type 42, Sheffield class – all highly manoeuvrable – but the loss of *Sheffield* and *Coventry* to Argentine Exocet missiles demonstrated the inadequacy of their damage control systems. Type 42s were armed with **Sea Dart** systems, whose medium level capability obliged Argentine aircraft to fly at extremely low altitude.

Destroyers played a vital role in the campaign – bombarding targets in and around **Stanley** airport and other installations, serving as lead vessels of detached naval forces performing specific duties, as command and control centres using their sophisticated SATCOMM, and providing air defence and fighter direction. Both Type 22s and Type 42s were stationed at various times to the north of Falkland Sound and off the north coast of both islands as radar pickets, providing not only early warning of imminent air attack but also serving as a 'missile trap'.

Royal Navy destroyers first came into action on 1 May, when they began shelling Stanley airport and the facilities around it. Two of the eight destroyers serving in the South Atlantic were sunk; an Exocet missile struck *Sheffield* on 4 May, killing twenty officers and men; and *Coventry* succumbed to bombs that set her alight on 25 May, leaving nineteen men dead.

Douglas

A tiny settlement on East Falkland situated at the north-west corner of Port Salvador Bay. Driven from **Fanning Head** by **Special Boat Squadron** on 21 May, the Argentines' Combat Team Eagle retreated east to Douglas, which it reached four days later before departing. Early on 28 May, **45 Commando** reached the settlement during its **yomp** from **Port San Carlos** to **Mount Kent**.

Dumbarton Castle, HMS

A Castle class fishery protection vessel, she constituted one of two offshore patrol vessels brought to the South Atlantic, the other being *Leeds Castle*. She left Portland on 1 May and arrived at **Ascension** ten days later. From there she served as a dispatch vessel between Ascension and the Falklands before finishing service at Rosyth on 20 August.

D

Commander:	Lieutenant Commander N.D. Wood	
Builders:	Hall Russell (Aberdeen)	
Launched:	3 June 1981	
Commissioned:	26 March 1982	
Displacement (tons):	1,250 Standard	1,450 Full Load
Dimensions: length × beam; feet (metres):	266 × 38 (81 × 11.5)	
Draught:	3.4m	
Propulsion:	2 diesel engines	5,640bhp = 20 knots
Armament:	1 × 40mm AA gun	
	2 × 7.62mm GPMG	

Eburna, MV

A motor tanker chartered from Shell (UK) on 13 April for fleet refuelling and consequently one of a large fleet of **Ships Taken Up From Trade**, and supplied with a Naval Party from the **Royal Fleet Auxiliary**. She departed from Santa Anna Bay, Curaçao, on 8 May and took up station in the Tug, Repair and Logistic Area (TRALA). Her service ended on reaching Rosyth on 31 July.

Commander:	Captain J. Beaumont	
Launched:	1979	
Tonnage:	19,763 Gross Register	31,375 Deadweight
Dimensions: length × beam; feet (metres):	558 × 85 (170 × 26)	
Propulsion:	1 diesel engine	11,200bhp = 14.5 knots

Elk, MV

A roll-on/roll-off motor cargo vessel requisitioned on 5 April from P&O and therefore one of the many **Ships Taken Up From Trade** to serve in the campaign. Built in 1977 and furnished with Naval Party 2050 under Commander A.S. Ritchie, on Operation **Corporate** she transported aircraft and ordnance. Much of the reserve ammunition, and bridging and signalling equipment of **3 Commando Brigade** went in *Elk*, including 100 vehicles, 2,000 tons of ammunition, and hundreds of tons of stores. She departed from Southampton on 9 April and arrived at **Ascension** on the 20th. She served in Falklands waters from 19 May and finished her service at Devonport on 12 July.

Commander:	Captain J.P. Morton	
Launched:	1977	
Tonnage:	5,463 Gross Register	8,652 Deadweight
Dimensions: length × beam; feet (metres):	495 × 71 (151 × 21.3)	
Propulsion:	2 diesel engines	15,600bhp = 18.5 knots
Armament:	2 × 40mm AA guns	
Aircraft Cargo (Ascension to **Total Exclusion Zone**):	3 × **Sea King** HC4 3 × **Scout** AH1	

Endurance, HMS

Originally built in Denmark as the *Anita Dan* in 1956, she was purchased in 1967 by the **Royal Navy** and converted to serve under the name *Endurance* as the Falkland Islands guardship and ice patrol vessel. Painted with distinctive red and white upper works for ease of recognition in Antarctic waters, she carried two unarmed **Wasp**

HMS *Endurance* with a Wessex HAS3 bearing an underslung load. (AirSeaLand Photos)

E

helicopters and, indeed, her only armament consisted of two 20mm Oerlikon guns, which remained stowed until required. She also carried a dozen **Royal Marines**. Her essentially peaceful responsibilities included transporting the small team of the British Antarctic Survey (BAS) who worked on **South Georgia**, 800 miles south-east of the Falklands.

In 1981 the Government announced that *Endurance* would be withdrawn from service the following year, effectively leaving the South Atlantic without a British naval presence. As part of her final commission, *Endurance* stopped in Argentina in February 1982, where she was well received. She stopped again, at **Stanley**, on 25 February before sailing south to South Georgia for her final contact with the BAS team before returning to the UK for the last time via Stanley, Montevideo, Buenos Aires, Barbados and the Azores.

The Argentine invasion of South Georgia altered these plans. While at Stanley on 19 March, Captain Barker learned from the BAS base commander at South Georgia that the scrap metal merchants meant to dismantle the old whaling station at Leith had raised the Argentine flag and failed to report their presence on the island as required. The Governor of the Falklands, Rex Hunt, ordered the Argentines to withdraw from South Georgia and, in response to the Argentine presence there, *Endurance* sailed for the island on the morning of 21 March with twenty-two Royal Marines.

Endurance's Wasp inserted an observation team on the 24th and monitored Argentine activity, while the ship herself followed the movements of the *Bahia Paraíso* over the course of the following days until Royal Marines detachments received orders to land at King Edward Point, whereupon *Endurance* put to sea but continued to carry out reconnaissance with her two Wasps until the fall of the island to the Argentines. *Endurance*, however, returned during Operation **Paraquet**, during which she played an important role in the campaign, not least when her embarked Wasp

HAS1 attacked the Argentine submarine *Sante Fe* in Grytviken harbour on 25 April. *Endurance* arrived in Chatham on 20 August.

Commander:	Captain N.J. Barker	
Builders:	Krögerwerft (Denmark)	
Launched:	May 1956 as the *Anita Dan*; Purchased by the Admiralty February 1967; Commissioned as *Endurance* 28 June 1968	
Displacement (tons):	2,640 Gross Register	3,600 Full Load
Dimensions: length × beam; feet (metres):	307 × 46 (93.58 × 14)	
Draught:	5.5m	
Propulsion:	1 diesel engine	3,220bhp = 14.5 knots
Armament:	2 × 20mm Oerlikons	
Aircraft:	2 × Wasp HAS1	

Engadine, RFA

The sole helicopter support ship in theatre, this **Royal Fleet Auxiliary** vessel carried a mixed force of 270 **Royal Navy** and **Royal Air Force** personnel. Carrying four badly needed **Wessex HU5 helicopters**, she departed Devonport on 10 May, reaching **Ascension** on the 25th, and **San Carlos Water** on 9 June. She also carried crews from helicopters that had previously reached the **Total Exclusion Zone** aboard other recently arrived vessels, such as *Atlantic Causeway*. The helicopters aboard *Engadine* established themselves ashore at the Forward Operating Bases at **Port San Carlos** and at **Teal Inlet**, respectively. *Engadine's* personnel provided vital maintenance support for shore–based helicopters and handled more than 1,600 deck landings. She arrived back in Devonport on 30 July.

Commander:	Captain D.F. Freeman	
Builders:	Henry Robb (Leith Docks, Edinburgh)	
Launched:	15 September 1966	
Commissioned:	15 December 1967	
Tonnage:	3,640 Light Displacement	8,960 Full Load
		6,380 Gross Register
Dimensions: length × beam; feet (metres):	424 × 58 (129.3 × 17.9)	
Draught:	6.7m	
Propulsion:	1 diesel engine	5,500bhp = 16 knots
Armament:	Improvised – 14 × 7.62mm machine guns	
Aircraft:	4 × Wessex HU5	

Europic Ferry, MV

A roll-on/roll-off motor ferry requisitioned on 19 April from Townsend Thoresen as a troop transport. One of many **Ships Taken Up From Trade** employed in the campaign, she was built in 1968 for Atlantic Steam Navigation and furnished with Naval Party 1720 under Commander A.B. Gough RN. *Europic Ferry* carried the ammunition, stores and support equipment for **2 Para**.

She departed Portland on 25 April, reached **Ascension** on 7 May and appeared off the Falklands on the 16th. She was in **San Carlos Water** for the first day of the landings on 21 May, but withdrew late that evening in company with *Norland* and escorted by the damaged *Antrim*, to the relative safety of a holding area approximately 170 miles north-east of **Stanley**. She returned to San Carlos Water on the 23rd to continue unloading troops and stores. Her service in the campaign ended when she reached Southampton on 17 July.

Commander:	Captain C.J.C. Clark	
Launched:	1968	
Tonnage:	4,190 Gross Register	2,784 Deadweight
Dimensions: length × beam; feet (metres):	451 × 70 (137.6 × 21)	
Propulsion:	2 diesel engines	13,360bhp = 19.25 knots
Aircraft cargo (UK to San Carlos):	3 **Scout** (AAC) (transferred to *Elk* for Ascension – **Total Exclusion Zone** 'leg')	

Exeter, HMS

One of eight **destroyers** that served in the South Atlantic, the others being *Antrim*, *Bristol*, *Cardiff*, *Coventry*, *Glamorgan*, *Glasgow* and *Sheffield*. *Exeter* belonged to the Type 42, Sheffield class Batch 2 laid down in the 1970s and designed for area air defence. She was powered by a dual set of engines, both designed by Rolls-Royce: the gas turbine Tyne for cruising, and the Olympus for full power, which could be achieved after approximately thirty seconds. Armed with the **Seacat** system, she could keep Argentine aircraft flying low, close to the surface of the sea. Her Type 1022 air warning **radar** system was more advanced than the other destroyers in theatre.

After patrolling off Belize on guardship duties since March, on 7 May she was ordered to sail with all haste to the South Atlantic to bolster the British naval presence in the South Atlantic in light of the loss of *Sheffield*, struck by an Exocet missile on 4 May. Accordingly, she departed Antigua on 7 May, arrived at **Ascension** exactly a week later, and entered the **Total Exclusion Zone** on 21 May. *Exeter* did not take part in the landings on that day nor did she, technically, speaking, replace either *Sheffield* or *Ardent*, since *Exeter* remained with the **Carrier Battle Group** for most of the campaign.

HMS *Exeter* firing a Sea Dart. (AirSeaLand Photos)

On 30 May at about 1732Z an Exocet launched from a Super Etendard failed to hit its target – probably as a result of chaff diverting it – and landed in the sea between *Exeter* and *Avenger*, which were 10 miles apart. This constituted the last air-launched Exocet in the Argentine armoury.

On 7 June, while in Falkland Sound, *Exeter* fired two **Sea Dart** missiles at Learjets flying at high altitude taking photographs of ships in the anchorage. She brought down one of them at 1203Z, which crashed on to **Pebble Island**. At about 1635Z on 8 June, while near **San Carlos**, *Exeter* detected the presence of Argentine aircraft (whose intended targets were the *Sir Galahad* and *Sir Tristram*) near **Fitzroy** and issued the warning 'Air Raid Red', although this proved too late to allow enough notice for their intended targets, with tragic results. *Exeter* reached Portsmouth on 28 July.

Commander:	Captain H.M. Balfour LVO	
Builders:	Swan Hunter	
Launched:	25 April 1978	
Commissioned:	19 September 1980	
Tonnage:	3,150 Standard	4,100 Full Load

Dimensions: length × beam; feet (metres):	410 × 47 (125 × 13.3)	
Draught:	5.8m	
Propulsion:	2 Rolls-Royce Olympus gas turbines	54,400shp = 30 knots
	2 Rolls-Royce Tyne gas turbines	8,200shp = 18 knots (cruising)
Armament:	1 × 4.5in Mark 8 gun	
	2 × 20mm Oerlikon AA guns	
	1 × Sea Dart system (GWS 30)	
	2 × triple Mark 46 ASW torpedo tubes	
Aircraft:	1 × **Lynx** HAS2	

E

Exocet

Designed by the French firm Aerospatiale, the MM.38 Exocet was a ship-launched, anti-ship missile system with an active **radar** terminal homing capability and inertial mid-course guidance. The two County class **destroyers** *Antrim* and *Glamorgan* were armed with four MM.38 Exocets. Five Type 21 **frigates**, *Active*, *Arrow*, *Alacrity*, *Ardent* and *Avenger*, also carried four MM.38 Exocet launchers each.

The solid-fuel rocket booster could propel the 17ft (5.2m), 1,540lb (700kg) missile at 700mph at sea-skimming elevation – rendering it very difficult to detect – for at least 20 miles (37km), with a maximum range of 45. Before launching, the bearing and range of the target were inputted into the memory of the computer guidance system. On approaching its target, the radar locked on and detonated its 365lb charge upon breaking through the ship's casing.

Fanning Head

A 768ft tussock-covered promontory overlooking the northern approaches of Falkland Sound and the narrows into **San Carlos Water**, and therefore a position from which the Argentines could potentially control the neck into this strategically important water feature. A small force of Argentines – twenty men, an 81mm mortar and a 105mm recoilless rifle – established an observation post there at the end of April to report any British activity. The presence of this combat team, dubbed by the British the 'Fanning Head Mob', was detected on 14 May by signals intelligence and confirmed by an **Special Boat Squadron** patrol near **Port San Carlos**.

With supporting gunfire from *Antrim* commencing at 0452Z on 21 May, thirty-two men from 3 SBS with night-vision equipment were inserted by *Antrim*'s **Wessex** HAS3 and another helicopter from 845 NAS to neutralise them just prior to the landings. This team was supported by armed reconnaissance flights conducted by two GPMG- and SNEB rocket-fitted **Gazelle AH1s** of 3 Commando Brigade Air Squadron from the *Sir Tristram* and functioning as gunships. Some Argentines were killed, others fled and lived wild for the next three weeks in the area of San Carlos Water, although a small number in poor condition were captured by a **40 Commando** while **patrolling** on 8 June. Four wounded **prisoners** were evacuated to a ship in San Carlos Water. With Fanning Head secured, the **landing craft** could proceed to disembark the main force, which took place at 0530Z.

Farnella, HMS

A motor trawler requisitioned and converted as a minesweeper for **Royal Navy** service, she served in the waters off **South Georgia**. She departed from Portland on 27 April, reached **Ascension** on 11 May and arrived off Grytviken on 27 May.

Commander:	Lieutenant R.J. Bishop	
Builders:	J. Marr & Son (Hull)	
Launched:	1972	
Commissioned:	26 April 1982	
Tonnage:	1,238 Gross Register	
Dimensions: length × beam; feet (metres):	230 × 42 (70.2 × 12.7)	
Propulsion:	1 diesel engine	3,250bhp = 16.5 knots

Fearless, HMS

A Fearless class assault ship and sister ship to *Intrepid*, the only two Landing Platform (Docks) (LPD) in the **Royal Navy**, contained four **landing craft** and a **Lynx** helicopter. In 1982 defence cutbacks were threatening her existence, as with

Intrepid, and after an exercise in north Norway with **42 Commando** in February she had reverted to a training ship the following month. She and *Intrepid* could serve as emergency landing platforms for **Sea Harriers** low on fuel or suffering from mechanical problems, but in the event only one aircraft made use of this facility, on 13 June.

On 19 May, two days before the landings in **San Carlos Water**, **40 Commando** was cross-decked in Falkland Sound from *Canberra* to *Fearless* aboard landing craft. She carried the **CVR(T)s** of the **Blues and Royals** before transferring them to her landing craft on 21 May. *Fearless* and *Intrepid* took part in the landings in San Carlos Water on 21 May and three days later escaped the bombs of several waves of Argentine aircraft, suffering only superficial damage from strafing.

She departed on 6 April with Brigadier **Thompson** and **3 Commando Brigade** HQ, and Commodore Amphibious Warfare, Commodore Michael Clapp, and his staff, as well as vehicles and heavy equipment, sailing ahead of the **Amphibious Task Group** to reach **Ascension** on 17 April and meet up with the Commander, **Carrier Battle Group**, Admiral **Woodward**.

Fearless arrived off the Falklands on 16 May. Three days later part of 40 Commando and **3 Para** were cross-decked aboard from *Canberra*. On the morning of 21 May, with *Fearless* south-west of Chancho Point at the opening of San Carlos Water, 40 Commando embarked into landing craft, and Thompson went ashore and established 3 **Commando Brigade** HQ at **San Carlos**.

On 27 May, *Fearless* left San Carlos Water to rendezvous with *Antrim* and collect Major General **Moore**, Brigadier **Wilson**, CO of **5 Infantry Brigade**, and their respective staffs, with Moore establishing his HQ in the Amphibious Operations Room. *Fearless* re-entered San Carlos Water three days later.

As part of the effort of shifting 5 Infantry Brigade to **Bluff Cove**, on 4 June, *Fearless* took aboard the **Scots Guards**, who had landed only two days earlier, although on the 5th instructions from Admiral **Fieldhouse** dictated that the ship was not to depart from San Carlos Water except under cover of darkness. *Fearless* departed on the 7th, entering Falkland Sound at 2330Z accompanied by *Penelope* and *Avenger*. On the same day she also conveyed the **Welsh Guards** from San Carlos Water to Elephant Island, where at 0200Z on the 8th, with Major Ewen Southby-Tailyour's LCUs having missed the rendezvous, half the Welsh Guards proceeded to **Port Pleasant** in two *Fearless* landing craft. *Fearless* herself then departed at 0415Z and returned to San Carlos with two companies of the Welsh Guards and some of its supporting elements.

Brigadiers Thompson and Wilson, together with Major General Moore, were aboard *Fearless* on 8 June discussing the **strategy** to be adopted in capturing **Stanley** when their conference broke up upon news of the attack on *Sir Tristram* and *Sir Galahad*, from both of which **Scout** and **Gazelle helicopters** casevaced some of the injured to *Fearless*. She arrived in Devonport on 13 July.

Commander:	Captain E.J.S. Larken	
Builders:	Harland & Wolff	
Launched:	19 December 1963	
Commissioned:	25 November 1965	
Displacement (tons):	11,060 Standard	
	12,120 Full load	
	16,950 Dock Flooded	
Dimensions: length × beam; feet (metres):	520 × 80 (158.5 × 24.4)	
Draught:	7.0m forward; 9.8m aft	
Propulsion:	2 sets geared steam turbines	22,000shp = 21 knots
Armament:	2 × 40mm AA guns	
	4 × **Seacat** systems (GWS 20)	
	2 × 20mm Rheinmetall RH202 AA guns (fitted in early June)	
Aircraft:	Various combinations of **helicopters**; up to 4 **Sea King** Mark 4 operated	
Assault Force:	1 Royal Marines Commando (650 men) + logistic elements	
	1 Commando Light Battery, **Royal Artillery** (6 × 105mm guns)	
	4 × Landing Craft, Utility	
	4 × Landing Craft, Vehicles & Personnel	

Landing Craft (Utility)

Displacement (tons):	75 Standard	176 Full Load
Dimensions: length × beam; feet (metres):	84 × 21 (25.7 × 6.5)	
Draught:	1.7m	
Propulsion:	2 Paxman diesel engines	624bhp = 9 knots
Armament:	1 × 7.62mm GPMG	
Assault Load:	100 tons cargo or two tanks or 140 men	
Crew:	SNCO + 6 ratings	

Landing Craft (Vehicles & Personnel)

Displacement (tons):	8.5 tons	
	Empty (fuelled)	13.5 tons Full Load
Dimensions: length × beam; feet (metres):	43 × 10 (13.1 × 3.1)	
Propulsion:	2 diesel engines	200bhp = 9 knots
Assault Load:	5 tons of cargo or one vehicle or 35 men	

Fieldhouse, Admiral Sir John

Commander-in-Chief (C-in-C) Fleet during the war, by virtue of which position he was appointed Commander, **Combined Task Force 317**, with headquarters based at Northwood, just outside London. As **Task Force** Commander he was responsible for the planning and direction of Operation **Corporate**. Answerable directly to the

Chief of the Defence Staff, Admiral Lewin, his remit was to conduct operations in order to recover the Falkland Islands from Argentine control.

Fieldhouse was born on 12 February 1928 and joined the **Royal Navy** in 1941, attending the Naval College at Dartmouth and joining the Submarine Service in 1948. Having passed the Commanding Officer's Qualifying Course in 1955 he took his first submarine command in *Acheron*. He later commanded the submarines *Tiptoe* and *Walrus* and, in 1964, of *Dreadnought*, the first nuclear submarine in the Royal Navy's service. He remained in the Submarine Service for the most part until appointment as second-in-command aboard the aircraft carrier *Hermes* in 1967. The following year Fieldhouse served at Faslane as captain of a squadron of Polaris submarines, and later with the rank of commodore as Commander of the Naval Standing Force Atlantic, a NATO command. In 1973 he became Director of Naval Warfare and three years later Flag Officer Submarines and NATO Commander Submarines Eastern Atlantic. In 1981 he served as C-in-C Fleet, NATO C-in-C Eastern Atlantic Area and Allied C-in-C Channel during the period when the Nott Review had dictated drastic cuts in the Navy's shipping. Six months after the Falklands War he became First Sea Lord and Chief of the Naval Staff, reversing some of the damage inflicted on his Service by Whitehall. He was a strong advocate for the continuing role of Britain as a sea power and supported the replacement of Polaris with Trident as the UK's independent nuclear deterrent.

Quite in contrast to many in the Ministry of Defence, Fieldhouse shared the view of the First Sea Lord, Admiral Sir Henry Leach, that retaking the Falklands was attainable. At the outbreak of the war, Fieldhouse was in the Mediterranean with Rear Admiral **Woodward** engaged on Exercise **Springtrain**. After Woodward sailed south with the first element of the Task Force, Fieldhouse flew to **Ascension** to meet him, Brigadier Thompson and Commodore Clapp on 17 April to devise a **strategy** for the campaign, although he possessed very little intelligence of Argentine dispositions or strength. He expressed to Thompson and Clapp his opposition to Operation Paraquet, the recapture of **South Georgia**, although in the event his objections were overridden.

Returning to Northwood, Fieldhouse requested another brigade – which was granted in the form of **5 Infantry Brigade**, a decision not approved by the War Cabinet until 2 May – and worked under considerable pressure, with the government keen for victory in short order and with minimal casualties, all the while conscious that the public took a great interest in the course of the campaign.

At Woodward's request, Fieldhouse authorised the sinking of the Argentine cruiser, *General Belgrano*. Fieldhouse accepted Thompson's and Clapp's plan to land troops in **San Carlos Water** despite knowledge that in the absence of local air superiority Operation **Sutton** carried with it considerable risk of defeat if the Argentines could offer resistance on the ground. Fieldhouse maintained his nerve during the various periods of crisis characterising the campaign – such as the loss of *Sheffield* and other vessels to **Exocets** and bombs, a consequence of the lack of long-range airborne early warning capability and the inadequacy of anti-aircraft defences both at sea and on land.

Fieldhouse was promoted Admiral of the Fleet in August 1985 and three months later became Chief of the Defence Staff. He retired in December 1988 and died on 17 February 1992.

Fitzroy

A small settlement on the southern coast of East Falkland, approximately 20 miles by track from **Stanley**. On the morning of 3 June, as the start of the southern thrust across the island, **2 Para** was landed at Fitzroy, starting with C (Patrol) Company, followed later by the rest of the battalion. B Company established itself on Fitzroy Ridge, just north of the settlement and Battalion HQ was fixed in Fitzroy itself.

A further element of the southern thrust involved Commodore Michael Clapp's plan to send the **Scots Guards** and half the **Welsh Guards** to the **Bluff Cove** area, but some of the remaining units of **5 Infantry Brigade** were to go aboard *Sir Tristram* to Fitzroy as the Brigade Forward Maintenance Area. These would include the rest of the Welsh Guards, a **Rapier** detachment, the Brigade War Maintenance Reserve and a **Mexeflote**. Rapiers and other essential stores and equipment were to be delivered to Fitzroy by *Sir Tristram* and unloaded, in daylight if necessary.

After the Scots Guards landed at Bluff Cove, Brigadier Wilson and Lieutenant Colonel Michael Scott, the unit's commanding officer, arrived at Fitzroy by **helicopter** where 5 Infantry Brigade established its HQ in the sheep-shearing shed. The large presence of British troops now made possible repair to the bridge at Fitzroy that spanned the western neck of Port Fitzroy Inlet. Using explosives the Argentines had damaged the 150m structure, leaving a 66ft gap at its eastern end. Over two days 1 Troop, 9 Parachute Squadron **Royal Engineers** strengthened it sufficiently to accommodate the 10-ton load of **CVR(T)s**.

On the morning of 8 June, the second half of 1 Welsh Guards arrived at **Port Pleasant**, the inlet just south of Bluff Cove, but closer to Fitzroy, aboard *Sir Galahad*. At about 1300Z the ship received direct hits from Skyhawks, resulting in heavy casualties. Two other bombs struck *Sir Tristram*, but failed to explode. The wounded were evacuated to the beach and thence to the community centre.

All available helicopters immediately went to the stricken ships' assistance, together with a **landing craft** and several ships' boats. Amid thick, swirling black smoke that limited visibility, **Sea King** helicopters winched up survivors from *Sir Galahad* and flew them to shore, while the pilot of a **Wessex** positioned his helicopter between a dinghy and the burning LSL to use the downdraft of his rotor blades to stop the boat and its passengers drifting towards the flames. The Sea Kings soon assisted similarly, pushing several other dinghies away from danger. Only the aft section of

Sir Galahad caught fire, making the rescue of survivors able to reach the forward section of the ship much easier, but others had to be plucked from the decks of the smoke-filled stern. **Scouts** and **Gazelles** soon joined in the search and rescue and casevac operation, flying casualties to *Fearless* or direct to the field hospital at **Ajax Bay**. Rescue operations continued into the hours of darkness involving helicopters equipped with passive night vision goggles (PNGs).

In the late afternoon of the same day four more Skyhawks appeared over Fitzroy, but air defences issued such intensive ground fire, including surface-to-air missiles, that all the aircraft were damaged and made their escape without carrying through their attack.

In the days following, the build-up of supplies continued apace; on 9 June, for instance, Sea Kings of 846 NAS moved ammunition and supplies from Ajax Bay to forward positions at Fitzroy.

5 Infantry Brigade

Formed in December 1981 as an 'out-of-area' formation – that is, capable of deployment outside the likely NATO operating area and therefore not committed to either NATO or Northern Ireland like the remainder of the Army – 5 Infantry Brigade, with headquarters based in Aldershot and commanded by Brigadier Tony **Wilson**, formed the second major land component dispatched on Operation **Corporate**. It initially consisted of 2 **Para** and 3 **Para**, 1/7 **Gurkha Rifles** and supporting arms, but this order of battle would change before deployment to the South Atlantic. Earlier in the year it had been converted from a mixed Regular/Territorial Army home defence formation into an all-Regular formation. The brigade contained no organic artillery, but ultimately sailed with 4th Field Regiment under Lieutenant Colonel Tony Holt.

It was given notice of deployment to the South Atlantic on the day of the invasion, 2 April. Five days later the Ministry of Defence reduced the notice to move from the standard seven days to three, whereupon 5 Infantry Brigade cancelled Easter leave. Shortly thereafter 2 Para and 3 Para were transferred to **3 Commando Brigade**, necessitating replacement of those units with two infantry battalions. A solution emerged at a HQ United Kingdom Land Forces (HQ UKLF) conference at Wilton; cognisant that Britain had to maintain its NATO Priority One commitment against the Warsaw Pact, the General Officer Commanding, London District, Major General Sir Desmond Langley, suggested the detachment of two of his Guards battalions.

There were three available: 1st Battalion **Welsh Guards**; 2nd Battalion **Scots Guards**, serving on public duties; and 2nd Battalion Grenadier Guards, recently returned from a tour in Germany as mechanised infantry. Only one battalion stood in reserve in the UK, the 1st Queen's Own Highlanders.

With the inclusion of 1 Welsh Guards and 2 Scots Guards, 5 Infantry Brigade returned to a strength of three battalions, including 1/7th Gurkhas and 2 Para.

Troops of 5
Infantry Brigade.
(AirSeaLand
Photos)

Brigadier Julian **Thompson** RM and Commodore Michael Clapp RN first became aware that 5 Infantry Brigade would be dispatched from UK shores when Admiral **Fieldhouse** held a conference aboard *Hermes*, off **Ascension**, on 17 April. But the War Cabinet did not approve it until 2 May. The original proposed strength was to have been 3,961 men, 1,067 tons of ammunition, 1,129 tons of supplies (for thirty-five days), 205 vehicles and nineteen **helicopters**, but owing to a shortage of shipping the brigade was reduced by about 1,000 personnel and the requisite number of vehicles and freight support, with most of the personnel to travel in the Cunard liner *Queen Elizabeth 2*. The Brigade was later supplemented with an additional 355 troops, 200 tons of freight and dozens of vehicles.

Given that the Ministry of Defence chose two battalions currently on ceremonial duties it would appear that planners regarded 5 Infantry Brigade as a reserve for 3 Commando Brigade rather than a formation to be committed to fighting across a particularly unforgiving landscape against well-entrenched defenders. In all likelihood 5 Infantry Brigade would provide at least some of its troops to garrison the islands upon successful liberation.

On 12 May, 5 Infantry Brigade sailed from Southampton aboard the *QE2*, together with two ro-ro ferries, *Baltic Ferry* and *Nordic Ferry*, and *Atlantic Causeway*. The *QE2* stopped briefly at **Freetown**, Sierra Leone, circled Ascension on 21 May – where she took on stores – and then made a rendezvous with HMS *Antrim*, aboard which she transferred Major General **Moore** and Brigadier Wilson and their respective staffs. The vessels carrying the brigade with its supporting arms anchored off Grytviken, **South Georgia**, on 27 May and proceeded to cross-deck troops and supplies on to *Canberra* and *Norland*, a process that took more than twenty-four hours. These ships then proceeded in company of *Baltic Ferry* to a point off the **Blue Beaches** in **San Carlos Water**, where they were landed via ships' boats and **landing craft** (LCUs) beginning on the night of 31 May. The two Guards battalions left *Canberra* on 2 June and went ashore on LCUs. Owing to poor visibility as a consequence of low cloud and patches of fog, no Argentine air raids took place on 3 June against the ships unloading troops from 5 Infantry Brigade.

On 5 June, Wilson and Clapp ordered part of the brigade to proceed by ship to **Bluff Cove**. The **Scots Guards** accordingly embarked on *Intrepid* that evening. Owing to the risks, Northwood would not authorise *Intrepid* to proceed east of Lively Island, and thus when under the command of Major Ewen Southby-Tailyour the LCUs were retracted at about 0230Z 2 miles west of Lively Island, the 150 men in each of the four vessels were obliged to endure a journey of several hours in four landing craft exposed to the cold and wet through waters not under friendly control. Owing to the failure of Brigade HQ to inform **Royal Navy** vessels in the area of impending inshore naval operations, in the early hours of 6 June, the destroyer *Cardiff*, detecting their presence on radar, fired six star shells in quick succession over the unidentified craft before ordering them to 'heave to' and identifying them as friendly. This averted a potentially disastrous **'Blue on Blue'** incident involving about 600 men.

At last, after a nine-hour journey in pitching landing craft, freezing winds and drenched in sea-water spray, the Scots Guards reached their destination of Bluff Cove, where in the absence of their own commanding officer, the CO of 2 Para, Lieutenant Colonel Chaundler, ordered them to move north and dig in. This completed Phase One of the 5 Infantry Brigade move. Wilson and Scott arrived by helicopter and set up Brigade HQ in the sheep-shearing shed.

On the evening of 7 June, 1 Welsh Guards proceeded aboard HMS *Fearless* to a position south of Elephant Island where they were meant to rendezvous with four *Intrepid* LCUs coming from Bluff Cove led by Major Ewen Southby-Tailyour RM. When these did not materialise, the plan changed whereby half the battalion proceeded in two *Fearless* LCUs to Bluff Cove under Southby-Tailyour's direction – although they were supposed to be bound for **Fitzroy**.

The remaining two companies and other supporting elements returned at 0415Z in *Fearless* to **San Carlos**. Thus, over two days, 2 Scots Guards and half of 1 Welsh Guards, plus some supporting elements, had been ferried to Bluff Cove, but this still left Phase Two of Clapp's move incomplete.

The remainder of the Welsh Guards were moved by RFA *Sir Galahad*, although Brigade HQ were unaware of their arrival, believing that the two companies that had arrived the previous evening constituted the entire battalion; this circumstance caused consternation since no arrangements had been made for their disembarkation at Fitzroy on 8 June. Southby-Tailyour came aboard and explained his grave anxiety at the vulnerability of the troops to air attack and strongly urged their immediate disembarkation. The two company commanders declined, wishing instead for their troops to be spared the march to their ultimate destination – Bluff Cove.

After several hours aboard ship the troops were finally disembarked. During this process, however, Mirage III jets distracted a **Sea Harrier combat air patrol** over **West Falkland** around 1645Z, enabling five Skyhawks to carry on to **Port Pleasant** and attack the anchorage there. Most of the troops and equipment were still onboard *Sir Tristram* and *Sir Galahad*, which sat exposed in a mostly undefended inlet, with little supporting ground fire offered and only one ineffectual ground-based surface-to-air missile fired.

The stern of the *Sir Galahad* took three hits – 500lb bombs from the same Skyhawk – causing a raging fire from ignited fuel and ammunition. *Sir Tristram* sustained two hits from another Skyhawk, although neither of the bombs exploded. A third bomb did explode, however, blowing off the rear loading ramp. Fires broke out, forcing the crew to abandon ship, but *Sir Tristram* escaped terminal damage. While five Skyhawks withdrew without suffering serious damage, their attack rendered half the Welsh Guards *hors de combat*, their two devastated companies replaced by **Royal Marines** from **40 Commando** for the final operation of the war: clearing **Sapper Hill**.

Notwithstanding the disaster at Port Pleasant, 5 Infantry Brigade continued to form an important part of the advance on **Stanley**: the Scots Guards, with reinforcement from the Gurkhas, protected the flank of the **42 Commando** assault on **Mount Harriet** on 11–12 June; the Gurkhas patrolled towards **Mount Tumbledown** and **Mount William** and had orders to attack the latter if the Argentines did not surrender; and of course the occasion of the Scots Guards sweeping the Argentines from Mount Tumbledown on the night of 13–14 June. The few Argentines on William fled, leaving the Gurkhas to occupy that position without opposition. After the Argentine surrender on 14 June, most of the Brigade returned to Fitzroy, apart from the Gurkhas, who went to **Goose Green**.

Total casualties for 5 Infantry Brigade during the campaign amounted to fifty-seven killed in action, eighty-six wounded in action, twenty-five injured (e.g. broken limbs sustained on patrol), and nine out of action due to illness.

Fleet Air Arm

The air assets available to the **Royal Navy**, which in the case of the Falklands War involved the **Sea Harrier** and various types of helicopter, were deployed across a range of vessels, including the **aircraft carriers** *Hermes* and *Invincible*. All such aircraft were all organised into Naval Air Squadrons (NAS), which in 1982 included approximately 250 **helicopters**, almost 200 of which served in the **Total Exclusion Zone**, and thirty Sea Harriers, of which twenty-eight were deployed south.

The helicopters were responsible for carrying troops and conducting anti-submarine warfare operations, resupply, and casualty evacuation. The Sea Harriers provided air defence to the **Task Force** and, once air superiority was achieved in late May, support to ground forces. Sea Harriers could take off and land vertically, thus requiring a much smaller carrier flight deck than conventional aircraft. The Sea Harrier used the ski-jump ramp fitted to *Hermes* and *Invincible* to get airborne while at sea. Those operating from **Ships Taken Up From Trade** did so on specially reinforced decks fitted to bear the weight and pressure of these remarkable aircraft.

The obvious and vital need for the maximum number of deployable helicopters on Operation **Corporate** not only led to a reorganisation of the available force, but in an increase of naval air squadrons and the absorption of a small number of **Royal Air Force** pilots to boost Fleet Air Arm numbers. Seven RAF pilots fully qualified to fly the Sea Harrier already existed, and two more underwent training during the journey south. To top up the numbers, training squadrons gave up aircraft for deployment south.

In all, fifteen Fleet Air Arm squadrons served in the South Atlantic, containing between them **Wessex, Lynx, Wasp, Sea King** and Sea Harriers.

F

Fleet Oilers

Carrying all three types of fuel as well as fresh water, these formed part of the **Royal Fleet Auxiliary**, with five fleet oilers serving during the war: *Olmeda, Olna, Tidepool, Tidespring* and *Blue Rover*.

A Sea Harrier FRS1 of the Fleet Air Arm, one of the two types of aircraft in theatre with a remarkable vertical take off and landing capability. (AirSeaLand Photos)

Fleet Replenishment Ships

Supplying ammunition, food and dry stores, five such vessels of the **Royal Fleet Auxiliary** served in the South Atlantic: *Regent, Resource, Stromness, Fort Austin* and *Fort Grange*.

Forrest, MV

A Falkland Islands Company motor coaster built in 1967 owned by the government and which on 1–2 April made two sorties to conduct radar sweeps after word came of imminent invasion. The Argentines subsequently seized her for use during their occupation.

Tonnage:	144 Gross Register	140 Deadweight
Dimensions: length × beam; feet (metres):	86 × 23 (26.2 × 7)	
Propulsion:	1 diesel engine	320bhp = 10 knots (eorgan.)

Fort Austin, RFA

Fort class **fleet replenishment ship**, one of five such vessels of the **Royal Fleet Auxiliary** to serve in the South Atlantic, the others being *Regent, Resource, Stromness,* and *Fort Grange*.

At the outbreak of war she was rapidly recalled from the Persian Gulf to Gibraltar and then dispatched south to replenish *Endurance*, which carried stores and provisions for only another three weeks. *Fort Austin* arrived at **Ascension** on 6 April carrying various types of **helicopters**, including **Lynx** specially fitted to fire the **Sea Skua** missile, and embarked Special Forces for the operation to recapture **South Georgia**.

She arrived off the Falklands on 3 May. On the 24th, while stationed in **San Carlos Water**, *Fort Austin* narrowly escaped being bombed by several waves of Argentine aircraft. The following day she took aboard 263 survivors from *Coventry*. Her service in the conflict ended upon arrival at Devonport on 28 June.

Commander:	Commodore S.C. Dunlop CBE	
Launched:	9 March 1978	
Builders:	Scott-Lithgow (Greenock)	
Commissioned:	11 May 1979	
Tonnage:	15,300	
	Light Displacement	22,750
	Full Load	16,000
	Gross Register	8,300 Deadweight
Dimensions: length × beam; feet (metres):	603 × 79 (183.8 × 24.1)	

Draught:	14.9m	
Propulsion:	1 diesel engine	23,200bhp = 20 knots
Armament:	Improvised – GPMGs and rifles	
Load:	3,500 tons of ammunition, stores and spares	
Aircraft:	2 × **Sea King** HAS5	
	3 × helicopters of various types embarked	

Fort Grange, RFA

A Fort class **fleet replenishment ship**. Five such vessels of the **Royal Fleet Auxiliary** served in the South Atlantic, the other four being *Regent*, *Resource*, *Stromness*, and *Fort Austin*. She mainly carried aircraft spares, ammunition and food, departed Devonport on 14 May and joined the **Carrier Battle Group** on 3 June, transferring stores ashore in **San Carlos Water**. She arrived back in Devonport on 3 October.

Commander:	Captain D.G.M. Averill CBE	
Builders:	Scott-Lithgow (Greenock)	
Launched:	9 December 1976	
Commissioned:	6 April 1978	
Tonnage:	15,300 Light Displacement	22,750 Full Load
	16,000 Gross Register	8,300 Deadweight
Dimensions: length × beam; feet (metres):	603 × 79 (183.8 × 24.1)	
Draught:	14.9m	
Propulsion/Machinery:	1 diesel engine	23,200bhp = 20 knots
Armament:	Improvised – GPMGs and rifles	
Load:	3,500 tons of ammunition, stores and spares	
Aircraft:	2 × **Sea King** HAS2A	
	3 × other **helicopters** of various types embarked	

Fort Toronto, MV

A motor chemical tanker chartered from Canadian Pacific (Bermuda) on 7 April as a fresh water supply tanker. Like most **Ships Taken Up From Trade**, she carried a Naval Party supplied by the **Royal Fleet Auxiliary**. *Fort Toronto* departed Southampton on 19 April and reached Falklands waters in mid–May. She did not return to the UK until April 1984.

Commander:	Captain R.I. Kinnier
Launched:	1981

Tonnage:	19,982 Gross Register	31,745 Deadweight
Dimensions: length × beam; feet (metres):	556 × 89 (169.6 × 27.2)	
Propulsion:	1 diesel engine	11,200bhp = 15 knots

40 Commando Royal Marines

See Royal Marines

42 Commando Royal Marines

See Royal Marines

45 Commando Royal Marines

See Royal Marines

Fox Bay

A settlement on the east coast of **West Falkland**, containing an Argentine garrison that elements of both the **Special Air Service** and the **Special Boat Squadron** monitored. An air attack was launched against Argentine positions at Fox Bay – on 20 May a **Sea Harrier** cluster bomb attack destroyed a large number of petrol and oil drums – but otherwise the place remained undisturbed for the duration of the conflict. On the afternoon of 15 June an officer from *Avenger* arrived by helicopter and accepted the surrender of the 950 Argentine troops, mostly of the 8th Regiment, in the settlement.

Freetown

A port city and capital of Sierra Leone, on the West African coast. On the journey south, *Norland*, carrying **2 Para** from **3 Commando Brigade**, and *Queen Elizabeth 2* and other vessels carrying the troops of **5 Infantry Brigade** briefly anchored there to take on stores during their journey south.

Friendly Fire

See 'Blue on Blue'

Frigates

There were fifteen **Royal Navy** frigates deployed to the South Atlantic, performing two principal roles: protecting the troop carriers during the landings and, for the duration of the conflict, the capital ships of the **Task Force**. Frigates on Operation **Corporate** belonged to three types: six Type 12s: *Plymouth, Yarmouth, Argonaut, Minerva, Penelope*, and *Andromeda*; seven Type 21s: *Active, Alacrity, Ambuscade, Antelope, Ardent, Arrow* and *Avenger;* and two Type 22s: *Brilliant* and *Broadsword.* All frigates carried one or two **Lynx helicopters** as their main anti-submarine weapon system, with the exception of *Active*, which had a **Wasp**. Two Type 21s were lost, both from bombing: *Ardent* on 21 May, and *Antelope* on the 23rd, with several others sustaining damage of varying degrees.

Their design intended them mostly for an Anti-Submarine Warfare (ASW) role. Boasting a range of **naval armament**, all but the Leander class (*Argonaut, Minerva* and *Penelope* – Batch 2; and *Andromeda* – Batch 3) still had 4.5in guns (either Mark 6 or Mark 8) used to bombard targets on land or to repel aircraft; that is to say, the older Type 12 Rothesay class and the Type 21 Amazon class. More recent frigates served effectively as missile launching platforms, such as the Type 22 Broadsword class. The newer Leanders, *Penelope, Minerva, Argonaut* and *Andromeda*, had no turrets with 4.5in guns and thus served entirely as anti-submarine and anti-aircraft ships, armed with three quadruple **Seacat** surface-to-air launchers and four **Exocet** launchers, a Lynx helicopter with ASW capability, two triple torpedo tubes and a pair of Bofors 40mm guns.

The Type 22 Broadsword class frigates were more modern than the Leanders and were fitted as command and control ships. They, like the Leanders, possessed no 4.5in main armament, instead carrying two **Sea Wolf** systems, four Exocet launchers, two triple torpedo tubes, two 40mm Bofors guns and two Lynx helicopters. *Broadsword* and *Brilliant* were larger than their predecessors, with the latter commissioned less than a year before Operation **Corporate**.

The ageing *Plymouth* and *Yarmouth*, both belonging to the Rothesay class, were more than twenty years old in 1982 and ranked as the smallest frigates to serve in the conflict, with 4.5in Mark 6 guns, two 20mm Oerlikon anti-aircraft guns, a Seacat missile system and, unique within the fleet, an anti-submarine mortar.

Gazelle AH1

A light helicopter carrying a crew of two and up to three passengers, the Westland Gazelle AH1 was employed in a range of duties including casualty evacuation, reconnaissance, communications and light attack. However, its most critical role was in the fundamentally vital function of **logistics**. This involved ferrying light loads over secured ground, and was essential in areas bereft of roads and consequently impassable to most vehicles. Fifteen Gazelle AH1s served in the Falklands, ten operated by 3 Commando Brigade Air Squadron and five by 656 Squadron Army Air Corps. In 3 CBAS, the average flying time for each Gazelle between 21 May and 24 June amounted to just over 146 hours. When escorting unarmed transport helicopters, Gazelles carried SNEB rockets, but otherwise they flew without this armament. The Gazelle could be fitted as a gunship, such as two in 3 CBAS fitted with GPMGs and SNEB 68mm rockets to support the **Special Boat Squadron** raid against **Fanning Head** on 21 May.

Their many missions cannot all be recounted, but some examples will serve to highlight their many roles. On the day of the landings, 21 May, a Gazelle flew from RFA *Sir Galahad* to recce locations for **Rapier** sites, while others protected **Sea Kings** bringing stores ashore. With so many **helicopters** aloft on the first day of the landings it was perhaps inevitable that some would be lost. Two Gazelles, for instance, were shot down on that day; in one case, Lieutenant Ken Francis RM and Lance Corporal Brett RM were shot down near **Port San Carlos**, killing both crew. A third Gazelle was lost to a British **Sea Dart** in a **'Blue on Blue'** incident. A week later, two Gazelles were present at **Goose Green** to support 2 Para's attack. Both flew forward to collect the body of the fallen commanding officer, Lieutenant Colonel Jones, but one was shot down by two Pucaras and the other escaped. On the night of 5 June, a Gazelle piloted by Staff Sergeant Christopher Griffin of 656 Squadron and carrying Major Forge and Staff Sergeant Joe Baker, was accidently shot down near Pleasant Peak by a Sea Dart fired by *Cardiff*, whose radar operator mistook the aircraft for an Argentine C-130. Gazelles played an important part in assisting with casevac operations at **Port Pleasant** after the attacks against the *Sir Galahad* and *Sir Tristram* on 8 June.

Geestport, MV

A motor refrigerated cargo ship requisitioned from Geest Line on 7 May for use as a food and provisions transport. One of dozens of **Ships Taken Up From Trade** and supplied with a Naval Party from the RNSTS, *Geestport* left Portsmouth on 21 May and first served off **South Georgia** during the conflict and then off the Falklands from 21 June – a week after the end of the fighting, reaching Portsmouth on 19 August.

Commander:	Captain G.F. Foster	
Launched:	1982	
Naval Party:	Mr R.A. Reeves RNSTS	
Tonnage:	7,729 Gross Register	9,970 Deadweight
Dimensions: length × beam; feet (metres):	522 × 70 (159 × 21.4)	
Propulsion:	1 diesel engine	13,100bhp = 19.5 knots

Gemini

Inflatable and collapsible craft equipped with an outboard motor, used by Special Forces for water-borne insertion, specifically by the **Special Boat Squadron** in the operation to recapture **South Georgia**.

G

Glamorgan, HMS

One of two County class guided missile **destroyers** on Operation **Corporate**, the other being *Antrim*. At the end of March, *Glamorgan* was engaged on Exercise **Springtrain** off Gibraltar, together with four other destroyers. She immediately made her way to Gibraltar and after cross-decking supplies and taking on personnel and aircraft led the initial **Task Force** south, arriving off the Falklands on 1 May.

Going into action the same day, together with the **frigates** *Alacrity* and *Arrow*, off Cape Pembroke, *Glamorgan* briefly shelled **Stanley** airfield, when the ships were attacked by three Dagger As. As none of the warships' **radar** had detected the approach of hostile aircraft they were caught unprepared, although neither of the two 500lb parachute-retarded bombs released struck the ships. *Glamorgan* nevertheless suffered minor damage below the waterline caused by bomb explosions nearby. She managed to fire a single **Seacat** missile but failed to hit any of the Daggers.

On the evening of 14–15 May, in company with *Broadsword* and *Hermes*, *Glamorgan* supported the **Special Air Service** raid on **Pebble Island**, providing covering fire during extraction before sailing north-east at full speed to avoid being near the coast at dawn.

As part of the **Carrier Battle Group**, *Glamorgan* was not directly involved in the landings in **San Carlos Water** on 21 May, but rather played a diversionary role off the east coast of East Falkland. From there she fired 100 rounds of 4.5in shells towards **Berkeley Sound** in an effort to persuade senior Argentine commanders that the landings were taking place near Stanley. At the same time, her **Wessex HAS3** approached the coast to reinforce this impression.

On the night of 27–28 May, by way of diverting Argentine HQ's attention away from the attack at **Goose Green**, *Glamorgan*, together with *Alacrity* and *Avenger*, bombarded Argentine positions around Stanley, firing a total of 250 rounds. *Glamorgan* also fired a **Seaslug** missile at Stanley airfield, but in its ship-to-shore capacity it flew unguided.

At 1700Z on 11 June *Glamorgan*, together with *Avenger* and **Yarmouth**, left the Tug, Repair and Logistic Area (TRALA) and positioned herself off **Fitzroy** to support the night-time attack on **Two Sisters** and **Mount Harriet** with naval gunfire. With the attack under way she ceased firing and at about 0635Z on the 12th, while approximately 17 miles south-west of Stanley, she detected an approaching **Exocet** missile – in this case ground-based – prompting her to begin evasive manoeuvring and to fire a Seacat missile to intercept it. Two minutes after its launch the surface-to-air missile exploded ineffectually, upon which the Exocet bounced off the ship's flight deck and entered her hangar, exploding and causing an intense fire that destroyed her Wessex HAS3 and killed thirteen sailors. *Yarmouth* immediately dispatched her **Wasp** over with medical assistance and a fire-control team. Other damage sustained included a 3yd x 5yd hole in her port side, a second and larger one in the weather deck, damage to the galley, destruction of a Seaslug launcher and damage to a Seacat launcher. Over the next few hours **Sea Harriers** of 801 NAS conducted regular Combat Air Patrols over the damaged ship for her protection. Yet despite her travails, *Glamorgan* made a rapid recovery, setting out for the TRALA at about 1000Z to undertake repairs care of the *Stena Seaspread*. She was therefore able also to support the **Scots Guards** during their attack on **Mount Tumbledown** on the night of 13–14 June. *Glamorgan* departed the Falklands on 21 June and arrived in Portsmouth on 10 July.

Commander:	Captain M.E. Barrow	
Launched:	9 July 1964	
Commissioned:	11 October 1966	
Displacement (tons):	5,440 Standard	6,200 Full load
Dimensions: length × beam; feet (metres):	520 × 54 (158.5 × 16.5)	
Draught:	6.3m	
Propulsion:	2 sets geared steam turbines, 2 G6 gas turbines	30,000shp + 15,000shp = 32.5 knots
Armament:	2 × 4.5in (114mm) Mark 6 dual purpose guns (surface/AA)	
	2 × 20mm Oerlikon AA guns	
	1 × **Seaslug** 2 system (GWS 10)	
	2 **Seacat** systems (GWS 22)	
	4 × MM.38 Exocet	
Aircraft:	1 × Wessex HAS3 (destroyed; replaced by 1 × Wessex HU5)	

Glasgow, HMS

One of eight **destroyers** that served in the South Atlantic, she belonged to the Type 42, Sheffield class laid down in the 1970s and designed for area air defence. *Glasgow* was powered by a dual set of engines, both designed by Rolls-Royce: the gas turbine Tyne for cruising, and the Olympus for full power, which could be achieved after approximately thirty seconds. Her **Seacat** system, designed for medium-level capability, could force Argentine aircraft to fly close to the surface of the sea.

In late March 1982 *Glasgow* numbered among five destroyers on Exercise **Springtrain** off Gibraltar; as such, she was available to sail with the initial **Task Force** after transferring aircraft and personnel and cross-decking stores at HM Dockyard, Gibraltar. She arrived at **Ascension** on 11 April and reached Falklands waters on 1 May.

On 3 May, while off the north coast of East Falkland, *Glasgow* dispatched her **Lynx** HAS2 against a vessel that turned out to be an Argentine patrol boat, the *Alferez Sobral*, which was damaged by four **Sea Skua** missiles, two each from *Glasgow*'s and *Coventry*'s Lynx.

A week later, on the 10th, *Glasgow*, in company with the frigate *Brilliant*, relieved *Broadsword* and *Coventry* from radar picket and bombardment duties off **Stanley**. Both ships struck the area of the airfield, firing 222 rounds with the aid of a forward observer from the **Royal Artillery** operating from a Lynx.

On 12 May, while about 15 miles south of Stanley in company with *Brilliant* and returning from their bombardment of the area, two A-4B Skyhawks attacked each of the two warships. *Glasgow*'s 4.5in gun had developed a fault earlier in the day; worse still, after the Skyhawks were detected on radar, it was found that *Glasgow*'s **Sea Dart** launcher had malfunctioned, leaving the ship's defence entirely to *Brilliant* and her **Sea Wolf** capability. This brought down two attackers, while a third struck the sea while trying to evade a missile. The last Skyhawk escaped, having failed to strike its target with two 500lb bombs, one of which, however, bounced off the sea and over *Glasgow*'s stern. Her Oerlikon 20mm gun jammed just before this attack, which meant all her firing systems had failed, apart from small arms- and machine-gun fire offered by some of her crew.

At 1715Z four more Skyhawks attacked both ships, one against *Brilliant* and three against *Glasgow*. The latter's Sea Dart system remained inoperable but her main armament was back in action and fired at her assailants. Meanwhile, *Brilliant* found herself unable to fire any further Sea Wolf missiles owing to a computer fault. *Brilliant* remained undamaged by two bombs dropped by one of the Skyhawks, but one of the bombs hit *Glasgow* amidships 3ft above her waterline, puncturing her skin, crashing through the auxiliary machinery room and striking a fuel tank, thereafter smashing its way out of the ship to explode upon hitting the sea. Other bombs dropped by two further aircraft qualified as near misses but caused no additional damage to *Glasgow*, which later repaired her Sea Dart system and main armament.

She was obliged to remain on operations but with the arrival of the Bristol Group, she was free to undertake badly needed extensive repairs; on 26 May she sailed to the Tug, Repair and Logistic Area (TRALA) to undergo repairs care of the *Stena Seaspread*, but when that vessel's resources proved inadequate to the task *Glasgow* was sent back to the UK the following day, covering the entire journey on her secondary engines and only arriving at Portsmouth on 20 June, six days after the conclusion of the campaign.

Commander:	Captain A.P. Hoddinot OBE	
Builders:	Swan Hunter	
Launched:	14 April 1976	
Commissioned:	24 May 1979	
Dimensions: length × beam; feet (metres):	410 × 47 (125m × 13.3)	
Draught:	5.8m	
Propulsion:	2 Rolls-Royce Olympus gas turbines	54,000shp = 30 knots
	2 Rolls-Royce Tyne gas turbines	8,200shp – 18 knots (cruising)
Armament:	1 × 4.5in Mark 8 Dual Purpose gun	
	2 × 20mm Oerlikons	
	1 × Sea Dart system (GWS 30)	
	2 × triple Mark 46 ASW torpedo tubes	
Aircraft:	1 × Lynx HAS2	

Goat Ridge

A long, narrow, east–west running position, about 600ft in elevation situated roughly half a mile between **Mount Harriet** and **Two Sisters**. During the attack of **42 Commando** on Harriet, Goat Ridge was held by a platoon from A Company, 4th Infantry Regiment. It was captured by K Company, 42 Commando after the fall of 'Zoya', the main position on Harriet.

Goosander, RMAS

A mooring vessel in the **Royal Maritime Auxiliary Service** employed from the end of May to lay buoys and moorings at **Ascension**.

Commander:	Captain A. MacGregor	
Launched:	1973	
Displacement:	750 Standard	1,200 Full Load
	283 Deadweight	
Dimensions: length × beam; feet (metres):	186 × 36.5 (55.4 × 12.2)	
Propulsion:	2 diesel engines	550bhp = 10 knots

Goose Green

Site of the largest ground engagement of the campaign, fought on 28 May, Goose Green was the most populated of the few settlements on the Falklands, yet numbered only 127 residents, with another twenty-five at **Darwin**, about 5 miles to the north. The whole community was involved in sheep farming. An Argentine force known as Task Force Mercedes arrived there on 3 April, established a small airbase for Pucara ground attack aircraft around the 400yd grass airstrip, and eventually detained nearly all the area's residents in the Community Centre.

After the Second Battalion, the **Parachute Regiment** (2 Para) came ashore in **San Carlos Water** just after dawn on 21 May it immediately ascended **Sussex Mountain** and established defensive positions amid cold and windy conditions, with the ground too hard to dig trenches. On the same day as the landings, a G Squadron **Special Air Service** (SAS) patrol conducted a diversionary raid on the northern approach to the Darwin–Goose Green isthmus, about 15 miles to the south, to pin the troops there in place, denying the possibility of a disruption to the landings further north.

On the 23rd Brigadier Julian **Thompson**, commanding **3 Commando Brigade** and Lieutenant Colonel 'H' Jones, commanding officer (CO) of 2 Para, discussed the possibility of launching a battalion-sized raid against the Argentine garrison at Darwin and Goose Green, the only sizeable Argentine formation within close proximity to the **San Carlos** bridgehead. The main Argentine elements consisted of the 12th Infantry Regiment of about 650 men, mostly conscripts, which had arrived on 28 April, C Company from the 25th Regiment, which had arrived on 3 April, a platoon from the 8th Infantry Regiment and various Air Force personnel. They had two pack howitzers and several anti-aircraft guns: two 35mm Oerlikons and six Air Force 20mm cannon, all near the airfield and the settlement itself, plus one 105mm recoilless rifle and two 81mm mortars elsewhere. The defenders had laid mines along Salinas Beach, at the northern end of the airfield, on both sides of the inlet north of the schoolhouse and between Middle Hill and Coronation Ridge. A line of trenches extended across the isthmus, many along Darwin Ridge at whose eastern end stood Darwin Hill. A strike at Goose Green, only 15 miles away, would be consistent with Major General **Moore's** orders to establish moral domination over the Argentines. With only six **Sea King** HC4s and five **Wessex** HU5s available, Thompson did not possess enough air lift assets to carry the troops south; they would have to move on foot. With Goose Green and Darwin situated on an isthmus, a landing by sea seemed the obvious choice; but with rocks lining the coast of Brenton Loch, the presence of minefields and the risks of detection if employing **radar** for purposes of aiding navigation, rendered this option laden with risk.

Still, moving on foot was perfectly feasible and Jones strongly wished to move forward and engage the Argentines; armed with Thompson's orders for a raid, Jones sent C Company under Major Roger Jenner south on the morning of the 24th to recce a route to Darwin. It reached the unoccupied Canterra House, 6 miles from Sussex Mountain, from where it sent back intelligence of the presence of one Argentine company and a troop carrier. Thus informed, Jones ordered the raid against Goose Green to be conducted early on the 26th, with fire support provided by three 105mm light guns from 8 (Alma) Commando Battery, **Royal Artillery**. At sunset on the 25th, D Company, with responsibility for securing the start line, left Sussex Mountain, joined with the platoon (12 Pl) from C Company that had remained at Canterra House, and carried on south for Camilla Creek House.

In the event, after appreciating that the raid represented an unwelcome diversion to the main effort of pushing east, and that with the required helicopter lift to **Mount Kent** he could no longer supply the three guns envisaged for it, Thompson cancelled it accordingly, much to Jones's fury. At 1000Z on the 26th Jones ordered D Company under Major Philip Neame to be airlifted by helicopter to Camilla Creek House – but there were none available owing to bad weather. 12 Platoon was recalled and returned to 2 Para's position at Camilla Creek House, as did D Company.

This brought only a very temporary halt to a strike on Goose Green. There is little doubt that in the wake of the losses on 25 May of *Coventry* and *Atlantic Conveyor*, Downing Street and Northwood wished for immediate action by way of a counterstrike, if only to allay public opinion that Britain had not lost the initiative. Communicating with London via satellite link from **Ajax Bay**, Thompson received clear orders from Admiral **Fieldhouse** to resume the attack on Darwin–Goose Green, notwithstanding the absence of sufficient fire support. Accordingly, Thompson ordered Jones to capture the settlements, having

Lieutenant Colonel 'H' Jones, commanding officer of Second Battalion, The Parachute Regiment. (AirSeaLand Photos)

ascertained from Fieldhouse that the new operation now envisaged more than a raid but a full-scale assault – a notion having been suggested to Fieldhouse by General Stanier, Commander-in-Chief, UK Land Forces, when the latter visited Northwood and stated his belief that the Argentine position could be seized by a battalion. Jones made his preparations accordingly, in the knowledge that the most recent intelligence indicated an Argentine order of battle of three companies of infantry, two 105mm guns and several anti-aircraft guns – much in contrast to SAS intelligence that, after its diversionary raid of the 21st, had reported the presence of a mere company.

By way of support, 2 Para would still depend upon the firepower provided by the three 105mm guns of 8 (Alma) Commando Battery originally earmarked for the raid, to be flown forward on the night of the attack; and **naval gunfire support** from *Arrow*, anchored in San Carlos Water and capable of delivering 4.5in shells from its main armament. The only **helicopters** available consisted of two **Scouts** of 3 Commando Brigade Air Squadron (3 CBAS).

At first light on 26 May, 2 Para moved off Sussex Mountain with C Company in the lead, and marched to Camilla Creek House, around which it dug in. Believing that **CVR(T)s** could not negotiate over the boggy ground, Thompson declined to deploy the **Blues and Royals** in support. Upon arriving at Camilla Creek House just before dawn on the 27th, the men of 2 Para stuffed themselves in every conceivable space in the house and its ten outbuildings for the sake of some protection from the cold. At 1400Z, however, the BBC World Service announced that a Parachute Regiment battalion was preparing to assault Goose Green, astonishing everyone, infuriating Jones, and evaporating all hope of attacking with the element of surprise – although in the event the Argentines believed it to be a hoax, since they considered it inconceivable that anyone would reveal their own plans. As a precaution against air attack or artillery bombardment, Jones ordered the men to disperse.

The battalion remained in position for the whole of the 27th, sending out patrols to gather intelligence on Argentine positions. Two patrols clashed with an Argentine platoon, whereupon, around 1430Z, three **Harriers** came in support of one of the patrols. In the event, Argentine gunners shot down Squadron Leader Bob Iveson who, after bailing out, spent three days in hiding before being rescued by a **Gazelle**. A four-man Argentine patrol in a commandeered Land Rover tasked with investigating activity north of Camilla Creek House drove along the track to **San Carlos**, only to be captured by a 2 Para patrol, who learned that the Argentines at Goose Green were aware of the impending assault.

A battalion Orders Group was called for 1500Z, but with the unit spread across a wide area this did not assemble until 1800Z. In his impatience to get on with the brief, Jones interrupted his Intelligence Officer, Captain Alan Coulson, and proceeded to explain the plan of attack, a six phase, night/day, silent/noisy battalion assault. In Phase One, Support Company, led by Major Hugh Jenner, would fix itself at the western end of Camilla Creek while Major Roger Jenner's C Company secured the start line running between Camilla Creek and a stream known as Ceritos Arroyo, after which they would assume the role of Battalion reserve. In Phase Two, to commence at 0600Z, A Company, under Major Dair Farrar-Hockley, would attack the right flank near Darwin Hill while B Company under Major John Crosland, would assault the Argentine left flank in the area around the ruins of Boca House. In Phase Three, at 0700Z, A Company would advance and engage the Argentine positions on Coronation Point, while D Company would advance on the Argentine left to seize high ground about 1,000yd north of Boca House. In Phase Four, at 0800Z, B Company was to attack the Boca House position. A Company would exploit to Darwin in Phase Five at 0900Z, while C Company would move through B and D Companies to capture the airfield. In Phase Six, at 1000Z, A Company was to capture Darwin, B Company to attack the schoolhouse, C Company to establish a blocking position south of Goose Green, and D Company was to liberate the inhabitants in the settlement by sunrise.

Preparations for battle in terms of air support took place throughout 27 May, with two Gazelle AH1s of 3 CBAS moving ammunition, rations and other supplies to the 2 Para positions around Camilla Creek House. Artillery support was to come in the form of three 105mm guns of 8 (Alma) Commando Battery, Royal Artillery, which, after sunset, a Sea King HC4 shifted to Camilla Creek House. Naval support was to be supplied by the 4.5in gun of the frigate *Arrow* in San Carlos Water.

A Company reached the start line and would begin its advance thirty-five minutes late. Support Company was next to move off, leaving Camilla Creek House at 2300Z on the 27th and establishing itself in its desired position overlooking Camilla Creek by 0200Z on the 28th. There it waited until 0730Z before it stood in a position to engage the Argentines. Finally, A Company left Camilla Creek House at 0220Z. All movement took place over sodden ground, which soaked the men's feet in icy water, the discomfort exacerbated by bitterly cold temperatures and rainfall beginning in the early hours of the morning. The night was completely black and no one could see the objective.

A Company was first into the attack – in complete darkness, but not throughout, as the fighting was destined to last a staggering fourteen hours. As A Company reached Burntside House the gun crews lifted their fire – which, in the event, had failed to hit the house – and redirected it on the second target area. *Arrow*, on whose heavy weight of fire so many in 2 Para depended, began her mission by firing star shells to help illuminate the battlefield. Although no light emerged from Burntside House and no fire originated from within, 3 Platoon took no chances and fired two 84mm Carl Gustav anti-tank missiles at the structure. The first round missed, while two further attempts ended in frustrating misfires, whereupon 2 Platoon sought the same result with rifle, machine gun and 66mm rocket fire. Four civilians were inside but, lying on the floor, miraculously remained unscathed, despite a grenade exploding in one of the bedrooms. An Argentine platoon had indeed been present in the area, but had left either during or immediately prior to the assault.

With A Company's objective secure – and without casualties – Jones now ordered Crosland's B Company to begin its advance. Crosland's men did not find it difficult to reach their start line, which required only that they follow a track leading south down a narrow section of land between Camilla Creek and Burntside Pond. Their start line stood only 100yd from the Argentine position, a point chosen by the Patrols Platoon around midnight. The men began their move at 0700Z, en route to their objective, Boca House, 5,500yd distant.

Employing machine guns against the trenches, followed by grenades, Crosland's men maintained the momentum of the attack throughout, making early contact with their opponents. Three minutes after leaving their start line, the leading sections destroyed a machine gun post as the whole company continued to move forward, clearing trenches as they advanced. Inevitably, B Company came under mortar and artillery fire and amidst the gloom it took forty-five minutes alone to clear an Argentine position containing mortars and anti-aircraft missiles, which B Company had bypassed on its flank. Thus, notwithstanding the problems inherent in trying to maintain their cohesion in darkness, with Argentine resistance relatively light B Company had made significant progress during this opening phase of the attack – and all without loss to themselves. The company carried forward, although Crosland had no idea where he actually was. Around 0900Z he began the lengthy process so characteristic of night actions, of reorganising and reassembling his men in preparation for their continued advance toward Boca House.

Nevertheless, Jones's plan had fallen considerably behind schedule. Major Philip Neame's D Company was meant by this time to have reached the knoll near Camilla Creek, while A Company, to be examined later, was supposed to have reached Coronation Point and gone into reserve. A Company had in fact met no resistance, but both B and D Companies had been held up by Argentine resistance, eating into the time allotted by Jones for the achievement of each objective.

By sunrise 2 Para still had a good deal of ground yet to take; Jones's timings were completely out, with most of the objectives for the early phases of his plan not yet achieved, and from the time since A Company had begun its advance the battalion stood only halfway to Goose Green. 2 Para now faced ten hours of daylight ahead of it, with totally bare ground to its front, most of it occupied by forces well dug in.

Meanwhile, D Company, acting as the reserve and the last of the four companies into action, proceeded from its assembly area at Camilla Creek House towards its start line, losing its way in the blackness. Nevertheless, this was eventually put to rights, and D Company would soon encounter a series of trenches meant to be assaulted by Crosland's men. Thus, in the confusion caused by darkness and poor timings, D Company now found itself ahead of B Company, poised to take on the right and rear of the Argentine formation to its front.

Jones's original plan was going awry – hence his decision around 0950Z to push D Company forward to make up for lost time. He had originally envisaged the battalion reaching the outskirts of both settlements around 1000Z – only sixty minutes away. But with precious time lost while B Company reassembled its scattered elements – a process that was taking longer than actually expelling the defenders from their positions – he needed to accelerate the pace of progress. Thus far, 2 Para had crossed 1,600yd of ground, but another third of that distance remained, and the main Argentine defensive position had yet to be reached. D Company soon came under fire, with tracer filling the air, but not before it had reached as near as 30 or 40yd from the Argentine firing line, which inflicted 2 Para's first casualties of the battle, one of them a mortal wound. Argentine mortar fire now began to descend, adding another two casualties.

Since 0730Z, A Company had remained motionless west of Burntside House, but an hour later Farrar-Hockley received an order over the net to resume the advance – now with the support of artillery, which had shifted periodically to assist other companies in light of the malfunction of *Arrow*'s main armament shortly after her barrage began. His objective was Coronation Point, 1,100yd away, although a track and a fence could be conveniently used to help navigate the company through the cold, wet and darkness. By 0845Z A Company now constituted the leading company, while the others continued to regroup to the west. Strangely, Farrar-Hockley did not initially encounter any opposition, although he expected to confront a series of defended trenches. This was a logical conclusion, given the previous experience of other companies. Thus, by the time A Company reached the northern edge of Darwin inlet at 0920Z, it stood within less than 600yd of the settlement itself, which lay just across the water.

On reaching Coronation Point at 0920Z, A Company discovered it was unoccupied. Thus far, Farrar-Hockley had sustained no casualties, sunrise was not due for more than an hour and Darwin Hill stood only 1,000yd away. If A Company continued to make progress at this rate, it was likely it would reach that feature, which overlooked the settlement, by first light. This would conform to Jones's plan, since he wanted A Company to capture the settlement when the sun was up. But the timetable came to a juddering halt, for Farrar-Hockley waited an hour before resuming his advance, owing to the fact that A Company, now in control of Coronation Point, was much further advanced in its progress than B and D. When he radioed for authority to move ahead, Farrar-Hockley was told to await the commanding officer's presence, for Jones would not allow his plan to be altered without his own assessment of the situation. It seemed odd that the Argentines had chosen not to defend Coronation Point, leaving the eastern side of the isthmus virtually undefended compared with the centre and west. Jones's decision to see matters for himself may have been sound, but of course the time required for him to arrive on the scene caused further delay to A Company's progress. After reviewing Farrar-Hockley's position, Jones ordered his rapid advance, in so doing gaining ground where the other rifle companies had not. By this time it was nearly dawn, so all possible speed was required to reach the settlement before light exposed A Company to any defenders on the eastern side of the isthmus. Accordingly, the lead platoon advanced down the gorse-covered gully that approached Darwin Hill, from which Darwin settlement could be easily seen with, beyond it, the airstrip and Goose Green.

A Company now began to cross the open ground in a gorse gully towards Darwin Hill, with a view to reaching high ground and acquiring for itself a clear view of the settlement. From this position, and with one platoon providing supporting fire from the causeway, the settlement was very likely to fall. Light now began to emerge along the horizon, highlighting the fact that the ground lay totally open, covered only by grassy hummocks, irregular in shape and difficult for one's footing – the treacherous 'babies' heads'. Darwin Hill was low, with a gully to its left filled with high gorse, and to the left of the lower slope of Darwin stood the opening of a re-entrant. Then, at 1030Z, A Company took heavy machine-gun fire, obliging it to take whatever cover it could find. One section rushed for the re-entrant, defended by an Argentine platoon, which wounded two Paras in the increasing light and forced the section to return to the gorse gully. Farrar-Hockley was not facing any enemy on the face of Darwin Hill, which overlooked the gully, and this would otherwise have rendered the attack a very costly one. Men of A Company proceeded to attack trenches situated on a spur to the right of the gully entrance using grenades, 66mms and a General Purpose Machine Gun (GPMG), but engaging the Argentines at close range denied the Paras the benefit of supporting artillery fire since incoming shells could strike friendly forces. The Paras quite naturally attempted to execute a left flanking movement around the spur, but heavy machine-gun fire rendered this impossible.

A Company had encountered only a portion of the fourteen or more bunkers and trenches stretching across the isthmus, and high-explosive rounds from supporting mortar fire largely proved themselves substantially ineffective, burying themselves in the soft ground and causing little damage.

Quite sensibly, Farrar-Hockley deployed considerable firepower with GPMGs, but he had no artillery in support so long as the guns continued to direct their fire missions against those Argentine positions that were impeding B Company's efforts to take Boca House. When at last A Company did receive some support from the guns they soon went silent, as forward observation officers (FOOs) began to appreciate the very real risks of putting down fire with the Argentines so close to both companies. Moreover, *Arrow* had left the area, her gun still jammed. This left Farrar-Hockley with the final option: to call in a Harrier strike, which he did at 1125Z, aware that their cluster bombs could wreak havoc on the trenches stretching across the open ridge. Yet when his request reached the **aircraft carriers**, he received a refusal: foggy conditions rendered take-off and landing impossible. A Company had now reached an impasse: the guns were supporting B Company, which needed them for its advance against Boca house; naval gunfire was unavailable; aircraft could not fly owing to adverse weather conditions; and only two mortars were available, and these were incapable of laying down sufficient firepower to produce the results required. In addition, the defenders enjoyed a clear field of fire for much of the approach, forcing Farrar-Hockley's men to huddle in what dead ground they could, for what so far had accounted for a frustrating ninety minutes. An option, as yet untried, now presented itself: A Company could make recourse to the difficult business of neutralising trenches in succession with 66mms and grenades. This was a slow process that offered some hope of making up for lost time. A Company had already been held up well beyond Jones's timetable.

Jones, of course, now long aware of A Company's difficulties in getting forward, was growing increasingly angry and frustrated, for no sooner had the sun come up than both A and B Companies had been stalled on reaching the main Argentine position – A at Darwin Hill and B near Boca House. This situation was exacerbated by the ineffective fire of his guns and his staff's ignorance of the Argentines' dug-in positions. Compounding Jones's problems, shells continued to rain down, yet he could direct no counter-battery fire or air assets against the three guns firing from unidentified positions. This left 2 Para to cope almost entirely on its own, leaving its CO to find a solution to the deadlock.

As Jones adhered to the philosophy that an officer, whatever his rank, must lead from the front, that is precisely what he resolved to do. On the other hand, most officers agree that the place of a CO is well behind the frontline, in a position to observe 'the bigger picture', analyse the situation, devise a plan and issue orders accordingly – as opposed to maintaining a physical presence in the midst of the action where he cannot influence events except at a very local level. This sort of micro-management style of leadership, many contend, constitutes the responsibility of the company and platoon commanders but, above all, the section commanders. By contrast, even as a battalion CO, Jones believed he must observe events personally, assess the situation and take a personal hand in the outcome of his decisions. In this way, he could impose his will upon a given situation and thus lead by example. As Farrar-Hockley reported that intense Argentine fire was pinning his men down and holding up the advance, Jones felt he must reverse his fortunes – an objective requiring his presence in no less than the frontline.

In the critical situation confronting Jones, he could not break the deadlock by introducing greater firepower: he had none to add. Neither air strikes nor naval gunfire were available, artillery was in short supply, and most of the unit's heavy weapons were not present on the battlefield, apart from the MILANs ('Missile Infanterie, Leger, Anti-char'/Missile, Infantry, Light, Anti-tank) and machine guns available from Support Company, still uncommitted in the rear. While he had the option of committing reserves to break the deadlock in the form of C or D Companies, Jones decided to end the impasse by inspiring and encouraging his men forward in the style so tragically characteristic of the exploits performed in no-man's-land during the First World War. In short, he headed for the gorse gully with Tac 1 (his immediate command team), which consisted of a dozen men, and found what little cover there was to be had while small arms and machine guns rattled away, and artillery and mortar fire continued to rain down on the positions held by A, B and D Companies.

By radio, Jones, now in the gorse gully 500yd north-east of A Company's position and 1,100yd east of B Company's, instructed Farrar-Hockley to press on. About this time, Pucaras appeared and fired on the artillery and Camilla Creek House. At about the same time, 2 Para's two mortars came into action, but with insufficient weight of fire and with not enough mortar bombs to hand. The three guns continued to fire in support of B Company, shifting later to help A Company – but often inaccurately owing to difficulties for the FOOs in observing the fall of shells and the prevalence of strong winds. At the same time, C Company was advancing down the axis track, just east of D Company, approaching the gently elevated ground west of Coronation Point. Jenner offered to deploy his light machine guns to assist in supporting Farrar-Hockley, still pinned in the open facing Darwin Hill as daylight gathered. Again, Jones intervened, this time addressing the C Company second-in-command, Lieutenant Peter Kennedy, to stay off the net – bluntly asserting that he desired no interference while he sought to sort out the problem.

Significantly, Jones took an hour to determine his next course of action. Finally, rather than commit his reserve too early, without Support Company yet on the field, and frustrated by the ineffectiveness of the guns and mortars, he decided to make a dash forward himself. At about 1230Z he ran towards the gorse gully, produced a smokescreen with white phosphorus grenades, and came within 200yd of A Company's position, outpacing the rest of Tac 1 in the process. He found Farrar-Hockley, by which time A Company had cleared about seven trenches on the western side of the spur. Other Argentine positions further west, however, continued to issue fire across the top of the spur with such violence that A Company's continued efforts to skirt round the spur or to approach it frontally failed. No progress from the gully, it seemed, could be made with GPMG fire alone; Farrar-Hockley needed artillery or, even more effective, aircraft, to break the impasse. Argentine artillery had now set fire to much of the gorse, not far from where Jones hugged the ground with Tac 1, with Farrar-Hockley and staff, around him. D Company, meanwhile, had reached the western side of the isthmus and now stood 300yd from the water. Neame got on the radio and suggested his company make an attempt to outflank the Argentine line by skirting it along the shore. This, he reckoned, would break the deadlock involving A and B Companies and turn the whole Argentine position on the ridge; to this Jones replied caustically that Neame was not to interfere with the CO's conduct of the battle.

At about 1300Z Support Company reached a position around 1,300yd from Darwin Ridge, bearing its MILANs and machine guns, but with instructions to remain *in situ*; unaccountably, Jones turned down a suggestion that the MILANs come forward. The colonel wanted A Company to achieve the breakthrough unassisted, driving off the Argentine defenders in the middle of the ridge. While A Company was making forward movement only very gradually, it was clear that the schedule Jones had outlined at his Orders Group the previous day was now irrelevant, with the battalion two and a half hours behind schedule as a consequence of resistance offered to A and B Companies. If the Argentines had chosen to counter-attack at this point, they might very well have either driven 2 Para back, or in any event compromised any further progress. A Company in particular stood in a vulnerable predicament in front of Darwin Hill. Before the Argentine commander, Lieutenant Colonel Italo Piaggi, lay a generous window of opportunity, stretching from about 1130Z until as late as 1600Z; it remained to be seen if he would act upon it.

At about 1300Z the mortars ran out of ammunition and a small group from A Company, including Farrar-Hockley, ran up towards the spur of Darwin Hill. This resulted in three Para deaths and their repulse, for the defenders swept the top with a withering fire. At this point, it appears Jones believed that he could alter the situation by moving ahead himself around the right of the spur and towards the closest trenches. At about 1330Z he duly ran forward, shouting 'Follow me!', shortly after which he fell from a single shot. Sergeant Norman was the first to arrive on the scene to assist him, with others following, including Sergeant Blackburn, also from Tac 1, who radioed the second-in-command, Major Chris Keeble, the coded message, 'Sunray is down'. After being carried on a makeshift stretcher to a spot deemed suitable as a helicopter landing site, from which to evacuate him to the regimental aid post for urgent medical attention, Jones died. Forty-five minutes later, two Scout helicopters flew forward from Camilla Creek House in a casualty evacuation role, but Pucaras appeared and shot one of them down with its 7.62mm machine gun, killing the pilot and badly injuring the crewman. The other Scout returned to Camilla Creek House without any of the wounded – or the CO's body.

A Company meanwhile continued to make slow progress, deploying its 66mm rockets to good effect against bunkers and trenches, and causing the occupants of various trenches to throw up their hands in surrender about fifteen minutes after Jones was shot. Farrar-Hockley's men discovered twenty-three trenches on the central part of the ridge, of whose occupants nearly twenty lay dead and twice that number wounded. A Company suffered six dead in the attack on the gorse gully and the spur, plus eleven wounded – a one in five casualty rate. The extent to which Jones's solo charge had broken the deadlock has been the source of controversy ever since, but it is relevant to state that no one but Sergeant Norman was within easy reach of him when he charged, with only a few personnel from Tac 1 some distance behind. In this respect, he did not personally carry any elements of A Company with him, or at that immediate moment inspire their forward movement, as none of the company's personnel were aware of Jones's dash. He had not sought to take any soldiers with him and Farrar-Hockley was not aware of his movement.

Turning to B Company's attack on the Boca House position, when the sun inched over the horizon around 1030Z, B Company still remained held up in its advance, with the emerging light promising to render its reception all the more unpleasant. The ground was gently undulating, with some dead ground, but the Argentines could engage from more than 1,000yd with their mortars, machine guns and snipers in a clear field of fire. At about 1200Z, two Pucaras, flying out of **Stanley** – all others had been withdrawn from the airfield at Goose Green before the battle – attacked Camilla Creek House with rockets and then proceeded towards the gun position, missing their target and only just dodging **Blowpipe** guided missiles, before returning to Stanley. Three hours later, two more arrived over Camilla Creek House, shooting down a helicopter with cannon and machine-gun fire and killing the pilot, while the second one successfully evaded destruction. One of the Pucaras crashed into Blue Mountain when the pilot became lost owing to poor visibility; the other reached Stanley safely.

Meanwhile, B Company faced stiff opposition opposite Boca House, especially now that the sun was up. Even the new recruits among the defenders could and did put up a respectable fight, with a clear field of fire available for several hundred yards, no threat from the air and very little from guns and mortars. The latter ran short of ammunition, leaving the Paras with no proper smokescreen with which to mask their advance in the clear light of day. Moreover, the soft ground absorbed much of the explosive power of the bombs and only a lucky, direct hit on a trench would result in any serious damage to the defenders. Progress was actually only achieved with direct fire weapons, especially MILANs fired against bunkers, but 2 Para's observers still could not identify the location of the Argentine guns – three 105mm pack howitzers deployed on the northern edge of Goose Green. These were well concealed, and with no British aircraft over the battlefield at this stage, the attackers had no hope of silencing them. Similarly, the mortars, placed on the outskirts of Goose Green on a small peninsula east of the settlement, continued to fire with impunity, their locations as yet unknown to the British.

It should be observed that Boca House, B Company's objective, was in fact not a house at all, but merely the foundations of a structure no longer standing, and thus the position not only offered no visible point of recognition, but could furnish no protection to a defender. In this area, the Argentines had deployed troops on slightly elevated ground on the western side of the isthmus, south-east of the ruins. As B Company approached, the defenders offered a brisk fire from rifles, machine guns, and mortars, bringing the advance to a halt – but leaving no option to retire, either – and obliging many of Crosland's men to take what little cover they could from the gorse line just north of the Boca House position. Still, resistance on the west end of the line began to break just before 1600Z as the Paras of B Company attempted to

G

outflank the position along the beach, employing MILANs to good effect as they did so. Some took advantage of the scarce cover available from the gorse line just north of Boca House, together with elements from D and Support Companies nearby. At last, at about 1600Z, Boca House, and the 50ft hill south of it, fell almost exactly as A Company broke through Darwin Ridge and crushed resistance there, leaving the Argentine main defensive position in tatters.

Around 1345Z, Keeble learned with dismay that the CO was dead, devolving command on him, a circumstance complicated by the fact that he stood at Battalion HQ, 1,600yd away from the CO's position. Time was also required to ascertain the situation from the two forward companies, A and B, for without this he could not make a decision on the use of reserves.

At 1445Z Keeble and his staff started down the track towards Crosland's B Company, which they did not reach until sometime after 1500Z. There was still no possibility of assistance from Harriers owing to poor weather out to sea and, with other units of 3 Commando Brigade on their way east, Keeble could not expect any reinforcements. Nevertheless, all were confident of success and despite the loss of their CO there was never any question but that the Paras, for whom attaining the mission is always paramount, would continue to prosecute the attack.

By the time Keeble reached B Company around 1400Z, the situation for 2 Para had undergone a remarkable turn for the better: A Company stood in possession of the gorse gully and spur, where the Argentines there had surrendered, leaving the whole of the eastern end of their main defensive line neutralised. B Company had used MILANs as 'bunker-busters', in skilful combination with GPMGs, while Neame's D Company had outflanked the Argentine position along the beach at the extreme west, with rocks partly covering its advance and the area mercifully free of mines. This development, in turn, established it in a position also to present flanking fire with MILANs and machine guns against the trenches on Darwin Ridge, precipitating capitulations there. Thus, between the close-quarter fighting by A Company in the gorse gully and the efforts of B and D Companies further west, aided by effective use of heavy weapons and a flanking movement, 2 Para achieved the required breakthrough. This resulted in twelve dead and fifteen prisoners; a handful escaped towards the airfield and most of the rest were taken unhurt.

Now, around 1600Z, almost ten hours after the fighting had begun and seven and a half since dawn, 2 Para had finally overcome the main Argentine positions. According to Jones's original plan, the battle ought to have ended with the capture of Goose Green hours ago, but there was still much fighting left to be done – all in the cold light of day.

With the fall of Darwin Ridge and the area around Boca House, the Argentines' position was contracting to include an area covering the airfield, about 1,500yd south of the gorse line; the school, which sat at the head of an estuary with a bridge across it; and Goose Green settlement. The key to this area's capture was the school, through which ran a shoreline track and, east of the airstrip, an area designated the 'flagpole position' – a simple flag flying from the mast on high ground – which, owing to its position, dominated a track extending north–south. If 2 Para approached via this track they would have to capture both the flagpole position and the school to reach Goose Green; sub-units that proceeded south to capture the flagpole position would need to seize, or at least neutralise fire from, the school to prevent flanking fire reaching them from a distance of little more than 300yd.

Despite the collapse of their defensive position further north, Argentine fortunes appeared to be recovering, for the intervening ground extending south from Darwin Ridge to the airfield and the school was virtually flat, furnishing the defenders with excellent fields of fire. Several bunkers dotted the area around the airfield, plus, just to the south, six 20mm anti-aircraft guns capable of serving in a ground role could offer devastating fire to a range of 2,100yd, with a staggering rate of fire of 1,000 rounds a minute.

Around Goose Green itself, the Argentines maintained 112 residents in the Community Centre, with the buildings surrounded by bunkers and mortar positions; this deployment successfully deterred the attackers from firing into the settlement in the course of the battle. Other prominent features of the defence included the two Oerlikon anti-aircraft guns, positioned just east of the settlement on the peninsula, which juts out into Choiseul Sound. Like those deployed near the airfield, these guns could be used to fire horizontally against ground troops and enjoyed a range of 1,100yd.

Keeble was determined to maintain the momentum of the attack following the breakthrough at Boca House and Darwin Ridge. So long as the Argentines could be kept under pressure, the prospect of victory loomed large for 2 Para, despite the presence of defences around the airfield and schoolhouse. In this last phase of the battle, Keeble directed A Company into reserve on Darwin Hill; the taking of the settlement itself, which was not occupied, could occur later. B Company was instructed to advance south along the western side of the isthmus and move past the airfield, before finally shifting east in a wide arc, taking it to the coast south of the settlement. Roger Jenner's C Company was to move against the airfield and Neame's D Company was to take the school and establish itself just outside the settlement itself. Keeble's plan meant that all rifle companies would be simultaneously on the advance, including one platoon from A Company detached to Jenner's formation, leaving Farrar-Hockley's other two platoons on Darwin Hill. Keeble wished to keep the Argentines under pressure, capture the airfield and envelop Goose Green – that is clear – but the various companies would have to cross, depending on their particular route, between 1,100 and 2,200yd of completely open ground, which, if the Argentines chose to defend with any degree of determination, could prove costly. 2 Para still had poor indirect fire support in terms of mortars and artillery, and continued impatiently to await the massive firepower offered by air assets. Keeble's worries also extended to the problems inherent in fighting within a confined area, for with all the rifle companies on the move across it, they faced the genuine risk of intermingling, so disrupting the momentum of attack as a result of the ensuing confusion and increasing the risk of direct fire support weapons accidentally inflicting casualties on friendly troops.

Shortly after 1600Z, C Company and the attached platoon from A Company, with fixed bayonets, began to move to cover the 1,600yd to the airfield, the whole area completely bereft of cover. D Company unexpectedly crossed in front of it, demonstrating the danger of so many rifle companies operating in such a small area. The sight proved an inviting one for the crews of the 20mm anti-aircraft guns, backed by mortars and heavy machine guns, and all enjoying a perfect view of assailants who lacked the benefit of supporting fire, much less smoke to conceal their movement, as they advanced in open order over a flat, featureless landscape.

The Argentines, confident of their strength and evidently undeterred by the fall of their initial line of defence, unleashed a withering fire with mortars, artillery, heavy machine guns, rifles and anti-aircraft guns, forcing C Company to ground. Without supporting fire over such a long distance, the advance stalled until mortar fire silenced the 20mm anti-aircraft gun on the western end of the airfield, but the crew declined to engage the artillery on the outskirts of Goose Green for fear of inflicting casualties on civilians. Still, clearly the defenders were determined to fight, bolstered as they were by a company of reinforcements helicoptered in from Stanley. Jenner called in fire support, only to be told by Keeble that none was to hand. Jenner, like Crosland during his struggle to take the Boca House position, strongly felt the absence of artillery support. C Company nonetheless persisted in the advance, although shells from the 105s near Goose Green wounded Jenner and killed or wounded eleven others in the process. Support Company now sought to engage the Argentines, albeit at extreme range from the forward slope of Darwin Hill. The Anti-Tank Platoon fired a missile at the two 35mm Oerlikons on the peninsula, and although the wire reached its limit 80yd short of the target, it frightened the crew off the position. While some platoons preserved their cover in the undulations of Darwin Ridge, others made a dash forward over the more than 400yd of ground separating them from the schoolhouse, only to suffer several casualties and retire. Gains did occur elsewhere: by 1630Z two companies from C Company had reached the footbridge that allowed access across the estuary and along the track leading to Goose Green; yet with one Para killed and eleven wounded in just a few minutes of the assault, and still with 650yd to cross to reach the airfield, a good deal remained to be done.

D Company, in the meantime, was forward of C Company, the former moving east and the latter moving south. A strong degree of confusion reigned, not least owing to D Company adopting a line of advance towards Goose Green that crossed C Company's objective, the airfield, so mixing personnel from both companies. D Company achieved progress by proceeding along a shallow depression, which offered cover from the anti-aircraft fire, and although exposed mines slowed Neame's men, one of his platoons reached the outskirts of the airfield, there to encounter abandoned sangars. In short order it came under fire from the area around the flagpole, situated on a ridge just east of the airstrip, and withdrew. Elsewhere, while C and D Companies carried on towards their respective objectives, B Company proceeded in its effort to swing east, enabling it to reach a position south of the airfield. In so doing, one of its platoons suppressed fire from the airfield and sent the anti-aircraft gunners scurrying for the protection of the settlement, leaving behind empty bunkers around the airfield and enabling B Company to approach from the south-west to within about 450yd of Goose Green itself as darkness began to descend.

Turning to the efforts to capture the schoolhouse and the fighting around the flagpole, with elements of both C and D Companies, some of which, as related, had become intermingled, confusion arose, rendering impossible any form of co-ordinated attack, which was now taking place twelve hours into the fighting. The school and the flagpole position offered points from which the Argentines could deny access from the north to Goose Green, their opponents' ultimate objective. C and D Companies were determined to capture them. A series of trenches and bunkers were situated around the flagpole, along which ran a track leading to Goose Green. In order to capture it, Neame sought first to seize the school more than 300yd away, so securing his flank before he could turn to attack the flagpole area. This area, however, was swept by small arms and artillery fire and became the site of the death of Lieutenant Jim Barry, commanding 12 Platoon, D Company, as he tried to arrange the surrender of troops holding the flagpole area. Accounts do not agree on the circumstances surrounding his death; some suggest he approached men signalling their intention to surrender, while others say he misinterpreted the situation and encountered Argentinian 2nd Lieutenant Centurion, who told him in clear English to return to his lines. Whatever the actual intention of the defenders, it seems clear that when someone fired a machine gun, probably sited on Darwin Ridge, at long range, the Argentines opened fire at their closest target, killing Barry at point-blank range.

At the same time, elements of both C and D Companies were tasked with attacking the school, although neither attempted any form of co-ordination and the whole affair became a confused effort. The details of this are not clear, since sub-units became intermingled in a contest that began around 1700Z and occurred simultaneously with the challenge for possession of the airfield. The assault on the school began when Paras proceeded from the western end of the estuary and rapidly reached an area housing a dairy and outbuildings, as well as the school itself – all positions defended by troops in nearby trenches. As at Boca House and along Darwin Ridge, fighting involved the now indispensable 66mm rocket, as well as grenades and rifles. The school soon caught fire and the survivors from within fled south in the direction of the settlement. The defenders answered with anti-aircraft guns situated on the Goose Green peninsula, hitting the blazing school building with accurate fire but failing to impede the Paras' advance. After more confused fighting near the school and at the airfield, by around 1900Z the fighting amid these positions slackened and finally subsided as the Argentines withdrew into the settlement. Keeble instructed Neame not to advance further, but to assume a defensive position.

At about the same time, two Aermacchi jets appeared over the isthmus and strafed D Company with cannon fire, dispersing the men but inflicting no damage as they dived for cover. One aircraft was downed by a Blowpipe fired by Support Company and the other disappeared from view, giving the briefest of respites from air attack. Then, a few minutes later at about 1915Z, two Pucaras approached from the north-west and dropped napalm canisters, narrowly missing a D Company platoon position, although causing consternation as the intense heat momentarily drew away the troops' oxygen and warmed their faces and hands. A hail of small arms fire brought down one of the Pucaras, leaving some of Crosland's men doused in aviation fuel as the plane descended and the pilot ejected, gliding into captivity. The other Pucara managed to reach Stanley, albeit heavily damaged. The hitherto absence of British aircraft was the consequence of poor visibility at sea; that now changed, so that the Paras had hardly seen off the Pucaras and MB-339s when at around 1930Z three Harriers roared overhead, long awaited by 2 Para as a decisive means with which to neutralise the two 35mm Oerlikons on the peninsula east of Goose Green. As these were close to the settlement, the pilots had to take extreme care to avoid civilian casualties; possibly as a result, both Harriers missed, dropping their cluster bombs into the sea, but causing an impressive spectacle as the water reacted violently to the detonations. The third Harrier managed to hit some Argentines on the peninsula, although crucially not the guns, which continued to fire.

At about 2000Z, as the light began to fade, it was by no means clear to 2 Para that the battle was over. A Company stood on Darwin Hill and occupied that position through the night; B Company had succeeded in executing its wide movement south of the airfield and now stood slightly over a mile south-west of Goose Green, from where the Argentines continued to fire until darkness set in. Worse still, as night descended eight Argentine helicopters offloaded reinforcements of approximately 100 men to the south-west of B Company's position. Crosland was worried: D Company were far off – in fact 2,200yd away – and his company was short of ammunition and severely fatigued after almost sixteen hours of uninterrupted fighting. He therefore sensibly ordered his men to withdraw to higher ground and dig in, thus seeking protection from possible counter-attack. They carried on with their work until 0600Z on the 29th, exhausted, hungry and huddled together against intense cold and the first signs of snowfall. C Company, meanwhile, withdrew to the gorse gully to reorganise after the attack on the school had succeeded, but the impetus of Jenner's assault had run its course and, in any event, the Argentines had retreated into the comparative safety of the settlement as darkness approached.

Neame's D Company had orders to regroup and not to advance any further that night. All the Paras thus spent the freezing night completely worn out, hungry, short of water and gravely low on ammunition. This constituted their third night with practically no sleep, a minimal amount of food and a great physical and psychological toll exacted on them since before they had even reached Camilla Creek House. Some still had plenty of work to do: the known wounded not yet evacuated were to be removed by Land Rover and helicopter, and men from all companies went out in search of the unrecovered wounded.

The situation was, therefore, mixed: the battalion had driven the Argentines from their positions, but had not yet taken Darwin and Goose Green. The men were desperate for rest and resupply, and had lost sixteen dead and thirty-one wounded. The Argentines had been reinforced by a company, which reached Goose Green in the dark but whose presence was probably not sufficient to embolden Piaggi to renew the fighting the following morning. In short, with his men scattered across the isthmus and exhausted, Keeble could not be certain that the gains of 28 May would go unchallenged on the 29th.

He appreciated, however, that Argentine spirits must be low – perhaps close to breaking point – and therefore decided to encourage their surrender. He received a promise from Brigadier Thompson for reinforcements and additional firepower, the combination of which Keeble planned, if necessary, to employ in the form of a demonstration of force to overawe the defenders, imbue in them a sense of the futility of further resistance, and thereby force a capitulation. Barring that, Keeble had no choice but to assault the settlement and finish the job the hard way – although he certainly did not wish to exercise the latter option, particularly in light of the civilian casualties inevitably to be caused. Accordingly, before dawn, a radio message was sent to the Argentines in Goose Green that a party bearing a flag of truce would approach their position around first light. Two prisoners were duly sent forward to present the terms, written in Spanish, with stress placed on the issue of the civilians' safety, which Piaggi was reminded, barring the residents' release from captivity, remained his responsibility under the rules of war. To Keeble's considerable relief, Argentine commanders agreed to assemble near the airfield to discuss the terms of surrender. The fact was that, despite having been reinforced, Piaggi found himself surrounded and could not possibly put up a successful defence on the 29th. Consequently, at 1330Z a meeting took place between senior officers from both sides, during which the British delegation persuaded their counterparts that, having fought well, they could lay down their arms with honour. Keen to encourage this impression among the vanquished, Keeble permitted them to conduct a ceremony, complete with a speech and a chorus of their national anthem, before approximately 1,100 personnel (961 accounted for, including eighty-one held at Camilla Creek House, plus perhaps fifty Argentine bodies discovered and buried) grounded arms in a field near the church.

An enormous boost to British morale and a great blow to Argentine spirits, the Battle of Goose Green cost sixteen dead to 2 Para, including its commanding officer, plus a Royal Marine and a Royal Engineer, both on detached duty from their respective units. The Argentines lost fifty-five killed and several times that number wounded.

Green Beaches

Designated 'One' and 'Two' these unexplored beaches lay off **Port San Carlos** settlement in **San Carlos Water** and received **3 Para** and **42 Commando**, respectively on D-Day, 21 May.

Grenades

See Infantry Weapons

Grytviken

See South Georgia, Operations on

Gurkha Rifles

Recruited in Nepal, with (in 1982) only one candidate in thirty selected, the Gurkhas are a regular formation of the British Army, comprised of hardy, physically robust men accustomed to training in extreme weather conditions ranging from the freezing temperatures of the Himalayas to the humidity of the jungles of Brunei. One of the three infantry battalions comprising **5 Infantry Brigade**, the 1st Battalion 7th (Duke of Edinburgh's Own) Gurkha Rifles, better known as the 1/7th Gurkha Rifles, was commanded by Lieutenant Colonel David Morgan, who joined the battalion at the end of 1981, bringing with him experience from the Borneo confrontation and as Brigade Major of 48 Gurkha Brigade in Hong Kong. The Gurkha Rifles were based at Church Crookham, near Aldershot, in Hampshire. In early 1982 some companies were on exercise in Belize, and others in Cyprus, but the battalion was ready for overseas service when war began on 2 April.

The unit contained four rifle companies – whereas other British infantry battalions contained three – plus a support company comprising four platoons: mortar, recce, pioneer and anti-tank. Support weapons consisted of eight 84mm mortars, the MILAN wire-guided anti-tank missile, and the Browning .50 calibre machine gun, carried by the mortar, anti-tank and the (converted) motor transport platoons, respectively.

Gurkhas with a captured 20mm anti-aircraft gun. (AirSeaLand Photos)

G

The battalion travelled south aboard the *Queen Elizabeth 2* from Southampton on 12 May, landed near **San Carlos** and established positions there, apart from D Company which on 2 June was flown to **Goose Green** in order to guard the approaches to Choiseul Sound and release J Company **42 Commando** to rejoin its unit. Three days later, Brigadier **Wilson** assigned D Company as his Brigade Patrol/Recce Company with the task of discovering the location of an artillery and radar unit believed to be somewhere in the vicinity of Port Harriet. It duly marched to **Darwin** and was ferried to **Fitzroy** on 7 June aboard the MV *Monsunen*. In the period prior to 5 Infantry Brigade's landing in the **Port Pleasant** area, a Gurkha patrol searched Lively Island for land-based **Exocets**.

After a British **Gazelle** helicopter was mistakenly shot down by a **Sea Dart** fired by *Cardiff* on the evening of 5 June, the Gurkhas were sent to the Wickham Heights/Pleasant Point area to destroy the Argentine patrol erroneously believed to have been responsible.

At the same time, Gurkhas, supported by Scout AH1 **helicopters** of 656 Squadron were combing **Lafonia** for Argentines believed to be present there monitoring helicopter routes and to capture or kill any troops detached by, or who had fled from, the previous garrison at Goose Green. Patrols systematically searched all residences and other structures in Lafonia to clear the peninsula entirely of Argentine troops.

At 1705Z on 7 June two **Sea King** helicopters carrying a Gurkha patrol landed near Egg Harbour House near Elephant Bay on the west coast of Lafonia in response to a report of an Argentine presence. This proved correct; upon discovery the occupants left the house and hid in a gully. A Scout AH1 fired an SS–11 missile, which led to the surrender of eight Argentine soldiers.

On 8 June, minus C Company left at Goose Green on rear security duties, and D Company, still in the Port Pleasant area, the Gurkhas were flown to Little Wether Ground, an area north of Fitzroy Ridge. In the late afternoon others, under the 2i/c Major Bill Dawson, boarded the *Monsunen* at Goose Green to be ferried to Fitzroy. Over the following two days the remainder of the battalion was helicoptered in to Fitzroy.

As part of 5 Infantry Brigade's advance on **Stanley**, the Gurkhas were to patrol aggressively towards **Mount Tumbledown** and **Mount William** with the intention of inducing the defenders to surrender. Should the Argentines fail to do so, the Gurkhas were to attack Mount William in tandem with the assault of the **Scots Guards** on Mount Tumbledown, the Gurkhas to prosecute their assault not later than sunrise on 14 June. Once Tumbledown and William had been secured, the Gurkhas were to advance on to Stanley Common, to be facilitated by the anticipated capture of **Sapper Hill** by the **Welsh Guards**.

Early on 10 June, D Company advanced to **Mount Challenger** to establish a patrol base against Mount William, whereupon the Argentines shelled the former position, causing four wounded. The remaining companies arrived in advance of the uninformed Welsh Guards, as a result of which the two sides nearly inadvertently exchanged fire as a result of poor **radio communication** and a failure of unit co-ordination.

Helicoptered forward on the 13th to a position just south of **Two Sisters**, they then proceeded along the line of **Goat Ridge** just to the north of Mount Tumbledown during the Scots Guards' fighting there. During their progress the Gurkhas suffered losses from artillery fire and with dawn approaching on the 14th and Tumbledown yet to be secured, it seemed the Gurkhas would have to fight in daylight to take Mount William. However, to their great disappointment, they found the Argentines had withdrawn from Mount William before an engagement could take place.

After the Argentine surrender on 14 June the Gurkhas were moved to Goose Green, where they lost a soldier killed on 24 June when a grenade exploded while he was filling in a trench. The Gurkhas left the Falklands on 18 July aboard *Uganda*, arriving at Southampton on 9 August. Total casualties during the campaign amounted to eight wounded and one killed on battlefield clearance duty after the Argentine surrender, as noted above.

Harrier GR3

A remarkable **Royal Air Force** ground-attack aircraft capable of vertical take-off and landing, the British Aerospace Harrier GR3 of No 1 (F) Squadron, based at RAF Wittering, Cambridgeshire, proved exceptionally manoeuvrable and airworthy. With only twenty-eight **Sea Harrier** FRS1s available for service with the **Royal Navy** in the South Atlantic, it was natural to supplement them with the ten Harrier GR3s that belonged to 1 Squadron.

The Harrier could carry three 1,000lb bombs or up to five cluster bomb units (CBU), two **Sidewinder** missiles (one under each wing) and 30mm cannons. Towards the end of the conflict their 1,000lb bombs were replaced with Paveway laser-guided bombs (LGBs). The Harrier could be refuelled in flight and had a maximum speed of 690mph at low altitude, but carried no early warning **radar**, obliging the pilot to depend on his own sight to locate an adversary.

To render the GR3s fit for service in the South Atlantic, in only three weeks they underwent modification by engineers at various locations in the UK. Specifically, alterations enabled the Harrier to operate from aircraft carriers and pilots received refresher training in the tactics of air-to-air combat. Engineering modifications included substantial changes to the inertial navigational system, adding Sidewinder missiles and fitting radar transponders to make the RAF system compatible with the Royal Navy. Pilots received training at the Royal Naval Air Station at Yeovilton in Somerset to familiarise them with operating from the deck of an aircraft carrier and in taking off from the training ski-ramp there. They also studied the characteristics, tactics and capabilities of Argentine aircraft.

H

A Harrier prepares to land on the deck of HMS *Hermes*. (AirSeaLand Photos)

Six Harrier GR3s went south aboard the *Atlantic Conveyor*, while the other four executed an extraordinarily long flight from **Ascension** to *Hermes* using in-flight refuelling.

On 3 May, three Harriers set off from RAF St Mawgan in Cornwall on the 4,600-mile flight to Ascension carrying 330-gallon ferry tanks, most of which required up to five in-flight refuellings in case the Harriers had to divert to an airfield in an emergency. Refuelling took place via **Victor** tankers. Two Harriers flew non-stop, while the third briefly stopped at Banjul in Gambia. Another three Harriers left the UK on the 4th for a non-stop flight to Ascension, although one developed a fault and had to return after stopping at Madeira. The last four Harriers left St Mawgan on the morning of the 5th for Ascension, completing 1 Squadron's initial deployment. One of these, however, diverted to Banjul and would arrive at Wideawake later than scheduled.

Three Harrier GR3s were fitted with AIM-9 Sidewinders at Ascension and remained on post to provide air defence cover until relieved by the arrival of **Phantom** FGR2s on 24 and 26 May. In theatre, the ten Harrier GR3s all operated from *Hermes*, but even with only eighteen ground crew they achieved an exceptional record of serviceability.

Unlike the Sea Harrier, which mainly flew **combat air patrols** and engaged in toss-bombing, the Harrier GR3 performed low-level close air support – a ground-attack role – and interdiction, and regularly bombed the airport at **Stanley**, as a consequence of which the type suffered heavier losses than its naval counterpart.

The first operational missions carried out by the Harrier GR3 took place from the decks of *Hermes* on 19 May, with combat training and familiarisation sorties, since the pilots were not accustomed to operating at sea. On 20 May, on the eve of the landings, there were six GR3s available to the **Task Force**.

On D-Day, 21 May, two Harriers struck a helicopter hide on **Mount Kent**, damaging several fixed-wing and rotary aircraft. On the same morning, Flight Lieutenant Jeff Glover was shot down during his solo attack on **Port Howard**. Severely wounded during his ejection and impact with the sea, he was rescued from the water and taken prisoner – earning the dubious honour of being the only British **prisoner of war** captured after the initial Argentine invasion.

Squadron Leader Bob Iveson was shot down over **Goose Green** on 27 May, but managed to evade capture until he was rescued on 30 May, the same day that Harriers first deployed laser-guided bombs in a raid on **Stanley** airfield. Still, the attack proceeded without the assistance of a ground-based forward air controller and thus they achieved little.

On 1 June, two Harriers flew an eight hour and twenty minute mission from Ascension to *Hermes*, a distance of 3,900 miles, an impressive achievement that required refuelling on occasions by four Victor K2s. Neither pilot had ever landed on the deck of an aircraft carrier before.

Harriers sometimes used 'Sid's Strip' (so-called by the RAF, together with 'RAF West Wittering', but known as 'HMS *Sheathbill*' by the Royal Navy), an improvised landing area that came into operation on 5 June near **Port San Carlos**, although after several problems there some combat air patrols reverted to using the carriers. On a few occasions a Forward Operating Base (FOB) became non-operational, such as, most dramatically, on 8 June, when at the Port San Carlos strip a Harrier GR3 experiencing partial engine failure crash-landed across the runway, tearing up a portion of the aluminium planking. Repairs were completed by the end of the day, but in the meantime all Sea Harrier Combat Air Patrols were obliged to originate and finish from one of the two carriers lying more than 200 miles east of the Falklands, a process depriving pilots of much-needed loiter time. On the morning of 12 June, however, the Port San Carlos FOB had to be closed owing to foggy and icy conditions, obliging the Harriers attacking **Sapper Hill** that day to return to *Hermes*.

Once **3 Commando Brigade** and **5 Infantry Brigade** moved eastwards from **San Carlos Water**, from 9 June the Harriers began to carry out sorties against Argentine troop positions on **Mount Longdon** and artillery positions on Sapper Hill, and the following day conducted low-level **photographic reconnaissance** of **Two Sisters**, Mount Longdon and Stanley. In the closing days of the war Harriers attacked positions on Sapper Hill, while at sea *Contender Bezant* brought an additional four machines to the South Atlantic as a reserve.

All told, Harriers flew 126 operational sorties over the Falklands, with pilots averaging two sorties daily. During the course of the campaign three Harriers were hit by ground fire and a fourth crashed owing to engine failure. A further three suffered damage caused by ground fire; hence, only three aircraft finished the war completely unscathed.

Headquarters UK Land Forces (HQ UKLF)

Based at Wilton in Wiltshire, HQ UKLF held a conference at which strategists had to weigh up the troop requirements for Northern Ireland and the NATO Priority One commitment against the Warsaw Pact.

Hecla, HMS

Hecla, a **Royal Navy** survey vessel, together with *Herald* and *Hydra*, was used as an ambulance ship to ferry casualties from the combat area to the hospital ship *Uganda* and from there to Montevideo for onward aeromedic **VC10** C1 transport to naval and military hospitals in Britain. She departed Gibraltar on 20 April, reached **Ascension** on 2 May and arrived in Falklands waters on 14 May. In one example of her role, *Hecla* arrived at Montevideo on 2 June with British and Argentine wounded, the former of which were then flown home on a VC10 that arrived at Brize Norton the following day. *Hecla* then arrived back in the **Red Cross Box** on 6 June. Her service in the campaign ended on her reaching Devonport on 29 July.

Commander:	Captain G.L. Hope	
Builders:	Yarrow (Blythswood)	
Launched:	21 December 1964	
Commissioned:	8 September 1965	
Displacement (tons):	1,915 Standard	2,733 Full Load
Draught:	4.7m	
Dimensions: length × beam; feet (metres):	260 × 49 (79.23 × 14.94)	
Propulsion:	3 diesel engines supplying 2 electric motors	2,000hp = 14 knots
Armament:	none	
Aircraft:	1 × **Wasp** HAS1 – no ordnance carried	

Helicopters

Without doubt helicopters played a crucial – indeed a decisive – part in the British effort during the Falklands War.

A Wessex HAS3 on the deck of HMS *Antrim*. (AirSeaLand Photos)

Roles

Helicopters performed many functions including communications, liaison duties between units, search and rescue, casualty evacuation, anti–submarine operations, artillery and naval gunfire observation, surveillance, anti–surface (ship) attack, logistic support, cross-decking and troop transport. Some specific operational examples of these roles may be instructive:

Helicopters could serve as naval gunfire observers, such as in the case of the destroyer *Coventry*, whose **Lynx** HAS2 on 9 May provided targeting information for the bombardment of a temporary helicopter base near the burnt out **Royal Marines** barracks at **Moody Brook**.

In the Search and Rescue (SAR) role, helicopters, particularly **Sea Kings**, played a key role in carrying away the survivors of ships struck by bombs or missiles, such as an aircraft of 826 NAS that evacuated some of the crew of *Sheffield*, struck by an **Exocet** on 4 May. Similarly, Squadron Leader Bob Iveson, flying a **Harrier**, was shot down near **Goose Green** on 27 May, spending three days on the move until finally settling in the unoccupied Paragon House about 7 miles north-west of the settlement, where a **Gazelle** AH1 from 3 Commando Brigade Air Squadron (CBAS) discovered and rescued him.

The importance of the casualty evacuation role played by helicopters cannot be overestimated, with many lives saved by their timely efforts. Casualty evacuation (casevac) duties were usually performed by the lighter Gazelle, **Wessex** and **Scout**. During the rescue operation at **Port Pleasant** on 8 June, Scouts, Gazelles, Wessex, Sea Kings and **Chinooks** all took part. During the night assaults of 11–12 June on **Mount Longdon**, **Mount Harriet** and **Two Sisters**, for example, helicopters evacuated eighty-five casualties from these areas.

Logistic support proved an indispensable part of the helicopter presence during Operation **Corporate**. Owing to the boggy ground and the almost total absence of roads, rotary aircraft were employed to bring up ammunition, food and medical supplies, as well as to transport troops. Examples are legion; hundreds of thousands of pounds of stores, guns, **Rapier** fire units and more than 500 troops went ashore by helicopter on the first day of the landings alone. During the first week of June, moreover, Wessex, Sea Kings and Chinooks shifted tons of stores, ammunition, artillery, and equipment to **Teal Inlet**, **Mount Kent** and elsewhere along the route of the northern thrust in support of the advance of the **3 Commando Brigade** break-out from **San Carlos Water**.

The same effort was required in the first two weeks of June on behalf of **5 Infantry Brigade** as its troops moved from San Carlos Water to forward positions at **Fitzroy** and **Bluff Cove** in their advance on **Stanley** via the southern route. Accordingly, forward operating bases were established for helicopters at sites such as Fitzroy from 12 June.

Heli-borne stores were normally placed on pallets and then lifted using rope, cables and underslung nets. As for artillery, without the use of motor transport their crews depended entirely on helicopters to move their guns, a battery of which, together with 100 rounds for each gun and the gunners themselves required at least forty-five lifts. Wessex could carry only twenty-four rounds of 105mm shells, a Sea King, forty-eight, and a Chinook, 192.

Special Forces reconnaissance teams were inserted by helicopter on numerous occasions throughout the conflict. By 18 May, Sea Kings HC4s of 846 NAS alone had flown twenty-five night sorties to insert, recover and resupply Special Forces on the islands. Passive night vision goggles (PNGs) (four Sea Kings from 846 NAS were thus equipped) aided these operations, most of them nocturnal, assisting with difficult navigation flown across featureless terrain totally deprived of ambient light. 846 NAS moved ashore from *Intrepid* on 29 May as a result of the break-out from **San Carlos**, establishing a Forward Operating Base (FOB) in a small river gully just north of the **Ajax Bay** medical facility. Many more missions followed, including insertions on **West Falkland** on 9 June to investigate reports of the arrival of Argentine reinforcements and supplies on the island. While 846 NAS possessed the most advanced version of PNGs, with five sets at its disposal, earlier versions were available to a limited number of other helicopter crews. Night-vision capability proved extremely valuable, with only three 846 NAS missions failing to locate their objectives.

In the last few days of the war Special Forces teams came within very close proximity of Stanley, with at least one team moving by PNG-equipped Sea Kings from Estancia House to **Beagle Ridge**, only 4 miles north of the capital.

Type, Number and Service Allocation

Five types of helicopter (some of two or more 'marks' or variations) supported British forces in the Falklands. The Gazelle AH1, Wasp HAS1, Lynx HAS2 and Scout AH1 were fast, light helicopters, but highly vulnerable to Pucaras and small arms fire. The more robust but slower Wessex HU5, Wessex HAS3, Sea King HC4, and Sea King HAS5 were all medium-lift transport helicopters. The twin-rotored Chinook HC1, with its impressive load capacity, served as the only heavy-lift helicopter in theatre.

The **Royal Navy** employed four types of helicopter: Sea King, Lynx, Wessex and Wasp. Those deployed to **Ascension**, **South Georgia** and/or the Falklands in the course of the campaign numbered as follows: Lynx HAS2 (twenty-four); Sea King HC4 (fourteen) Sea King HAS2A/2A (sixteen); Sea King HAS5 (twenty); Wasp HAS1 (eleven); and two variations of Wessex: HAS3 (two) and HU5 (fifty-four).

The Royal Marines of 3 CBAS operated eleven Gazelle AH1s and seven Scout AH1s, while 656 Squadron of the **Army Air Corps** operated six Gazelle AH1s and eight Scout AH1s.

The Royal Air Force flew the Chinook HC1 (only one of which survived the sinking of *Atlantic Conveyor* on 25 May) in the **Total Exclusion Zone** (TEZ) and operated a single Sea King at Ascension.

The Scout was a sturdy, reliable utility machine used on and off the battlefield whose main function was in reconnaissance and casualty evacuation. With its SS-11 missile capability it could strike bunkers and sangars as a substitute for its principal target – armoured vehicles. With greater lift and more recently taken into service than the Scout, the Gazelle performed a reconnaissance and communications role, but the exigencies of the campaign later required it to move troops and stores to forward areas and evacuate the wounded, a task for which this light helicopter was not well suited. In all, fifteen Scouts served on Operation Corporate, divided between 3 CBAS and 656 Squadron Army Air Corps.

The total number of helicopters aboard the vessels of the **Amphibious Task Group** for the landings in San Carlos Water on 21 May amounted to one Wessex HAS3, five Lynx HAS2s, two Wasp HAS1s, twelve Sea King HC4s, four Sea King HAS5s, nine Gazelle AH1s, and nine Scout AH1s. On the same day the **Carrier Battle Group** carried a total of eighteen Sea King HAS5s, seven Lynx HAS2s and one Wessex HAS3. Other ships in or close to the TEZ at the same time carried a total of twenty-two helicopters: two Lynx HAS2s, two Wasp HAS1s, two Sea King HAS2As, twelve Wessex HU5s, and four Chinook HC1s.

The Exocet missile attack on *Atlantic Conveyor* resulted in the painful loss of ten helicopters, including three Chinook HC1s, six Wessex, and one Lynx. One Wessex, normally resident aboard *Fort Austin*, happened to be aloft at the time, and thus avoided destruction, as did the only surviving Chinook in theatre, ZA718 of 18 Squadron. These losses severely affected the process of moving stores between ships and shore, but its most profound impact came with respect to campaign **strategy** as two units, **3 Para** and **45 Commando**, were now forced to proceed east on foot from the San Carlos area.

The total number of helicopters available on 26 May for the planned break-out from San Carlos was only thirty-two, only half of which constituted transport helicopters: nine Scout AH1s, seven Gazelle AH1s, five Wessex HU5s, ten Sea King HC4s and one Chinook HC1.

With the arrival of *Atlantic Causeway* in the TEZ on 29 May, carrying twenty-eight helicopters, some of the losses of the 25th were made good. On 2 June, however, eight Wessex HU5s of 847 NAS remained aboard when she sailed to the Tug, Repair and Logistic Area (TRALA) to act as a floating reserve. Four more Wessex arrived in San Carlos Water on 9 June aboard the helicopter support ship, *Engadine*, distributing her load between the FOBs at **Port San Carlos** and the settlement at Teal Inlet.

By 3 June, with the recent arrivals of vessels from the UK, the number of helicopters based ashore reached sixty-eight, consisting of twenty-six Sea Kings, seventeen Wessex, one Chinook, eleven Scouts and thirteen Gazelles. More were en route for the Falklands from Ascension aboard *Contender Bezant*, totaling four Chinook HC1s, two Wasp HAS1s, one Sea King HAS2A and two Gazelle AH1s.

Platforms and Operating Bases

Helicopters operating from **frigates** and **destroyers** used the helicopter pads aft, with facilities for their maintenance located in the hangar. Those aboard **aircraft carriers** used the flight deck like fixed-wing aircraft. In the days following the landings on 21 May, with weather conditions deteriorating – fog, mist and high winds growing more prevalent as winter progressed – 'Eagle' bases were established just over 2 miles north of San Carlos settlement at Old House Creek forward operating base. Camouflaged, these bases became refuges for ships' helicopters ferrying troops and stores ashore to avoid exposing them to air attack aboard ship, or served simply as positions closer to the target, thus offering an alternative to returning to the carriers. A few days later a new FOB was established at Fern Valley Creek, 1½ miles south of Old House Creek. Another FOB was created on 1 June when Sea King HAS2As arrived from *Atlantic Causeway*. On 3 June, six Gazelles newly arrived aboard *Nordic Ferry* established themselves at a new FOB at Clam Valley, south-east of San Carlos settlement, while Sea Kings arrived from *Fort Austin* to existing FOBs.

In terms of helicopter support, the ground crews in all cases worked extraordinarily hard to provide a remarkable record of serviceability under harsh winter conditions both aboard ship and onshore; even in the course of the journey to the South Atlantic some helicopters were stored below decks to protect them from the saltwater corrosion that affected all aircraft and shipping. *Engadine* served as the helicopter support ship, carrying mechanics and spare parts.

Sea Kings could refuel while still aloft using the HIFR refuelling system, which involved hovering over the stern of a frigate while the helicopter crew lowered a hook to hoist up a fuel line. This innovation was first employed on 1 May by Sea King HAS5s of 826 NAS on ASW work off the north coast of East Falkland.

Herald, HMS

Herald was a Hecla class **Royal Navy** survey vessel that, together with *Hecla* and *Hydra*, was used as an ambulance ship to ferry casualties to the hospital ship *Uganda* and from her to Montevideo for onward aeromedic **VC10** flights to naval and military hospitals in Britain. She left Portsmouth on 24 April and arrived off the Falklands on 25 May. Her service in the conflict ended upon reaching Portsmouth on 21 July.

Commander:	Capt R.I.C. Halliday	
Builders:	Robb Caledon	
Launched:	4 October 1973	
Commissioned:	31 October 1974	
Displacement (tons):	2,125 Standard	2,945 Full Load
Draught:	4.7m	

Dimensions: length × beam; feet (metres):	260 × 49 (79.23 × 14.94)	
Propulsion:	3 diesel engines supplying 2 electric motors	2,000hp = 14 knots
Armament: none		
Aircraft:	1 × **Wasp** HAS1 – no ordnance carried	

Hercules C1

Based at Lyneham in Wiltshire and the mainstay of transport aircraft belonging to the **Royal Air Force**, the Lockheed Hercules C1 (and those modified as either C1Ks or C1Ps) transported vast amounts of personnel and stores to **Ascension**, supplementing the already formidable **logistics** achievement of the transport vessels of the **Royal Fleet Auxiliary** and **Ships Taken Up From Trade**. Capable of carrying up to ninety fully armed troops or more than 25,000lb of freight, including **helicopters** and vehicles, the Hercules also carried equipment, provisions and ammunition in urgent need, as well as mail, to ships en route to the Falklands or already in the **Total Exclusion Zone**. It employed airdrops to resupply ships with high priority freight, such as to the frigate *Minerva*, to which in the early hours of 6 June Hercules C1P XV196 flew a refuelled sortie that took a staggering twenty-four hours in total. In a few instances they transported personnel who parachuted from the rear into the icy waters of the South Atlantic, such as Lieutenant Colonel David Chaundler, the new CO 2 **Para**, who on 1 June parachuted from 800ft out of a Hercules into the sea near *Penelope* in order to reach the Battle Group and replace Lieutenant Colonel Jones, killed at **Goose Green** four days earlier.

Twin auxiliary tanks were fitted to provide an additional three to four hours' flying time, and some aircraft had an additional two added, although the additional weight in fuel reduced the payload capability of the aircraft. Six Hercules were modified with the new in-flight refuelling probe, the first of these aircraft arriving at Wideawake on 14 May and flying its first sortie two days later, when it dropped 1,000lb of special stores and eight Special Forces troops to *Antelope*. The 6,300-mile journey took twenty-four hours to complete, refuelled on the outbound journey by two **Victor K2** tankers and by three more on the return flight to **Ascension**. Similarly, on 18 May, Hercules C1 XV291 flew almost seventeen hours from Ascension to airdrop a new camshaft to *Leeds Castle* after she experienced engine trouble.

Many of these journeys, including forty-four long-range air drop missions to the **Task Force** and made more accurate by the installation of improved navigational equipment, involved extremely long periods in the air over great distances – a total of 13,000 hours in the air for all Hercules combined – thus requiring air-to-air refuelling.

Another 4,000 hours were clocked by other RAF transport aircraft, including **VC10s**, and three chartered civilian aircraft – ex-RAF Belfasts capable of carrying

H

40 tons each and flying a total of twenty-one flights with vehicles, helicopters and a range of miscellaneous cargo – to compensate for the shortfall in capacity of the RAF. All told, RAF transport aircraft carried to Ascension 7,000 tons of cargo, including 100 vehicles, plus 5,500 civilian and military personnel.

Hermes, HMS

Twenty-two years in service by the time of the war, *Hermes* was one of the two **aircraft carriers** in the operational theatre, the other being *Invincible*, and she provided close air support and **combat air patrols**.

Originally designed to carry fixed-wing aircraft, *Hermes* was converted in 1971–73 to a commando carrier as a successor to *Albion*, though she continued her capacity as a carrier for anti-submarine **helicopters**. Refitted again in 1976, now as an anti-submarine support ship, or CVS, she underwent a third transformation in 1980–81 to render her capable of deploying **Harriers**, preserving however her secondary and short-term capacity to carry a commando force.

In 1981 *Hermes* went on exercise with **Sea Harriers** and a complement of 130 Marines from 41 Commando. Early the following year, she practised her amphibious capability on the south coast of England with more than 900 **Royal Marines** embarked during two major landing exercises. For amphibious exercises conducted at a considerable distance from home shores *Hermes* had to offload her Sea Harriers and ASW **Sea Kings** to accommodate the troops aboard and their stores, but these additional assets did not displace the four LCVPs slung in davits meant to facilitate this extra capacity, which happened to suit admirably the needs of the forthcoming campaign. Just prior to the Argentine invasion of the Falklands, *Hermes* conducted anti-submarine exercises in the south-western approaches and was fortuitously back in Portsmouth on 19 March for dockyard maintenance.

Hermes carried a crew of 960 officers and men, but could embark large numbers of troops. Her flight deck stood at an angle of 6.5 degrees, with a 7 degree ski-jump ramp. Her communications equipment consisted of WSC-3 SATCOMM, bought from the United States, and this was to serve her well during the war. Although *Hermes* could play various roles on operations, Northwood decided to employ her chiefly as a 'Harrier Carrier' to maximise the number of these aircraft.

At the outset of the conflict *Hermes* was under maintenance, with many of her crew on leave and the structure under scaffolding. The dockyard workers at Portsmouth performed miracles in preparing her for operations by round-the-clock refitting and loading stores, supplies and ammunition in only three days when the ordinary tempo of such preparations would have taken three weeks. She departed on 5 April and her presence with the fleet enhanced air capability considerably, with, on disembarkation, eleven Sea Harriers aboard from 800 and 899 NAS, and eighteen Sea Kings from 826 NAS (ASW) and 846 NAS (Commando), together

Sea Harriers crowd the deck of HMS *Hermes* as a Chinook prepares to land. (AirSeaLand Photos)

H

with A Company, **40 Commando** Royal Marines. Her five **Harrier** GR3s of 1 Squadron RAF would deploy aboard *Hermes* by flying from **Ascension**, to which they had flown from the UK in early May.

She arrived at Ascension on 16 April, upon which she became the flagship of Rear Admiral **Woodward** after he transferred from *Glamorgan*. The following day, *Hermes* became the site of an important strategy meeting held between Admiral **Fieldhouse**, Brigadier **Thompson**, Commodore Clapp and others.

She arrived off the Falklands on 1 May, positioned about 95 miles east-north-east of **Stanley**. She first launched her Sea Harriers against targets on the Falklands on that day, nine attacking Stanley airport and three attacking the airfield at **Goose Green**.

On the evening of 14–15 May, *Hermes*, together with *Broadsword* and *Glamorgan*, detached from the **Carrier Battle Group** to support the **Special Air Service** raid on **Pebble Island**. With *Hermes* laying about 40 miles of the coast in order to reduce the distance to be covered by **helicopters**, at 0225Z on the 15th four Sea King HC4s of 846 NAS carrying forty-five men of D Squadron and their fire support team left the deck and dropped them with the reconnaissance patrol inserted earlier. After the raid, the men were returned to *Hermes*, which sailed rapidly north-east to avoid being caught near shore at sunrise. Back at her post as part of the Carrier Battle Group north-east of Stanley, *Hermes* was not directly involved in the landings in **San Carlos Water** on 21 May.

While approximately 60 miles north-east of Stanley on the afternoon of 25 May, *Hermes* launched all her available Sea Harriers to oppose two approaching Super Etendards that fired two **Exocets**, probably intended for both aircraft carriers. Chaff fired from *Ambuscade* appears to have diverted both missiles, one of which hit *Atlantic Conveyor* instead of *Hermes*.

In early June, she retired to the east out of the **Total Exclusion Zone** for boiler repairs, leaving less loiter time over the Falklands for her aircraft and thus inadvertently exposing ships at **Fitzroy** to greater danger. Nevertheless, remarkably considering her age, *Hermes* developed no serious mechanical defects. The carrier arrived in Portsmouth 21 July to a rapturous homecoming from the public.

Commander:	Captain L.E. Middleton ADC	
Builders:	Vickers (Barrow)	
Launched:	16 February 1953	
Commissioned:	18 November 1959	
Displacement (tons):	23,900 Standard	28,700 Full load
Dimensions: feet (metres):	Hull 744 × 90 (227.9 × 27.4); Flight Deck 600 × 112 (182.9 × 34.1)	
Draught: 8.8m	Flight Deck angled 6.5 degrees with 7 degree ski-jump ramp	
Propulsion:	2 sets of Parsons geared steam turbines	76,000shp = 26 knots (pprox.)
Armament:	2 × **Seacat** systems (GWS 22)	
	4 × LCVP (**Landing Craft**, Vehicles & Personnel) on davits	
Complement:	143 officers, 1,027 ratings (excluding embarked troops)	
Aircraft (as of 21 May):	15 × Sea Harrier FRS1	
	6 × Harrier GR3	
	6 × Sea King HAS5	
	2 × **Lynx** HAS2	
	1 × **Wessex** HU5	

Hospital Ship

See Uganda, SS

Hydra, HMS

Hydra, a Hecla class **Royal Navy** survey vessel, together with *Hecla* and *Herald*, was used as an ambulance ship to ferry **casualties** from the battle area to the hospital ship *Uganda* and on occasion from her on the four-day journey to Montevideo for onward aeromedic **VC10** flights to naval and military hospitals in Britain. She departed Portsmouth on 24 April and arrived at **Ascension** on 8 May. Operating from Falklands waters as of 19 May, among several journeys to Uruguay, one involved her leaving for Montevideo from the **Red Cross Box** on 2 June and arriving on the 6th with fifty-one wounded. By 11 June, now loaded with medical supplies collected in Montevideo that had been flown over from the UK, she was back in company with *Uganda*, now anchored in Falkland Sound instead of the Red Cross Box. This greatly reduced the transit time for the large number of casualties that were initially taken to **Ajax Bay** from the actions at **Mount Longdon**, **Mount Harriet** and **Two Sisters**. *Hydra*'s services continued in the South Atlantic well after the cessation of hostilities and she did not arrive back in Portsmouth until 24 September.

Commander:	Commander R.J. Campbell	
Builders:	Yarrow (Blythwood)	
Launched:	14 July 1965	
Commissioned:	5 May 1966	
Displacement (tons):	1,915 Standard	2,733 Full Load
Dimensions: length × beam; feet (metres):	260 × 49 (79.23 × 14.94)	
Draught:	4.7m	
Propulsion:	3 diesel engines supplying 2 electric motors	2,000hp = 14 knots
Aircraft:	1 × **Wasp** HAS1 – no ordnance carried	

H

Infantry Weapons

British infantry and **Royal Marines** were armed with a variety of weapons that together enabled them to offer a substantial amount of firepower. They carried the standard infantry rifle, the reliable and robust 7.62mm calibre L1A1 SLR, or self-loading rifle (SLR), which weighed 5kg when loaded with its standard 20-round box magazine. With an effective range of 850yd, the SLR was an adaptation of the Belgian FAL (*fusil automatique leger*). Its principal difference from the original lay in a modification that removed the automatic fire capability in favour of single-shot fire, thus encouraging the soldier to fire with greater accuracy and reducing the instinct to fire in a sustained manner, which expended larger amounts of ammunition. The Argentine counterpart, also a variant of the FAL, was capable of firing in bursts. To ensure accuracy and sight alignment, soldiers 'zeroed' their personal weapons. It could be fitted with a Trilux night sight, although many soldiers found them heavy and ineffective. Special Forces preferred the American M-16, while snipers used the L42 sniper rifle.

The rifle could be fitted with the L1A1 bayonet, whose blade measured 204mm (8in), and this would see extensive use in the close-quarters fighting characterising all six ground engagements.

Battalions also carried the fully automatic, belt-fed 7.62mm calibre General Purpose Machine Gun (GPMG), popularly referred to as the 'Gimpy'. This weighed 24lb (13.85kg) and had a 50-round belt that could, of course, be linked to any length, but it was too light for the sustained fire support role and yet too heavy when carried over any distance.

Each rifle company section employed this weapon in the sustained fire role to support the infantry. In this role it was mounted on a lightweight bipod unless grouped together in the Machine Gun Platoon, in which case it was mounted on a heavyweight tripod, with recoil buffers that allowed long bursts of fire, and two spare barrels to hand in case the fitted barrel overheated. Gimpys, with a rate of fire of 750 rounds per minute, employed belts of 100 round link ammunition for an effective range of 800m in the light role and 1,800m in the sustained fire role. The weapon was also fitted with a dial sight that facilitated firing against pre-registered targets when obscured from view.

Selected infantry carried a 66mm light anti-armour weapon, the L1A1 rocket launcher, which weighed only 5lb and fired a 2lb projectile capable of 'bunker busting' – demolishing light field entrenchments such as trenches and sangars. For more formidable dug-in positions, the heavier Carl Gustav medium anti-tank weapon (MAW) – an 84mm recoilless gun with a 6½lb high-explosive anti-tank (HEAT) round – proved more effective.

The severe weather conditions in the Falklands demanded that soldiers constantly check and clean their weapons since the damp affected both the rifle and its ammunition. This required the men to empty their magazines and clips regularly to prevent rust and verdigris from forming on brass. Failure to do so could result in stoppages. In peacetime the personnel of the Machine Gun Platoon in **3 Para** served as drummers and buglers in the regimental band, although some believed this a misallocated role for gunners and thought they ought to specialise entirely on their operational role. A soldier carrying a LMG might have two dozen magazines – no inconsiderable weight. Machine guns were supplied with tracer rounds to track the trajectory of their fire.

Some radio operators, MILAN and mortar crews and other specialist troops burdened with heavy equipment and otherwise encumbered by the SLR could choose instead the 9mm L2A3 Sterling submachine gun (SMG), whose curved thirty-four-round magazine loaded from the left. Its stock could be folded from 690mm to 483mm for easier stowage and its magazine held either ten or thirty-four rounds. Impressive for its rate of fire, it was however effective only at close quarters.

A soldier from 3 Para on Mount Longdon manning a General Purpose Machine Gun (GPMG). (AirSeaLand Photos)

Of French manufacture, the newly issued, wire-guided, anti-tank weapon system known as 'MILAN' ('Missile Infanterie, Leger, Anti-char'/Missile, Infantry, Light, Anti-tank) offered excellent support to the rifle companies and consisted of a control/firing post and missile fired from a launch tube. MILANs were grouped together in the anti-tank platoon in the respective Support Companies of both battalions. The MILAN was not light to carry: the missile itself only weighed 6.65kg, but the complete unit rose to 16.5kg, so that generally the firing post was carried by one of the crew and its ammunition by others.

The warhead contained about 3kg of hollow charge high explosive, which could penetrate armour 25.6in (650mm) in thickness at up to 2,000yd. 3 Para had only just received the MILAN prior to being called up for service in the South Atlantic, and had only three men in the entire battalion trained in its use, with the remainder trained during the journey south.

The MILAN system was limited at night by a dependence on sufficient light for the firer to see his target, a light that could be provided by requesting the fire of illuminating rounds (parachute flares) from either mortars or artillery. The MILAN enjoyed a number of advantages over the Wombat, being smaller and less cumbersome to transport, easier to camouflage, and blessed with a greater range.

3 Para's Anti-tank Platoon was also armed with six Wombat 120mm recoilless anti-tank guns, although these were never fired in the Falklands. Wombat was an acronym for 'Weapon of Magnesium Battalion Anti-Tank', required a four-man crew to operate and a Land Rover. Although it could be shifted for short distances on its two wheels, it was normally moved by and fired from a vehicle, but it served its function best when dismounted and dug in. It fired high-explosive squash head (HESH) rounds.

In 3 Para, each rifle platoon and each Wombat crew carried an 84mm 'Carl Gustav' MAW, similar to the 66mm light anti-tank weapon (LAW) but larger, heavier and capable of being reloaded rather than having to be disposed of after a single use. Soldiers found it cumbersome and its greater weight disproportionate to its effectiveness. The American-made LAW fired a short range rocket from the shoulder using a disposable tube, using a smaller HEAT warhead than MILAN that could be employed very effectively against bunkers as well as armoured targets.

Specialised infantry companies were equipped with the L16A2 81mm mortar employed in an indirect fire role, firing high-explosive shells to a range exceeding 5,000yd at a rate of twelve rounds a minute, but to a maximum of fifteen. With a weight of 38kg, the mortar weighed more than twice the MILAN and therefore posed a challenge to any infantry forced to carry it in the absence of ground or air transport. Mortar fire was usually directed by a mortar-fire controller; rounds sometimes failed to explode when they embedded in the boggy ground.

Snipers were armed with the 7.62mm calibre L42A1 sniper rifle, consisting of a manual bolt action mechanism based on the Lee Enfield, whose origins stretched

Royal Marines firing their SLRs in weapon training on Ascension. (AirSeaLand Photos)

back to the late nineteenth century. It retained the Mark 3 telescopic sight and mounting from its Second World War predecessor, the .303 calibre rifle. Snipers employed this weapon while on patrol, performing escort duties and during battle. It weighed 4.43kg when loaded and carried a magazine containing ten rounds. Snipers worked best in pairs.

Few officers were armed with pistols; those who were carried the Browning FN High Power Pistol, which when loaded carried a magazine with fourteen rounds and weighed just over a kilogram. Most officers carried either a rifle or submachine gun with several magazines, and sometimes grenades and even bandoliers of additional ammunition.

Grenades were either high-explosive (HE) fragmentation or white phosphorus (WP), the latter of which, on detonation, sprayed burning particles of phosphorus, thus providing an instant smokescreen during attack or withdrawal, as well as a means of setting foliage and structures on fire. International law forbade the use of the WP grenade as a weapon specifically deployed against enemy personnel.

Intrepid, HMS

One of two Fearless class **amphibious assault ships** (Landing Platform Dock, or LPD) of the **Task Force**, the other being *Fearless*, both of which contained four **landing craft** (Landing Craft Utility or LCUs) and a **Lynx** helicopter. Due to

Ministry of Defence cutbacks, specifically the 1981 Defence Review, when war broke out *Intrepid* had already been paid off and was moored in Portsmouth awaiting its fate either as a reserve vessel or for disposal. As a result, several weeks were required to return her to operational capacity with the **Amphibious Task Group**.

She departed from Portland on 26 April, arrived at **Ascension** on 5 May and reached the Falklands on the 16th. **3 Para** was cross-decked by landing craft on to *Intrepid* on 19 May, two days before the landings. On D-Day itself she and her sister ship *Fearless* took part in the landings, launching her landing craft, and while laying south of Chancho Point at the opening of **San Carlos Water** she fired **Seacat** against attacking aircraft.

On 5 June, the **Welsh Guards** and the **Scots Guards** embarked on *Intrepid* bound for **Bluff Cove**, although on instructions from London the assault ships were ordered not to depart from San Carlos Water in daylight. Accordingly, Captain Dingemans embarked on the evening of 5 June and, owing to the dangers associated with retracting his LCUs in a swell on the open sea, decided to launch them to the leeward side of Lively Island, where the waters were calmer.

Intrepid and *Fearless* could serve as emergency landing platforms for **Sea Harriers** low on fuel or suffering from mechanical problems, but in the event only one aircraft made use of this facility, on 13 June. *Intrepid*'s South Atlantic service ended when she arrived at Devonport on 13 July.

Commander:	Captain P.G.V. Dingemans
Launched:	25 June 1964
Commissioned:	11 March 1967
Builders:	John Brown
Displacement (tons):	11,060 Standard
	12,120 Full load
	16,950 Dock Flooded
Dimensions: length × beam; feet (metres):	520× 80 (158.5 × 24.4)
Draught:	7.0m forward; 9.8m aft
Propulsion:	2 sets geared steam turbines 22,000shp = 21 knots
Armament:	2 × 40mm AA guns
	4 × Seacat systems (GWS 20)
	2 × 20mm Rheinmetall RH202 AA guns
Aircraft:	Various combinations of **helicopters** up to 4 × **Sea King** HC4
Assault Force:	1 RM Commando (650 men) = logistic elements
	1 Commando Light Battery RA (6 × 105mm guns)
	4 × Landing Craft, Utility
	4 × Landing Craft, Vehicles & Personnel

Landing Craft (Utility)

Displacement (tons):	75 Standard	176 Full Load
Dimensions: length × beam; feet (metres):	84 × 21 (25.7 × 6.5)	
Draught:	1.7m	
Propulsion:	2 Paxman diesel engines	624bhp = 9 knots
Armament:	1 × 7.62mm GPMG	
Crew:	SNCO + 6 ratings	
Assault Load:	100 tons cargo or two tanks or 140 men	

Landing Craft (Vehicles & Personnel)

Displacement (tons):	8.5 tons Empty (fuelled)	13.5 tons Full Load
Dimensions: length × beam; feet (metres):	43× 10 (13.1 × 3.1)	
Propulsion:	2 diesel engines	200bhp = 9 knots
Assault Load:	5 tons of cargo or one vehicle or 35 men	

Invincible, HMS

One of two **aircraft carriers** involved in the conflict – the other being *Hermes* – *Invincible* was of a lighter class, only two years old in 1982. The first modern through deck carrier in the **Royal Navy**, her aircraft provided close air support and **combat air patrols**. Two other carriers, *Illustrious* and *Ark Royal*, were then under construction. The Ministry of Defence had considered selling *Invincible* to the Royal Australian Navy, but the outbreak of hostilities ended all such aspirations.

The first aircraft carrier of a new class to be constructed since the Second World War, *Invincible* was built as a through deck cruiser furnished with as many as ten medium-sized **helicopters** operating against **submarines**. *Invincible* could also function as a Command and Control Ship, with her operations room equipped with Action Data and Automated Weapons System (ADAWS). Other sophisticated equipment included Marconi ICS-3 communications, Type 992Q target indication **radar**, Type 1006 navigational radar, and Type 1022 air warning radar. Like *Hermes*, she had a 6-degree angled deck and 7-degree ski-ramp. Her principal armament consisted of one **Sea Dart** missile system, which used radar guidance.

Invincible's first exercise in her anti-submarine role and involving **Royal Marines** and embarked **Sea Harriers** took place in 1981. Space proved a premium in accommodating much of **40 Commando**, but at the sacrifice of comfort lessons were learned about operating amphibiously. In February and March 1982 she went on an anti-submarine exercise with the regulation number of aircraft: five Sea Harriers and nine ASW **Sea King** 5s, but two days after the Argentine invasion 801 NAS increased her load of Sea Harriers to eight and when she sailed from Portsmouth on 5 April *Invincible* carried additional Sea Dart missiles.

Invincible arrived at **Ascension** on 16 April and entered Falklands waters with the **Carrier Battle Group** on 1 May, serving for the duration of the war as the Anti-Air Warfare Co-ordinator tasked with defending the fleet and as a platform for Sea Harriers conducting combat air patrols and helicopters performing a range of functions.

Two examples of her operations may be instructive. On 18 May, escorted by *Broadsword*, *Invincible* detached herself from the Carrier Battle Group and proceeded west. Sea King HC4 ZA290 left her deck at 0315Z carrying an **Special Air Service** team bound for the Argentine mainland in a planned raid on Rio Grande air base, home of Exocet-equipped Super Etendard aircraft. She then returned to the **Task Force**. A week later, on the afternoon of the 25th, while *Invincible* lay about 60 miles north-east of **Stanley** in company with *Hermes* and other vessels, all her available Sea Harriers and **Lynx** set off to intercept two approaching Super Etendards whose **Exocets**, probably intended for the two carriers but apparently diverted by a combination of chaff and jamming, concentrated instead on the ill-fated aircraft container ship *Atlantic Conveyor*. In the course of the attack, *Invincible* fired a salvo of six **Sea Dart** missiles, though none of them intercepted either of the two incoming Exocets.

Returning home after relief from the newly commissioned *Illustrious*, *Invincible* had spent a remarkable 166 days continuously at sea, reaching Portsmouth on 17 September.

Commander:	Captain J.J. Black MBE	
Builders:	Vickers (Barrow)	
Launched:	3 May 1977	
Commissioned:	11 July 1980	
Displacement (tons):	16,000 Standard	19,500 Full load
Dimensions: length × beam; feet (metres):	Hull: 678 × 90 (206.6 × 27.5)	Flight deck: 590 × 105 (180 × 31.9)
Draught:	7.3m	Flight deck angled 6 degrees with 7-degree ski-jump ramp
Propulsion:	4 × Rolls-Royce Olympus TM 3B gas turbines	112,000shp = 29+ knots
Complement:	131 officers, 869 ratings (excluding Air Group)	
Armament:	1 × 2 Sea Dart (GWS 30)	
	2 × 20mm Phalanx CIWS	
	2 × 20mm Oerlikon	
	(14 × 7.62mm GPMGs added)	
Aircraft (as of 21 May):	10 × Sea Harrier FRS1	
	9 × Sea King HAS5	
	1 × **Lynx** HAS2	

Iris, CS

A motor cable vessel requisitioned from British Telecom in April, *Iris* carried Naval Party 1870 under Lieutenant Commander J. Bithell RN. She departed Devonport on 29 April and arrived off **South Georgia** on 25 May. Five days later, she reached Falklands waters. Her service ended upon arrival at Southampton on 30 November.

Commander:	Captain G. Fulton	
Launched:	1976	
Tonnage:	3,874 Gross Register	2,150 Deadweight
Dimensions: length × beam; feet (metres):	319 × 49 (97.3 × 15)	
Propulsion:	2 diesel engines	5,200bhp = 15 knots
Helicopter platform – no embarked aircraft		

Irishman, MV

An ocean-going motor tug requisitioned from United Towing on 7 April, *Irishman* contained a Naval Party from the **Royal Maritime Auxiliary Service**. She had two sister ships, *Yorkshireman* and *Salvageman*, also requisitioned tugs. On 10 April *Irishman* left Portsmouth loaded with towing and salvage gear. She was called to the stricken *Atlantic Conveyor* for work after the latter was struck by an **Exocet** missile on 25 May. *Irishman* returned to the UK in November.

Commander:	Captain W. Allen	
Launched:	1978	
Tonnage:	686 Gross Register	
Dimensions: length × beam; feet (metres):	138 × 38 (42 × 11.6)	
Propulsion:	2 diesel engines	2,000bhp= 13 knots

Junella, HMS

A motor fish factory trawler requisitioned on 26 April and converted to a minesweeper, *Junella* departed from Portland on 27 April and arrived at **Ascension** on 11 May. She then proceeded to **South Georgia**, reaching the island on the 27th. Her service in Falklands waters did not begin until 21 June, a week after the cessation of fighting. Her South Atlantic service ended upon arrival in Rosyth on 11 August.

Commander:	Lieutenant M. Rowledge	
Launched:	1975	
Builders:	J. Marr & Son (Hull)	
Tonnage:	1,615 Gross Register	
Dimensions: length × beam; feet (metres):	217 × 43 (66.3 × 13.1)	
Propulsion:	1 diesel engine	3,180bhp = 15.5 knots

Klepper canoe

Small craft capable of being dismantled, the Klepper canoe was employed by a recce team of D Squadron, 22 **Special Air Service** prior to the raid on **Pebble Island**. In the event, an eight-man Boat Troop patrol deployed four Kleppers at Purvis Bay on the night 11–12 May, but owing to very rough seas had to dismantle and carry them to Deep Ferny Valley. They laid up there, establishing an observation point over Pebble Island before reassembling their canoes and crossing 2km of water to Phillips Cove.

Lafonia

A peninsula attached to the southern part of East Falkland, to which it is joined by an isthmus about 1.6 miles (2.5km) wide, on which are situated the settlements of **Darwin** and **Goose Green**. Almost uninhabited, Lafonia is largely grassland on gently undulating ground.

In early June, soldiers from the **Gurkha Rifles** supported by 656 Squadron searched Lafonia for Argentines suspected of gathering intelligence on helicopter flight routes and others who may not have figured in the tally taken at the Goose Green capitulation on 29 May. A **Scout** helicopter spotted a group of Argentines at Egg Harbour House and when heli-borne Gurkha reinforcements arrived on the scene from Goose Green and an SS-11 missile was fired at their new position in a nearby gully, eight men surrendered themselves and a surface-to-air missile.

Landing craft ferrying troops ashore from either LSL *Fearless* or *Intrepid*. (AirSeaLand Photos)

Landing Craft (LCU/LCVP)

British landing craft in the Falklands War consisted of two types: Landing Craft (Utility) and Landing Craft (Vehicles and Personnel). Four LCUs accompanied the assault ships *Intrepid* and *Fearless*, which served as the mother ships. Each LCU could carry about 150 men. *Fearless* and *Intrepid* also carried four Landing Craft Vehicle and Personnel (LCVPs). LCU navigation could be inhibited by poor visibility and large kelp formations. Retracting LCUs involved flooding the tank deck of the assault ship with several thousand tons of sea water, which dropped the stern, and by decreasing speed to a few knots. Landing craft personnel consisted of a Royal Marines Assault Squadron composed of approximately eighty **Royal Marines** and **Royal Navy** personnel, including an Amphibious Beach Unit.

Troops embarking on to the LCUs on the morning of 21 May found it a very difficult enterprise, having to jump from the LSL after carefully timing the roll and pitch of the two vessels lest they injure themselves while fully equipped with Bergen and weapons. Seven LCUs, sailing initially in line astern before shifting to line abreast as they approached the assault beaches, brought troops ashore on D-Day. **3 Para** occupied four LCUs, two of them carrying **Scorpions** and **Scimitars**.

After the landings, the LCUs remained in **San Carlos Water**, ferrying supplies ashore, although two were later assigned to **Teal Inlet** to support the **3 Commando Brigade** BMA there. The other six remained at **San Carlos** unloading the stores of the newly arrived **5 Infantry Brigade**.

The plan to move the **Welsh Guards** to **Fitzroy** involved the four LCUs from *Intrepid* rendezvousing with *Fearless* off Elephant Island on the evening of 7 June, but when the LCUs did not appear, half the battalion were loaded on to two landing craft from *Fearless* for the 19-mile journey to **Bluff Cove**. They then proceeded, together with one *Intrepid* LCU, under Major Ewen Southby-Tailyour's direction, to Fitzroy, where he discovered the three *Intrepid* LCUs that had missed the rendezvous. At the same time, the other two LCUs from *Fearless* were at Teal Inlet, although these were soon recovered.

LCU 'Foxtrot 4', embarked from **Goose Green** on the morning of 8 June bound for Fitzroy with six Land Rovers of 5 Infantry Brigade HQ and the Signal Squadron. This movement was against the orders of Southby-Tailyour not to sail in daylight. Just after 1830Z, about a mile south of Johnson Island near the mouth of Choiseul Sound, a 500lb bomb from a Skyhawk struck the stern, killing six Royal Marines and RN sailors and wounding one Royal Marine. Three Skyhawks were shot down with **Sidewinder** missiles by two 800 NAS **Sea Harriers** around 1945Z. A Mayday radio call to Brigade HQ resulted in the appearance of a **Sea King**, which winched on board the eleven survivors of the burning craft. Later the same day, *Monsunen*, bound from Goose Green to Fitzroy, was ordered to locate and tow the stricken LCU, as she carried sensitive cryptographic material and valuable radio vehicles. After several hours' search, 'Foxtrot Four' was discovered drifting south-east of Lively Island. A tow rope was duly fastened, but a trailing rope snagged on *Monsunen*'s propeller and in any event the LCU eventually sank, with the additional loss of the radio vehicles.

Landing Force Group

Code-named CTG 317.1, the Landing Force Group (LFG) consisted of **3 Commando Brigade** commanded by Brigadier Julian **Thompson** RM, reinforced by the

3rd Battalion, the **Parachute Regiment** (3 Para), and several smaller units from the Army and **Royal Air Force**. Thompson had three tasks: landing his troops; establishing a beach-head; and defeating Argentine ground forces. Upon the appointment of Major General Jeremy **Moore** RM as Commander, Land Forces Falkland Islands, and the creation of a divisional headquarters, LFG was divided into its two components of 3 Commando Brigade and **5 Infantry Brigade**. After arriving at **Ascension**, the LFG spent the next three weeks restowing equipment and training. It rendezvoused with the **Carrier Battle Group** for the first time in the early hours of 20 May. After dark that evening, it sailed into Falkland Sound and remained outside the narrows of **San Carlos Water**, sending the troops of 3 Commando Brigade ashore in the early hours of the following day.

Landing Platform Dock (LPD)

See Amphibious Assault Ships

Landing Ships (Logistic) (LSL)

Manned by the **Royal Fleet Auxiliary**, six LSLs were deployed on Operation **Corporate**, all named after Knights of the Round Table: *Sir Bedivere*, *Sir Galahad*, *Sir Geraint*, *Sir Lancelot*, *Sir Percivale*, and *Sir Tristram*. So essential were these vessels to the campaign, together with the **amphibious assault ships**, that it simply could not have been mounted without them.

Built to embark and disembark troops and heavy vehicles, they exercised regularly in the Mediterranean and north Norway with **3 Commando Brigade**. Fitted with bow and stern doors, the LSL functioned as a roll-on/roll-off ferry, with a complement of about seventy officers and men, many of the ratings being Chinese. The LSLs could carry as many as 400 troops and 340 tons of stores or vehicles, with two **Mexeflotes** – powered rafts designed to ferry men, stores and equipment ashore. Lightly armed with only two 40mm Bofors guns, LSLs could reach a speed of about 17 knots. Their two heli-pads, positioned amidships and aft, accommodated light **helicopters**. All the LSLs played a part in the landings on 21 May and remained in **San Carlos Water** where necessary to continue the process of offloading. Both *Sir Galahad* and *Sir Tristram* were bombed on 8 June at **Port Pleasant** near **Fitzroy** while unloading the **Welsh Guards** and medical supplies.

Leeds Castle, HMS

A Castle class North Sea fishery protection vessel converted for the campaign into one of two offshore patrol vessels, the other being *Dumbarton Castle*.

She departed Portsmouth on 29 April and arrived at **Ascension**, initially acting as the island's guardship, on 9 May. *Leeds Castle* eventually accompanied *Dumbarton*

Castle in proceeding south with essential supplies, entering Falklands waters on the 21st and thereafter serving as a dispatch vessel, shuttling between the Falklands, **South Georgia** and Ascension. At South Georgia she served as a floating helicopter refuelling platform. She experienced engine trouble while sailing for the **Total Exclusion Zone** as a dispatch vessel on 18 May, but managed to undertake successful repairs thanks to the airdrop of a new camshaft carried out by a **Hercules** C1. Her South Atlantic service ended upon arrival at Rosyth on 20 August.

Commander:	Lieutenant Commander C.F.B. Hamilton	
Builders:	Hall Russell (Aberdeen)	
Launched:	29 October 1980	
Commissioned:	27 October 1981	
Displacement (tons):	1,250 Standard	1,450 Full Load
Dimensions: length × beam; feet (metres):	266 × 38 (81 × 11.5)	
Draught:	3.4m	
Propulsion:	2 diesel engines	5,640bhp = 20 knots
Armament:	1 × 40mm AA gun	
	2 × 7.62mm GPMG	

Logistics

Logistics in a military and naval context consist of the movement, supply and maintenance of armed forces. The Falklands presented extraordinary challenges by land, sea and air, owing to the formidable distance to the islands and the difficult ground, changeable weather and the absence of airfields, roads or a useable port (**Stanley** being, of course, in Argentine hands). In short, Operation **Corporate** encompassed prosecuting a campaign on remote islands 8,000 miles from the UK with a requirement to support a tri-service force of more than 100 ships, 300 aircraft and more than 10,000 men.

Co-ordinating this extremely complex, gargantuan effort all required considerable planning, with the urgent need to rapidly dispatch the **Task Force**, an effort rendered all the more difficult by the need to locate and allocate the correct amount of food, ammunition, fuel, cold and wet weather clothing and stores required and pack them efficiently to ensure speedy distribution when required.

No contingency plans existed to support an expeditionary operation to the South Atlantic, and speed was of the essence owing to the approach of a Southern Hemisphere winter; yet within a day of receiving orders to put stores in motion, the war maintenance reserve for 3 **Commando Brigade** consisted of thirty days' stocks of combat supplies at limited war rates and sixty days' stocks of technical and general stores. Thousands of tons of supplies were drawn from major depots throughout the UK and dispatched by road – given British Rail's short-term inability to reposition rolling stock – to Portsmouth, Southampton and elsewhere. Similarly, the **Royal**

Navy and the **Royal Air Force** immediately began to send food, ammunition and stores to wherever required.

Logistical support came in many guises and from many sources, not least the Royal Army Ordnance Corps and the Royal Corps of Transport, which had to draw upon Territorial Army vehicles and drivers, and chartered nearly 100 40ft flat-bed trucks. In the opening days, 39,108 tons of freight were shifted by road and much less by rail. Still, by the second week, with the rail authorities now able to redirect some of their rolling stock, logistic personnel had hired forty-four special trains. Even before the Task Force left the UK, thousands of people collectively put in a prodigious effort at HM Dockyards involving civilian contractors and builders busily converting merchant ships after requisitioning, while Territorial units trucked supplies across the country and British Rail trains moved stores. In the event, with time at a premium, many stores were not packed tactically and would have to be cross-decked and repacked at a later stage, mostly in the safe anchorage off **Ascension** or on the island itself. In the meantime, allocated shipping for the 4,350 men to be carried, plus service transport, could meet most of this need, with 1,700 men, 150 tons of stores and approximately sixty vehicles to be moved later.

The value of Ascension as an essential supporting point for supplying the Task Force was immediately appreciated and the island rapidly became a vital logistic hub, with cargo aircraft requisitioned from civilian firms to speed the movement of supplies. To facilitate transit to the **Total Exclusion Zone**, a tanker supply train was established to resupply the Task Force; **Royal Fleet Auxiliary** tankers carrying fuel and fresh water thus played a vital logistic role in the war.

The logistics plan for landing 3 Commando Brigade at **San Carlos Water** was laid out by Major Gerry Wells-Cole, Deputy Chief of Staff to Brigadier **Thompson**, aboard *Fearless* on 13 May. In the course of those landings, code-named Operation **Sutton** and conducted on 21 May, the **Commando Logistic Regiment** under Colonel Ivar Hellberg established a large Brigade Maintenance Area (BMA) ashore at **Ajax Bay**, which included a massive ammunition dump and a field dressing station, the whole responsible for supporting five major units ashore – two battalions of the **Parachute Regiment** and three commandos of **Royal Marines**, plus ancillary formations.

By the end of the 21st, almost 1,000 tons of supplies had been landed by sea without opposition. In the same period, seven **helicopters** of 846 NAS had lifted tens of thousands of tons of stores and 520 troops – 288 loads in total, shuttled from ship to shore, mostly slung in nets beneath **Sea King** helicopters; and by the evening of the 24th, the beachhead boasted 5,500 British troops safely ashore and a massive stockpile of equipment and stores. However, owing to the strength of Argentine air attacks that day, it was decided to withdraw several of the transport vessels, including the **Landing Ships Logistic** (LSLs), during the night despite their having yet to put ashore all their cargo, thus compromising the carefully planned unloading procedure, with new schedules worked out as circumstances allowed.

As the main logistic hub for Corporate, the BMA in San Carlos Water became the main storage area for aviation fuel, stored in floating rubberised bags moored offshore, with a small pipeline employed for pumping it to a landing area established for **Harriers** and **Sea Harriers** known as 'Sid's Strip' to the RAF and 'HMS Sheathbill' to the Royal Navy. The BMA also served as the point of concentration for the build-up of supplies required to support a break-out from the bridgehead, a process thought likely to take five days.

With troops now ensconced on East Falkland, moving supplies proved extremely problematical, with only a small number of **BV 202E** oversnow vehicles deployed and almost no Land Rovers on the false belief that even these vehicles might experience problems on the boggy ground. With virtually no roads on the island, the helicopter would become the mainstay of the logistic effort on land.

To compound the already enormous strain on the logistic machine, serious problems arose on 25 May with the loss of the container ship *Atlantic Conveyor*, containing ten helicopters – a particularly bitter blow – thus requiring 3 **Para** to **tab** and **45 Commando** to **yomp** considerable distances on foot in the course of the break-out from San Carlos Water that began two days later. Pressure on the logistic chain became all the greater with the unexpectedly high number of Argentine prisoners taken at **Goose Green**, since no supply of spare clothing or shelter existed for them.

After the arrival of **5 Infantry Brigade** in San Carlos Water on 2 June, logistic arrangements came to a near standstill owing to a severe shortage of **landing craft** to unload ships in an otherwise crowded anchorage. Compounding this, as 5 Infantry Brigade contained no counterpart to the Commando Logistic Regiment, Hellberg's formation was called upon to manage this additional burden, with supply lines soon to lengthen even further with the opening of a southern offensive against Stanley and 3 Commando Brigade already on the move. Accordingly, in the first week of June, **Wessex**, Sea Kings and a **Chinook** shifted tons of stores, ammunition and guns to **Teal Inlet** and **Mount Kent** in support of Thompson's northern advance towards Stanley, while to the south problems arose when, for instance, **2 Para** advanced alone to the **Bluff Cove/Fitzroy** area and consequently required reinforcement. Helicopter support for 3 Commando Brigade was duly diverted to the south, leaving Thompson's troops severely short of rations, warm clothing and fresh water; some personnel were deprived of their bergens – containing the men's precious sleeping bags and extra clothing – for nearly five days in sub-zero temperatures.

The movement east of 3 Commando Brigade and 5 Infantry Brigade naturally required the establishment of Forward Administrative Areas, which duly sprang up at Teal Inlet and Fitzroy to meet the needs of these respective formations. LSLs sailed back and forth between San Carlos Water and these points, resupplying ships at sea and the two forward areas. Later, supplies went ashore via landing craft (specifically, LCVPs) and Rigid Raiding Craft. Meanwhile, by air, helicopters moved vast quantities of ammunition, supplies and 105mm guns of the **Royal Artillery**, with the requirement to resupply troops all the greater during the phase of heavy fighting from 11 to 14 June, and to site guns in newly captured positions.

Feeding thousands of troops posed considerable problems, not least owing to the fact that they depended on Arctic ration packs, which required 8 pints of water to reconstitute into consumable form, a circumstance that led to a severe shortage of fresh water. Although water is plentiful on the Falklands, the presence of vast numbers of sheep render it unfit to drink without boiling and sterilisation tablets.

Petrol and diesel were also required in vast amounts, yet in chronic short supply, these fuels being required to satisfy an array of needs: vehicles, small landing craft, battery chargers, oversnow vehicles, **CVR(T)s** and **Rapier** firing posts. Bulk fuel was held in the ten 4-ton Unit Bulk Refuelling Equipment vehicles of Transport Squadron, with each vehicle carrying 3,000 litres.

Although ground units went into action with sufficient rifle and machine gun ammunition, in several instances they found themselves low by morning. Artillery shells were especially in short supply and the means to transport them posed a perennial problem throughout the campaign, not least because of their prodigious weight and rapid rate of expenditure in action. Palleted when transported by helicopter, ammunition represented an impressive burden even in small quantities; thus, a Wessex could carry only twenty-four rounds of 105mm rounds, a Sea King forty-eight, and a Chinook, 192. The lack of artillery ammunition figured as one of the reasons that Major General **Moore** postponed by twenty-four hours 3 Commando Brigade's attack meant to begin on the night of 10 June.

By war's end – quite apart from everything shifted down to the South Atlantic – over 9,000 tons of stocks had been moved within East Falkland alone. Without question, the herculean effort by all those connected with the logistic effort of Operation Corporate represents one of the greatest achievements of the campaign.

Lycaon, MV

One of many **Ships Taken Up From Trade**, *Lycaon* was a motor cargo ship requisitioned from China Mutual Steamship Company on 26 April for use as an ammunition transport vessel. Naval Party 1900 under Lieutenant Commander D.J. Stile RN served aboard her. She departed Southampton on 4 May and reached **South Georgia** on the 28th. Her service in Falklands waters did not begin until 11 June, three days before the end of the fighting, and she arrived in Hull on 21 April 1983.

Commander:	Captain H.R. Lawton	
Launched:	1976	
Tonnage:	11,804 Gross Register	13,450 Deadweight
Dimension: length × beam; feet (metres):	533 × 73 (162.5 × 22.3)	
Propulsion:	1 diesel engine	10,600bhp = 18 knots
Helicopter platform – no embarked aircraft		

Lynx HAS2

The Westland Lynx, the principal workhorse of British **helicopters** in theatre, formed the mainstay of rotary wing aircraft embarked on **destroyers** and **frigates**, with its tasks including anti-submarine warfare (ASW) and operations in the anti-surface, anti-Exocet ESM, reconnaissance and gunship roles.

Carrying a pilot, observer and aircrewman and up to eight passengers, it had twin engines, was capable of operating in practically all weather conditions, and could land on a deck rolling up to 20 degrees. Equipped with Seaspray surface search **radar**, the Lynx supplemented the capabilities of its parent ship. Some of those that served on Operation **Corporate** were fitted with **Sea Skua** anti-ship missiles. In the right hands, this light helicopter could prove extremely manoeuvrable, such as when Lieutenant Chris Clayton in *Cardiff*'s Lynx successfully evaded attacks by two Daggers on 13 June.

Most Type 42 destroyers and frigates embarked a Lynx. Many of their sorties were short, often between ships, but they were numerous: between 1 April and 30 June, *Brilliant*'s two Lynx chalked up 490 flying hours and performed 860 deck landings. 815 NAS supplied all Lynx – twenty-two in all – of which three were lost when the ships on which they were deployed were sunk.

Machine Guns

See Infantry weapons

Maritime Exclusion Zone

See Total Exclusion Zone

Medical Services

As early as 2 April, the day of the Argentine invasion, Northwood mobilised medical staff and ordered their increase, while those in the **logistics** chain packed and dispatched medical war stores. The Royal Naval Hospitals at Haslar and Devonport in particular swung into action to supply these needs to the imminently departing **3 Commando Brigade**, while in due course units of the **Royal Army Medical Corps** (RAMC), largely 16 Field Ambulance, would form part of **5 Infantry Brigade** when the government increased the size of the **Task Force** to include that formation.

During the voyage south, medical personnel trained troops in basic combat life support and battlefield first aid. As a consequence, by the time the men were ashore they possessed considerable knowledge in these subjects, doubtless saving many lives as a result. Staff also provided tutorials on survival in the freezing conditions soon to be faced in the South Atlantic, where hypothermia posed a great threat, as well as advice on measures to avoid trench foot. Blood supplies were augmented by voluntary offerings from troops; aboard *Canberra* alone troops from the **Parachute**

M

A casualty at Bluff Cove taken from a Scout AH1. (AirSeaLand Photos)

Regiment and **Royal Marines** filled 900 half-litre bags. During the same period, Royal Marines Bandsmen were trained as stretcher bearers and helicopter marshals.

To increase patients' chances of survival, it was deemed essential to provide surgical facilities in reasonable proximity to the battle area. With the establishment of the bridgehead at **San Carlos Water** on 21 May, the main medical facility remained afloat initially, medical staff having prepared *Canberra* as a hospital ship to supplement *Uganda*. On that day, for instance, *Canberra* took aboard **casualties**, such as those from *Ardent*, with the use of her **Wessex**, while others arrived care of the **Sea Kings** of 846 NAS. In the course of the war medical staff aboard the converted passenger ship would treat 174 patients, eighty-two British and ninety-two Argentine, all of whom survived. However, when air superiority was not achieved by the time of the landings on 21 May, for her protection *Canberra* was moved out of San Carlos Water during the pre-dawn hours of the 22nd and plans were rapidly devised for a large medical facility ashore.

Surgeon Commander Rick Jolly, a Royal Marines doctor who commanded the Medical Squadron of 3 Commando Brigade, accordingly established the main field dressing station at the disused refrigeration plant at **Ajax Bay**, with generators suppling light and heat to the facility, outside of which hung a sign reading 'Welcome to the Red and Green Life Machine' to signify the joint efforts of the commando and Para doctors and staff, who co-operated well, with mutual respect and a dedication to a common purpose.

The first casualties arrived with the attacks on *Coventry*, *Ardent*, *Antelope* and *Atlantic Conveyor*, many with burns and often suffering from exposure after being plucked from the freezing water. Large numbers of wounded Paras also arrived as a consequence of their attack on **Goose Green** on 28 May. Work carried on at Ajax Bay despite the air attack on 27 May that left two unexploded bombs in the medical facility, one in the pipework and the other in the ceiling. It was a great testament to soldiers' battlefield first aid training and the skilfulness of medical staff at Ajax Bay that not a single casualty who arrived alive ever died while receiving care there.

SS *Uganda*, a P&O Liner, had been converted to a hospital ship, with Queen Alexandra's Royal Naval Nursing Service providing some of the staff. For most of the conflict *Uganda* remained confined to the **Red Cross Box** – a protected zone for the medical teams of both belligerents into which helicopters flying casevac missions brought the wounded and sick, but she would anchor in **Berkeley Sound** each morning at dawn to receive new patients. Three survey vessels were used as ambulance vessels: *Hecla*, *Herald* and *Hydra*. All of these ships made the four-day journey to Montevideo to offload casualties for repatriation to the UK. *Hecla*, for instance, arrived on 2 June, with her load of British wounded transferred to a **VC10** C1 for onward movement to RAF Brize Norton. Several such repatriation flights took place during the conflict aboard aircraft specially painted with Red Cross markings.

Men of Naval Party 8901, reconstituted as J Company 42 Commando, raise the Falklands flag at Government House, 14 June. (IWM 2049)

Ground crew service a Royal Navy Sea King in the snow-covered mountains around Stanley. (IWM 2097)

Heavily laden Royal Marines of 45 Commando, each carrying in excess of 120lb, enter Stanley on 14 June. (IWM 2040)

45 Commando march towards Stanley on the final day of the war. (IWM 2028)

Two Sea Harrier FRS1s of 801 Naval Air Squadron in flight. (IWM 2102)

Brigadier Julian Thompson, Commander of 3 Commando Brigade (left), Major General Jeremy Moore, overall commander of British forces on the Falklands (centre) and Colonel Brian Pennicott, Commander, Royal Artillery, at an impromptu open-air meeting. (IWM 1288)

A Royal Navy Wessex HU5 delivers mortar ammunition to the front line just west of Stanley during the final phase of the war. (IWM 117)

Men of 5 Infantry Brigade silhouetted at dusk during the landings at San Carlos on 2 June. (IWM 349)

Royal Marines of HQ Company 45 Commando cross a muddy field after leaving Teal Inlet on the last leg of their yomp to the foot of Mount Kent. (IWM 2270)

The sinking of HMS *Antelope* in San Carlos Water. The explosion of the second Argentine 1,000lb bomb on board the ship broke its back and caused the frigate to sink. Two bomb disposal officers had been attempting to defuse the bomb at the time. (IWM 1241)

3 Para disembark from a landing craft at San Carlos, 21 May. (© Graham Colbeck (IWM 2744))

Aerial view of San Carlos Water showing merchant shipping at anchor. (IWM 1218)

Chinook HC1 (ZA718), call sign 'Bravo November' of 18 Squadron RAF, flown by Squadron Leader Dick Langworthy, at Teal Inlet, shortly before transporting an Argentine prisoner back to Brigade HQ on 29 May. (© Graham Colbeck (IWM FKD 2753))

Chinook HC1 with call sign 'Bravo November' brings supplies to Fitzroy at sunset. Bravo November played a key role in the taking of Fitzroy settlement, transporting 156 men of 2 Para from Goose Green. (IWM FKD 357)

Lieutenant Commander Dante Camilette, an Argentine marine, taken prisoner on 27 May having been discovered observing British warship movements from a concealed position above San Carlos Water. (IWM FKD 2024)

A Royal Navy Sea Harrier comes in to land on HMS *Hermes* at sunset. (IWM FKD 2375)

The ice patrol ship HMS *Endurance* at Cumberland Bay, South Georgia. (IWM FKD 748)

The Cunard passenger liner *Queen Elizabeth 2* lies in the mist off Grytviken, South Georgia, with a converted trawler minesweeper alongside. *QE2* cross-decked 3,300 troops from 5 Infantry Brigade onto SS *Canberra* and MV *Norland* on 27 May for transport from South Georgia to San Carlos Water. (IWM FKD 342)

The P&O liner *Canberra* during the transfer of 5 Infantry Brigade from the Cunard liner *Queen Elizabeth 2* at Grytviken, South Georgia. The effects of the South Atlantic weather on *Canberra* are clearly visible. (IWM FKD 340)

Mount Longdon after the battle. Sergeant Chris Howard inspects a sangar containing three Argentine dead. (IWM FKD 2772)

Aerial view of RAF aircraft lined up on the apron at Wideawake Airfield, Ascension. Four Nimrod aircraft sit in the foreground with Victor tankers in the background. (IWM FKD 1170)

With the movement of 3 Commando Brigade east while the Main Dressing Station remained at Ajax Bay, a forward Brigade Maintenance Area was established at **Teal Inlet**, including an Advanced Dressing Station staffed by 1 Field Surgical Team, with the same facilities, including a surgical unit, constructed at **Fitzroy** on 5 June with staff supplied by 6 Field Ambulance RAMC. The medical services found themselves under particular pressure as large numbers of casualties arrived at dressing stations and aboard hospital ships as a result of the attacks on *Sir Galahad* and *Sir Tristram* on 8 June at **Port Pleasant**, with many of the wounded suffering from severe burns and in most cases initially treated at the medical facility at Fitzroy. Within a few days to these were added the wounded resulting from the simultaneous attacks launched against **Mount Longdon**, **Mount Harriet** and **Two Sisters** on the night of 11–12 June. After **Mount Tumbledown**, many **Scots Guards** casualties were flown by Sea King to the **aircraft carriers** for medical attention, while medical evacuees from the fighting on **Wireless Ridge**, fought simultaneously, were initially flown by **Scout** for treatment at Fitzroy.

In the course of the conflict over 1,000 casualties were received in the Main Dressing Station and the forward stations at Teal and Fitzroy, about two-thirds of which constituted wounds sustained in combat, and of whom only three subsequently died. In the course of the war staff at Ajax Bay performed 202 major operations, with a further 108 between Teal, Fitzroy and aboard *Uganda*, with almost a third of all patients being Argentine.

Apart from battlefield wounds, illness and injury arose from a variety of sources. Although plentiful on the Falklands, the water was unsafe to drink and had to be boiled and sterilised, barring which soldiers often contracted diarrhoea. Trench foot and other foot ailments plagued large numbers of the troops equipped with the Direct-Moulded Sole (DMS) boot, notoriously prone to absorbing and retaining water. Unlike many of their colleagues in 3 Commando Brigade, the men of 5 Infantry Brigade wore overboots, which protected them from trench foot. Cold-weather injuries were common owing to the cold and constant damp, wet clothing and feet. Abrasions and blisters impeded movement and sometimes led to trench foot. Drying and powdering the feet paid dividends, but conditions often made this impossible. Sickness rates rose as a consequence of exposure and hypothermia.

Mexeflote

A three-part (bow, centre and stern), multi-purpose pontoon specifically designed for saltwater operations and used as a raft or joined together to form jetties, causeways and breakwaters. Each Mexeflote had its own specialised diesel engine. They were operated by 17 Port Regiment, Royal Corps of Transport. The six **Landing Ships Logistic** (LSLs) each carried two Mexeflotes, which greatly aided the **logistics** effort.

MILAN

See Infantry weapons

Minerva, HMS

One of fifteen **frigates** in the South Atlantic, but the only one of three of the Batch 2 Leander class of this type of vessel, the others being *Argonaut* and *Penelope*. She departed Devonport on 10 May and reached **Ascension** eight days later. Appearing in Falklands waters on 26 May, it was *Minerva*, stationed in **San Carlos Water**, which on 1 June detected the reconnaissance flight of an Argentine C-130E Hercules north of **Pebble Island**, so triggering the response by two **Sea Harriers**, which shot the transport aircraft down. *Minerva* arrived back in Devonport on 3 August.

Commander:	Commander S.H.G. Johnston	
Builders:	Vickers-Armstrong	
Launched:	19 December 1964	
Commissioned:	14 May 1966	
Displacement (tons):	2,650 Standard	3,200 Full load
Dimensions: length × beam; feet (metres):	372 × 41 (113.4 × 12.5)	
Draught:	5.8m	
Propulsion:	2 sets geared steam turbines	30,000shp = 28 knots
Armament:	2 × 40mm Bofors AA guns	
	3 × **Seacat** systems (GWS 22)	
	4 × MM.38 **Exocet**	
	2 × triple Mark 32 ASW torpedo tubes (STWS)	
Aircraft:	1 × **Lynx** HAS2	

Mines and Minefields

See Royal Engineers

Minesweepers

The **Royal Navy** took up from trade and commissioned five fishing trawlers and converted them to minesweeping vessels with Royal Navy crews: *Cordella*, *Farnella*, *Northella*, *Junella* and *Pict*. These vessels therefore constituted the only **Ships Taken Up From Trade** to fly the White Ensign. HMS *Ledbury* and HMS *Brecon*, both Hunt class minesweepers, did not arrive off the Falklands until 10 July. HMS *Farnella*, a motor freezer trawler requisitioned and converted as a minesweeper, did not arrive in the Falklands until 21 June.

In the event, the Argentines laid few mines at sea – quite in contrast to those they sowed on East Falkland, but minesweeping remained a necessary prerequisite to laying plans for selecting the main landing site. An area off Cape Pembroke at the eastern end of East Falkland close to Stanley appeared to be the only area sewn with mines and these were partly cleared after the war, the remainder by Royal Navy mine hunters.

The 'Ellas' (i.e. minesweepers whose names ended thus) departed from the UK on 27 April as the 11th Minesweeping Squadron, joined later by the *Pict*, stopping at **Ascension** before proceeding to **South Georgia**. In both locations they served as dispatch vessels, cross-loading troops and stores between ships at anchor. From 1 May they inserted **Special Air Service** and **Special Boat Squadron** patrols nocturnally on the Falklands and were present in Falkland Sound during the landings on 21 May, on hand to sweep for mines if required.

Monsunen, MV

A 230-ton merchant coastal freighter built in 1957 and owned by the Falkland Islands Company. Abandoned off Lively Island, the Argentines requisitioned and employed her to ferry supplies. On 23 May, the **frigates** *Yarmouth* and *Brilliant* pursued her off the south coast of East Falkland, firing star shells and forcing her to run aground in Lively Sound, from whence a party from *Fearless* refloated her with the assistance of a local diver, and towed her into **Darwin** on the 23rd. Initially Major Robert Satchell, the senior Engineer staff officer under Brigadier **Wilson**, had charge of the vessel, but anxious that the Navy rather than the Army retain control of her, he appointed a small crew consisting of Lieutenant Ian McLaren and three naval ratings from *Fearless*, and designated Naval Party 2160, answerable directly to Commodore Clapp and with instructions only to sail in darkness.

At about 0200Z on 8 June, B Troop, Royal Signals embarked from **Goose Green** on the *Monsunen* for a night passage to **Fitzroy**, where it set up HQ **5 Infantry Brigade**. D Company 1/7th **Gurkha Rifles** was also aboard, plus a handful of **2 Para** who had remained behind at Goose Green while the rest of the battalion had moved forward to the **Port Pleasant** area. All told, about 200 troops were aboard, with a voyage of four hours to Fitzroy. *Monsunen* also had orders to locate the abandoned **landing craft**, Foxtrot Four, struck by a Skyhawk earlier that day. This was discovered drifting off Lively Island, but the trailing rope became entangled in *Monsunen's* propeller, requiring divers from *Yarmouth* to assist. *Monsunen* was then ordered back to Goose Green, from whence the Gurkhas were flown to Fitzroy by the sole-surviving **Chinook** in theatre.

Tonnage:	230 Gross Register	240 Deadweight
Dimensions: length × beam; feet (metres):	139 × 21 (42.3 × 6.5)	
Propulsion:	1 diesel engine	240bhp = 8.5 knots

Moody Brook Barracks

Residence of **Naval Party 8901** assigned to the Falklands. On the morning of the Argentine invasion on 2 April the structure stood empty while Major Mike Norman's men put up what resistance they could muster in and around **Stanley** against the overwhelming numbers of invaders. Unaware that Moody Brook Barracks stood unoccupied, at 0600Z Argentine forces riddled them with small arms- and machine-gun fire and grenades.

On the evening of 9 May, *Coventry* and *Broadsword*, situated more than 30 miles to the north-east of Stanley, bombarded various targets in and around the capital, including Moody Brook Barracks, where the Argentines had established a temporary helicopter base after the British attack on their previous position near **Mount Kent**.

On the afternoon of 10 June, two **Harriers** dropped cluster bombs on positions around Moody Brook based on **photographic reconnaissance** collected earlier that day. At about 1830Z on 13 June two Harriers dropped cluster bombs on a 105mm gun position near the barracks.

Moore, Major General John Jeremy, RM

Commander, Land Forces Falkland Islands (CLFFI), with overall responsibility for **3 Commando Brigade** and **5 Infantry Brigade**, Moore was born on 5 July 1928 into a military family and educated at Cheltenham College. He joined the **Royal Marines**, serving with **40 Commando** in Malaya during the communist insurgency there, earning the MC in 1952 for distinguished service. He held various training appointments thereafter and became a company commander in **42 Commando** in 1962 during the Brunei revolt, rescuing hostages from the rebels. In 1964 he graduated from the Australian Army Staff College and served on the staff of a Gurkha division then involved in the confrontation with Indonesia on Borneo.

Moore later served at the Ministry of Defence in London, thereafter commanding 42 Commando on two tours of Northern Ireland in 1972–73, including Operation Motorman, which saw the destruction of the IRA's attempts to enforce no-go areas in cities across Ulster, with distinguished command of 42 Commando leading to the award of an OBE. After serving as commandant of the Royal Marines School of Music – despite his own admission of having no musical talent whatsoever – Moore was appointed to command 3 Commando Brigade, at which post he increased the Royal Marines' responsibility for defence of the northern flank of NATO from a commando group to a full brigade. On promotion to major general in August 1979 he was appointed to command Commando Forces, with HQ at Plymouth.

Major General Moore proudly displays the Argentine instrument of surrender. (AirSeaLand Photos)

At the outbreak of hostilities Moore was actually on the point retiring from service with the Royal Marines, having taken temporary command from the Commandant General, Lieutenant General Sir Steuart Pringle, who had been on leave convalescing from an IRA bomb attack that cost him his leg. As Moore was also still in command of Commando Forces the time of the Argentine invasion, he appointed Commander, Land Forces Falkland Islands on 20 May. In short, the decision at Northwood to include 5 Infantry Brigade, under Brigadier **Wilson**, with its own brigade headquarters, in the **Task Force** along with 3 Commando Brigade, necessitated the creation of a divisional headquarters, and the appointment of a divisional commander above Brigadier Julian **Thompson** RM in the form of Moore.

Moore flew to **Ascension** and travelled south from there aboard *Queen Elizabeth 2*, together with Wilson, and cross-decked to *Antrim* at **South Georgia**. On 27 May *Fearless* left **San Carlos Water** to rendezvous with *Antrim* and collect Moore, Wilson and their respective staffs. *Fearless* re-entered **San Carlos Water** on 30 May, although Moore and his HQ staff remained aboard until a Tactical HQ went ashore on 10 June. Moore was therefore not in theatre during the amphibious landings on 21 May or off the Falklands at the time of the Battle of **Goose Green** on the 28th, and thus found himself, owing to faulty communications aboard *QE2*, unaware of the orders sent to 3 Commando Brigade during his ten days *incommunicado*. By that time, moreover, Thompson's axis of advance had already been decided – although Moore approved of the plan.

Upon arriving in theatre, Moore assumed command of all ground forces, but so as not to betray preference between the Army and the Royal Marines, he wore a Norwegian summer cap (issued to all the winter-trained personnel in 3 Commando Brigade for wear in Norway) in theatre instead of a green beret. His reports back to Northwood were optimistic in tone, consistent with his belief that while they should reflect the truth, they must also meet government (and public) expectations of regular progress.

Moore believed in the principle of mission command – explaining to his subordinates his intent and leaving them to achieve the stated objective as they saw fit. His strategy involved 3 Commando Brigade operating in the north against **Mount Longdon** – with possible exploitation to **Wireless Ridge** – and separate but simultaneous assaults against **Two Sisters** and **Mount Harriet**, followed by a 5 Infantry Brigade attack on **Mount Tumbledown** and **Mount William**, with a follow-up on to **Sapper Hill**. The start of this offensive began on the night of 11–12 June, with the second phase on 13–14 June, all leading to the surrender of Argentine forces on the 14th according to terms negotiated by Moore.

After the war he served briefly as Director General of the Food and Drink Federation, thereafter lecturing, pursuing consultancy work and holding three non-executive directorships. Moore died on 15 September 2007.

Mountain and Arctic Warfare Cadre

Commanded by Captain Rod Boswell RM and composed of specially trained **Royal Marines** skilled in mountain and winter warfare, survival, long-range reconnaissance and cliff-climbing techniques, all in adverse conditions as their name implies. As such, they were eminently suited to service in the Falklands. Based in Plymouth, the M & AWC served as the recce troop for **3 Commando Brigade** and performed a vital role in operating in areas beyond those normally patrolled by Royal Marines reconnaissance troops, or even of forward patrols of the **Special Air Service** and **Special Boat Squadron**. With long experience of training on the NATO northern flank in Norway, the men of the M & AWC possessed the right weapons, clothing and equipment and mindset for the South Atlantic environment. As well as conducting numerous patrols ahead of 3 Commando Brigade's move east, the M & AWC fought at **Top Malo House** on 31 May, the only action against Argentine Special Forces conducted in daylight.

On 2 June, a patrol from the M&AWC on **Smoko Mount** spotted and reported the **Chinook** carrying elements of **2 Para** from **Goose Green** to the **Fitzroy** area. Heavy mist nearly resulted in a **'Blue on Blue'**, or 'friendly fire', artillery fire mission.

Mount Challenger

An 800ft position near **Mount Kent** and about 12 miles west of **Stanley**, first occupied by a detachment from D Squadron 22 **Special Air Service** on the night of 27 May, and then again in strength three days later by L Company **42 Commando** and a party of sappers. From there they established an observation post on **Mount Wall**.

Mount Harriet

This 800ft position 6 miles from **Stanley** became a focus of attention when on 9 June Major General **Moore** issued operational orders for **3 Commando Brigade** to attack towards Stanley in three phases, to include an assault on **Mount Harriet** during Phase One. The following day, **Thompson** tasked **42 Commando** with this objective, with elements of the **Welsh Guards** in reserve, and with the possibility of supporting **45 Commando** should that unit succeed at **Two Sisters** and proceed against **Mount Tumbledown**.

Preparations for the assault on Mount Harriet began when 42 Commando, commanded by Lieutenant Colonel Nick Vaux, arrived on **Mount Kent** on 31 May and began to patrol the surrounding eminences: **Mount Challenger**, **Mount Wall**, **Goat Ridge** and, finally, Mount Harriet. With winter now reaching its height, temperatures continued to fall, but 42 Commando enjoyed the advantage of two weeks with which to conduct reconnaissance, identify Argentine positions and minefields, and formulate plans for the best route of attack. **Patrolling** produced extremely valuable intelligence over successive nights, some featuring brief clashes with hostile patrols, enabling Vaux to establish an excellent understanding of Argentine positions on and around Harriet, held by B Company, 4th Infantry Regiment, sections from the 1st Cavalry Regiment, 3rd Infantry Brigade Defence Platoon and a platoon from Combat Team Solari.

M

Royal Marines near Mount Harriet. (AirSeaLand Photos)

At the same time, Forward Artillery Observers benefited from the many days' relative quiet prior to the battle to establish accurate ranges for their guns and to calculate the precise angles of fire necessary to clear that feature's crest lines. Vaux had three companies at his disposal: M Company, which had served in the operation to recapture **South Georgia**, had remained behind to secure the island, but J Company – comprising the Marines of **Naval Party 8901** captured but subsequently released by the Argentines – served in its place, together with K and L Companies.

Mount Harriet stood just north of the track connecting Stanley with **Fitzroy** (from which it continued on to **Goose Green**) and was well protected by minefields – nine in total – largely confined to its western and southern approaches, which the Argentines logically expected to be the most likely direction of attack. Just half a mile to the north lay Goat Ridge, a long and slender eminence also identified as one of 42 Commando's objectives, and designated as the unit's left flank boundary, meant to separate it from the area of responsibility assigned to 45 Commando, with its simultaneously planned attack on **Two Sisters**, immediately to the north. Given the risk posed by fire inadvertently issued by 45 Commando or deliberately by the defenders on Two Sisters, Vaux deemed it prudent not to attack Mount Harriet from the north, especially with darkness rendering unit identification effectively impossible. Nor did an approach from the west, even under cover of darkness, appeal, for this would require crossing 2,000yd of exposed ground, heavily laced with mines.

These constraints consequently left Vaux with the difficult but certainly best option: seeking to achieve the element of surprise by conducting a long march to the south of Harriet, bypassing a small lake and the minefields there before assaulting the position from the rear; specifically, from the south-east, with K Company in the lead. This manoeuvre depended upon very accurate intelligence gleaned from patrolling, thus facilitating correct route marking and the establishment of a secure start line.

The Welsh Guards were to play a small part in the coming battle as well. On the afternoon of 11 June, two of its companies still operational after the disaster at Fitzroy moved to a position to the south of Mount Harriet where they could protect 42 Commando's right flank. Their Recce Platoon then proceeded east across open ground to 42 Commando's forming up place, but doing so in clear view of the Argentines attracted artillery fire and threatened to unhinge Vaux's plan to concentrate Argentine attention on Mount Challenger; that is, to the immediate west of Harriet, and thus facilitate an undisturbed southern approach skirting the minefields south of Harriet.

42 Commando assembled in the small gap between Mount Challenger and Mount Wall, about 3 miles from their start line. J Company had established its mortars on Mount Wall, code-named 'Tara' (one of Vaux's daughters). Mount Harriet itself was nicknamed 'Zoya', after Vaux's wife, and Goat Ridge as 'Katrina', his other daughter. While **Mount Longdon** and Two Sisters were to be 'silent' attacks, i.e. no preparatory bombardment from artillery or naval guns, 42 Commando's assault would be 'noisy'

as laid down in Vaux's deception plan involving a pre-assault artillery barrage on Harriet and machine-gun and mortar fire from J Company's position in front of Mount Wall. This was intended to persuade the defenders that the attack would come from the west. K Company would seize the eastern summit while L Company would take the western one. Should 45 Commando capture Two Sisters rapidly with the intention of proceeding with an attack on Mount Tumbledown, L Company was then to exploit to Goat Ridge. Vaux could call for fire from HMS *Yarmouth* and 7 (Kirkee) Commando Battery, **Royal Artillery** while 2 Troop, 59 Commando Squadron **Royal Engineers**, stood ready to offer direct support. A single air attack was launched in preparation for the ground assault: at 1450Z on 11 June two **Harrier** GR3s took off from *Hermes* and dropped a cluster bomb unit on Argentine positions on Mount Harriet.

With dusk descending, at 2015Z, K Company descended Mount Challenger and proceeded across the 8 miles of ground to Harriet, with a Troop of Royal Engineers to guide them through the first minefield, crossed the Stanley–Fitzroy track and formed up north of the road near a lake. At approximately 2130Z, L Company set off from the forming-up position, with the shelling of Harriet by 7 Commando Battery now under way. The Welsh Guards Recce Platoon was meant to have secured the start line at about 0230Z on the 12th, but when communications broke down between it and 42 Commando they failed to locate one another in the dark, setting back the timing of the attack by an hour, by which time the moon had appeared, denying the attackers some of the advantage of concealment that they desired. By this time the attacks on Longdon and Two Sisters had already begun. When at last the two met at the start line, K Company crossed it at 0200Z, as *Yarmouth* began her bombardment of Harriet. Meanwhile, L Company had lost its way, but believed itself capable of reaching the start line on time. On Mount Wall, the diversion started by 9 Troop attracted machine-gun fire from the Argentines to the east, while mortars and MILAN struck 'Zoya'.

About half an hour after leaving the start line, K Company, still unseen in the darkness after crossing 700yd, began to enter Argentine positions at the eastern end of Harriet, encountering defenders almost immediately and soon coming under mortar fire. Although the appearance of the commandos took them by surprise, the Argentines offered serious resistance as Captain Peter Babbington's men proceeded to clear bunkers and trenches along the lower eastern sections of Harriet, overrunning the Argentine mortar platoon position. As they penetrated further, two troops of K Company became intermingled and, in places, pinned down by growing resistance from snipers and machine guns. Employing rifle, bayonet and grenade, the men of K Company eventually prevailed and the eastern end of Harriet fell into their hands as Argentine artillery fire rained down on them.

L Company, meanwhile, crossed the start line at 0300Z on the 12th, with, as a result of the artillery fire, the Argentines fully vigilant to repel an attack from the south, the company's direction of approach. Crossing 600yd of unobscured ground sown with mines, L Company received heavy fire from troops defending the central southern slopes within the first minute or two of advance. MILAN fire cleared several machine gun positions, but such were the difficulties involved in operating in the confines of the rocks that the fighting became a business of troop and section, several hours passing until L Company finally reached its objective at the western end of the mountain. At 0600Z Vaux then altered his plan, ordering L Company to seize Goat Ridge, which the Argentines soon abandoned after artillery began to descend on their position, though sporadic fighting carried on until after 0700Z against isolated positions and snipers.

The Argentines on Mount Harriet suffered ten killed and approximately fifty-three wounded, plus about 300 lost as prisoners. The rest escaped to the temporary protection of Tumbledown. Royal Marines losses amounted to only two killed and thirteen wounded. With dawn close but darkness still reigning, Vaux contacted Brigadier **Thompson** by radio, requesting permission to exploit to Tumbledown; this was refused on account of low stocks of ammunition for the guns and the fact that the assaults on Longdon and Two Sisters were still under way. The capture of Mount Harriet, together with Mount Longdon and Two Sisters, signified the fall of the Argentines' Outer Defence Zone and demonstrated the utility of highly trained, highly motivated and physically fit troops expected to operate at night in winter conditions.

Mount Kent

An elevated, strategically important feature approximately 10 miles west of **Stanley**. Lightly defended by the Argentines, its seizure by British forces held the key to opening the way to Stanley as a staging post for offensives against more heavily defended positions nearby. It provided an excellent observation point from which to monitor Argentine activity and study their fixed positions near the capital. British occupation of Mount Kent would deny the Argentines a valuable position between the northern and southern routes of the intended British advance.

On the night of 24–25 May, Major Cedric Delves and 3 **Special Air Service** troopers recced Mount Kent with the expectation of the rest of the squadron arriving within twenty-four hours. An 846 NAS **Sea King** inserted an SAS team on Mount Kent in the early hours of the 27th, but owing to severe weather it had to be extracted shortly thereafter. Success was achieved on the night of the 27th, when practically the whole of D Squadron arrived on Mount Kent and **Mount Challenger**, thus laying the groundwork for reinforcement from **42 Commando**.

Brigadier **Thompson** accordingly ordered 42 Commando to produce accordingly. Arriving by helicopter, K Company (Captain Peter Babbington), had orders to seize the summit, with L Company (Captain David Wheen), a 7 (Sphinx) Commando Battery section, mortar platoon and a **Blowpipe** section to reinforce them from a second helicopter. In the event, K Company left after dark on the 28th in four

846 NAS Sea Kings, but was forced to turn back to **San Carlos** owing to near zero visibility in heavy snow showers.

K Company arrived on the night of 29 May, around the time of another clash between the SAS and an Argentine patrol. L Company followed, with the remainder of 42 Commando following over the next two nights, together with engineers and the rest of the battery. The Argentines withdrew from the position on the 30th, leaving the British in a good position overlooking Stanley and a base from which to strike at **Mount Longdon, Mount Harriet** and **Two Sisters**. On the 30th the troops were supplemented by three 105mm field guns brought in by the **Chinook** HC1 of 18 Squadron.

By 5 June, artillery ammunition was being shifted by Chinook to existing gun positions on Mount Kent to support the coming attacks, and two days later **3 Commando Brigade** established its HQ on the west side of the feature. On the 10th, Thompson issued his orders for his part in Major General **Moore's** three-phase attack against Stanley.

Mount Kent featured on a number of occasions in the air campaign, beginning on the first day, 1 May, when an air raid executed against a temporary Argentine helicopter base nearby damaged one machine; just before dawn on 21 May, **Harriers** of 1 Squadron attacked Argentine Army helicopters sited at a forward operating base just north of Mount Kent, damaging and destroying several of them; at dawn on 10 June, three Pucaras attacked artillery positions on the slopes of Mount Kent and at Murrell Bridge; and at 1515Z on 13 June three Skyhawks dropped bombs on the lower slopes of Mount Kent, narrowly missing HQ 3 Commando Brigade containing Moore and Thompson.

Mount Longdon

Only 5 miles north-west of **Stanley** and the site of a major ground engagement conducted by **3 Para** on 11–12 June, Mount Longdon had been an objective in the strategic plans of Brigadier **Thompson** as early as May owing to the requirement to avoid, at minimum, enfilading fire against his right flank from the south or, worse still, an Argentine flanking counter-attack.

As part of the break-out from **San Carlos Water**, 3 Para conducted a long **tab** beginning on 27 May, which by the 31st brought it to Estancia House, from where it began also to occupy both Mounts Estancia and Vernet on 2 June in preparation for an attack on Mount Longdon. From there 3 Para possessed a dominating view of Stanley from observation posts, while patrols sent out regularly collected intelligence about Argentine strength and dispositions.

Overanxious to make contact with the Argentines, 3 Para moved east on 2 June, only to be ordered back by Thompson, who reminded Lieutenant Colonel Hew Pike that the plan envisioned a co-ordinated brigade attack to include **Mount Harriet**

Soldiers of 3 Para after their struggle for Mount Longdon of 11–12 June. (AirSeaLand Photos)

and **Two Sisters**. The battalion dispatched patrols from its defensive position west of Murrell Bridge, one of which ambushed an Argentine counterpart on the morning of 6 June, but had to withdraw under heavy mortar and machine-gun fire. With a week to collect information, those planning the assault on Longdon acquired a fairly clear understanding of the ground to be covered and of the forces opposing them.

For the attack on Longdon, Thompson decided on a night assault – a sensible decision based on a number of considerations. He knew the Argentines controlled all the prominent positions covering the western approaches to Stanley, and appreciated that each could provide mutual support to the others, often with flanking fire. The ground over which his forces had to move was invariably open, highly exposed and easy to defend. It was impossible to be certain of the level of resistance to be encountered, but regular units of the Argentine Army were known to be in the area and even if some of the conscripts could not withstand a determined attack, Thompson had to be careful not to assume a victory would come as quickly as it had at **Goose Green**. Still, 3 Para was experienced in night fighting and exceptionally well motivated.

The axis of attack against Longdon was necessarily restricted by several factors: a large minefield south of the position that protected the western approach to Stanley; the narrow frontage of the ridge that could only accommodate a single infantry company attack; and the Argentine occupation of nearby **Wireless Ridge**. Pike sought both to capture Longdon and to advance as far east as he could.

He had the following fire support at his disposal: the 4.5in main armament of the frigate *Avenger* and the guns of 79 (Kirkee) Commando Battery. As the Wombats were still aboard ship, the Wombat platoon was broken up into General Purpose Machine Gun (GPMG) support groups assigned to each rifle company. D Company provided six sustained-fire GPMGs and one Light Machine Gun (LMG), and five MILAN posts, with personnel drawn from various supporting corps serving as stretcher-bearers and ammunition porters. He also had five **BV 202Es**, three requisitioned tractors and trailers and four civilian Land Rovers to carry the mortar platoon, part of the regimental aid post, a section of **Royal Engineers** and a **Blowpipe** section.

Ten hours were available for Pike's troops to reach their objectives, and full use of the time available was necessary given the inherent difficulties of moving and fighting over broken ground, which always slowed the advance and usually increased the casualty rate. He therefore determined that the attacks should be conducted in silence without supporting artillery fire, thus preserving, if possible, the element of surprise. Any opponents unfamiliar with fighting at night would be bewildered and less effective and this would be to the attackers' advantage. From approximately 0015Z on the 12th, the moonlit night would provide at least a silhouette of the elevated ground, so offering a modicum of direction as 3 Para advanced. Moreover, the attack would be aided by guns of the **Royal Artillery**, which had 11,000 shells at its disposal, as well as **naval gunfire support**, consisting of up to 1,400 rounds to be directed by forward observers. **Harriers** could supply close air support as soon as dawn emerged.

Longdon consisted of a long ridge running east to west, with open ground leading up to it from all directions for more than 1,000yd. Minefields, discovered by patrols, lay on the southern flank and reports indicated that the Argentines were well dug in on Wireless Ridge, about 1,000yd to the east. Pike had effectively no option but to attack west to east, so avoiding accidental contact with **45 Commando** to his right and probably enabling him to isolate defenders on the western end of the ridge from any potential support from the eastern end. 3 Para proceeded just after nightfall, around 2000Z. This gave it four hours of movement before the moon rose, providing it with some cover of darkness during its approach to the line of departure, which consisted of a small stream running north–south and therefore perpendicular to the line of attack.

Pike devised a simple plan of attack: two companies forward to be pitted against what he anticipated to be elements of 601 Marine Company, a well-trained and disciplined unit, and B Company of 7th Regiment – consisting of 287 men, supported by three 105mm guns at **Moody Brook** and at least one 155mm on **Sapper Hill**. Some of the Argentines were equipped with night sights with sufficient intensity to provide a near-daylight view. This, combined with the open ground extending over half a mile from the base of Longdon, offered the defenders an exceptionally good position and offered no option to 3 Para but to cross this expanse before ascending slopes that rose several hundred feet. According to Pike's plan, B Company would lead the attack by moving straight along the ridge bearing the nickname 'Fly Half' with its objective the 500ft eastern spur known as 'Full Back'. At the same time, A Company, to the left, would advance up the northern spur known as 'Wing Forward'. Once these objectives fell, C Company, still positioned on the start line with the battalion's 81mm mortars, would proceed to capture Wireless Ridge, which lay 1,000yd further east, since Thompson desired that attacking units meeting with success should exploit and continue their advance, thus adhering to the doctrine of maintaining the momentum of attack.

The attack got under way fifteen minutes late at 0015Z because of problems in crossing the Murrell River and the absence of 5 and 6 Platoons, which got temporarily lost in the total darkness. But the advance proceeded well, with the Paras moving quietly up the slope. The light of the moon soon illuminated the summit and the heights before them, with silence reigning for the moment. When, however, the two platoons were within 500yd of the formation, Corporal Ian Milne trod on a mine, ending the silent attack and resulting in a barrage of fire from the defenders.

The Argentines responded quickly with artillery fire, but by 0330Z B Company had occupied the western end of Longdon with minimal resistance in that sector, with many defenders caught completely by surprise. Yet if B Company found the assault against the western end of Longdon much less arduous an affair than expected, they received a much hotter reception on the lower eastern end, where a 105mm gun and heavy machine guns forced the foremost attackers to ground. 4 Platoon cleared an Argentine position and took its gun, but elements of 4 and 5 Platoons became pinned down when they attempted to capture another machine gun and were forced to withdraw. Supporting fire directed in by a forward observer rained down on the defenders, and B Company's commander, Major Mike Argue, halted the attack to consolidate his position.

Meanwhile, A Company had proceeded to the left and made its way to the crest of the northern spur, there to find itself under heavy fire from the same defenders blocking B Company's advance. The Argentines had positioned themselves well, holding points on the reverse slope and supported by well-directed artillery fire. A Company then pressed through B Company's positions on Fly Half and proceeded towards Full Back with supporting mortar, artillery and machine-gun fire. 1 and 2 Platoons spearheaded the attack, clearing the ridge by ejecting the defenders from their trenches and sangars with small arms fire, bayonets and grenades, taking prisoners as they advanced towards the eastern end.

The men advanced without their webbing, moving at the crawl and carrying only their SLRs, grenades, ammunition for their rifles, and ammunition for the machine guns where possible. Working in pairs, one advancing and the other offering covering fire, they systematically cleared positions, directing machine-gun fire as they slowly advanced among the rocks. When about 100yd had been cleared, 3 Platoon then advanced through the other two platoons to establish itself on the slope, which extended in the direction of Wireless Ridge slightly to the south-east.

At about 1028Z, dawn broke just after the conclusion of the fighting, which had raged for eight hours. Wireless Ridge was beyond the means of 3 Para, for daylight rendered further movement too hazardous, particularly with Tumbledown, immediately to the south, still in the hands of troops capable of offering enfilading fire. Instead, exhausted by their efforts, the Paras dug in on the reverse slopes north-west of Longdon in expectation of a response from Argentine artillery. The rocky outcrops made digging in an arduous affair, so in many cases the troops resorted to constructing sangars to protect themselves from the elements, artillery bombardment and possible counter-attack.

At 1150Z on the 12th Pike radioed 3 Commando Brigade HQ requesting to advance to Wireless Ridge, but Thompson refused owing to the flanking fire that the Argentines on Tumbledown could bring down on 3 Para. Remaining in position, at around 1515Z 3 Para came under continual artillery fire, which killed four men and wounded another seven.

The Battle of Mount Longdon represented a sound victory for 3 Para, with the Argentines putting up a respectable defence and inflicting a heavy toll of eighteen killed and forty wounded during the assault and a further four killed and several wounded during the shelling that followed. The defenders lost more than fifty killed and about the same number as prisoners.

Mount Tumbledown

Situated about 4 miles west of **Stanley** and the site of a major ground engagement conducted by the **Scots Guards** on the night of 13–14 June. The three battles of 11–12 June – **Mount Harriet**, **Mount Longdon** and **Two Sisters** – may be seen collectively as a remarkable success for the British, who had defeated a numerically superior force in its main defensive positions. However, the fighting had been more prolonged than expected, rendering impossible further exploitation eastwards. All told, the British suffered twenty-eight fatal casualties and approximately seventy wounded, with a disproportionate share falling on **3 Para**, with eighteen dead from the difficult frontal assault against Longdon, juxtaposed with the **Royal Marines'** two assaults that employed flanking approaches and resulted in only five men dead.

Major General **Moore**, Commander Land Forces, had intended to renew his offensive on the following night – 12–13 June – with assaults on Mount Tumbledown, **Mount William** and **Wireless Ridge**, but so rapid a renewal of the fighting could not be undertaken because the Scots Guards and the **Gurkha Rifles**, tasked to assault Tumbledown and Mount William, respectively, had not completed their reconnaissance and observation. Moore agreed to postpone operations, but only for twenty-four hours, with the newly available time spent bringing up batteries of artillery and ammunition for both the guns and the infantry. The artillery duly bombarded Argentine positions, with returning fire killing four soldiers on Mount Longdon.

On the evening of 13 June the offensive resumed, with the main effort to come from **5 Infantry Brigade** in the south against the Stanley defences, involving the Scots Guards against Mount Tumbledown and 1/7 Gurkhas against Mount William. Further north, **2 Para**, which had been transferred back to **3 Commando Brigade**, was tasked with assaulting Wireless Ridge. The **Royal Artillery** would furnish five batteries of guns to support these three attacks, together with four warships and four **CVR(T)s** of the **Blues and Royals**, the latter of which had proceeded across the island from **San Carlos**.

Only one sortie was flown against Argentine positions on Tumbledown prior to the ground attack, conducted on the afternoon of 13 June by two **Harriers** with laser-guided bombs, one of which fell short by 400yd, but the second of which struck the target – a company HQ – marked by a forward air controller. The second Harrier then dropped its cluster bomb units on the target area, after which the pair returned to *Hermes*.

Tumbledown constituted a very formidable position held by elements of the 5th Marines – perhaps the best sizeable unit the Argentines possessed on the islands – holding the key post in the defences west of Stanley. Two companies stood on the mountain itself, with troops also deployed on Mount William and to the south near the track leading into the capital.

Scots Guardsmen on Mount Tumbledown celebrating news of the Argentine surrender on 14 June. (AirSeaLand Photos)

As a prelude, the **Mountain and Arctic Warfare Cadre** had already carried out scouting missions and acquired valuable intelligence on the area west of Tumbledown. Opening moves began on the morning of 13 June, when helicopters conveyed the Scots Guards from **Bluff Cove** to the western end of **Goat Ridge**, there to be briefed extensively on Argentine strength and dispositions. In his assessment, the battalion's commander, Lieutenant Colonel Michael Scott, thought that an attack across the exposed southern slopes of the mountain posed too great a risk to his unit, so he instead chose a western advance along the summit ridge without the benefit of supporting fire, thereby ensuring as quiet an approach as possible. In phase one, a diversionary raid carried out along the **Fitzroy–Stanley track** would precede G Company's seizure of the western end of the eminence, while in the second phase, Left Flank (LF) Company was to proceed through G Company and capture the area around the summit. Lastly, Right Flank (RF) Company would skirt around LF Company to take the eastern end.

Thirty minutes before the main assault Major Richard Bethell launched a diversionary attack with approximately thirty members of the Recce Platoon, preceded by **Royal Engineers** in charge of mine clearance. This was followed by the two **Scorpions** and two **Scimitars** of No 4 Troop, the Blues and Royals, providing fire support. A mine disabled one tank, whose crew evacuated and joined the second, which then withdrew amid Argentine artillery fire attracted by the sound of the explosion. The surviving tank proceeded to fire on Mount William, the defenders' mortar position. Bethell's infantry engaged bunkers with rifles and grenades, losing two dead and seven wounded, but killing ten before wandering into a minefield, from which engineers later extricated them. However, their action succeeded in its purpose.

Naval gunfire support came in the form of 856 rounds in total fired by the frigates *Active* and *Avenger* on the night of 13–14 June.

Half an hour after the start of the diversionary attack, G Company began its advance amid freezing conditions, taking its first objective by 0230Z, whereupon this new ground served to support LF Company.

LF Company under Major John Kiszley moved against the middle third of Tumbledown, where all remained quiet for the first thirty minutes until the defenders unleashed a thunderous, continuous hail of small arms fire directed with the aid of night sights. The attackers were forced to take cover among crags with no communication apart from shouting in the darkness. LF Company remained pinned down among the rocks for more than three hours until part of 13 Platoon climbed the northern side of the ridge, overlooking the main Argentine position, from where they put down fire with machine guns, rifles, and rocket launchers, supported by artillery. Strongly aided by this devastating covering fire, 14 and 15 Platoons advanced through the Argentine positions. Hard fighting followed, involving anti-tank weapons against Argentine bunkers, with progress still severely held up despite the efforts of Guardsmen to use grenades at perilously close range. Around 0630Z the attackers called in artillery support in order to break the impasse, which required several instances of hand-to-hand combat. A handful of men from LF Company finally reached the summit at 0905Z – but only after a seven-hour fight, complete with bayonets blooded.

In the third and final phase of the battle, RF Company, under Major Simon Price, having remained stationary for over five hours, now assumed the lead and advanced, making extensive use of its 84mm Carl Gustav medium anti-tank weapons (MAW) and light anti-tank weapons (LAW), to destroy sangars. Price deployed 1 Platoon high up in the rocks to the north in order to offer fire support, while 2 and 3 Platoon began the main attack with a right hook over fairly open ground. Advancing by half sections, the company cleared trenches, sangars and machine gun positions. With six men wounded but no fatalities, RF Company captured the final eminence more than eleven hours after the Guardsmen had crossed their start line.

Fighting did not cease until about 1215Z on the 14th, long after sunrise, in the course of which the Scots Guards suffered eight killed and thirty-five wounded. It took just over eleven hours from the moment they left their start line for the Guardsmen to wrest the ridge from the Argentines, of whom forty-five were made prisoner and approximately sixteen were killed. The victory represented a significant achievement, although it took much longer than the plan envisioned since the best Argentine units were deployed there; little now remained in the path of the British offensive. With the fall of Tumbledown went the key feature in the Argentine defence of Stanley, and Wireless Ridge, contested simultaneously by 2 Para, fell the same morning.

Mount Wall

A position near **Mount Challenger**, on which, on 30 May, L Company 42 **Commando** established an observation post named 'Tara', the name of one of its commanding officer's daughters. In heavy fog on the night of 3 June, a 42 Commando patrol was forced off this position, abandoning much of its equipment.

Mount William

A 500ft rocky feature 3 miles south-east of **Stanley** designated for capture by the **Gurkha Rifles** as part of the **5 Infantry Brigade** advance on Stanley in June. If the Argentines defending Mount William failed to surrender as a consequence of the Gurkhas' aggressive **patrolling**, the latter were to seize this position by daylight on the 14th while the **Scots Guards** simultaneously assaulted **Mount Tumbledown**. Accordingly, on the 13th the Gurkhas were helicoptered forward from an area south of **Mount Challenger** to a position just south of **Two Sisters**, ready to attack Mount William; but with the success of the Scots Guards on Tumbledown, the Argentines on Mount William fled the scene, denying the approaching Gurkhas the fight they so keenly desired. Mount William was declared secure at 1705Z.

Naval Air Squadrons

See Fleet Air Arm

Naval Armament

As the last ship-to-ship engagement had not occurred since the Battle of Jutland in 1916, naval guns were used for shore bombardment and in support of ground operations, such as the numerous salvoes fired on **Stanley** airfield and other targets, damaging or destroying parked aircraft and facilities.

Most **frigates** serving in the South Atlantic carried the Vickers 4.5in (114mm) gun, *Yarmouth* and *Plymouth* (Rothesay class) armed with the twin-mounted Mark 6 and the Amazon class carrying the single-barrelled turret Mark 8 gun, both a fully automatic, quick loading main armament firing a 55lb high-explosive shell (with close-proximity fuses, air burst against aircraft or ground troops, or star shell). The Mark 6 had a range of up to 17,500yd (16km) and a rate of fire of sixteen rounds per minute, with the capacity of changing the type of fuse in a matter of seconds. The Mark 8 fired at up to twenty-five rounds per minute to a maximum range of 22,000yd (20km). In the course of the campaign more than 8,000 rounds were fired in support of ground operations, directed in most cases by forward observation teams of the **Royal Artillery**.

Some of the frigates serving on Operation **Corporate** including *Argonaut*, *Minerva*, *Penelope*, *Andromeda*, *Brilliant* and *Broadsword*, carried the 40mm 60-calibre Bofors anti-aircraft gun, consisting of a single-barrelled power-driven armament firing a 2.2lb (1kg) high-explosive anti-aircraft shell. The Bofors could fire 100–120 rounds per minute up to 4,000yd (3.6km).

The two Type 12 Rothesay class frigates *Yarmouth* and *Plymouth* both carried the Limbo ASW Mortar Mark 10, which could fire three 450lb projectiles a minute to a range of 2,000yd.

All the **destroyers** serving in the conflict carried the 20mm (65-calibre) Oerlikon Mark 7 anti-aircraft gun – a single-barrelled, manually operated mounting that fired a 4oz (120g) high-explosive or solid round at a rate of 470 per minute to an effective range of 1,200yd (1.1km).

The Corvus Broadband chaff rocket was fitted to some vessels as a self-defence system and consisted of metallised strips launched by rocket at close range to deflect an incoming missile by confusing its **radar** homing system. The cloud produced by dispersion served as a decoy or produced a false echo, on to which the missile locked instead of on the intended target.

Some destroyers, including *Cardiff*, *Coventry*, *Exeter*, *Glasgow* and *Sheffield*, and all frigates except *Plymouth* and *Yarmouth*, carried two triple torpedo tubes mounted on either side of the ship and designed to fire the Mark 46 homing torpedo as an anti-submarine measure.

N

Naval Gunfire Support

Naval gunfire support played an important part in the ground operations of the war, from the bombardment of **Fanning Head** and **Stanley** airport to preparatory and supporting fire for the infantry assaults during the six major ground engagements.

Naval gunfire support was facilitated through a Naval Gunfire Officer (NGFO), who directed the firepower of ships accurately on to targets on land. Five naval gunfire support parties and, towards the end of the fighting, forward air control, was supplied by 148 Commando Forward Observation Battery, **Royal Artillery**, three teams going ashore with Special Forces well before the landings on 21 May and the other two taking part in the recapture of **South Georgia**. Thereafter they moved regularly between units as required, especially in the course of battle.

While most naval gunfire support was directed from the ground, some observers worked from **helicopters**, such as 148 (Meiktila) Commando Forward Observation Battery, RA, which on 9 May operated from a **Lynx** from *Broadsword*.

The naval gunfire support provided by *Antrim* and *Plymouth* against the Argentine garrison on South Georgia on 26 April is acknowledged to have played a decisive role in its decision to surrender. HMS *Arrow* very briefly aided the **2 Para** attack at **Goose Green** in the early hours of 28 May, but her gun jammed and when daylight approached she was forced to withdraw further out to sea. On the night of 11–12 June, British warships bombarded shore positions with almost 800 rounds, including against **Moody Brook Barracks** where an Argentine UH-1H (Huey) helicopter was put out of action. In the course of this barrage naval gunfire rendered all but six Hueys at Stanley airport unfit for service. On the same night, the destroyer *Glamorgan* and the frigate *Yarmouth* fired between them 428 high-explosive shells against **Two Sisters**, **Mount Harriet** and **Mount Tumbledown** (although the last would not come under attack until the evening of the 13–14th), while the frigate *Avenger* supported **3 Para** at **Mount Longdon** with her 4.5in main armament. Prior to the assault on **Wireless Ridge**, *Yarmouth* and *Ambuscade* bombarded that position, while in preparation for the **Scots Guards** attack on Mount Tumbledown the frigates *Active* and *Avenger* fired more than 850 rounds between them before the attack commenced; during the assault itself, *Yarmouth* and *Glamorgan* hit the position with 261 rounds fired by the former vessel alone.

Naval Party 8901

See Royal Naval Parties; Stanley

Nimrod MR1/2 and R1

British Aerospace Nimrods served in the anti-submarine warfare (ASW) role for the **Task Force** when its vessels remained within range of **Ascension**, but they also monitored the Argentine surface fleet. With its in-flight refuelling probe the Nimrod could fly missions of up to nineteen hours. Although its weapons were never fired, the Nimrod carried the Harpoon anti-ship missile and the AIM-9L **Sidewinder**, the latter specially fitted for a modicum of self-protection since fighter escort could not be provided over such extraordinary distances. In the course of the campaign Nimrods executed 130 maritime patrol sorties from Ascension, totalling 1,148 hours and fifty-two minutes in the air.

Sixteen Nimrod were modified for in-flight refuelling, being designated as MR2Ps. This capability rendered this aircraft – already blessed with an extended range – more capable of long-range surveillance or search and rescue coverage over the vast expanses of the South Atlantic.

The Nimrod's in-flight refuelling for service was not approved until 5 May, but within twenty-four hours the first long-range test occurred, consisting of a twenty-hour flight involving refuelling by **Victor K2** tankers. The first Nimrod with this capability arrived at Ascension on 7 May, flying non-stop from RAF Kinloss. Two days later, the first operational sortie left Ascension, flying 2,750 miles south to give ASW cover for the **Amphibious Support Group** bound for the Falklands, involving in-flight refuelling by three Victors. A second Nimrod arrived at Ascension on the 9th, bringing the strength up to allow long-range flights for MR2Ps from Ascension every day.

Nimrods performed some remarkable sorties during the war. On the morning of 15 May, for instance, XV232 of 201 Squadron left Wideawake Airfield on long-range reconnaissance along the Argentine coast to ascertain if the Argentine fleet had entered international waters. This remarkable achievement required the support of twelve Victor tanker sorties, with two Victors flying two sorties apiece, one on the passage to the South American coast and the other on the return flight. Flying as close as 60 miles to the Argentine coast in a northerly direction, the MR2P employed its **radar** to determine the positions of Argentine naval vessels, by which it discovered that none had left port. The sortie lasted nineteen hours in the air and reached Ascension after covering 8,300 miles, all the while very fortunate not to have been intercepted. Other such sorties followed, flown at night, to determine if Argentine warships could potentially threaten the Amphibious Support Group as it approached the Falklands.

The longest Nimrod sortie of the war (and the longest ever operational sortie by a **Royal Air Force** aircraft at the time) took place on the night of 20–21 May, when XV232 left Ascension to monitor Argentine activity around the Falklands as preparation for the landings the following day. The flight took eighteen hours and fifty minutes, covered 8,453 miles and required fourteen Victor K2 tanker sorties to refuel the aircraft.

Nordic Ferry, MV

A motor ro-ro ferry requisitioned from Townsend Thoresen on 1 May for use as a troop and helicopter transport, *Nordic Ferry* constituted one of a large fleet of **Ships Taken Up From Trade**. She carried with her Naval Party 1950 under Commander M. Thorburn RN. With **Baltic Ferry**, which conveyed part of **5 Infantry Brigade** to the South Atlantic, she sailed from Southampton on 12 May carrying vehicles, stores, and troops. She arrived in **San Carlos Water** with six **Gazelles** aboard at 1030Z on 3 June, a day after *Baltic Ferry* had already begun to unload vehicles and stores for 5 Infantry Brigade. She later served off **South Georgia** from 8 July, arriving back in Southampton on the 29th.

Commander:	Captain R. Jenkins	
Launched:	1978	
Tonnage:	6,455 Gross Register	8,704 Deadweight
Dimensions: length × beam; feet (metres):	495 × 71 (151 × 21.7)	
Propulsion:	2 diesel engines	15,600bhp = 17 knots
Aircraft cargo (UK to San Carlos Water):	6 × Gazelle AH1	

Norland, MV

A motor ro-ro ferry requisitioned from P&O North Sea Ferries on 16 April for use as a troop transport and carrying Naval Party 1850 under Commander C.J. Esplin-Jones RN. One of the most prominent of the **Ships Taken Up From Trade**, she sailed from Portsmouth on 27 April – a day late owing to delays in the fitting of her helicopter pad and a workers' strike at Hull – with **2 Para** aboard and arrived at **Ascension** on 7 May.

She reached Falklands waters on 20 May and the following day, D-Day, she offloaded 2 Para on to **landing craft** and then lay just off Chanco Point at the opening of **San Carlos Water**. Late in the evening of 21 May, at the end of the first day of the landings, *Norland* left San Carlos Water and took refuge in a holding area approximately 170 miles north-east of **Stanley**, well beyond the range of mainland-based aircraft. From there, in company with *Canberra*, she sailed before sunrise on the 22nd to **South Georgia**. Five days later, in a process off **Grytviken** taking more than twenty-four hours, she embarked troops from **5 Infantry Brigade**, which had travelled south aboard **Queen Elizabeth 2**. *Norland*, in company with *Canberra*, arrived back in San Carlos Water on 2 June and began disembarking her precious cargo.

After the surrender, *Norland*, together with *Canberra*, loaded 1,000 Argentine **prisoners of war** at San Carlos Water and conveyed them to Stanley, from where on the 18th *Norland*, carrying 2,000 prisoners, arrived off Puerto Madryn two days later.

Norland left the Falklands on 25 June carrying 2 and **3 Para**. She arrived at Ascension on 5 July, from whence the Paras flew on to Brize Norton. Returning to the Falklands on 19 July, she embarked the **Scots Guards** and **Welsh Guards**, which she conducted to Ascension, arriving at the end of the month and from which those units flew home. *Norland* did not arrive back in Hull until 31 January 1983.

Commander:	Captain M. Ellerby	
Builders:	A.G. Weser (Bremerhaven)	
Launched:	1974	
Tonnage:	12,998 Gross Register	4,036 Deadweight
Dimensions: length × beam; feet (metres):	502 × 83 (153 × 25.2)	
Propulsion:	2 diesel engines	18,000bhp = 19 knots
Aircraft:	1 × **Sea King** HC4 (Ascension to San Carlos Water)	
	2 × Sea King HC4 (21–23 May)	

Northella, HMS

A motor freezer trawler owned by J Marr & Son, *Northella* was commissioned on 26 April and converted into a minesweeper. Departing from Portland on 27 April, she arrived off **Ascension** on 11 May. She served at **South Georgia** from 27 May, not reaching Falklands waters until 21 June, a week after the cessation of hostilities. She was decommissioned and returned to her owners after arriving at Rosyth on 11 August.

N

Commander:	Lieutenant J.P.S. Greenop	
Launched:	1973	
Tonnage:	1,238 Gross Register	
Dimensions: length × beam; feet (metres):	230 × 42 (70.2 × 12.7)	
Propulsion:	1 diesel engine	3,250bhp = 16.5 knots

Offshore Patrol Vessels

Two newly commissioned offshore patrol boats, *Leeds Castle* and *Dumbarton Castle* were employed as dispatch vessels carrying essential supplies south.

Olmeda, RFA

A **Royal Fleet Auxiliary** oil tanker, *Olmeda* departed from Devonport on 5 April in support of the **Carrier Battle Group**, arriving off **Ascension** on the 16th. On 1 May she reached Falklands waters, where she spent most of the campaign until detached to **South Georgia**. From there she accompanied *Endurance* during the operation to recapture **Southern Thule**. During Operation **Corporate**, *Olmeda* conducted a total of 185 replenishments at sea before arriving back in Devonport on 12 July.

Commander:	Captain A.P. Overbury	
Builders:	Swan Hunter	
Launched:	19 November 1964	
Commissioned:	18 October 1965	
Tonnage:	10,890 Light Displacement	
	33,240 Full Load	
	18,600 Gross Register	22,350 Deadweight
Dimensions: length × beam; feet (metres):	648 × 84 (197.5 × 25.6)	
Draught:	11.1m	
Propulsion:	2 sets geared steam turbines	26,500shp = 19 knots (service speed)
Capacity:	18,400 tons FFO; 1,730 tons diesel oil; 3,730 tons Avgas	
Armament:	Improvised – machines guns and rifles	
Aircraft:	2 × **Sea King** HAS2A	

Olna, RFA

A Royal Fleet Auxiliary oiler commissioned on 1 April 1966, during her time in Falkland Sound she conducted 143 replenishments at sea and seventy replenishments in harbour. She departed from Portsmouth on 10 May, reached **Ascension** eight days later, and arrived off the Falklands on the 25th. Her South Atlantic service ended on 17 September, when she sailed into Portsmouth harbour.

Commander:	Captain J.A. Bailey	
Builders:	Hawthorn Leslie	
Launched:	28 July 1965	
Tonnage:	10,890 Light Displacement	
	33,240 Full Load	
	18,600 Gross Register	22,350 Deadweight
Dimensions: length × beam; feet (metres):	648 × 84 (197.5 × 25.6)	

Draught:	11.1m	
Propulsion:	2 sets geared steam turbines	26,500shp = 19 knots (service speed)
Capacity:	18,400 tons FFO; 1,730 tons diesel oil; 3,730 tons Avgas	
Armament:	Improvised – machines guns and rifles	
Aircraft:	2 × **Sea King** HAS2A	
	1 × **Wessex** HU5	

Onyx, HMS

An Oberon class diesel-electric patrol submarine, *Onyx* was the last built of her class before the war and carried a crew of six officers and sixty-two ratings. She was the only diesel-electric submarine to serve in the **Task Force**. The other five were designated 'Fleet' **submarines**, whereas *Onyx* was designated 'Patrol'. Accordingly, her principal function was to patrol in coastal waters, collect intelligence and insert and extract Special Forces teams, although she could, like other submarines, detect and destroy her counterparts and surface vessels. Recharging her diesel engines required surfacing at regular intervals, although her snorkel also performed this function. *Onyx* had two stern tubes and six forward tubes, these firing the Mark 8 homing torpedo with a weight of 3,375lb and running at up to 45 knots at a depth of 60ft.

 Onyx departed Gosport on 26 April and, on arriving in the **Total Exclusion Zone**, enabled the **Special Boat Squadron** and **Special Air Service** to use her for their operations as an alternative to small surface vessels that were more easily detected. She arrived on the evening of 31 May in **San Carlos Water**, escorted by *Avenger* and *Arrow*. Three months after the war, on 21 October, *Onyx* torpedoed the Argentine transport *Bahia Buen Suceso* captured at the fall of **South Georgia** and towed out to sea over deep water.

O

Commander:	Lieutenant Commander A.P. Johnson	
Builders:	Cammell Laird	
Launched:	18 August 1966	
Commissioned:	20 November 1967	
Displacement (tons):	1,610 Standard	
	2,030 Full Load, Surface	
	2,400 Submerged	
Dimensions: length × beam; feet (metres):	295 × 26.5 (89.9 × 8.11)	
Draught:	5.5m	
Propulsion:	2 sets of diesel-electric motors	7,360shp = 17.5 knots (surface)
		6,000shp = 15 knots (submerged)
Speed:	15 knots (submerged)	
Complement:	6 officers, 62 ratings	
Armament:	6 × 53cm bow torpedo tubes	
	2 × stern tubes	
	21in torpedoes	

Parachute Regiment

With a distinguished service record dating from its formation during the Second World War, through the Malayan Emergency, Aden, Borneo, Cyprus, Northern Ireland and elsewhere, the Parachute Regiment had not performed an airborne role in combat since parachuting on to an Egyptian airfield during the Suez Crisis in 1956. In order to earn his 'wings', each soldier had to complete at least eight jumps, but although airborne-trained they performed a normal infantry role. With their strong regimental ethos and exceptionally tough training regime – much of it carried out in Arctic, desert and jungle conditions – they enjoyed an elite status only rivalled within the Army by the **Special Air Service**, and they were thus some of the fittest and best-trained troops in the world. Continuously ready for 'out-of-area' operations, the Parachute Regiment sent two of its three battalions south.

2nd Battalion

Abbreviated as 2 Para and based in Aldershot, Hampshire, the battalion had served for two years in Northern Ireland until April 1981. From March of that year its new commanding officer was Lieutenant Colonel Herbert 'H' Jones, formerly of the Devon and Dorset Regiment. In September 1981, 2 Para was on exercise in Denmark, and two months later one company trained in Kenya, consistent with its capacity to fight in all terrain and conditions.

The battalion's advance party was in Belize in early April 1982 to prepare for the unit's imminent exercise there, but was immediately recalled. The rest of the battalion was on leave but returned rapidly to Aldershot. Just prior to its departure, the battalion's signallers received the new Clansman radio, with whose use they familiarised themselves during the long journey south. The battalion also requested and was supplied with twice the normal allocation of General Purpose Machine Guns as well as a limited number of American M79 grenade launchers, both of which were to provide the unit with a much-appreciated level of extra firepower.

2 Para contained three rifle companies of approximately 100 men each, with a fourth, C Company, known as Patrol Company, divided into two platoons: Recce and Patrol, which gathered information and intelligence. Support Company was equipped with machine guns, 81mm mortars and MILAN anti-tank missiles.

2 Para was given seventy-two hours' notice to move on 15 April, as a consequence of which it was transferred from **5 Infantry Brigade** to **3 Commando Brigade**. It departed from Portsmouth on 26 April aboard the requisitioned MV *Norland*, with most of its equipment carried in *Europic Ferry*. It arrived at **Ascension** on 7 May, where it spent a day field firing and conducting a landing exercise. Throughout its passage south the men maintained their fitness by running around the decks, practised combat first aid techniques, engaged in Argentine aircraft recognition and in other forms of training, all of which were to pay dividends in the field.

A soldier of 2 Para. (AirSeaLand Photos)

2 Para landed on Blue Beach One near **San Carlos** settlement on 21 May and immediately tabbed up **Sussex Mountain**, where it held defensive positions until first light on 26 May. It then moved south to Camilla Creek House before launching an attack down the **Darwin** and **Goose Green** isthmus on the 28th, losing its commanding officer and adjutant in the process. Major Chris Keeble, the 2i/c, assumed command and accepted the Argentine surrender the following morning. It suffered sixteen killed plus one attached Royal Marine and one Royal Engineer.

After Goose Green, 2 Para reverted back to 5 Infantry Brigade. Keeble assumed command until the arrival of Lieutenant Colonel David Chaundler, who gave his approval for a heli-borne advance to **Bluff Cove**. Accordingly, on 2 June, an advanced party of 155 Paras led by Major John Crosland, OC B Company, arrived by helicopter at **Swan Inlet House**, about halfway to **Fitzroy**, and discovered by telephone that Fitzroy and Bluff Cove were free of an Argentine presence, thus triggering the forward movement of the battalion from Goose Green. The first to arrive were A Company HQ and two platoons, B Company HQ and a platoon, and mortar and anti-tank platoons detachments, flown by **Chinook** in two groups of eighty-one and seventy-five personnel, respectively. A nearby **Mountain and Arctic Warfare Cadre** patrol, unable to positively identify these arriving troops, called in a fire mission against them, as HQ 3 Commando Brigade had not been informed of 2 Para's move. When a break in the mist revealed two British **Scout** helicopters accompanying the Chinook, the fire mission was cancelled. A and B Companies arrived by Chinook later that evening.

As part of the plan devised by Brigadier **Wilson** to move 5 Infantry Brigade forward on the southern flank approach to **Stanley**, he ordered D Company 2 Para to move off from its position east of Bluff Cove Inlet and for the remainder of the battalion to pull back to Fitzroy as Brigade Reserve, thus making space available for the imminent arrival of the **Scots Guards**, **Welsh Guards** and **Gurkha Rifles**.

The remainder of 2 Para was flown forward from Goose Green on the morning of 3 June. C (Patrol) Company was dropped at Fitzroy instead of the intended destination, Bluff Cove; D Company was taken to a position on the eastern shores of Bluff Cove Creek, 2 miles from the intended landing site and within easy sight of Argentine-held **Mount Harriet**. In time, the battalion settled its dispositions thus: A Company defending Bluff Cove; B Company on Fitzroy Ridge, just north of the settlement; C Company defending the approaches from the north-east; and D Company deployed across Bluff Cove to cover an Argentine approach from the east. Battalion HQ was located at Fitzroy. By this time the battalion came under Chaundler's command, who was already earmarked as Jones's successor if circumstances required it. Called away from his post at the Ministry of Defence, he was flown to **Ascension** and then to the waters held by the **Carrier Battle Group** by an RAF **Hercules**, from which on 1 June he parachuted into the sea, to be collected by HMS *Penelope*.

The Scots Guards arrived at Bluff Cove on 6 June, followed shortly by Wilson, upon which Chaundler suggested the Scots Guards remain within the confines of the settlement while 2 Para returned to Fitzroy. This would enable 2 Para to consolidate in a single location and prepare for any future engagement into which the battalion might be committed.

Accordingly, the four **landing craft** that had brought the Scots Guards were used to ferry 2 Para across Bluff Cove Inlet to Fitzroy – but only after Keeble forcefully overrode orders from Major Ewen Southby-Tailyour that the LCUs remain until further notice. This venture failed, however, as a consequence of the presence of extensive kelp, poor visibility, and faulty radar, and within two hours they were back at Bluff Cove.

2 Para reverted to 3 Commando Brigade in early June and on the afternoon of the 11th six **Sea Kings** transported the battalion from Fitzroy to Bluff Peak near **Mount Kent**, where they were to act in reserve for the attacks on **Mount Longdon** and **Two Sisters**. They lent their mortars to **3 Para** for their sister battalion's attack on Longdon and drove the Argentines from **Wireless Ridge** on 13–14 June, killing as many as 100, but with only seventeen prisoners, the rest of the defenders having fled. 2 Para lost three dead and eleven wounded.

2 Para constituted the first unit into Stanley, followed by 3 Para and **42 Commando**. The battalion departed aboard *Norland* from the Falklands on 25 June, arriving at Ascension on 5 July, from whence it flew by **VC10** to Brize Norton on the 6th.

Total casualties sustained by 2 Para up to 23 June amounted to eighteen killed, thirty-nine wounded, twenty-one injured and three out of action through illness.

3rd Battalion

Commanded by Lieutenant Colonel Hew Pike and stationed at Tidworth in Wiltshire, 3 Para also possessed experience of service in Northern Ireland and had recently taken part in exercises in Canada and parachute drops in the UK, one with 2 Para on Salisbury Plain. As recently as January 1982, a quarter of the battalion was on exercise in Oman in preparation for its forthcoming role as Spearhead battalion, a rapid deployment role. From December 1981 it joined 5 Infantry Brigade, designated for 'Out of Area' operations, but was transferred to 3 Commando Brigade on 3 April, having been put on notice for service in the South Atlantic the day before.

On 9 April, SS *Canberra* embarked with 3 Para aboard, together with **40 Commando** and 42 Commando, a potentially disastrous arrangement involving the mixing of red and green berets, but which in the event caused no serious difficulties. Most of the battalion's stores went in the *Elk*. Aboard ship, 3 Para practised using their newly issued Clansman radios, developed fitness regimes, and undertook battlefield medical and other forms of training. The battalion disembarked at Ascension on 20 April, practising embarkation and disembarkation with landing craft, conducting field firing and undertaking other training during their two-week stay aboard *Canberra*, anchored off the island.

On 19 May, two days before the landings in San Carlos Water, 3 Para was cross-decked to *Fearless* by landing craft. Two days later, the battalion landed at **Green Beach** One from four LCUs, proceeded to secure **Port San Carlos** and dug in at nearby Windy Gap.

Men of 3 Para aboard landing craft off Port San Carlos. (AirSeaLand Photos)

As part of Brigadier **Thompson's** break-out from the beachhead, 3 Para left Port San Carlos on its famous **tab** on 27 May, reaching **Teal Inlet**, a tiny settlement on Port Salvador Bay on the night of 29 May. The following night it proceeded to Estancia House, which it reached on 31 May, and from where it occupied Mounts Estancia and Vernet on 1 June as part of its preparations for an attack on Mount Longdon. On the morning of 2 June it advanced further east until Thompson ordered the battalion to halt, reminding Pike, who appeared to him overly enthusiastic to seek a major engagement, that the **strategy** involved a brigade, and not a battalion, attack on the Argentine outer ring.

After Major General **Moore** issued his operational order on 9 June for a three-phase attack on Stanley, the following day Thompson revealed 3 Para's part: to capture Mount Longdon and exploit to Wireless Ridge if possible. In the event, on 11–12 June the battalion captured Longdon against stiff resistance, suffering eighteen killed and forty wounded and coming under artillery fire in its wake, which caused a further four killed and several wounded.

3 Para left the Falklands on 25 June aboard *Norland*, together with 2 Para, arriving at Ascension on 5 July. Both battalions then flew by VC10 to Brize Norton the following day.

Casualties for 3 Para up to 23 June amounted to twenty-two killed, fifty-six wounded, forty-five injured and seven out of action due to illness.

Patrolling

A fundamentally important feature of British operations in the Falklands, especially from 31 May when, with the capture of **Mount Kent**, aggressive patrolling dominated the ground in the days prior to the assaults on the Argentines' outer defences – **Mount Harriet, Two Sisters** and **Mount Longdon**.

Patrols gathered information on Argentine positions and strength, probed their defences, and screened British positions. These were carried out by elements of all infantry formations, but especially the **Mountain and Arctic Warfare Cadre**, the **Special Air Service** and the **Special Boat Squadron**.

Innumerable examples of patrolling may be cited. In the days immediately prior to the attack on Two Sisters, for example, **45 Commando** pushed out patrols that probed positions held by the 4th Infantry Regiment, successfully engaged Argentine patrols, and discovered a useful track connecting Mount Kent with Two Sisters. On the morning of 6 June, a **3 Para** patrol ambushed an Argentine patrol, killing several troops, but was forced to withdraw under heavy machine gun and mortar fire.

Similarly, after **42 Commando** established itself in the area around Mount Kent, it sent out patrols in the direction of its ultimate objective, Mount Harriet, engaging several times with patrols from 4th Infantry Regiment. On 3 June, in heavy fog, a recce troop patrol was forced off **Mount Wall**, leaving behind most of its equipment, and the following day patrols from K and L Companies sustained casualties from mines while recceing the area south of Harriet.

Paraquet, Operation

See South Georgia

Pearleaf, RFA

One of five Leaf class support tankers chartered to the **Royal Fleet Auxiliary**, together with *Bayleaf, Plumleaf, Appleleaf* and *Brambleleaf.* She departed Portsmouth on 5 April, reached **Ascension** on the 22nd, and arrived off the Falklands on 16 May. She was detached for service off **South Georgia** on 4 June and completed her service on Operation **Corporate** upon arrival in Devonport on 13 August.

Commander:	Captain J. McCulloch	
Builders:	Blythwood (Scotstoun)	
Launched:	15 October 1959	
Commissioned:	January 1960	
Tonnage:	12,353 Gross Register	18,797 Deadweight
Dimensions: length × beam; feet (metres):	568 × 72 (173.1 × 22)	
Draught:	9.2m	
Propulsion:	1 diesel engine	8,000bhp = 15 knots
Capacity:	1,410 tons fuel	

Pebble Island

A successful **Special Air Service** raid on 14–15 May was conducted against a grass airstrip on Pebble Island containing Argentine aircraft in an operation that mirrored those conducted by the regiment in North Africa during the Second World War.

Situated north of **West Falkland**, Pebble Island features low terrain, especially in the east, which has several lakes and large ponds. The settlement contained approximately two dozen inhabitants engaged in shepherding 25,000 sheep. A track ran west from the settlement to a croft on the lower southern slopes of Marble Mountain Peak. Pebble Island contained two airstrips, a grass runway to the east of the settlement and another on a southern stretch of beach at Elephant Bay.

The Argentines established a naval air station on the island on 24 April, occupying the sheep-shearing shed, the guesthouse and an unoccupied house. On 27 April, the first Argentine ground forces arrived on the Island, imposing a dawn to dusk curfew and requisitioning all Land Rovers. After the **Black Buck** raid on **Stanley** airport on 1 May, the Argentines diverted six Pucaras to Pebble Island, joining the Mentors already there.

Situated only nineteen minutes' flying time to **San Carlos Water**, Argentine occupation of the island posed a threat to the British anchorage to be established there on 21 May, as a consequence of which Rear Admiral **Woodward** requested on 10 May that the SAS neutralise the threat by the 15th since **helicopters** would not be available for that purpose after that date. The SAS liaison officer suggested three weeks of preparation, but Woodward insisted on five days, to which the SAS acceded, setting in train events that would call for the sort of raid not carried out since 1945.

Captain John Hamilton was put in command and given three options for insertion. The first involved transport by helicopter straight to the eastern end of Pebble Island; this was rejected on the grounds of possible detection by **radar**. The second option involved using **Gemini** craft, but was also rejected owing to D Squadron's poor experience with outboard engines at **South Georgia**. It was also difficult to conceal Geminis. The final option was chosen: using **Klepper canoes** to be employed by the recce team, which would then call in the assault team by helicopter.

The original plan envisioned dropping an eight-man Boat Troop patrol led by Captain Burls with four Kleppers at Purvis Bay on the night of 11–12 May. They would then proceed by paddling to Deep Ferny Valley and establish a laying up position from which to observe activity on the island before crossing 1¼ miles (2km) of water by night. Although the raid was meant for 0630Z on 15 May, foul weather delayed the recce patrol deployment until the night of 12–13 May, when an 846 NAS **Sea King** HC4 inserted an eight-man reconnaissance team near Port Purvis, east of Pebble Island, from where the team carried its disassembled canoes overland to Deep Ferny Valley. The team had hoped to establish an observation post on the night of its arrival, but given the delay in dismantling the canoes and the two journeys required to move by foot – which of course involved carrying personal equipment as well as its transport – the team ran out of the cover of darkness and had to lay up in Deep Ferny Valley during the daylight hours of the 12th. All this denied it the opportunity for observation and set its schedule back by a day. Still, the team managed to proceed as planned thereafter and, on the night of 12–13 May, moved to an observation post that enabled it to view the eastern end of Pebble Island, with its particular interest drawn to the area around Phillips Cove – where it intended to land.

After the wind calmed, the patrol returned to Deep Ferny Valley, where it assembled the canoes and paddled across Phillips Cove. There, it beached and split into two four-man patrols, with one remaining behind to dismantle and conceal the canoes and the other dispatched to observe the airfield and settlement. At sunrise, it identified eleven aircraft spread across the runway as well as an ammunition dump and a fuel storage facility, although it possessed no information about the strength of the garrison.

Major Cedric Delves, the squadron commander, radioed Hamilton to proceed with the raid. Woodward in turn detached *Hermes*, the destroyer *Glamorgan* and the frigate *Broadsword* from the **Carrier Battle Group** to make for Pebble Island in haste. For the attack itself, the raiding party totalled forty-five men, including a

Naval Gunfire Officer. The plan called for Mobility Troop to raid the airfield, while Air Troop would engage whatever Argentine forces occupied the settlement itself. Mountain Troop would stand in reserve together with the 60mm mortar detachment. The attack would commence with *Glamorgan* firing her 4.5in gun. At approximately 2225Z on the 14th, the two troops boarded four Sea Kings on the deck of *Hermes*. With lights out and the helicopters flying low over the sea, the men arrived in Phillips Cove at 0345Z – an hour late. Moving rapidly in single file over 5 miles of ground, Mobility and Mountain Troop lost contact with each other, leaving the latter to proceed with the attack and Mobility Troop to remain in reserve with the mortar.

At the appointed time, *Glamorgan* fired on the airfield to disrupt any Argentine counter-attack; fires erupted when shells ignited fuel and struck some of the aircraft. As a consequence, the garrison dispatched men with firefighting equipment. Driving the Argentines – who returned fire – back into shelter, Mountain Troop then entered the airstrip, firing on a manned bunker as they proceeded, with the mortar offering supporting fire. In seven two-man teams the men of Mountain Troop climbed on to the wings of the parked aircraft, ripping out essential wiring, destroying fuel lines with gunfire, placing explosives and employing grenades. Their small arms fire proving ineffective, the Argentines detonated an explosive charge under the runway as the SAS team was about to withdraw, causing injury to one man by concussion while another received an accidental gunshot wound from a fellow trooper. The Argentines continued to fire as the SAS departed, at 0740Z, boarding four Sea Kings and reaching *Hermes* at approximately 0930Z. The team had damaged or destroyed all eleven aircraft, rendering them incapable of threatening the landings at San Carlos Water a few days later. Other light aircraft still remained at **Goose Green**, but the Pebble Island raid proved an overwhelming success.

Several air attacks followed the raid: on 23 May three **Harriers** dropped cluster bomb units and parachute-retarded 1,000lb bombs on the airstrip to deny its future use to aircraft on resupply missions and to Pucaras; at about 1238Z on 29 May two **Sea Harriers** took off from *Hermes* to bomb the airstrip on Pebble Island, and another two left *Hermes* at 1735Z against the same target. On 3 June the frigate *Avenger* fired her main armament against the Argentine post on Pebble Island.

Penelope, HMS

One of fifteen **frigates** in the South Atlantic, but only one of three of the Batch 2 Leander class of this type of vessel, the others being *Argonaut* and *Minerva*. She departed Devonport on 10 May, reached **Ascension** eight days later and arrived off the Falklands on the 25th.

On 1 June *Penelope* picked up Lieutenant Colonel David Chaundler after he parachuted from a **Hercules** C1 into the sea near the **Carrier Battle Group**, in order to replace Lieutenant Colonel 'H' Jones, the commanding officer of **2 Para** killed at

Goose Green on 28 May. On 7 June at 1930Z she entered Falkland Sound together with *Fearless* and *Avenger*. *Penelope* arrived back in Devonport on 10 September.

Commander:	Commander P.V. Rickard	
Builders:	Vickers-Armstrong	
Launched:	17 August 1962	
Commissioned:	31 October 1963	
Displacement (tons):	2,650 Standard	3,200 Full load
Dimensions: length × beam; feet (metres):	372 × 41 (113.4 × 12.5)	
Draught:	5.8m	
Propulsion:	2 sets geared steam turbines	30,000shp = 28 knots
Armament:	2 × 40mm Bofors AA guns	
	3 × **Seacat** systems (GWS 22)	
	4 × MM.38 **Exocet**	
	2 × triple Mark 32 ASW torpedo tubes (STWS)	
Aircraft:	1 × **Lynx** HAS2	

Phantom FGR2

Admiral **Woodward** advocated establishing an airstrip on **West Falkland** to accommodate such aircraft, together with **Hercules**, but the plan never came to fruition. Three Phantoms served to defend **Ascension** from 26 May until they returned to RAF Coningsby in July.

Photographic Reconnaissance

Despite the fact that the Falklands constituted a British Overseas Territory – and a measure of the degree to which an invasion was totally unanticipated – no aerial photographs were available of the islands until the last days of the war. In general, photographic reconnaissance proved problematic owing to Argentine anti-aircraft measures and the low-level approach required by the **Sea Harrier**. After the first of the **Black Buck raids**, for instance, poor weather in the form of rain under a 1,200ft cloud base prevented proper damage assessment. Even after the **Task Force** arrived in the South Atlantic with air assets, foul weather prevented air recce of the Argentine positions atop the eminences just west of **Stanley**, although two **Harrier** GR3s left *Hermes* at 1631Z on 10 June to conduct photographic reconnaissance of **Stanley**, **Two Sisters** and **Mount Longdon**.

Pict, HMS

A motor freezer trawler requisitioned from British United Trawlers by the Ministry of Defence and converted as a minesweeper. Commissioned on 26 April, she departed Portland the following day and arrived off **Ascension** on 11 May. She served off

South Georgia from the 27th and anchored off the Falklands the day after the cessation of hostilities. Arriving in Rosyth on 11 August, *Pict* was decommissioned and returned to her owners.

Commander:	Lieutenant Commander D.G. Garwood	
Launched:	1973	
Tonnage:	1,478 Gross Register	
Dimensions: length × beam; feet (metres):	2309 × 42 (70.1 × 12.9)	
Propulsion:	1 diesel engine	3,246bhp = 13.5 knots

Plumleaf, RFA

One of five Leaf class support tankers chartered to the **Royal Fleet Auxiliary**, together with *Pearleaf, Bayleaf, Appleleaf* and *Brambleleaf,* she departed Portland on 19 April and reached **Ascension** on 1 May, refuelling the ship in the South Atlantic en route to and from the Falklands. On finishing her service, she arrived in Gibraltar on 22 July and in Portsmouth on 26 August.

Commander:	Captain R.W.M. Wallace	
Builders:	Blyth Drydock	
Launched:	29 March 1960	
Commissioned:	July 1960	
Tonnage:	12,549 Gross Register	19,200 Deadweight
Dimensions: length × beam; feet (metres):	560 × 72 (170.7 × 21.9)	
Draught:	9.2m	
Propulsion:	1 diesel engine	9,500bhp = 15 knots
Capacity:	684 tons fuel	

Plymouth, HMS

One of two Type 12 (Rothesay class) **frigates** to serve with the **Royal Navy** in the South Atlantic, the other being *Yarmouth*. In all, fifteen frigates served on Operation **Corporate**. She left Exercise **Springtrain** on 2 April, arrived at **Ascension** eight days later, and proceeded to **South Georgia**, whose waters she reached on the 21st. *Plymouth*'s embarked **Wasp** HAS1, together with that of *Endurance*, attacked the Argentine submarine *Santa Fe* off Grytviken on 25 April and the following day contributed decisively to the decision of the garrison to surrender in the wake of her naval bombardment, in tandem with that of *Antrim*.

Plymouth accompanied the **landing craft** (both LCUs and LCVPs) on their approach to the assault beaches in **San Carlos Water** on 21 May, offering **naval gunfire support**.

At about 1650Z on 8 June, while en route to Chancho Point to issue naval gunfire against a suspected Argentine observation post on Mount Rosalie on **West Falkland**,

Plymouth was attacked by five Daggers, whose cannon damaged the hydraulic and electrical cables providing power to the frigate's 4.5in main armament. The aircraft scored four hits with their 500lb bombs, although none exploded. One, however, set off a depth charge that started a fire in the chief petty officers' mess and galley. Another travelled down the ship's funnel but failed to explode, while the remaining two bounced off the water, pierced the hull and punched through the other side, miraculously without exploding but seriously damaging the ship's mortar launcher in the process. *Plymouth's* five wounded were evacuated by helicopter to the medical facility at **Ajax Bay**. The crew managed to control the resulting fire within forty-five minutes and brought her back into San Carlos Water to effect emergency repairs prior to sailing to the Tug, Repair and Logistic Area (TRALA) for full damage recovery. *Plymouth* arrived in Rosyth on 14 July.

Commander:	Captain D. Pentreath	
Builders:	HM Dockyard (Devonport)	
Launched:	20 July 1959	
Commissioned:	11 May 1961	
Displacement (tons):	2,380 Standard	2,800 Full load
Dimensions: length × beam; feet (metres):	370 × 41 (112.8 × 12.5)	
Draught:	5.3m	
Propulsion:	2 sets geared steam turbines	30,000shp = 28 knots
Armament:	2 × 4.5in Mark 6 guns	
	2 × 20mm Oerlikon AA guns	
	1 × **Seacat** system (GWS 20)	
	1 × Limbo ASW Mortar Mark 10	
Aircraft:	1 × **Wasp** HAS1	

Port Howard

A sheep-farming settlement situated on an inlet on the east coast of **West Falkland** containing about two dozen residents in 1982 and occupied by the Argentine 5th Infantry Regiment. Both the **Special Air Service** and **Special Boat Squadron** monitored activity there, but the place did not attract significant attention. On 8 May, for instance, two **helicopters** from HMS *Brilliant* fired their GPMGs at Argentine troop positions there, while on the 17th *Alacrity's* **Lynx** dropped flares over the settlement to divert the attention of the garrison to the landing of **naval gunfire support** spotting teams in anticipation of the landings on the opposite side of Falkland Sound on the 21st.

While on a **photographic reconnaissance** run over Argentine positions at Port Howard on 21 May, Flight Lieutenant Jeff Glover in a **Harrier** GR3 was downed, apparently by a **Blowpipe** surface-to-air missile. Glover was injured, recovered from the water and taken prisoner. Five days later, two Harrier GR3s attacked Argentine troop positions with cluster bomb units, with unknown results, and on the 27th, *Yarmouth* fired 300 rounds at Argentine positions in the area around Port Howard. On 10 June, Captain John Hamilton, in command of a concealed SAS observation post at Many Branch Point, a ridge above Port Howard, was killed when overwhelming forces brought fire against his position. The Argentine garrison there surrendered to B Company **42 Commando** on 15 June.

Port Pleasant

An inlet just south of **Bluff Cove**, but actually closer to **Fitzroy**, on the south coast of East Falkland. In spite of the many misidentifications of Fitzroy and Bluff Cove as the site of the catastrophic air attacks against *Sir Galahad* and *Sir Tristram* on 8 June, Port Pleasant remains the true position.

Port San Carlos

When the decision was reached to land in **San Carlos Water**, Port San Carlos settlement, of which Alan Miller served as manager, was chosen as one of the three sites. It is not to be confused with **San Carlos** settlement; the former faces the opening of San Carlos Water, while the latter lies to the south, deep on the eastern side of the inlet. **3 Para** and **42 Commando** landed on **Green Beaches** One and Two, respectively, on 21 May, causing about forty Argentines in the area to withdraw to the high ground to the east without offering resistance.

Port Stanley

See Stanley

Prisoners of War

British service personnel who fell into Argentine hands included the twenty-two **Royal Marines** and thirteen civilians taken on **South Georgia** on 3 April and transported by sea to Bahia Blanca, where they arrived on 13 April, and those comprising **Naval Party 8901** captured during the initial invasion and fall of **Stanley** on 2 April (sixty-nine all ranks, plus eleven **Royal Navy** personnel from *Endurance's* survey parties and one ex-Royal Marine living on East Falkland who re-enlisted) – with the final six coming in from the hinterland three days later – all of whom were repatriated via Montevideo and reached RAF Brize Norton on 5 April. During the period following the arrival of the **Task Force** in the **Total Exclusion Zone**, only one British serviceman fell into Argentine hands: Flight Lieutenant Jeff Glover, whose **Harrier** GR3 (XZ972) was shot down over **Port Howard** on 21 May. He

Argentine prisoners at Stanley airfield. (AirSeaLand Photos)

ejected over the sea at 600mph at such a low altitude that he struck the surface before his parachute could fully deploy. Suffering a range of injuries – a broken left arm, shoulder and collarbone, severe shock and bruising to his face – he was plucked from the water and spent his captivity in Argentina until released on 8 July.

By contrast, British forces captured the entire garrisons of South Georgia and of the Falkland Islands, the former numbering 151 naval personnel and marines and thirty-nine civilian scrap metal workers. All of these were put aboard the *Tidespring* and taken to **Ascension**, where they arrived on 12 May. The following day they were flown to Montevideo aboard a red cross–bearing **VC10** C1 before repatriation on the 14th.

The second large influx of prisoners into British hands took place at **Goose Green** on 29 May, when approximately 1,100 Argentine Army and Air Force personnel laid down their arms outside the settlement. The one remaining **Chinook** from the sinking of *Atlantic Conveyor* was employed in ferrying some of these prisoners to **San Carlos**, but in the absence of bedding, tentage or provision for feeding them they were soon repatriated by ship. Nor had thought been given to providing British forces with Spanish-speaking interpreters, leaving the *ad hoc* approach of employing the handful of troops who happened to speak the language, such as Captain Rod Bell RM, whose services proved invaluable throughout the campaign.

The Regimental Police Troop of thirty Royal Marines, initially spread across a number of ships, were consolidated to handle the 1,100 prisoners taken at Goose

Green. They later worked in **Fitzroy** in tandem with the Royal Military Police from **5 Infantry Brigade**, guarding prisoners in a POW cage in a sheep shearing shed.

Wounded prisoners from Goose Green who received medical treatment aboard the hospital ship *Uganda* were transferred to an Argentine hospital ship in the **Red Cross Box** to the north of Falkland Sound. **Helicopters** just arrived with *Atlantic Causeway* in **San Carlos Water** moved about 800 Argentine prisoners from **Darwin** and Goose Green to RFA *Sir Percivale* on 1 June.

On 14 June General Menéndez surrendered the entire garrison of East and West Falkland, with approximately 8,000 prisoners immediately moved from Stanley to the airport, where they could be more easily managed. Major General **Moore**, already short of food and accommodation for his own troops, faced the priority of sending most of them home as soon as possible, apart from about 300 'special category' officers withheld as a guarantee against the Argentine government repudiating the surrender agreement. *Canberra* and *Norland* loaded 1,000 prisoners each at **San Carlos Water** and made for Stanley, where *Canberra* took aboard an additional 3,000 and departed for Argentina on the 18th, escorted the following day into Puerto Madryn by two Argentine destroyers, with the handover supervised by the International Red Cross. *Norland* left Stanley on the 18th with a total of 2,000 prisoners and arrived off the same port on the 20th, with many other Argentines reaching their homeland aboard the icebreaker *Bahia Paraíso*. The special category prisoners, held aboard *St Edmund*, were landed at Puerto Madryn on 30 June.

On 15 June, the 5th and 8th Infantry Regiments surrendered at **Port Howard** and **Fox Bay**, respectively, on **West Falkland**, after which all these prisoners were moved to San Carlos.

All told, on 14 June General Menendez surrendered 11,848 officers and men on East and West Falkland, but when to these were added the prisoners taken in the aftermath of Goose Green and subsequent actions the total rises to approximately 13,000.

P

Queen Elizabeth 2, RMS

A luxury steam passenger liner owned by Cunard – in fact the largest passenger liner afloat at the time – she was requisitioned on 4 April after returning from a cruise to Philadelphia. As soon as she reached Southampton, workmen from Vosper Thornycroft began shifts on a twenty-four-hour basis to refit and load her as a troopship, a process that took nine days and involved three months' supply of stores and constructing two helicopter pads, one aft and one forward over the swimming pool. She was also fitted with satellite communications and equipment for replenishment of fuel and water at sea.

Once converted, with a troop capacity of 3,000 and with most of her crew remaining on a voluntary basis, she departed with Naval Party 1980 under Captain N.C.H. James RN on the afternoon of 12 May, carrying most of **5 Infantry Brigade**, including Brigade HQ, 2 **Scots Guards**, 1 **Welsh Guards** and 1/7th **Gurkha Rifles**, as well as many support units and most of HQ staff Land Forces Falkland Islands – in all about 3,000 troops.

QE2 docked at **Freetown**, Sierra Leone, on 18 May to take on fresh water and fuel and reached **Ascension** on 20 May, where she embarked Major General Jeremy **Moore**.

With considerable prestige value and considered too vulnerable to offload troops in **San Carlos Water**, she sailed to the secure anchorage of Cumberland Bay, **South Georgia**, and from 27–29 May cross-decked troops mostly by boat and trawler, and vehicles and stores by heavy-lift helicopters, to *Canberra* and *Norland*, which had arrived from Falklands waters, so enabling the *QE2* to avoid the considerable risk she would face as such an obvious target to air attack in San Carlos Water. With the process completed on the afternoon of the 29th, *QE2* embarked 629 survivors from *Ardent*, *Antelope* and *Coventry*.

She arrived off Ascension on 4 June on her return journey to the UK. Those stores still aboard that could be useful to the **Task Force** were unloaded on to the island by a **Sea King** HAR3. The great liner arrived back in Southampton on 11 June to a tumultuous reception.

Commander:	Captain Peter Jackson	
Builders:	John Brown & Co. (Glasgow)	
Launched:	20 September 1967	
Tonnage:	67,140 Gross Register	15,976 Deadweight
Dimensions: length × beam; feet (metres):	963 × 105 (293.5 × 32.1)	
Propulsion:	4 sets geared steam turbines	110,000shp = 28.5 knots
Aircraft:	2 × Sea King HAS2A (UK to South Georgia)	

Queen Elizabeth 2 reaching port at Southampton on 11 June. (AirSeaLand Photos)

Radar

British land, sea and air forces employed a wide range of radar technology, only some of which can be covered here, but the most critical aspect of this subject concerns the grave deficiency in the capacity of the **Task Force** to provide Anti-Electronic Warfare (AEW) protection to the fleet, a feature lost when the carrier-borne aircraft the Fairey Gannet was retired, together with the aircraft carrier *Ark Royal*, only three years before the conflict in the South Atlantic.

As the UK naturally assumed any future conflict would occur in the North Atlantic, the **Royal Navy** expected to rely on the Americans for airborne radar coverage in the form of the US Navy Grumman E-2 Hawkeye, or from AWACS aircraft provided by the **Royal Air Force** and USAF. In the absence of these assets in the South Atlantic, **Sea Harriers** found themselves at a serious disadvantage in having to depend on the limited capabilities of Royal Navy vessels, whose radar systems provided little warning of hostile aircraft approaching over land or at low altitude.

British warships suffered accordingly, and in the absence of AEW, Sea Harriers found themselves deployed much more often and far less efficiently than circumstances required, since poor radar coverage obliged these short-range aircraft to mount barrier patrols on a very frequent basis, much of them fruitless since the warning provided to Argentine aircraft by their efficient ground-based radar system often enabled them to avoid those seeking their destruction.

Ships on radar picket duty off the Falklands tracked and, where possible, engaged Argentine aircraft intending to attack British targets on land or at sea. Amazon class **frigates**, for example, were equipped with Type 992Q (target indication) radar, which functioned poorly when vessels stood close inshore, such as in Falkland Sound or **San Carlos Water**, since the system could not distinguish between aircraft and the undulating ground over which they approached. The Leander class used the ageing Type 965 (AKE-1) long-range air warning radar, a system that did not respond well to Argentine fast jets in contrast to the subsonic bombers which the system was originally designed to track. Leander class frigates were also equipped with Type 993 medium range information radar and Type 975 surface warning radar.

Radio Communication

Radio communication proved absolutely essential to operations in the Falklands, with great distances to be covered and with units spread across wide areas.

Trained in both naval and army communications, a signals squadron staffed for the most part by **Royal Marines** was attached to **3 Commando Brigade**, while **5 Infantry Brigade** was supported by 205 Signal Squadron, 30 Signal Regiment. Signals personnel were also assigned to **Ships Taken Up From Trade** as experts in maritime communications.

Those radios that could not be man-packed generally found transport in the form of the 75 Volvo **BV 202E**, an oversnow vehicle used by 3 Commando Brigade in northern Norway that could easily traverse the Falklands boggy ground. 5 Infantry Brigade possessed very few such vehicles.

In the field, most ground forces operated the recently issued Clansman radio, replacing the Larkspur A43, so new that signallers had to learn its use during their passage south. This came in nine versions, man-packed and used one of three frequencies: HF, VHF and UHF. At section level signallers carried the 3lb PRC 349 with a range of 1,000yd, the PRC 350 at platoon level, and, with a range of 6 miles, the PRC 351 used by company commanders to communicate with their platoon commanders. Radio communication allowed for co-ordination of sub-units in battle, and for facilitating requests for reinforcements, resupply and other matters. The Larkspur nevertheless remained in limited use, and with its 100-mile range enabled Tactical Air Control Parties to speak with pilots to co-ordinate close air support with troops on the ground. Such man-packed radios generally survived the rough treatment meted out by signallers carrying them across open ground in harsh conditions, but the batteries were heavy and required regular charging, with supplies of petrol for this task in short supply.

In a few instances, Special Forces operating in the Falklands hinterland possessed their own secure High Frequency communication nets, including a portable satellite communication (SATCOM) radio that enabled them to speak directly with commanders at their base in Hereford, as well as a range of tactical communications for use in the field. It was with this specialised equipment that Lieutenant Colonel Mike Rose, CO 22 **Special Air Service**, was able to communicate directly with Admiral **Fieldhouse** back at Northwood and with the regiment's command post aboard *Fearless* during the negotiations for the Argentine surrender on 14 June.

As troops advanced west across East Falkland, relay stations were established to cope with communications extending over ever-lengthening distances. A 2 Signals Platoon rebroadcast team established itself on Wickham Heights on 2 June, in order to overcome the communications problems between **Fitzroy** and **Goose Green**.

For the first time, satellite communications provided senior commanders in the field the ability to speak directly to Northwood – not always a welcomed innovation, as those sitting 8,000 miles away could not always properly appreciate the complexities apparent to men on the spot who were best placed to make decisions at the tactical level. Prior to the Royal Signals establishing a satellite communications terminal – so heavy as to require a helicopter to transport it – near the Brigade Maintenance Area at **Ajax Bay**, Brigadier **Thompson** sent daily situation reports by hard copy signal, and continued to do so after the SATCOM link had been established ashore. He used the SATCOM link from HMS *Fearless* to talk to Northwood occasionally, but only about three times once it was ashore. Once Thompson moved his HQ forward to **Teal Inlet**, he never used it again. From 8 April, a communications centre was established on **Ascension** under **Royal Air Force** control.

Rapier

Rapier served as the principal short-range anti-aircraft missile defence system of the Army and the **Royal Air Force**, divided between twelve fire units of 'T' (Shah Shujah's) Battery, 12 Air Defence Regiment, Royal Artillery – the only unit to fire its Rapiers in anger during the campaign – and the eight units of 9 Battery, **Royal Artillery**, and 63 Squadron RAF Regiment.

The Rapier experienced a poor record of serviceability, partly owing to the fact that its crews left **Ascension** without some of their support equipment owing to lack of space on board the considerably over-subscribed transport vessels and based on the erroneous belief that their kit would follow in a timely fashion. The relevant equipment did not in fact arrive until the conflict had ended; in the meantime the weapon system performed badly, with a number of factors contributing to poor performance: most of the Rapier components were loaded in the first few days of the **Task Force** departure, which consequently denied the crews the ability to maintain them or train even with weeks of sea voyage ahead of them. No practice firing took place at Ascension, again forfeiting the chance of keeping the crews well-practised in handling the firing units. Damage sustained to the sensitive systems during loading, the voyage south and in helicopter transit from ship-to-shore during the landings in May all contributed to the various mechanical failures experienced during the campaign, exacerbated by the fact that in order to reduce the strain on the **logistics** chain, the DN181 Blindfire **radar** trackers were left in the UK, obliging the crews to depend on the organic surveillance system or in many cases to resort to optical tracking. Indeed, in most cases Rapier crews acquired their targets visually, since Argentine aircraft tended to approach at extremely low elevation, sometimes only 50ft above sea or land.

On 21 May great importance was attached to establishing the Rapier fire units on high ground around **San Carlos** to protect the vessels and troops newly arrived in the area from air attack. **Gazelles** from 3 CBAS recced possible sites before **Sea King** HC4s of 846 NAS transported units ashore in underslung loads. However, as the units had been loaded early aboard the *Sir Geraint* and were difficult to retrieve, the first fire unit did not emerge until about midday, by which time Argentine air attacks against shipping in Falkland Sound and **San Carlos Water** had already begun.

Having establishing themselves on elevated positions on shore at San Carlos Water on 21 May, Rapier operators were also severely hampered by the presence of large numbers of British aircraft operating in the area, moving supplies and performing other tasks. During the passage south these sensitive weapons were jostled numerous times, as a result of which they performed poorly on D-Day. Consequently, visually locating, identifying and tracking targets offered a surer method of avoiding tragedy than interpreting signals from ubiquitous aircraft of all descriptions and trying to distinguish between them as friend or foe.

A Rapier surface-to-air missile firing post from T Battery, 32 Air Defence Regiment, Royal Artillery. (AirSeaLand Photos)

By the end of the day, Sea Kings had air transported ten of the twelve Rapier fire units of 'T' Battery on to the hills around San Carlos Water, a task requiring sixty-three helicopter sorties. The poor performance of the Rapier systems owed much to their sensitivity to handling, with loading, long storage onboard ship and unloading delaying the process of rendering all twelve units operational, with further problems thereafter connected with their generators.

On 1 June, the recently arrived *Atlantic Causeway*, anchored in San Carlos Water, unloaded eight Rapier fire units of 63 Squadron, RAF Regiment, to protect ships therein and the logistic base, so enabling the twelve fire units of 'T' Battery, 12 Air Defence Regiment, sited around San Carlos Water to move four fire units south to **2 Para's** position at Goose Green, while another four were sent to the advanced logistic base at **Teal Inlet** to support the advance by 42 and **45 Commando** to the area around **Mount Kent** and Mount Estancia.

During **5 Infantry Brigade's** move to the **Port Pleasant** area in early June, Rapiers were taken to **Fitzroy** aboard *Sir Galahad*. Three were flown ashore on 8 June by a Sea King HC4 with the intention of setting them up quickly to provide air defence for the vessels and troops once ashore; indeed, *Galahad*'s Sea King was actually airborne close to the ship when Skyhawks attacked the anchorage there. Badly positioned and not fully prepared for the onslaught, the Rapier batteries could offer no adequate defence against the unexpected appearance of Argentine jets. At least two of these attempted to fire their missiles, but both failed.

Initial claims that Rapier missiles were responsible for shooting down fourteen Argentine aircraft have since been proven false; in fact, only one kill – a Dagger A shot down on 29 May during a raid against ships in San Carlos Water – can be positively accounted for by a Rapier. In fact, many of them failed to launch or took an erratic course before harmlessly striking the ground or the water. While Rapier may have constituted a source of concern for Argentine pilots, in practical terms it did not live up to expectations.

Red Beach

Situated in **Ajax Bay** in **San Carlos Water**, it was the landing site on 21 May for **45 Commando**.

Red Cross Box

An area at sea about 30 miles north of the Falklands designated by both belligerents as a safe haven for their respective hospital ships, *Uganda* and *Bahia Paraíso*. The International Committee of the Red Cross inspected both hospital ships there to ensure they met the criteria as non-combatant vessels.

Refuelling (in-flight)

The **Victor K2** tanker refuelled long-haul aircraft such as the **Hercules**, a procedure conducted with both aircraft descending slowly at the same altitude, with refuelling commencing at about 23,000ft and involving the transfer of perhaps 25,000lb of fuel. Upon separation, both aircraft would return to their previous higher elevation. The refuelling of ships at sea occurred on about 1,200 occasions and involved a gargantuan effort by **Royal Air Force** overseas agents, who had to secure vast quantities of fuel and oil from a host of international suppliers.

Regent, RFA

A **Royal Fleet Auxiliary** resource class **fleet replenishment ship**, one of five including *Resource*, *Stromness*, *Fort Austin* and *Fort Grange*. Carrying ammunition, stores and spares, she departed Portland on 19 April and arrived at **Ascension** ten days later. *Regent* was the first ship to enter the **Total Exclusion Zone** after the beginning of UK operations on 1 May and reached Falklands waters on the 12th. In the last days of the war she was dispatched to **South Georgia**, which she reached on 11 June, arriving back off the Falklands on 1 July. Her service ended at Rosyth on 15 September.

Commander:	Captain J. Logan	
Builders:	Harland and Wolff (Belfast)	
Launched:	9 March 1966	
Commissioned:	6 June 1967	
Tonnage:	23,000 Full Load	18,030 Gross Register
Dimensions: length × beam; feet (metres):	640 × 77 (195.1 × 23.5)	
Draught:	8.0m	
Propulsion:	1 set geared steam turbines	20,000shp = 19 knots
Armament:	Improvised – GPMGs and rifles	
Aircraft:	1 × **Wessex** HU5	

Repair Ships

See *Stena Inspector*, MV; *Stena Seaspread*, MV

Resource, RFA

Resource class **fleet replenishment ship** that carried ammunition, stores and spares. Four other vessels of the **Royal Fleet Auxiliary** served in the South Atlantic: *Regent*, *Stromness*, **Fort Austin** and **Fort Grange**. *Resource* departed Rosyth on 6 April and arrived at **Ascension** after an eleven-day journey. One of the first merchant vessels into **San Carlos Water**, *Resource* resupplied troops between 23 May and 26 May, and before proceeding south-east to **South Georgia** she took on refrigerated stores and fresh food from the liner *Saxonia*. Her service in the conflict ended upon arrival in Devonport on 19 July.

Commander:	Captain B.A. Seymour	
Builders:	Scotts SB (Greenock)	
Launched:	11 February 1966	
Commissioned:	16 May 1967	
Tonnage:	23,000 Full Load	18,030 Gross Register
Dimensions: length × beam; feet (metres):	640 × 77 (195.1 × 23.5)	
Draught:	8m	
Propulsion:	1 set geared steam turbines	20,000shp = 19 knots
Armament:	Improvised – GPMGs and rifles	
Aircraft:	1 × **Wessex** HU5	

R

Royal Air Force

Although its main responsibility lay in the defence of the UK and its commitment to NATO, particularly in West Germany, the RAF provided assets for 'Out of Area' operations and maintained units in Hong Kong, Belize and Cyprus.

In the Falklands War the RAF maintained both fixed-wing and rotary assets, the former consisting of the **Harrier** GR3, which satisfied the RAF's need for an aircraft that could be deployed in forward areas without the need for long runways. Harriers belonged to 1 (F) Squadron. Other aircraft included the **Nimrod** and **Victor** K2. **Helicopters** consisted of the **Chinook** HC1. A few RAF pilots operated with the **Fleet Air Arm**, which with the small contribution of the **Army Air Corps** and 3 Commando Brigade Air Squadron, constituted the British air commitment to the South Atlantic. All RAF units in the Falklands came under the umbrella of 18 Group RAF, with this formation reporting directly to Admiral **Fieldhouse** at Northwood.

Central to this role was the use of Wideawake Airfield on **Ascension** as a staging post and base, although all Harriers (and the Royal Navy's **Sea Harriers**) would have to operate from **aircraft carriers** or forward operating bases established ashore on East Falkland after the landings on 21 May.

The problems facing the RAF were obvious from the start: fighting a campaign 8,000 miles from home and outmatched numerically by an adversary operating from mainland bases only 400 miles from the Falklands – even after the Argentine aircraft carrier *Veinticinco de Mayo* withdrew to port for the duration of the campaign after the sinking of the cruiser *General Belgrano* on 2 May.

Fortunately for the RAF, highly trained Argentine pilots flying Daggers, Mirage, Super Etendards and Canberras could not operate from **Stanley** airport, limiting them to only a few minutes' loiter time over the western end of East Falkland after a 400-mile flight from the mainland; but their Pucaras, MB-339s and Mentors could operate from grass airstrips on the islands, such as those at **Goose Green** and **Pebble Island**. All told, the Navy's Sea Harriers and the RAF's Harriers were outnumbered by more than ten to one, yet they in combination with the air defence systems of the **frigates** and **destroyers** managed to achieve air superiority – although never air supremacy – within a week of the landings.

In addition to **combat air patrols** and ground-attack missions carried out by Sea Harriers and, to a lesser extent, Harriers, the **Vulcan**, refuelled by Victor tankers, executed five sorties (in fact, seven in total, with one aborted and another cancelled), known as **Black Buck raids**, against targets in and around Stanley. With in-flight refuelling, RAF Nimrods could operate continuously from Wideawake, providing early warning to the **Task Force** of the presence of Argentine ships and aircraft.

Two often unsung elements of the RAF deserve mention: the Explosive Ordnance Demolition Team – bomb disposal experts – which would help defuse one of the two unexploded bombs lodged in *Argonaut* and another protruding through the ceiling of the forward dressing station at **Ajax Bay**; and the ground crews and support units who provided an extraordinarily high level of serviceability, often in very difficult operating conditions, with all personnel working overtime to enable aircraft to operate at what probably amounted to four times their normal peacetime rates.

Royal Army Medical Corps

Commanded by Lieutenant Colonel John Roberts, the RAMC personnel of 16 Field Ambulance, provided **medical services** at dressing stations at **Ajax Bay**, **Teal Inlet**, **Fitzroy** and aboard *Uganda*, and elsewhere.

The long journey to the Falklands enabled medical officers to train the men intensively in advanced first aid, including resuscitation, applying a drip and the treatment of various types of wounds.

16 Field Ambulance was among the first to go ashore from *Sir Galahad* on 8 June and was thus spared the disaster that befell the **Welsh Guards** and others who were still on board when Argentine aircraft attacked around midday. Nevertheless, some RAMC personnel were still aboard *Galahad* during the attack, losing three dead and much of their equipment.

Royal Artillery

The Royal Artillery provided fire support to ground forces. Given the boggy and rocky nature of the ground, its 105mm light guns, with a range of more than 10 miles, were usually sited in earthworks and sangars rather than dug into position, with camouflage netting overhead. Forward observation officers (FOO) either on the ground or, less frequently, airborne in **helicopters**, directed both ground-based and naval gunfire by identifying targets and their co-ordinates. Co-ordination between the Army and Navy was the responsibility of the four Royal Artillery naval gunfire liaison officers operating ashore.

Each of the two infantry brigades contained artillery organised into batteries of six guns each. As the **Royal Marines** possessed no artillery of its own, **3 Commando Brigade** contained an organic Royal Artillery component in the form of 29 Commando Light Regiment RA, which saw the most action in the conflict and consisted of three batteries: 8 (Alma), 79 (Kirkee) and 145 (Maiwand), with a total of eighteen 105s. All Royal Artillery personnel attached to 29 Regiment underwent commando training like their Royal Marines colleagues.

5 Infantry Brigade contained no organic artillery, but prior to sailing received 4 Field Regiment, equipped with 105mm light guns, under Lieutenant Colonel Tony Holt. Owing to a shortage of FOOs in 5 Infantry Brigade, a third battery commander and two observation parties were created.

A 105mm gun of 29 Commando Regiment, Royal Artillery, which consisted of three batteries of six guns each, attached to 3 Commando Brigade. (AirSeaLand Photos)

97 (Lawson's) Field Battery also deployed with 5 Infantry Brigade, although the temporary absence of gun sights required them to rely on quadrants and prismatic compasses for several days.

T (Shah Shuja's Troop) Air Defence Battery, 12 Air Defence Regiment, consisting of twelve **Rapier** surface-to-air missile systems also deployed to the Falklands. On going ashore in **San Carlos Water** on 21 May, it sited ten of its fire units to defend the anchorage, together with the two sections of **Blowpipe**.

With the almost total absence of roads in the Falklands, 29 Regiment journeyed to the South Atlantic with **BV 202E** oversnow vehicles to tow its guns, although in the event the batteries relied much more heavily on helicopter transport both for their guns and ammunition resupply. The shortage of shipping deprived forward observers of vehicles altogether, requiring them to man-pack most of their equipment, although they too were often moved forward by air.

The effectiveness of the artillery depended on a combination of mobility and firepower; this, in turn, inevitably depended partly on the stock of available ammunition, in turn dictated by the numbers and types of **helicopters** to hand. A **Wessex** could carry only twenty-four rounds of 105mm rounds on pallets, a **Sea King** forty-eight, and a **Chinook** 192.

With the forward movement of 3 Commando Brigade and 5 Infantry Brigade, guns and Rapier batteries were flown forward via **Sea King**. Thus, three light guns from 7 (Sphinx) Commando Battery were brought by helicopter to support K Company **42 Commando** on **Mount Kent** on 29 May, with the rest arriving the following night. On 2 June, the battery nearly carried out a fire order based on a request from a **Mountain and Arctic Warfare Cadre** patrol on **Smoko Mount**, which spotted **2 Para** landing near **Fitzroy**, but was unable to distinguish them between friend or foe. Just before zeroing rounds were fired, they received word that the forces were friendly and the fire mission was cancelled.

Artillery fire was generally brought down accurately on Argentine positions, sometimes in close proximity (e.g. as close as 50yd) of attacking British troops, but in a few instances **'Blue on Blue'** resulted in the death of British personnel, such as the case of Private David Parr at **Wireless Ridge**. Eleven Royal Artillery personnel were wounded but none killed.

For the assault on the ring of Argentine defences around **Stanley**, 4 Field and 29 Commando Regiments (with thirty light guns between them) stated a desire for 1,000 rounds per gun, which required adding 700 shells to the existing stockpile of 300. However, since this would require four days of helicopter flying, Major General **Moore** decided that each gun would be allocated 500 rounds. In the event, in the course of the three battles on 11–12 June – **Mount Harriet, Two Sisters** and **Mount Longdon** – 8 Commando Battery alone fired 1,500 rounds, leaving insufficient numbers, in the view of Brigadier **Thompson**, to risk **3 Para** exploiting to Wireless Ridge after its success on Longdon.

During the last six days of the conflict, all guns between them fired approximately 12,000 rounds.

Royal Engineers

A highly versatile organisation, among their many tasks the Royal Engineers were employed to check for and clear mines and booby traps and assess the suitability of a beachhead to support a military force. They also dug latrines, repaired tracks and erected water points, demolished obstacles, built bridges, repaired water supplies and airfields, and disposed of bombs. One troop constructed a pumping and storage system at **Ajax Bay** to supply fuel for **helicopters**. They built field engineering works and laid airfield tracking and pipelines. Engineers also played an important role in identifying minefields and bringing back mines for analysis.

3 **Commando Brigade** possessed an integrated Royal Engineer component in the form of 59 Independent Commando Field Squadron RE that, like the **Royal Marines** themselves, possessed special training in mountain and Arctic warfare, and a recce troop of specialist forward engineer reconnaissance troops, complete with their own transport, supplies and communications. 3 Commando Brigade also contained

49 Explosive Ordnance Disposal Squadron. 9 Parachute Squadron supplied the Royal Engineers contingent to **5 Infantry Brigade**.

Myriad examples of the Royal Engineers' work may be cited:

On **Ascension**, in order to cope with the enormous strain on fuel supplies, sappers constructed a 4-mile pipeline to connect the storage farm to Wideawake Airfield.

A troop of sappers was attached to infantry units that went ashore on D-Day, but in the absence of mines in **San Carlos Water** on 21 May they first came to prominence a week later at **Goose Green**, where in groups of four they cleared mines and looked for booby traps.

Royal Engineers performed beach reconnaissance with the **Special Boat Squadron** to locate obstacles to amphibious landings, as they did on 5 June at **Bluff Cove**.

After the break-out from the beachhead engineers followed the advance east, clearing mines and establishing start lines for the units involved in the engagements fought on 11–12 and 13–14 June.

59 Independent Commando Squadron RE was tasked immediately after the landings with constructing a forward operating base for **Harriers** and **Sea Harriers**, which the **Royal Air Force** dubbed 'West Wittering' and later 'Sid's Strip', while the **Royal Navy** called it HMS *Sheathbill*. 11 Field Squadron, a specialist airfield construction unit that travelled down in RFA *Bedivere*, used hundreds of prefabricated 10ft x 2ft aluminium airfield surfacing panels to repair bomb damage and build a vertical take-off and landing pad. Their work, completed on 2 June, boasted an 850ft runway and a fuel pumping system capable of bringing ashore 40,000 gallons of aviation fuel. Poor weather prevented flying until the 5th, but from that day until the 14th, inclusive, this site facilitated 150 operational sorties.

Using equipment shipped from San Carlos Water by RFA *Sir Tristram*, 1 Troop, 9 Parachute Squadron (attached to **2 Para**) spent two days in dreadful conditions repairing the damage the Argentines had inflicted with explosives to the bridge at **Fitzroy**. Engineers performed their task so well that instead of carrying 4-ton loads in the form of farm vehicles, the bridge could handle 10 tons, thus accommodating **Scorpions** and **Scimitars**, which drove around the head of the creek to Bluff Cove.

Well after the Argentine surrender on 14 June, Royal Engineers were heavily engaged in mine clearance, discovering that anti-tank, anti-personnel and beach mines had been laid across wide swathes of the islands, in many cases indiscriminately, with no mine-maps to help locate them. 4 Field Squadron, for instance, had the unenviable task of clearing mines and booby traps from settlements on **West Falkland**.

Casualties included the deaths of two ordnance disposal experts who tried to defuse an unexploded bomb aboard HMS *Antelope*. Two Engineers were killed and eight wounded among those who had not yet disembarked from *Sir Galahad* during the air attack on **Port Pleasant** on 8 June. All told, seven Engineers were killed in action and seven wounded, with many more injuries sustained in the post-war clear-up of mines, booby traps, improvised explosive devices, unexploded bombs, shells and missiles scattered across the islands. In all, the Argentines are thought to have laid more than 12,000 mines, many of them defying easy detection owing to their manufacture from largely non-metallic materials. Many minefields remain *in situ*, cordoned off, while parts of the Falklands coastline are off-limits, with mines now long since shuffled in all directions by the tides and shifting sands.

Royal Fleet Auxiliary (RFA)

The RFA supplied twenty-seven ships, twenty-two of which served with the **Task Force** with a total of 2,500 personnel. Fifteen logistic supply vessels sailed under the flag of the RFA: the fleet tankers *Olmeda, Olna, Tidepool, Tidespring* and *Blue Rover*; the support oilers *Pearleaf, Plumleaf, Appleleaf, Bayleaf* and *Brambleleaf*; and the **fleet replenishment ships** *Regent, Resource, Stromness, Fort Austin* and *Fort Grange*. Six RFA-manned **Landing Ships Logistic**, all named after knights of the Round Table, served in the South Atlantic: *Sir Bedivere, Sir Galahad, Sir Geraint, Sir Lancelot, Sir Percivale* and *Sir Tristram*. The sole helicopter support ship in theatre, *Engadine*, also belonged to the RFA.

Royal Fleet Auxiliaries – Fleet Replenishment Ships

Royal Fleet Auxiliary (RFA) fleet replenishment ships, including the *Fort Grange, Fort Austin, Resource, Regent* and *Stromness*, were merchant ships operating under the authority of the Ministry of Defence to carry stores, victuals, ammunition, equipment and other items, all transferable to warships by a variety of means: Jackstay rigs, by helicopter, to smaller vessels alongside, or by vertical replenishment (VERTREP), although sometimes supplies were airlifted directly ashore. They were in turn resupplied by **Ships Taken Up From Trade** (STUFT) situated in the safety of the Tug, Repair and Logistic Area (TRALA). Although necessarily required to operate in hostile areas and coming under attack on a number of occasions, none sustained any damage in the course of the conflict. Effectively unarmed – with nothing more than General Purpose Machine Guns and rifles – most RFAs had helicopter pads, a single rotary aircraft and **Royal Navy** staff to fly and maintain it.

Royal Fleet Auxiliaries – Fleet Tankers and Support Oilers

Manned by a combination of **Royal Fleet Auxiliary** and merchant seamen, the fleet tankers (*Olna, Olmeda, Tidepool, Tidespring* and *Blue Rover*) and Support Oilers (*Pearleaf, Plumleaf, Appleleaf, Brambleleaf* and *Bayleaf*) provided the various types of fuels required by ships, aircraft and vehicles in theatre, including Furnace Fuel Oil (FFO) for some older vessels such as the aircraft carrier *Hermes*, diesel oil (DIESO) for most other warships, aviation fuel (AVCAT) for aircraft and a range of types for merchant vessels. Ordinary petrol (MOGAS) was required for vehicles in support of the ground campaign. These varying needs required tankers to carry a range of fuels and in the correct proportion to anticipated demand. Tankers such as *Olna* and *Olmeda* carried more than 20,000 tons of fuel and up to three different varieties. Various modifications such as hangars to accommodate **Sea King helicopters** and the mounting of machine guns on their superstructures prepared them for service in the South Atlantic, together with replenishment at sea (RAS) facilities.

Fifteen other **Ships Taken Up From Trade** tankers also carried fresh water, both for the troops ashore, where the local water was contaminated by sheep droppings, and for many of the ships that could not distill their own, such as the hospital ship *Uganda*. The *Fort Toronto* carried no fuel, in fact, but rather fresh water for the troops.

Royal Marines

Although dating back to the seventeenth century, the Royal Marines only became a commando force during the Second World War. They are employed in raiding enemy territory, as a spearhead to seaborne assaults and for particularly tough enterprises requiring exceptional standards of fitness, bravery and initiative. Trained for service at sea, particularly in an amphibious capacity, during the Falklands War and since the Royal Marines have also supplied small detachments to **aircraft carriers, frigates, amphibious assault ships** and other vessels. They train and

serve in all climates and conditions, from the jungles of Belize to the snows of northern Norway, and during 1982 were well accustomed to deployments on the streets of Northern Ireland. All Royal Marines have an intimate understanding amphibious warfare and regularly train on **landing craft**.

During the Falklands War, Royal Marines units belonged to **3 Commando Brigade** with its own HQ, the whole organisation falling under Headquarters Commando Forces based at Plymouth, responsible for planning and mounting operations and

A Royal Marine in Stanley after the Argentine surrender. (AirSeaLand Photos)

exercises for Royal Marines units. 3 Commando Brigade's units consisted of 40, 42 and **45 Commando**, each approximately the equivalent to an Army battalion, together with artillery, engineer, logistic, air, headquarters and signals components. Unlike in the Army, a Royal Marine may move between different commandos, acquiring the skills and learning the culture of each, yet still maintaining the same cap badge throughout the Corps, thus producing an extremely close-knit formation even at the strength, in 1982, of more than 7,000 officers and men. All Army and **Royal Navy** personnel serving in 3 Commando Brigade were trained on the commando course at Lympstone in Devon and thus wore the coveted green beret like all Royal Marines. This consisted of a thirty-week training course composed of various elements including rope-climbing, an assault course, running, weapon handling, speed marching, attack exercises, a long cross-country march in full order, and a swimming test – all designed to assess endurance, cardiovascular fitness, strength, teamwork and other characteristics.

40 Commando

Commanded by Lieutenant Colonel Malcolm Hunt since September 1981 and based at Seaton Barracks, near Plymouth, in Devon, this unit was designated for 'Out-of-Area' operations. 40 Commando served and exercised abroad frequently, with recent jungle training in Brunei, amphibious training in the Caribbean and Europe, and recent tours in Northern Ireland. In the months preceding Operation **Corporate**, 40 Commando had conducted amphibious trials aboard *Hermes* and only two months before deployment to the South Atlantic the commando took part in landing exercises on the south coast of England.

On 9 April, SS *Canberra* embarked with 40 Commando aboard, together with 42 Commando and **3 Para**. 'Forty' went ashore at **Ascension** on 20 April for training and remained there a fortnight. On 19 May, two days before the landings in **San Carlos Water**, it was cross-decked to *Fearless* by landing craft. The commando landed on Blue Beach Two near **San Carlos** settlement on 21 May where, much to its frustration, it remained to defend the divisional supplies dump as Force Reserve for the remainder of the campaign, with other responsibilities such as, from 29 May, A Company guarding Argentine **prisoners** taken at **Goose Green**. The unit nevertheless served an important purpose, for it was well-positioned and prepared to repel any Argentine counter-attack from **West Falkland**. To that end, G Company inserted patrols to watch the garrisons at **Fox Bay** and **Port Howard**.

In the week before the attack on **Mount Harriet**, Brigadier **Thompson** had offered to remove 42 Commando from its very exposed positions in appalling weather around **Mount Kent** and replace it with 40 Commando, but 'Four-Two' was keen for a fight and declined. On 8 June, a patrol from 40 Commando captured a small group of Argentines, formerly part of the combat team on **Fanning Head**, which had fled the engagement with a team from the **Special Boat Squadron** on 21 May. After the devastation wrought against the **Welsh Guards** aboard *Sir Galahad* on 8 June, the remaining two companies plus A and C Companies of 40 Commando made up numbers as the reserve in support of 42 Commando's attack on Mount Harriet on 11–12 June. These companies, together with elements of the **Welsh Guards**, were flown to **Sapper Hill** on the 14th, meeting slight resistance before the general Argentine surrender later that day. On the following day, B Company crossed Falkland Sound to Port Howard on West Falkland to accept the surrender of the 5th Infantry Regiment. Up to 23 June, 40 Commando sustained one killed, six wounded and two out of action through illness.

The unit returned home together with 42 Commando and Z Company 45 Commando aboard *Canberra*, departing the Falklands on 25 June and arriving at Southampton on 11 July.

42 Commando

Commanded by Lieutenant Colonel Nick Vaux since December 1981 and based at Bickleigh, north of Plymouth, 'Four-Two' was responsible for 'out-of-area' operations and were fully trained in Arctic warfare, to which end it trained in southern Norway and Denmark in the spring and summer of 1981, respectively. Owing to financial constraints affecting Royal Marines training, 'Four-Two' was the only commando to train in Norway in early 1982, though 45 Commando constituted the other regularly winter-trained unit. Although it was on leave when hostilities broke out on 2 April, within seventy-two hours all but one Royal Marine reported for duty, with the last arriving in time to depart with his unit.

Embarked on 9 April aboard SS *Canberra*, together with 42 Commando and 3 Para, the unit went ashore at Ascension on 20 April for a fortnight's training. M Company would play a key role in the recapture of **South Georgia**, while the rest of the commando would serve on East Falkland. During the landings on 21 May, 42 Commando remained on board *Canberra*, forming a floating reserve, until later that day when it landed at **Green Beach** Two near **Port San Carlos**. On the night of 29 May, patrols from G Company reported that Mount Kent could be seized well ahead of the main thrust eastwards from the beachhead. D Squadron 22 **Special Air Service** was sent to Mount Kent on the night of the 27th to recce the possibility and came under fire the following day.

Thompson accordingly ordered 42 Commando to reinforce the SAS there. Arriving by helicopter, K Company had orders to seize the summit, with L Company, a 7 (Sphinx) Commando Battery section, mortar platoon and a **Blowpipe** section to reinforce it from a second helicopter. In the event, K Company left after dark on the 28th in four **Sea Kings**, but was forced to turn back to San Carlos Water owing to near zero visibility in heavy snow showers. The insertion succeeded on the night of 29 May, with K Company, Tac HQ and four 81mm mortars, followed by L Company. The Argentines thereupon abandoned the position. Over the next two nights the remainder of the commando arrived, together with engineers, the rest of the battery and 105mm ammunition. Around 30 May, L Company was shifted from Mount Kent to **Mount Challenger**, establishing an observation post on **Mount Wall**. On 2 June, the hybrid J Company rejoined 42 Commando from Goose Green, where it had replaced **2 Para** after the latter's movement east.

After Major General **Moore** issued operational orders on 9 June that involved a 3 Commando Brigade thrust against **Stanley**, Thompson explained 42 Commando's part the following day, involving an attack against Mount Harriet and possible support to 45 Commando if the latter was able to exploit as far as **Mount Tumbledown** after seizing **Two Sisters**. Elements of the Welsh Guards were to operate in reserve to 42 Commando. The attack against Mount Harriet on 11–12 June succeeded, with the unit suffering only light losses: two killed and thirteen wounded.

J Company, most of whose personnel had formerly comprised the captured **Naval Party 8901**, hoisted the Governor's flag over Government House on 14 June and six days later M Company accepted the surrender of the tiny Argentine garrison on **Southern Thule**.

On 25 June, 42 Commando, minus M Company, embarked for the UK aboard *Canberra*, together with 40 Commando and Z Company 45 Commando. It arrived at Southampton 11 July. M Company left aboard *Nordic Ferry*, departed from South Georgia on 8 July, arrived at Ascension and flew on to RAF St Mawgan. Up to 23 June, 42 Commando lost two killed, twenty-four wounded and five injured.

45 Commando

Specialising in Arctic warfare, including snow survival skills and military skiing – but also well-trained in jungle warfare – 45 Commando had been under the command of Lieutenant Colonel Andrew Whitehead since April 1981 and was based at Arbroath in Scotland. As with the other two commandos, 'Four-Five' boasted a long service record in the Middle and Far East in the 1950s and 1960s, plus tours in Northern Ireland as recently as 1981. The commando was just about to go on two weeks' leave and two of its companies were training abroad, but its personnel assembled rapidly back in Arbroath once recalled.

Most of the commando departed on 7 April aboard RFA *Stromness* and arrived at Ascension on the 17th, with J Company composed of the former **Naval Party 8901**, which the Argentines had repatriated after the capture of Stanley. On D-Day, 21 May, 45 Commando was cross-decked on to landing craft from *Stromness* and disembarked on **Red Beach** in **Ajax Bay**. It cleared the derelict refrigeration plant there and by '**yomp**' ascended the northern slopes of **Sussex Mountain** behind 2 Para. At dawn on 27 May, 45 Commando left this position and moved by LCU to Port San Carlos, from where it yomped 13 miles east to New House that night. Early the next day, it reached **Douglas** settlement and arrived at **Teal Inlet** by 0030Z on 31 May, resuming its march on 3 June and reaching a position just west of Mount Kent by 1700Z the following day.

45 Commando Royal Marines entering Stanley. (AirSeaLand Photos)

On 9 June, Major General Moore issued operational orders for a three-phase attack against Stanley. Accordingly, the following day Thompson instructed 45 Commando to execute an attack on Two Sisters on the night of the 11th to 12th, and to exploit to Mount Tumbledown and **Mount William** if circumstances permitted. The attack succeeded by dawn, thus precluding any further exploitation under cover of darkness, at a cost of only four killed and ten wounded.

Z Company 45 Commando returned home aboard *Canberra*, which departed the Falklands on 25 June and arrived at Southampton on 11 July. X and Y Companies left the Falklands in late June aboard *Stromness*, arrived at Ascension on 7–8 July and then flew back to the UK by **VC10**, landing near Arbroath on the night of the 8th–9th.

Up to 23 June casualties amounted to twelve killed, twenty-three wounded and two out of action through illness.

Royal Maritime Auxiliary Service (RMAS)

The RMAS supplied a tug, *Typhoon*, and a mooring vessel, *Goosander*, the latter of which was employed at **Ascension** from late May laying buoys and moorings.

Royal Naval Parties

In order to cope with the military requirements imposed on them by requisitioning, **Ships Taken Up From Trade** (STUFT) required their normal civilian crews to be supplemented by naval personnel, mostly from the **Royal Navy** itself but in some cases from ancillary services. These were to assist in, or be wholly responsible for, maintaining and operating newly installed naval communications systems, explaining naval procedures unknown to merchant vessels, operating cryptographic machines and managing replenishment at sea (RAS) facilities. Naval parties varied in size from two or three personnel to more than two dozen, depending on individual ship requirements.

Twenty STUFT carried embarked naval parties composed of Royal Navy personnel; four naval parties were supplied by the **Royal Maritime Auxiliary Service** (RMAS); the **Royal Fleet Auxiliary** provided eleven; and the Royal Naval Supply and Transport Service supplied parties to four vessels. A further two parties, both provided by the Royal Navy, were shore based: a Royal Navy Aircraft Servicing Unit on **Ascension** and the **Royal Marines** detachment best known as **Naval Party 8901**, serving as the garrison force in the Falklands. Finally, there were two Fleet Clearance Diving Teams: bomb disposal experts, who defused the unexploded ordnance aboard *Sir Galahad, Sir Lancelot, Antrim* and *Argonaut.*

Naval Party 8901 consisted of about thirty-five ranks and lived at **Moody Brook Barracks**, just west of **Stanley**, but the Argentine invasion happened to coincide with the annual changeover then under way between those present under Major Gary Noot and by the relieving party under Major Mike Norman, which meant that sixty-nine Royal Marines were present on East Falkland on 2 April (plus one ex-Royal Marine resident there who re-enlisted) – a force wholly inadequate to do more with a few rocket launchers and their own rifles than offer what resistance it could to the thousands of Argentine troops converging on Stanley from two directions. After having inflicted a number of casualties on the invaders from their main position at Government House, they reluctantly obeyed the orders of Governor Rex Hunt and laid down their weapons. Taken into captivity to Argentina, Naval Party 8901 remained there only very briefly, being repatriated to the UK and arriving at RAF Brize Norton on the 5th. Many of them returned to the Falklands, however, as the nucleus of J Company **42 Commando**.

Royal Navy

As the Falklands War constituted a mainly naval operation, the Royal Navy played a fundamentally important part in the success of the campaign, deploying thirty-three ships and six submarines to the South Atlantic, supported by twenty-two ships from the **Royal Fleet Auxiliary**, two from the **Royal Maritime Auxiliary Service** and five **Ships Taken Up From Trade** in Royal Navy service. Warships of the Royal Navy proper were organised into fifteen different classes, designated by function, type number or the name of the lead-ship of the class. The warships for Operation **Corporate** comprised two **aircraft carriers** (*Hermes* and *Invincible*); fifteen **frigates**, eight **destroyers**, and six **submarines**. Supplying a formidable **Task Force** composed of a good balance of ship types, the Navy nonetheless suffered its share of weaknesses; chief among these was its poor capability in defending its vessels against sea-skimming missiles such as the **Exocet**.

Royal Navy aircraft during the conflict consisted of **Wessex**, **Lynx** and **Sea King** helicopters, and the **Sea Harrier** FRS1. Seven RAF **Harrier** pilots were 'navalised' and attached to *Hermes* and *Invincible* to compensate for the shortage of Royal Navy fixed-wing pilots operating Sea Harriers, although two of these fliers went south while still in the early stages of their operational training.

Salvageman, MT

Salvageman, a motor tug requisitioned from United Towing on 6 April, contained a RMAS Naval Party under Captain B. W. Vere-Stevens. *Salvageman* departed from Portsmouth on 10 April loaded with towing and salvage gear, reaching **Ascension** on the 23rd. She assisted in the evacuation of *Sheffield* after she was bombed on 4 May and was called to the stricken *Atlantic Conveyor* on the 25th. Her services continued to be of use well after the war; she did not arrive back in Hull until 22 June 1984.

Commander:	Captain A.J. Stockwell
Launched:	1980
Tonnage:	1,598 Gross Register
Dimensions: length × beam; feet (metres):	227 × 49 (69.1 x14.9)
Propulsion:	4 diesel engines (2 propellers) = 17.5 knots

San Carlos

When the decision was reached to land in **San Carlos Water**, the settlement of San Carlos was chosen as one of the three sites. Located deep on the eastern side of the inlet, it should not be confused with **Port San Carlos**, which faces the mouth of San Carlos Water. Blue Beach One was designated the landing site for **2 Para**, while **40 Commando** landed at Blue Beach Two. Later, on 2 June, the **Welsh Guards** also landed at San Carlos.

San Carlos Water

During the course of their journey to **Ascension**, Commodore Clapp and Brigadier **Thompson** chose three possible beaches on which to effect a landing, one of which included San Carlos Water. Prime considerations included the desire, if possible, to execute an unopposed landing; with the main Argentine forces concentrated around **Stanley**, San Carlos Water looked favourable. In naval terms, planners sought an anchorage sheltered from air attack, particularly the **Exocet** missile, which required a line of approach that involved skimming the surface of the water; San Carlos Water again appeared to meet this requirement. The position also offered some shelter from strong and unpredictable winds and strong seas, thus facilitating the amphibious landings. The landings had to occur beyond the range of Argentine artillery fire and yet within reasonable distance of Stanley to render approach

Troops in landing craft in San Carlos Water on 21 May. (AirSeaLand Photos)

feasible and resupply possible. The beaches had also to accommodate **landing craft** – both LCUs and LCVPs – as well as **Mexeflotes**, and provide adequate exit routes into the area beyond the bridgehead. Finally, San Carlos Water represented an area easily defendable against possible counter-attack and was sufficiently large to accommodate the five major units comprising **3 Commando Brigade**: **40 Commando, 42 Commando, 45 Commando, 2 Para** and **3 Para**, plus their supporting arms and a Brigade Maintenance Area – ultimately established at **Ajax Bay** – containing massive stocks of food, ammunition and medical supplies; in short, all the sinews of **logistics**.

San Carlos Water established itself as the favourite as early as 29 April, and in conjunction with the desire of Admiral **Fieldhouse** to land on East rather than **West Falkland**, the decision was made on 10 May to approach through this position, thereafter designated as the Amphibious Operating Area (AOA), which provided a sheltered anchorage that **Royal Navy** vessels could defend by closing the entrances to Falkland Sound against Argentine surface and submarine penetration. Notwithstanding the fact that Stanley, the ultimate objective, lay 50 miles beyond as the crow flies, over very rough terrain, it was reckoned that an Argentine counter-attack was unlikely or at least limited by the numbers of their assault **helicopters**. In addition, the high ground surrounding San Carlos Water would prevent Argentine aircraft from deploying their Exocet missiles at the ships in the anchorage. However, the surrounding hills were a two-edged sword, for they would prevent detection of low-flying aircraft until only moments before they appeared over the high ground, thus requiring the establishment of a naval air defence screen to the west. The narrow confines of the anchorage also restricted the ability of vessels to manoeuvre.

Thompson's 'Design for battle' within San Carlos Water involved a silent night attack by landing craft with the object of securing all the high ground by first light. Once it became clear on 19 May that no political settlement could be reached with Argentina, Northwood designated Friday, 21 May as D-Day and 0630Z as H Hour. Once inside San Carlos Water, the landing craft proceeded the 5-mile distance to the assault beaches, accompanied by HMS *Plymouth* offering **naval gunfire support**.

The **Special Boat Squadron** (SBS) was meant to use torch signals in Morse to communicate with the landing force thus: Alpha – 'Beach safe'; Bravo – 'Be careful'; Charlie – 'Enemy on beach'; no light – 'Serious problem' or 'enemy on beach'. In the event, the SBS got the date wrong, so no signal was shone. The first landing craft beached at around 0730Z, several metres behind the waterline, as a result of which most of the commandos and Paras reached dry land with wet feet, subsequently causing serious problems for some of them, especially 2 Para, which proceeded immediately up **Sussex Mountain**. The landings went virtually unopposed and without a single British fatality; a minor clash involving the SBS occurred at **Fanning Head** and a brief exchange of fire involving 3 Para took place during the Argentine withdrawal from **Port San Carlos**.

For a week after the landings, San Carlos Water, dubbed '**Bomb Alley**' by journalists, became the scene of regular Argentine air attacks, resulting in the loss of the **frigates** *Ardent* and *Antelope*. **5 Infantry Brigade** arrived on 2 June and unloaded troops, stores and vehicles on to the **Blue Beaches**.

Sapper Hill

A small 450ft feature just outside **Stanley** and the last point of resistance by the Argentines during ground operations, it was held by C Company, 3rd Infantry Regiment and M Company, 5th Marine Infantry Battalion.

With 2 **Scots Guards** victorious on **Mount Tumbledown**, at 1330Z on 14 June, the commanding officer of 1 **Welsh Guards**, Lieutenant Colonel Johnny Rickett, received orders from Major General **Moore** to seize Sapper Hill, with transport available via **Sea King** and more than sufficient troops: one company of the Welsh Guards and A and C Companies of 40 **Commando**. Although the attack was to be carried out in daylight, Rickett was assured of support from **Harriers**, and by 3 Troop, the **Blues and Royals**. **Helicopters** were meant to drop the troops about 3 miles from Sapper Hill on a track south of Tumbledown, but this proved to be mined and the men instead arrived close to Sapper Hill itself. A ten-minute firefight beginning around 1545Z ensued involving the **Royal Marines** and the Argentines, in which two of the former were wounded, but when the general surrender became known the defenders simply withdrew from the hill.

As the Argentines were known to have a 105mm artillery position on Sapper Hill, at 1200Z on 7 June two Harriers attacked it unsuccessfully with rockets. Other missions were flown two days later. On 12 June, two days before the Argentine surrender and in the wake of the British successes at **Mount Longdon, Two Sisters** and **Mount Harriet**, pairs of Harriers of 1 Squadron flew three missions against Argentine positions on Sapper Hill, the first launched at 1145Z. Two Harriers took off from *Hermes* at 1500Z on 14 June, the last day of the war, to make a combined laser-guided bomb/cluster bomb sortie against Argentine positions on the hill, but when white flags appeared at 1550Z the mission was aborted just minutes before the attack was due to commence.

Saxonia, MV

A motor refrigerated cargo vessel chartered on 28 April from Cunard for use as a naval stores and provisions transport, and one of the few **Ships Taken Up From Trade** that carried a Naval Party supplied by the Royal Navy Supply and Transport Service. *Saxonia* departed Devonport on 8 May and arrived off **South Georgia** on the 23rd. Her South Atlantic service ended when she arrived in Portsmouth on 28 June.

Commander:	Captain H. Evans	
Launched:	1972	
Tonnage:	8,547 Gross Register	12,182 Deadweight
Dimensions: length × beam; feet (metres):	533.5 × 75 (162.6 × 22.8)	
Propulsion:	1 diesel engine	23,200bhp = 23.5 knots
Helicopter platform – no embarked aircraft		

Scimitar

One of two types of light armoured vehicles known as **CVR(T)s** employed by the two troops of the **Blues and Royals** in the Falklands, the Scimitar was slightly lighter than the **Scorpion**, mounting a small gun in the form of a 30mm Rarden cannon that could fire armour piercing or high-explosive shells on a flat trajectory with exceptionally high accuracy. It carried 165 rounds for the main armament and 3,000 rounds of ammunition for its coaxially mounted 7.62 mm General Purpose Machine Gun. Four Scimitars served in the conflict, two in each of the two troops, with Scorpions supplying the other four vehicles. The Scimitars came ashore on 21 May, each carried in separate **landing craft** for purposes of providing close fire support if necessary, which they provided at both **Wireless Ridge** and at **Mount Tumbledown**.

A Scorpion of the Blues and Royals. (AirSeaLand Photos)

Scorpion

A light tank, known as a **CVR(T)**, used for armed reconnaissance and employed, together with **Scimitars**, by the **Blues and Royals**. Fully loaded, the Alvis Scorpion weighed 17,500lb with sufficient protection to withstand 14.5mm projectiles and 7.62mm armoured-piercing rounds. The three crew consisted of the commander, who also served as loader, with seven periscopes and a roof mounted sight at his disposal; the gunner, who doubled as radio operator, employing two periscopes, a roof-mounted sight, and a passive night sight with image intensifier; and a driver with his own periscope. The Scorpion had a top road speed of 50mph with a maximum road range of 400 miles. Its main armament consisted of a 76mm L23 gun capable of firing three types of projectiles: high explosive (HE), high-explosive squash head (HESH), or smoke, with up to forty rounds, together with a coaxially mounted General Purpose Machine Gun with 3,000 rounds of ammunition.

Two Scorpions came ashore with **2 Para** on 21 May, each carried in separate **landing craft** for the purpose of providing close fire support if necessary. Two further Scorpions accompanied **3 Para** ashore. Like the Scimitar, its performance in cross-country progress across the boggy and irregular ground of East Falkland greatly exceeded pessimistic expectations. Scorpions served at both **Wireless Ridge** and **Mount Tumbledown**.

Scots Guards

The 2nd Battalion Scots Guards belonged to **5 Infantry Brigade** and was commanded by Lieutenant Colonel Michael Scott, whose long service included tours of Kenya, Canada, Aden and Northern Ireland. 2 Scots Guards normally formed part of the Household Division and was based at Chelsea Barracks in London on ceremonial duties, but the regiment's two battalions primarily served in Ulster and with the British Army of the Rhine (BAOR) in Germany. Although the unit's training, equipment and mindset was not designed for 'out-of-area' operations, on 14 April it was notified of its definite departure for the South Atlantic and transferred from London District to 5 Infantry Brigade to compensate for the shifting of **2 Para** and **3 Para** from that formation to **3 Commando Brigade**.

Although trained like other infantry units, the Scots Guards required further physical training to bring it up to the standard required for service almost certain to be conducted without the benefit of movement by air or motorised transport, though some **BV 202E** over-snow vehicles accompanied the unit south. As part of the effort to raise fitness standards and to attune the battalion to combat under trying climatic and topographical conditions, the Scots Guards took part in Exercise **Welsh Falcon** in the Brecon Beacons in late April and early May, returning to London on 3 May.

Scots Guards landing at San Carlos on 2 June. (AirSeaLand Photos)

S

The battalion embarked from Southampton in *Queen Elizabeth 2* on 12 May and cross-decked to *Canberra* off **South Georgia** on 27 May. Along with the rest of 5 Infantry Brigade, it was then put ashore on 2 June near **San Carlos** by **landing craft**, its vulnerable situation partly ameliorated from possible air attack by misty conditions.

As part of the plan of Brigadier **Wilson** for a southern advance on **Stanley**, he tasked the Scots Guards with taking over the forward position held by D Company, 2 Para east of Bluff Cove Inlet. Accordingly, on 5 June Commodore Clapp, Commander **Amphibious Task Group**, ordered the battalion to embark on *Intrepid* and land at **Bluff Cove** on the night of 6–7 June. It was retracted in landing craft from *Intrepid* off Lively Island and spent nine hours in rough seas before reaching Bluff Cove, freezing, wet and exhausted, with many suffering from severe exposure. Lieutenant Colonel Chaundler, CO 2 Para and present with his battalion at Bluff Cove, ordered the Scots Guards' 2i/c, Major Iain Mackay-Dick, to move north and dig in. When Wilson arrived by helicopter, however, Chaundler suggested that the Scots Guards remain to rest at Bluff Cove rather than take up defensive positions in open ground outside the settlement. Wilson agreed: the battalion remained while 2 Para returned to **Fitzroy** in the four LCUs in which the Scots Guards had recently arrived.

Within a day of arriving at Bluff Cove, the Scots Guards dispatched patrols and, on the basis of **Special Air Service** intelligence, actively searched for Argentine howitzer positions and a **radar** post thought to be sited at Port Harriet. In the event, the intelligence was faulty, and Operation Impunity discovered no such positions.

As part of 5 Infantry Brigade's southern thrust against Stanley, the Scots Guards, reinforced by D Company, 1/7 **Gurkha Rifles**, was to provide right-flank protection to **42 Commando** as the **Royal Marines** attacked **Mount Harriet**, which took place on the night of 11–12 June. The Scots Guards' own main effort against **Mount Tumbledown** took place on the night of the 13th to 14th.

After the surrender, most of the Scots Guards were moved to **West Falkland** until the arrival of the first garrison troops, 1st Battalion, The Queen's Own Highlanders, who reached the Falklands in the middle of July aboard *Norland*. The battalion then departed for home aboard that vessel, together with the **Welsh Guards**, on 19 July. It arrived at **Ascension**, from where it flew by **VC10** to Brize Norton the following day.

Total casualties sustained by the Scots Guards up to 23 June amounted to eight killed, thirty-nine wounded, ten injured and four out of action through illness.

Scottish Eagle, MV

A motor tanker chartered from the King Line on 12 May as a base fuel tanker. Launched in 1980 and under Captain A. Terras, *Scottish Eagle* was dispatched to the South Atlantic but did not arrive at **South Georgia** until 18 June. She departed Milford Haven Oil Refinery Terminal and served in South Georgia and Falklands waters for an extended period after the war, reaching Plymouth on 23 October.

Commander:	Captain A. Terras	
Launched:	1980	
Displacement (tons):	33,000 Gross Register	56,490 Deadweight
Dimensions: length × beam; feet (metres):	689 × 106 (210 × 32.3)	
Propulsion:	1 × diesel engine	17,400bhp = 16.5 knots

Scout AH1

Twelve Scout AH1 light **helicopters** served on operations in the South Atlantic, six from 3 Commando Brigade Air Squadron (CBAS) and six from 656 Squadron **Army Air Corps**.

Carrying a crew of two, a pilot and aircrewman/observer, the Westland Scout AH1 performed many functions, the most important of which was in ferrying vital supplies and ammunition over roadless terrain that most vehicles could not traverse, although they were also used in reconnaissance and in the light attack role: in the final days of the war Scouts were armed with Aerospatiale wire-guided SS-11 anti-tank missiles. In the absence of Argentine armour, their pilots deployed the SS-11 on several occasions against entrenched positions such as bunkers and sangars, and probably in at least one instance against an artillery piece. Scouts also worked busily in the casualty evacuation (casevac) role during the ground operations, ferrying the wounded directly from the battlefield to aid stations at **Ajax Bay**, **Teal Inlet** or **Fitzroy** as appropriate, as well as during the critical casevac operations on 8 June after the disaster at **Port Pleasant**.

All told, and with the exception of the single lost helicopter, the Scouts in 3 CBAS averaged a total of just over 110 hours in the air each between 21 May and 24 June. One Scout was shot down by a Pucara – the only British aircraft to be downed in an air-to-air engagement.

Seacat

Manufactured by Short Brothers & Harland, the Seacat surface-to-air missile system designed for short-range point defence was best used against low and medium level aircraft at ranges up to 6,000yd, although it could be deployed against ships as well. Seacat employed an optical (i.e. the operator using binoculars) or a **radar** command guidance system, with each missile measuring 4.75ft (1.47m) in length and weighing 150lb (68kg) with a high-explosive warhead. Its solid-fuel rocket gave it a range of 5,000yd (4.6km). The Seacat came in three variants: Visually Guided (GWS 20), Radar/Visually Guided (GWS 22), and TV guided (GWS 24). During the Falklands War, the Seacat was carried by the **destroyers** *Antrim* and *Glamorgan* and by the Amazon class **frigates** *Antelope*, *Active*, *Ambuscade*, *Arrow*, *Alacrity*, *Ardent* and *Avenger*.

The Seacat performed poorly for close air defence, responding too slowly to the nimble and fast Argentine jets, such as when on 21 May the system aboard

Ardent malfunctioned during an attack on that vessel. As such, it did not appear to have shot down any Argentine aircraft, although it may have been responsible for inflicting damage or aborting attacks. On the other hand, it held the advantage over the **Sea Wolf** in being capable of being fired within **San Carlos Water**, where the surrounding hills confounded the radar guidance of the Sea Wolf, a more advanced weapon system but subject to more operational breakdowns than Seacat.

Sea Dart

A third generation surface-to-air missile system built by Hawker-Siddeley Dynamics, the Sea Dart used a semi-active **radar** homing system (Type 909) against incoming missiles or fast-moving aircraft. With a length of 14.4ft (4.4m) and weighing 1,210lb (550kg), its missile could be fired by its ramjet motor with rocket booster to 11 miles (20km) at low altitude and to 34 miles (63km) at high altitude.

Responsible for shooting down seven Argentine aircraft, the Sea Dart served best in medium-range area defence and was capable of striking targets at 40,000ft from 20 miles' distance, with the weapon most effective over open sea. Its Type 965 radar proved much less effective at detecting aircraft at low altitudes or in proximity to land, owing to background clutter and radar reflections bouncing off the ground. This applied more to fast jets than to slow-moving **helicopters**, one of which, an Argentine Puma, was lost to a Sea Dart missile. Its aiming and firing system left something to be desired and it proved slow in acquiring targets. On 22 May, for instance, while the destroyer *Coventry* stood on picket duty north of **Pebble Island**, her Sea Dart system malfunctioned, allowing a passing Argentine Hercules to proceed to **Stanley** unharmed when only 8 miles distant.

On 25 May, a Sea Dart launched at long range from *Coventry* did bring down a Skyhawk over **West Falkland**; however, later the same day the ship's Sea Dart system failed to acquire two Skyhawks approaching low and fast over **West Falkland**. This was due to the system's inability to cope when the two aircraft split up, confusing the computer, which thought it was tracking a single target (in fact, it was two aircraft flying in close formation). Moreover, the Sea Dart radar failed to distinguish between the background terrain, coastline and hills, and the aircraft. In the confusion, the computer crashed, denying the technicians time in which to deploy the weapon again.

Also on the 25th, the aircraft carrier *Invincible* fired a salvo of six Sea Dart missiles at two **Exocet** missiles fired by Super Etendards north of Stanley, but neither of the incoming missiles was hit. On the afternoon of the 30th, *Exeter* fired three Sea Darts: one at an Exocet missile launched from a Super Etendard which missed its target, while the other two destroyed separate Skyhawks. *Exeter* achieved success again on 7 June when a Sea Dart destroyed an Argentine Learjet flying a reconnaissance mission over Falkland Sound, although a second missile malfunctioned and fell into the sea. A week later, on the last day of the war, a Sea Dart fired by *Exeter* downed a Canberra B62 bomber off the coast of East Falkland.

Sea Harrier FRS1

Manufactured by British Aerospace, this impressive single-seater vertical and/or short take-off and landing (V/STOL) aircraft served as part of the **Fleet Air Arm**, its primary function being reconnaissance and searching for, and attacking, enemy ships; but with the withdrawal of nearly all Argentine ships from the **Total Exclusion Zone** early in the conflict the Sea Harriers' role became less one of probing to one of air defence of the ships of the **Task Force**. Later still, after air superiority swung in favour of the British a week after the landings, Sea Harriers supported ground operations.

A total of only twenty-eight served on operations in the South Atlantic, although their numbers varied, so that on 20 May, for instance, the Task Force had twenty-five on hand. The Sea Harriers of 800 and 801 Naval Air Squadrons (NAS) (809 NAS also flew Sea Harriers, but was integrated with 800 and 801 NAS) performed vital service during the campaign out of all proportion to their numbers, flying 2,197 sorties between 5 April and 30 June. Most of these missions were flown from the decks of the **aircraft carriers** *Hermes* and *Invincible*: between 1 May and 16 June 737 sorties originated from the former and 598 from the latter. All told, Sea Harriers dropped 437 bombs in the course of the war.

The Sea Harrier was armed with twin AIM-9L **Sidewinder** missiles and two **Aden 30mm cannon**, scoring twelve and seven kills with them respectively. Sea

A Sea Harrier descends on to the deck of HMS *Hermes*. (AirSeaLand Photos)

Harrier XZ451 flown by Lieutenant Commander 'Sharkey' Ward was responsible for shooting down the only Argentine C-130E Hercules transport lost during the war when at 1346Z on 1 June, two aircraft downed it about 50 miles north of **Pebble Island** with a Sidewinder and 30mm cannon fire.

The Sea Harrier could substitute three 1,000lb bombs or as many as five BL755 cluster bombs in the place of Sidewinders and Aden cannons when attacking a large target area such as an airfield or **radar** installation at low level. In its own defence, the Sea Harrier could manoeuvre very effectively, change altitude rapidly and drop chaff.

Three Argentine aircraft were downed by cannon fire and one helicopter crashed while seeking to outmanoeuvre a pursuing Sea Harrier. All told, Sea Harriers accounted for twenty-three Argentine aircraft. Sea Harriers suffered a 25 per cent attrition rate, with four lost in operational accidents and two to ground fire. One of the accidents involved two 801 NAS Sea Harriers flown by Lieutenant Al Curtis and Lieutenant Commander John Eyton-Jones, respectively, who appeared to have collided in fog and low cloud while investigating a radar target to the south of the **Carrier Battle Group**, with no sign of the pilots or wreckage ever found. Not a single Sea Harrier was lost – much less damaged – in air-to-air combat. The first Sea Harrier lost in action was that flown by Lieutenant Nick Taylor in XZ450, which crashed during a raid on **Goose Green** after being hit by anti-aircraft fire.

In the absence of an early warning radar system, Sea Harrier pilots had to rely on their own vision to identify their foe. The aircraft enjoyed a remarkable record of serviceability for the duration of the war, with an average of 95 per cent of machines operationally fit every morning and 99 per cent of planned missions carried out, with pilots averaging three sorties daily – although some flew up to six. The aircraft was also impressive for its ability to fly missions in the adverse – even harsh – weather conditions of the South Atlantic, beyond the means of other fighters.

As the Sea Harrier possessed inadequate Airborne Early Warning (AEW) capability of its own it depended on what radar data friendly warships provided, usually via fighter directors. This dependency resulted from the poor capability of the pilot's Blue Fox radar in detecting low-level flights and aircraft flying over land since their signal became confused with features on the ground. This left the pilot largely to visually identify Argentine aircraft, with or without prior warning provided by ships out to sea.

A number of points relating to the Sea Harrier's operational service in the Falklands are worth noting: **Woodward's** decision to shift the Carrier Battle Group further east of the Falklands following the loss of *Sheffield* on 4 May meant that the Sea Harriers had a greater distance to operate on their **combat air patrols** (CAP) and therefore less flying time. In a few instances Sea Harriers attacked the handful of Argentine vessels that dared approach the Falklands. On 9 May, for instance, two Sea Harriers discovered the 1,400-ton Argentine stern trawler *Narwal*, used to gather intelligence on the movements of the ships and aircraft of the Task Force, about

60 miles south-east of **Stanley**. The Sea Harriers dropped both their 1,000lb bombs, one of which struck and damaged the ship but did not explode, being fused for release from a higher altitude. The *Narwal* was also damaged by strafing by 30mm cannon. A **Special Boat Squadron** team boarded her from **Sea Kings** and took the crew away to *Hermes*. The trawler sank in a storm on the 10th after the prize crew was airlifted away by Sea Kings.

From about 15 May, the two squadrons of Sea Harriers typically began to carry a single 1,000lb bomb when on CAP to be used against targets of opportunity, most notably in the area around Stanley, keeping the Argentines guessing as to their targets and thus causing consternation and sapping morale.

By the end of the first day of the landings, 21 May, the Sea Harrier had proven its efficacy, having flown fifty CAP sorties and accounting for ten of the thirteen Argentine aircraft shot down over Falkland Sound and **San Carlos Water**. As such, the aircraft performed very well, in tandem with the ships' air defences, in preventing air attacks from reaching the more vulnerable amphibious, transport and supply ships close inshore.

On 22 May, Sea Harriers flew sixty CAP sorties, most of these in defence of the warships moved that day from Falkland Sound into San Carlos Water to benefit from the collective protection now furnished by the twelve **Rapier** fire units established atop the hills around the beachhead.

From late May, Sea Harriers, together with **Harrier** GR3s, began to use, when circumstances suggested it more convenient not to return to the carriers, 'HMS Sheathbill', a temporary landing strip made of aluminium planks constructed near Port **San Carlos**.

Sea King HAS2A

Capable of carrying up to twenty-five passengers, the Westland Sea King HAS2A was flown by 824 and 825 Naval Air Squadrons, with five **helicopters** of the former on board RFA *Olmeda* and ten of the latter in RFA *Fort Grange*. 825 NAS was normally a **Royal Navy** anti-submarine warfare (ASW) training squadron but converted to the utility role, such as for moving ammunition and stores. A Sea King could, for instance, transport forty-eight rounds of 105mm artillery ammunition.

When deployed in its ASW role, it lowered its sonar device up to 150ft below the surface to detect **submarines** to a range of at least 8 miles. If targeting a submarine it deployed one of three different types of weapon: four Mark 46 or Stingray lightweight torpedoes, or four Mark 11 depth charges.

The HAS2A was also used in search and rescue and equipped with a **radar** system capable of over-the-horizon targeting up to 50 miles. Several HAS2As rescued seriously injured survivors from the burning deck of *Sir Galahad* on 8 June. It flew 394 sorties totalling 1,756 hours of flying time and executed 1,051 deck landings.

Sea King HAS5

More advanced than the HAS2A, in particular due to its improved Sea Searcher **radar**, with some equipped with sonar sweeps used for detecting enemy **submarines**, two squadrons (820 and 826 Naval Air Squadron (NAS)) of Westland Sea King HAS5s served in the conflict, spending more time in the air than the HAS2A.

The rush to get stores aboard vessels at Portsmouth, Plymouth and Southampton as quickly as possible would later require an enormous effort by Sea Kings to cross-deck and reload them in the best order for offloading during the landings. This gargantuan task was carried out by Sea King HAS5s while at **Ascension**, together with other **helicopters**.

Ten machines provided a continuous anti-submarine warfare (ASW) screen for the **Task Force** from its departure from Ascension on 18 April until three days after the surrender, during which period three HAS5s patrolled around the clock searching for Argentine submarines, unaware that the threat ended on 11 May when the *San Luis* left the **Total Exclusion Zone** and did not return.

Between them the two squadrons flew 2,253 sorties for a total of 6,847 hours in the air – about half in the tedious ASW role – with sorties averaging approximately three hours. Sea King HAS5s of 820 NAS dropped six torpedoes and ten depth charges, with each pilot flying more than 300 hours between April and June.

In the three-month period from the first day of the war, 826 NAS flew 3,300 hours, achieving a rate aloft five times that of peacetime, with one machine clocking 265 hours in a single month – equal to ten days' continuous flight. Severe malfunction of two machines rendered them both unserviceable.

Sea King HC4

The highly reliable Westland Sea King HC4s belonged to 846 Naval Air Squadron (NAS), which possessed fourteen such machines, and provided most of the logistic lift during the ground campaign, with the squadron shifting 6,550 tons of cargo and more than 9,000 troops and averaging 170 flying hours per month per machine. In the course of the conflict the squadron performed 1,818 sorties, 3,343 deck landings and spent 3,107 hours in the air – clocking between April and June as many flying hours in theatre as a twelve-month period during peacetime. The machine enjoyed an extremely high rate of serviceability due to the remarkable efficiency of the ground crews.

The HC4 differed from the HAS5 as a consequence of their differing roles; as a logistic support helicopter, the HC4 possessed a more spacious cabin, bereft of the dipping sonar and other equipment present in the anti-submarine warfare HAS5, and thus enabling it to carry as many as twenty-eight fully armed men, an underslung load of up to 7,500lb, a fully laden Land Rover or a 105mm light gun.

HC4s performed all manner of roles: operating from *Norland*, *Fearless* and *Canberra*, they carried **Rapier** fire units ashore in underslung loads for the defence of **San**

Carlos Water on 21 May, together with several 105mm guns, troops and equipment; HC4s ferried casualties from the Argentine air raid on Ajax Bay on 27 May to the hospital ship *Uganda*; a Sea King commanded by Lieutenant J.A.G. Miller winched onboard the survivors of LCU Foxtrot Four near Choiseul Sound on the afternoon of 8 June, the same day as the tragedy that befell the *Sir Galahad* and *Sir Tristram*. Sea King HC4 ZA313 was very close to *Sir Galahad* during the Skyhawk attack at Port Pleasant on 8 June and came to the crew's immediate rescue, hovering over the foredeck and winching up survivors before transferring them ashore.

846 NAS was unique among helicopter operators on Operation Corporate, being supplied with four sets of US-designed passive night vision goggles, whose image-intensifying capacity enabled low level night flying. This in turn allowed the HC4 to insert Special Forces teams into the Falklands countryside and elsewhere. On twelve nights between 1 May and 18 May, 846's Sea Kings flew twenty-six sorties involving the insertion of Special Air Service (SAS) and Special Boat Squadron (SBS) teams. Two Sea King HC4s were lost due to accidents and one, ZA290, was destroyed on the ground in Chile on 18 May by its crew during an abortive SAS operation. Other examples include the raid on Pebble Island: in the early hours of 15 May and using passive night vision goggles, four Sea King HC4s carried SAS troops from *Hermes* to Pebble Island to execute its overwhelmingly successful raid against the airstrip there. Four Sea Kings then extracted them back after the raid. It was an 846 NAS Sea King, flying between *Hermes* and *Intrepid*, which crashed into the sea on 19 May, killing eighteen SAS and two other military personnel. Another provided lift for 3 SBS before dawn on 21 May to Fanning Head to neutralise the small Argentine force there in anticipation of the landings in San Carlos Water.

Sea Lynx

See Lynx

Sea Skua

An anti-ship missile designed and built by British Aerospace, the helicopter-launched Sea Skua employed a semi-active radar homing system. Measuring 9ft (2.8m) long and weighing 460lb (210kg), it was propelled by a solid-fuel rocket to a range of about 5 miles (9km). Where a sortie required deployment of the Sea Skua, helicopters not fitted with the missile were substituted with one another aboard ship for specific missions. Thus, fitted to most, but not all, of the Lynx HAS2 fleet, while it could not inflict the kind of catastrophic damage associated with the Exocet or Harpoon, Sea Skua could disable small vessels such as the three against which it was fired. On 3 May, the Lynx helicopter aboard the destroyer *Coventry* fired two Sea Skua missiles at the Argentine patrol vessel *Alferez Sobral*, marking the first operational use of the new weapon. Shortly thereafter the Lynx operating from *Glasgow* struck the same vessel with its two Sea Skuas; although heavily damaged, the ship limped back to the Argentine mainland. A Sea Skua was also fired against the *Rio Iquazu*, and two against the 8,482-ton cargo ship *Rio Carcarana* on 23 May.

Seaslug

A surface-to-air missile, the Seaslug 2 (GWS 10) was designed and manufactured by Hawker-Siddeley Dynamics using a beam-riding Type 901 **radar** guidance system. The missile measured 19.5ft (5.9m) in length and weighed 1,980lb (900kg), and its solid-fuel rocket boosters could propel the projectile to a range of 15 miles (27.6km). The County class **Antrim** and **Glamorgan** were armed with Seaslug as well as **Seacat**, with the former providing a much longer range of about 15 miles (27.6km). Seaslug could also be fired in a ship-to-shore mode, as *Glamorgan* did against **Stanley** airport on 27 May, but travelled unguided when thus launched.

Sea Wolf

Designed and manufactured by British Aerospace as an advanced point defence short-range missile system deployable against missiles and aircraft, Sea Wolf used its Type 967/986 surveillance **radar** to identify its target and transmit guidance information to its launcher, which fired one of six missiles, guided in turn by its Type 910 tracking radar. Propelled by its solid-fuel rocket to a range of approximately 2,700yd (2.5km), the missile measured 6.25ft (1.9m) in length and weighed 180lb (82kg).

Only two ships in the **Task Force** were equipped with Sea Wolf – the **frigates** *Broadsword* and *Brilliant* – but in their role protecting the **aircraft carriers**, which never came under attack, they seldom fired the missile except when detached to work with a Type 42 **destroyer**. A combination of its operators' still being novices and its acquisition and tracking system not functioning optimally led to initial problems, but steady achievements were made through hard experience. When on 16 May, for instance, *Broadsword* test-fired her Sea Wolf system against 4.5in shells fired by *Yarmouth*, two of them were brought down, demonstrating the missile's potential effectiveness.

A Sea Wolf missile launched by *Brilliant* on 12 May shot down two Argentine aircraft and forced another to crash while the latter sought to outmanoeuvre it. Another missile accounted for one of thirteen Argentine aircraft shot down over **San Carlos Water** on the first day of the landings, 21 May, but many more were fired; its radar struggled to lock on to targets amid all the high ground of the surrounding area. At least one fired by *Broadsword* on 23 May failed to strike its target, possibly for this reason. Thus, although Sea Wolf was never fired at an **Exocet** missile during the war, in its secondary role against low- and medium-level aircraft it did account for at least three Argentine kills.

Self-Loading Rifle

See Infantry weapons

Sheffield, HMS

One of eight **destroyers** that served in the South Atlantic, she belonged to the Type 42, Sheffield class laid down in the 1970s and designed for area air defence. She was powered with a dual set of engines, both designed by Rolls-Royce: the gas turbine Tyne for cruising, and the Olympus for full power, which could be achieved after approximately thirty seconds. As with other Type 42s, she carried the **Sea Dart** system, which forced attacking aircraft to fly close to the water's surface.

In late March 1982, *Sheffield* numbered among five destroyers taking part in Exercise **Springtrain**, as a consequence of which, after cross-decking supplies and

HMS *Sheffield* ablaze on 4 May after being struck by an Exocet missile. (AirSeaLand Photos)

transferring aircraft and personnel at Gibraltar, she sailed as part of the initial **Task Force**, arriving at **Ascension** on 11 April and off the Falklands on 1 May.

On 4 May two Super Etendards took off from Rio Grande at 1245Z and approached **San Carlos Water** just above sea level to avoid radar detection, and with a low cloud base aiding them. *Glasgow* detected the two aircraft on her **radar** and although she immediately transmitted a radio warning to the other ships of the **Task Force**, these were not properly heeded by the anti-air warfare officer aboard the aircraft carrier *Invincible* owing to previous mistaken reports of the proximity of Argentine aircraft; thus, Air Raid Warning White – indicating no hostile aircraft within 100 miles – remained in place. When *Glasgow's* radar detected the Super Etendards' presence again a short time later, again the warning did not elicit an upgrade in the alert state. At approximately 1402Z, both attacking aircraft launched their **Exocets** when less than 20 miles from *Sheffield* and changed course for home, eluding two **Sea Harriers** already airborne.

Glasgow engaged her anti-ship defences by firing chaff, followed later by attempting but failing to launch a Sea Dart. The two incoming Exocets approached just above the surface of the sea. Meanwhile, since the Satellite Communication Onboard Terminal (SCOT) satellite uplink terminal aboard *Sheffield* was in use to contact London during this period, the ship's electronic warning equipment could not be used properly either to track approaching aircraft or to detect incoming missiles.

At 1404Z one of the missiles struck *Sheffield* 6ft above the waterline on her starboard side amidships. Notwithstanding the missile's failure to explode, it tore through the auxiliary machine room to the forward engine room, inflicting heavy damage and causing an uncontrollable fire started by unspent rocket fuel and spread by the proximity of the strike to the ship's fuel tanks. *Sheffield's* fire control system simply could not cope as a consequence of damage inflicted to her water main and power supply.

Ten minutes after the missile strike, a **Sea King** on anti-submarine warfare (ASW) patrol nearby lowered a crew member aboard *Sheffield* to determine the cause of the crisis, after which it radioed *Hermes*. After a concerted effort to control the fire over a four-hour period and with the flames nearing the Sea Dart magazine, the captain had no choice but to order the crew to abandon ship. *Arrow* manoeuvred alongside the stricken vessel and rescued most of the 266 survivors, with a handful coming off via an 826 Naval Air Squadron Sea King after *Arrow* rapidly left the scene under the false impression that a torpedo had been fired at her. *Sheffield* lost nineteen officers and crew killed, one civilian dead and twenty-four wounded. The calamity demonstrated the inadequacy of her damage control systems.

On the day following the attack, two **Wessex** collected survivors from *Arrow* and transferred them to *Resource* and *Fort Austin*. In due course, *British Esk* took the survivors to Ascension whence, on 27 May, two **VC10s** flew them to RAF Brize Norton.

Rather than scuttle or torpedo her, Admiral **Woodward** chose to leave *Sheffield in situ* as a decoy target, but the hulk was drifting by the 6th. In the early hours of the 9th, *Yarmouth* took *Sheffield* in tow to **South Georgia** to determine if she could be salvaged. Two days later, however, high seas flooded *Sheffield's* lower decks, causing her to go down 135 miles east of the Falklands, thereby constituting the first **Royal Navy** vessel sunk in action since the Second World War.

Commander:	Captain J.F.T. Salt	
Launched:	10 June 1971	
Commissioned:	16 February 1975	
Builders:	Vickers (Barrow)	
Displacement (tons):	3,150 Standard	4,100 Full Load
Dimensions: length × beam; feet (metres):	410 × 47 (125 × 13.3)	
Draught:	5.8m	
Propulsion:	2 Rolls-Royce Olympus gas turbines	54,400shp = 30 knots
	2 Rolls-Royce Tyne gas turbines	8,200shp = 18 knots (cruising)
Armament:	1 × 4.5in Mark 8 gun	
	2 × 20mm AA guns	
	1 × **Sea Dart** system (GWS 30)	
	2 × triple ASW torpedo tubes (STWS)	
Aircraft:	1 × **Lynx** HAS2	

Ships Taken Up From Trade

Merchant ships requisitioned by the government using emergency powers and deployed to support the **Royal Navy** separately from the **Royal Fleet Auxiliary** (RFA) were popularly known by the acronym STUFT. In times of emergency, government departments such as the Ministry of Defence – specifically the Lords Commissioners of the Admiralty – and the Department of Transport, in consultation with the General Council of British Shipping, had authority to requisition civilian vessels; this became all the more relevant when the Government's White Paper of 1981 announced severe cutbacks in the **Royal Navy's** surface fleet that were to take effect the following year, although the Falklands War stayed this process.

Although 'out-of-area' operations were considered extremely unlikely, some contingency plans existed, albeit not for the repossession of the Falklands. Nevertheless, plans did exist for requisitioning vessels from the civilian trade, and on the afternoon of 4 April, two days after the Argentine invasion, an Order in Council from the Queen set this process in motion.

Ships were immediately identified to match operational requirements and conversion and alterations began almost immediately, around the clock, involving dockyard workers, engineers, armourers, technicians, managers, logisticians, and specialists of all kinds. Priority was placed on fitting helicopter landing decks – substantial enough in some cases to accommodate even a fully laden **Chinook** – to enable supplies and troops to be cross-decked or transferred ashore in all weather conditions.

In some instances modifications were also required to accommodate large numbers of troops and their stores, as well as facilities to feed them and provide fresh water. Some vessels were required to carry three times as many personnel for which their normal capacity provided, not to mention their weapons and equipment. Refuelling and medical facilities in most vessels were also required. Communications, particularly UHF equipment suited to war conditions, and facilities for operating naval cryptography, required specialist personnel, as did the satellite communications fitted to some vessels. All STUFT were thus assigned a Royal Naval Party furnished by either the RFA or **Royal Maritime Auxiliary Service** to assist with communications and other matters of co-ordination with Royal Navy ships. As a consequence of the extraordinary efforts of thousands of individuals, most STUFT would sail with the **Task Force** before the end of the month.

STUFT included many varieties of vessel, such as *Atlantic Conveyor*, converted for aircraft transport, later joined by *Atlantic Causeway*, *Contender Bezant* and *Astronomer*. *Uganda*, an educational cruise ship, was converted to a hospital ship, while *Hydra*, *Hecla* and *Herald* were converted into ambulance ships. On the outbreak on hostilities, most STUFT crews were given the option to remain in service; nearly all accepted.

Forty-nine ships were taken up from trade and commissioned for Royal Navy service before 15 June, all but six of which saw service in the South Atlantic before the Argentine surrender. This included one hospital ship, one minesweeper support ship, one mooring vessel, two repair ships, three salvage tugs, fifteen logistic support vessels (twelve support oilers, two base storage tankers and one fresh water tanker), five stores ships, four aircraft transports, two dispatch vessels, and nine personnel and vehicle transports.

Ships taken up from trade and the RFA shifted between them an estimated 9,000 personnel, 100,000 tons of freight and ninety-five aircraft to the South Atlantic. Only one STUFT vessel was sunk – *Atlantic Conveyor* – hit by at least one **Exocet** missile on 25 May.

Sidewinder

The AIM-9L Sidewinder missile proved a highly effective weapon in the air war over the Falklands, with nineteen Argentine aircraft downed by **Sea Harriers** deploying this 165lb armament fitted with an infra-red homing device and high-explosive warhead capable of striking a target up to approximately 1,200yd. Twenty out of twenty-six Sidewinders launched struck their target, in every case while the attacker was pursuing an Argentine aircraft from behind, rendering this weapon very favourable in British eyes and a source of dread for their adversaries. One Sidewinder failed to launch during the pursuit of a Skyhawk over **San Carlos Water** on 21 May, while another was mistakenly fired when the pilot intended to drop bombs and initiated the wrong switch. On 8 June three Skyhawks were shot down in rapid succession over Choiseul Sound by two Sea Harriers firing Sidewinders.

Signals

See Radio communication

Sir Bedivere, RFA

One of six **Landing Ships Logistic** in theatre as part of the large contingent of **Royal Fleet Auxiliary** vessels on Operation **Corporate**, the others being *Sir Galahad*, *Sir Geraint*, *Sir Lancelot*, *Sir Percivale* and *Sir Tristram*. She departed Marchwood on 29 April, reached **Ascension** on 8 May and arrived off the Falklands ten days later. On D-Day, she lay due west of the opening of **San Carlos Water**, where she was hit by two bombs, both of which failed to explode and initially prevented her from landing her stores and vehicles. Her South Atlantic service ended upon arrival back at Marchwood on 16 November.

Commander:	Captain P.J. McCarthy	
Launched:	20 July 1966	
Commissioned:	18 May 1967	
Tonnage:	3,270 Light Displacement	5,674 Full Load
	2,400 Deadweight	4,473 Gross Register
Dimensions: length × beam; feet (metres):	366 × 60 (126.5 × 17.7)	
Propulsion:	2 diesel engines	9,400bhp = 17 knots
Armament:	2 × 40mm AA guns	
Assault load:	402 troops	
	340 tons of stores/vehicles	
	2 **Mexeflote** sections	
Aircraft:	3 × light helicopters (**Gazelle** or **Scout**)	
	2 × helicopter decks (amidships and aft)	

Sir Galahad, RFA

One of six **Landing Ships Logistic** in the South Atlantic, the others being *Sir Bedivere*, *Sir Geraint*, *Sir Lancelot*, *Sir Percivale*, and *Sir Tristram*. Many of her crew were Chinese. She departed Devonport on 6 April and arrived at **Ascension** on the 11th, remaining there until early May. She appeared off the Falklands on 19 May and two days later, at the time of the landings, she lay due west of the opening of **San Carlos Water**.

On 24 May, while she remained in San Carlos Water, a 1,000lb bomb dropped by a Skyhawk hit her port side but did not explode while she was carrying 300 men of the **Commando Logistic Regiment**. In fact, the bomb had first bounced off *Sir Bedivere* without exploding. The crew withdrew overnight while the bomb was removed and defused.

On the evening of 7 June she embarked a force of 470 men at **San Carlos** bound for **Fitzroy**, including two companies of the **Welsh Guards**, 16 Field Ambulance, Royal Army Medical Corps, 4 Field Troop, **Royal Engineers** and several smaller units, including a **Rapier** troop. She arrived at about 1150Z on 8 June to the surprise of Major Ewen Southby-Tailyour and Captain Green, both aboard *Sir Tristram*, who strongly urged the disembarkation of the Guardsmen and other troops owing to their extreme vulnerability to air attack and the limited number of **combat air patrols** owing to *Hermes* having retired east, decreasing loiter time over the islands for **Harriers** and **Sea Harriers**.

At about 1700Z on 8 June *Sir Galahad* was struck by three 500lb bombs dropped by one of five Skyhawks involved in an attack against both her and *Sir Tristram*. One bomb broke through a diesel ready-use tank astern but failed to explode, but the two others detonated with catastrophic effect, with most of the men on the tank deck waiting to disembark and crowded in by vehicles, trailers, ammunition, packs,

RFA *Sir Galahad* after being bombed at Port Pleasant, 8 June. (AirSeaLand Photos)

rifles and equipment. Others were caught in the process of climbing down into the **landing craft** alongside. The explosion not only caused fires, by which many men were badly burnt or suffocated from billowing black smoke, but wounded or killed many as a consequence of exploding ammunition, which in many instances carried away limbs. Captain Roberts soon ordered 'Abandon Ship'.

Rescue efforts began immediately: both a LCU and a **Mexeflote** took men off, while many clambered into the life boats, helped ashore by men from **2 Para**, and every available helicopter soon appeared to pluck men from the burning decks and from the water. The wounded were laid on the beach. *Sir Galahad* lost forty-two Army personnel and five civilians killed as a result of the blast or resulting fire, forty-three of whom died on the tank deck as a result of burning ammunition. Another fifty-seven men were wounded, many badly burned. On the 9th some of *Sir Galahad*'s wounded were flown from **Ajax Bay** to *Uganda* by **Wessex** and **Sea King**.

While the incident is often mistakenly associated with **Bluff Cove** or Fitzroy, in fact it took place in **Port Pleasant**, the inlet immediately south of Bluff Cove but actually closer to Fitzroy.

On 25 June, eleven days after the Argentine surrender, the tug *Typhoon* towed *Sir Galahad* to a position south-west of **Stanley** where the submarine *Onyx* torpedoed her as a war grave on the 26th.

Commander:	Captain P.J.G. Roberts	
Launched:	19 April 1964	
Commissioned:	17 December 1966	
Tonnage:	3,270 Light Displacement	5,674 Full Load
	2,400 Deadweight	4,473 Gross Register
Dimensions: length × beam; feet (metres):	366 × 60 (126.5 × 17.7)	
Propulsion:	2 diesel engines	9,400bhp = 17 knots
Armament:	1 × 40mm AA guns	
Assault load:	402 troops	
	340 tons of stores/vehicles	
	2 **Mexeflote** sections	
Aircraft:	3 × **Gazelle** AH1	
	2 × helicopter decks (amidships and aft)	

S

Sir Geraint, RFA

One of six **Landing Ships Logistic** in theatre as part of the large contingent of **Royal Fleet Auxiliary** vessels, the others being *Sir Bedivere*, *Sir Galahad*, *Sir Lancelot*, *Sir Percivale* and *Sir Tristram*. She departed Devonport on 6 April and arrived at **Ascension** eleven days later. *Sir Geraint* reached Falklands waters on 19 May and two days later, during the landings, lay due west of the opening of **San Carlos Water**, where she offloaded **Rapier** equipment by **Sea King**. Her South Atlantic service ended upon arrival at Marchwood on 23 July.

Commander:	Captain D.E. Lawrence	
Launched:	26 January 1967	
Commissioned:	12 July 1967	
Tonnage:	3,270 Light Displacement	5,674 Full Load
	2,400 Deadweight	4,473 Gross Register
Dimensions: length × beam; feet (metres):	366 × 60 (126.5 × 17.7)	
Propulsion:	2 diesel engines	9,400bhp = 17 knots
Armament:	2 × 40mm AA guns	
Assault load:	402 troops	
	340 tons of stores/vehicles	
	2 **Mexeflote** sections	
Aircraft:	3 × light **helicopters** (**Gazelle** AH1 or **Scout** AH1)	
	2 × helicopter decks (amidships and aft)	

Sir Lancelot, RFA

One of six **Landing Ships Logistic** in theatre as part of the large contingent of **Royal Fleet Auxiliary** vessels, the others being *Sir Bedivere*, *Sir Galahad*, *Sir Geraint*, *Sir Percivale* and *Sir Tristram*. She departed Marchwood on 6 April, reached **Ascension** on the 17th and arrived off the Falklands on 19 May. Five days later, while stationed in **San Carlos Water**, Skyhawks struck her with two bombs, both of which failed to explode. She arrived in Portsmouth on 18 August.

Commander:	Capt C.A. Purtcher-Wydenbruck	
Launched:	25 June 1963	
Commissioned:	16 January 1964	
Tonnage:	3,370 Light Displacement	5,550 Full Load
	2,180 Deadweight	4,400 Gross Register
Dimensions: length × beam; feet (metres):	366 × 60 (126.5 × 17.7)	
Propulsion:	2 diesel engines	9,400bhp = 17 knots
Armament:	2 × 40mm AA guns	
Assault load:	402 troops	
	340 tons of stores/vehicles	
	2 × **Mexeflote** sections	
Aircraft:	3 × **Scout** AH1	
	2 × helicopter decks (amidships and aft)	

Sir Percivale, RFA

One of six **Landing Ships Logistic** in theatre as part of the large contingent of Royal Fleet Auxiliary vessels, the others being *Sir Bedivere, Sir Galahad, Sir Geraint, Sir Lancelot* and *Sir Tristram*. She departed Marchwood on 5 April, arrived at **Ascension** on the 17th and reached Falklands waters on 19 May. On D-Day, she lay due west of the mouth of **San Carlos Water**. On 1 June, **Sea Kings** put aboard about 800 Argentine **prisoners of war** from **Goose Green**. *Sir Percivale* finished her service in the conflict upon arrival at Marchwood on 23 July.

Commander:	Captain A.F. Pitt	
Launched:	12 December 1966	
Commissioned:	23 March 1968	
Tonnage:	3,270 Light Displacement	5,674 Full Load
	2,400 Deadweight	4,473 Gross Register
Dimensions: length × beam; feet (metres):	366 × 60 (126.5 × 17.7)	
Propulsion:	2 diesel engines	9,400bhp = 17 knots
Armament:	1 × 40mm AA guns	
Assault load:	402 troops	
	340 tons of stores/vehicles	
	2 × **Mexeflote** sections	
Aircraft:	3 × **Gazelle** AH1	
	2 × helicopter decks (amidships and aft)	

Sir Tristram, RFA

One of six **Landing Ships Logistic** in theatre as part of the large contingent of **Royal Fleet Auxiliary** vessels, the others being *Sir Bedivere, Sir Galahad, Sir Geraint, Sir Lancelot* and *Sir Percivale*.

She was in Caribbean waters when war broke out and left Belize on 2 April, reaching **Ascension** on the 17th. She entered the **Total Exclusion Zone** on 19 May and two days later, during the landings, lay due west of the mouth of **San Carlos Water**. Two of *Sir Tristram*'s **Gazelle** AH1s, fitted as gunships, supported the **Special Boat Squadron** raid on **Fanning Head** that morning.

Stores used in repairing the damaged bridge at **Fitzroy** were carried aboard *Sir Tristram*, which began unloading in **Port Pleasant** on 8 June with the help of two **landing craft** and a **Mexeflote** with the intention of completing the task that day so she could return to San Carlos Water that night. However, at about 1700Z, five Skyhawks appeared over Port Pleasant, two of which attacked *Sir Tristram*, while the other two concentrated on *Sir Galahad*, which was hit by two bombs. Neither of these exploded, although a third narrowly missed her and blew off her rear. Three Army personnel and two Chinese ratings were killed aboard *Sir Tristram* and forty-six men were evacuated to **Ajax Bay** with serious wounds. The following day **Wessex** and **Sea Kings** flew some of her wounded from Ajax Bay to the hospital ship *Uganda*. While the episode is often associated with **Bluff Cove**, in fact it took place at Port Pleasant, the inlet immediately south of the cove but actually closer to Fitzroy.

Sir Tristram was refloated and towed to **Stanley**, where she remained as an accommodation ship until transported back to the UK for reconstruction, arriving on 13 June 1983.

Commander:	Captain G.R. Green	
Launched:	12 December 1966	
Commissioned:	14 September 1967	
Tonnage:	3,270 Light Displacement	5,674 Full Load
	2,400 Deadweight	4,473 Gross Register
Dimensions: length × beam; feet (metres):	366 × 60 (126.5 × 17.7)	
Propulsion:	2 diesel engines	9,400bhp = 17 knots
Armament:	2 × 40mm AA guns	
Assault load:	402 troops	
	340 tons of stores/vehicles	
	2 × **Mexeflote** sections	
Aircraft:	3 × light **helicopters** (**Gazelle** or **Scout**)	
	2 × helicopter decks (amidships and aft)	

Smoko Mount

A bleak, windswept position near **Fitzroy**, with visibility often obscured by wet mist. In late May a patrol from the **Mountain and Arctic Warfare Cadre** was positioned to watch the track for any Argentine troop movement or activity in the vicinity. From there they reported the Argentines preparing the demolition of the bridge at Fitzroy. It was from Smoko Mount that on 2 June the patrol spotted the **Chinook** carrying elements of **2 Para** on their move east from **Goose Green**, nearly precipitating a 'Blue on Blue' incident.

Southern Thule

A dependency of the Falkland Islands and near the southern extremity of a 150-mile-long chain known as the South Sandwich Islands, Southern Thule is an active volcanic island lying 350 miles east-south-east of **South Georgia** with a fiercely Antarctic climate and no permanent inhabitants.

The Argentines had established an illegal scientific station there in 1976 against the protests of the British government, which, however, declined to remove the occupiers by force until the end of the Falklands conflict. Operation Keyhole involved the frigate HMS *Yarmouth* and RFA *Olmeda*, which arrived at South Georgia on 17 June to collect a party of 16 **Royal Marines** from M Company **42 Commando** under the command of Captain Chris Nunn. The rest of the company had already left aboard *Endurance* and the tug *Salvageman*. Arriving off the island at 1350Z on the 19th, *Endurance*'s **Wasp** landed a small party near the Argentine base. When the following day *Yarmouth* threatened the Argentine garrison with bombardment, the latter, consisting of only eleven personnel, surrendered without resistance at 1224Z, marking the last incident involving armed force during the conflict.

South Georgia

A dependency of the Falklands lying 900 miles east-south-east of **Stanley** and covering 1,450 square miles, this 100-mile-long island is dominated by mountain ranges and glaciers, with near-Antarctic conditions. It contained no permanent residents – only the approximately two dozen staff of the British Antarctic Survey (BAS) who worked at King Edward Point, near the abandoned whaling station at Grytviken. As a dependency of the Falklands, South Georgia comprised part of Argentina's general claim to British possessions that included the extremely remote, uninhabited South Sandwich Islands, including **Southern Thule**, on which the Argentines had established an illegal meteorological station in 1976.

   The Argentines organised the occupation of South Georgia by stealth, arriving under the pretext of conducting a commercial operation authorised by the British government via its embassy in Buenos Aires. This arrangement permitted workmen to salvage scrap metal from the former whaling enterprise across several sites on the island, particularly at Leith and the main settlement, Grytviken. A small group of workmen duly arrived aboard the fleet transport *Bahia Buen Suceso* on 19 March, but they commenced work without conforming to the requirement of reporting first to the island's magistrate, the base commander of the BAS. The workmen raised the Argentine flag and, despite being called upon, refused to obtain proper authorisation for their presence. At the same time, the ice patrol ship HMS *Endurance* – the only **Royal Navy** vessel present in South Atlantic waters – entered **Stanley** harbour en route to Britain, her tour of duty in the South Atlantic having reached its end. On word of events on South Georgia, however, Fleet HQ in Northwood, near London, ordered *Endurance* to reverse course and make for South Georgia with her complement of thirteen **Royal Marines**, plus nine more from the Falklands garrison of **Naval Party 8901** that, by annual rotation of personnel, had furnished a protection force to the Falklands for the past thirty years. While diplomatic efforts got under way between Britain and Argentina to settle the dispute, the Argentine transport departed, leaving the complement of civilian workers. *Endurance* reached Grytviken on 23 March, evacuated the BAS team from Leith and inserted Royal Marines by **Wasp** helicopter.

No attempt was made to remove the scrap metal workers during the continuing phase of negotiations between Britain and Argentina, but the latter dispatched the icebreaker *Bahia Paraíso* to protect them, and on 25 March she arrived at Leith, disembarking about 100 marines under Lieutenant Alfredo Astiz. The situation escalated when, on 31 March, with negotiations deadlocked, *Endurance* landed a detachment of Royal Marines at King Edward Point to establish a defensive position. She then left Cumberland Bay, unobserved by *Bahia Paraíso*, and made for Stanley. When, two days later, the Argentines occupied that town as part of the descent on the Falklands themselves, *Endurance* altered course and headed back towards South Georgia. In the meantime, the Argentine frigate *Guerrico* had left the mainland to rendezvous with *Bahia Paraíso* as Task Force 60.

On 3 April, both Argentine vessels, with many of the marines re-embarked from Leith, anchored off Grytviken and radioed the magistrate with a call to surrender. He, in turn, devolved authority upon Lieutenant Keith Mills RM, who prepared to resist. Fighting began around noon, when an Argentine Puma from *Bahia Paraíso* landed about twenty men near King Edward Point. A second journey by the Puma, laden with marines, came under fire from the Royal Marines, who, although equipped with only small arms, badly damaged the helicopter just off the Point, killing two Argentines and forcing the stricken helicopter to lift off. The Puma only reached the other side of King Edward Cove before crashing, although the Argentines continued

The Argentine submarine *Santa Fe* lying crippled in the harbour at Grytviken. (AirSeaLand Photos)

to make use of an Alouette to ferry in more marines. However, the defenders faced poor odds, for *Guerrico* approached the shore in support of the landings and commenced firing on Mills's positions, prompting his men to return fire – small arms plus 66mm light anti-tank weapons and 84s (Carl Gustav medium anti-tank weapons) – causing the vessel to reverse course away from shore.

From her new position, *Guerrico* directed the fire of her 100mm gun against the garrison while Argentine marines began to encircle Mills's position by moving around the cover provided by the whaling station at Grytviken. Finding himself surrounded, with one man wounded and the satisfaction that he had at least offered sufficient resistance to justify the decision, Mills surrendered his force of twenty-two Marines and the thirteen British civilians at Grytviken. *Endurance* arrived later the same day, but obviously too late to take part in the engagement. She remained in South Georgia waters for two more days before sailing north on 5 April with orders to link up with the vanguard of the **Task Force** then assembling at Portsmouth and Southampton in response to the Argentine invasion of the Falklands, which had occurred three days before.

Margaret Thatcher's government, while appreciating that South Georgia constituted merely a dependency of the Falklands and not the primary focus of operations, nonetheless stood firm that its recovery was essential. Indeed, repossession would highlight the government's resolve to employ force if necessary to re-establish control over the Falklands while simultaneously boosting public support for the war at a time when the 'shuttle diplomacy' then being conducted by the US Secretary of State, Alexander Haig, was doing nothing to satisfy the British people's desire for an honourable outcome to the dispute. The leeward coast of South Georgia provided a degree of sheltered anchorages at which to establish a base for the island's reconquest. There was no question but that the demanding environment of the island required only the fittest troops, trained in mountain and Arctic warfare conditions.

On the afternoon of 6 April, Major General Jeremy **Moore**, in seeking a commando company group for operations on South Georgia, suggested to Brigadier **Thompson**, commander of **3 Commando Brigade**, that they deploy for this task the **45 Commando** detachment on jungle warfare training in Brunei. Thompson produced a better option: a contingent from **42 Commando**, fresh back from its annual winter deployment to Norway. Thus, the following day, Colonel Richard Preston, Chief of Staff, Commando Forces, issued orders to CO 42 Commando, Lieutenant Colonel Nick Vaux, to detach a company group equipped for winter warfare on six hours' notice to move. Vaux had to decide whom he should send, including which rifle company and which commander. He was not happy with this being detached under someone else's control, but Major Guy Sheridan struck him as eminently qualified as overall commander, having served in Aden, Borneo and Oman, and a very experienced mountaineer. He then considered whom to choose as the company commander for the South Georgia operation. Since Captain

Royal Marines in the harbour at Grytviken, South Georgia, with the old whaling station in the background just left of centre. (AirSeaLand Photos)

Chris Nunn had just completed winter training while in command of M Company, he seemed the natural choice. Sheridan then established the composition of the company group, to include a section from the Reconnaissance Troop, who were specialists in mountain and Arctic warfare. He also included two of the six 81mm mortars from Support Company, and requested a naval gunfire support team. Total numbers for M Company including all attached personnel totalled 132 of all ranks. As Landing Force Commander, Sheridan requested the addition of the **Mountain and Arctic Warfare Cadre**, Royal Marines, but instead was given Mountain Troop, D Squadron, 22 **Special Air Service** (SAS), commanded by Major Cedric Delves who, with extreme keenness to take part in operations in the South Atlantic, had by 5 April flown his squadron down to **Ascension** without any authorisation to do so.

The naval component of the South Georgia operation included the **destroyer** *Antrim*, then at Gibraltar, commanded by Captain Brian Young, whom Admiral **Fieldhouse**, Commander-in-Chief Fleet, appointed as Task Force Commander. Young was to proceed with haste to **Ascension** with the frigate *Plymouth* and the fleet oiler RFA *Tidespring*, both to rendezvous with *Endurance* to form Task Force South Georgia.

On 8 April, RFA *Fort Austin* arrived at Ascension, with M Company 42 Commando arriving the following day. Major Jonathan Thomson RM, commander of the **Special Boat Squadron** (SBS), received them and bore instructions to attach 2 SBS to the Landing Force. This unit embarked on *Tidespring*, while 42 Commando embarked on *Fort Austin*, joined by several other formations: two Naval Gunfire Forward Observation Parties, and 148 (Meiktila) Commando Observation Battery, **Royal Artillery**.

Admiral Fieldhouse recognised the recapture of South Georgia, known as Operation Paraquet (a long-tailed parrot), as sending a strong message to the Argentines. HQ 3 Commando Brigade formulated the initial plans, but it was informally renamed as Operation 'Paraquat', after the industrial rat poison. The operation gave the Task Force the opportunity to rehearse an amphibious assault, and thus Thompson and Commodore Michael Clapp, Commander **Amphibious Task Group**, saw in it some useful experience. Little was known of Argentine strength, but they did not appear to have been recently reinforced and were expected to be found in no more larger formation than a platoon. Nothing was known of what weapons they possessed. If the scrap metal workers were included in these rough calculations, the Argentines could field approximately two platoons.

On 11 April, Task Force South Georgia, left Ascension, with *Tidespring* conveying M Company and two **Wessex HU5 helicopters**. The following day, *Endurance* received supplies from *Fort Austin* and the rest of the Task Force left Ascension. On the 14th, Task Force South Georgia joined up with *Endurance*, enabling Captain Barker, with his extensive knowledge of the island, to join the planning group. The following day operational orders arrived from Ascension via a **Nimrod**. These orders, dated the 12th and drawn up by Fieldhouse, ordered Young to recapture the island based on a landing date of the 21st. In turn, Young passed his orders to Sheridan: to recapture Grytviken and Leith; to neutralise Argentine communications; and to capture or kill Argentine military personnel and arrest Argentine civilians. The plan involved inserting SAS and SBS recce patrols north and south of Grytviken, to be followed by a landing by M Company to reinforce the Special Forces or to constitute the main assault group. Unaccountably, there was no plan to call on the Argentines to surrender. Sheridan felt unease at the difficulties that he believed the SAS faced, based on the plans outlined by Delves, who ordered Mountain Troop to move by helicopter to a point 20 miles south-east of Stromness, there to undertake a series of challenging tasks. First, they were to recce Leith, Stromness, Husvik and East Fortuna Bay in preparation for an assault at squadron level; second, they were to find routes across Fortuna Glacier, Breakwater Ridge and Konig Glacier.

Having ascertained Argentine strength and dispositions, the Troop could engage on the basis that D Squadron were available as reinforcements. Given the fickleness of the weather, the plan was risky, but it proceeded, with the SBS to land three patrols at Hound Bay, to cross Cumberland Bay East in **Geminis** supplied by helicopter and establish an observation post overlooking Grytviken.

Fearless arrived at Ascension on 17 April, carrying Thompson and Clapp. They flew to *Hermes* and met with Fieldhouse for a strategy conference, at which Fieldhouse advised against undertaking the recovery of South Georgia and announced that **5 Infantry Brigade** would also be dispatched to the Falklands, with **2 Para** shifted to 3 Commando Brigade. Thompson found this a welcome addition, as confronting the estimated 10,000 Argentine troops in the Falklands demanded, in his view, two brigades, the deployment of which would require the establishment of a Divisional HQ. For this purpose Major General Jeremy Moore was appointed Commander, Land Forces Falkland Islands.

The fleet under Admiral Sandy Woodward departed from Ascension on 14 April while the **Amphibious Task Group** remained on the island to train as the ships offshore restowed equipment. On 20 April *Plymouth* and *Endurance* sailed for Cumberland Bay while *Antrim* and *Tidespring* stood off Stromness. The following day, *Endurance* arrived and sent a helicopter ashore to contact the few BAS scientists who had not been captured with Mills, but who however had no reports of sighting the Argentines.

At 1100Z on the 21st Mountain Troop, D Squadron SAS, boarded a **Wessex** and, in company with a second, flew to Fortuna Glacier, but strong winds, poor visibility and ice obliged the pilot not to put down. Two hours later they tried again and, despite violent squalls and white-out conditions, inserted Mountain Troop on to the glacier. At about 2130Z, a Wasp flown from *Endurance* inserted four men from 2 SBS at Hound Bay, around which area they patrolled but discovered no sign of Argentines. In the meantime, the SAS struggled with bergens weighing in excess of 70lb while dragging, in atrocious conditions, sledges each weighing 200lb, traversing a mere half a mile in five hours. As night began to descend they sought to erect their tents, but winds exceeding 100mph blew one away and snapped the poles of the others, forcing five men to seek shelter in the one remaining tent while the others improvised shelters with the sledges. At 0300Z on the 22nd, high winds, which imperiled the flight of a **Wasp**, also prevented the insertion of a second SBS patrol at Hound Bay, so *Endurance* sailed close enough to the shore to allow two Gemini to land the patrol during a brief period of calm weather and tide. The team soon landed and rendezvoused with the other, establishing a camp at Dartmouth Point.

On the morning of 22 April, Mountain Troop found themselves in grave difficulty in light of the high, freezing winds and radioed *Antrim* for help. Notwithstanding nearly impossible flying conditions, three Wessex arrived for the rescue attempt, only to discover at the first attempt that the SAS were nowhere to be seen. They returned to the ship to refuel, tried again and managed to discover the men at 1300Z. Nevertheless, fifteen minutes into their flight one of the Wessex, operating in white-out conditions, crashed, with all but one of the seven on board escaping uninjured. The men and crew then divided themselves between the other two helicopters, one of which also crashed when it hit a ridge, although without serious injuries. With the equipment abandoned, in a remarkable feat of flying conducted by Lieutenant Commander Ian Stanley, the surviving helicopter took aboard all personnel – fifteen – and crash-landed aboard *Antrim*, since the excess weight made hovering impossible. The remainder of Mountain Troop returned later that day via a separate operation.

Meanwhile, the SBS, finding Cumberland Bay East icebound, could not use their Geminis, and although a Wasp carried two such craft, when their outboard motors failed the SBS could make no progress for the next three days.

Undaunted by these various travails, early on the morning of 22 April, Young brought *Antrim* close to shore and disembarked fifteen men from Boat Troop SAS, under Captain Tim Burls, in five Geminis, enabling them to establish an observation post on Grass Island from which to watch South Georgia. Two of the outboard motors failed to start, however, requiring those craft to be towed, all the while with the weather rapidly changing, the wind converting from a breeze to gale force and causing waves that scattered the Geminis across Stromness Bay. The two towed Geminis broke away, one of which was rescued the following morning when a Wessex winched the men to safety. The other team reached Grass Island, establishing there an effectively camouflaged observation point. Around 0400Z on the 23rd, the nine SAS on Green Island tried to land near Stromness, but the engines of their Geminis yet again failed to start.

Meanwhile, signals intelligence indicated the imminent arrival of an Argentine submarine in South Georgia waters: *Santa Fe* was indeed en route, with the intention of landing twenty personnel on the island. As a result, Young was told on the evening of the 23rd to withdraw his vessels outside the exclusion zone around the island, apart from *Endurance*, which remained anchored in Hound Bay. To confront *Santa Fe*, the frigate **Brilliant** and the submarine **Conqueror** were on their way.

After Boat Troop SAS landed near Stromness on the 23rd, a patrol proceeded to Harbour Point so as to observe Leith harbour from an elevated position. As dawn of the 24th broke they observed Argentine marines and later saw the *Santa Fe* arrive. The following day, *Brilliant* reached the Task Force with two additional **Lynx**.

While in the process of leaving Grytviken on the morning of the 25th, *Santa Fe*, incapable of submerging owing to a damaged hatch, was attacked around 1300Z by a Wessex, which dropped a depth charge, damaging the submarine's aft ballast tanks. Later that day, a Lynx from *Brilliant* dropped a torpedo and raked the boat with her machine guns, with Wasps from *Endurance* and *Plymouth* adding to the submarine's woes with missile fire that damaged its fin. Struggling back to Grytviken, *Santa Fe* docked alongside the jetty at King Edward harbour, after being attacked en route by another Lynx from *Brilliant* firing its machine guns.

In the meantime, Sheridan had orders to recapture the island, a task that required concentrating his dispersed forces: M Company aboard *Tidespring* 50 miles out at sea and no naval vessels within distance to provide supporting fire for a ground attack. At his immediate disposal were D Squadron, Sheridan's Tac HQ, two mortars and two Naval Gunfire Officer teams to direct the fire of whatever ships could assist with bombardment.

With only about seventy-five men and two mortars – approximately half of the numbers he had hoped to muster – Sheridan issued orders for the attack to proceed. At 1400Z on the 26th, *Antrim* and *Plymouth*, their fire guided by an observation officer in a Lynx, bombarded the landing site, about 3 miles south of Grytviken, while forty-five minutes later two Lynx from *Brilliant*, awaiting the end of the barrage, set down with eighteen men from D Squadron. With the two **destroyers** directing their fire on the track heading into Grytviken, the SAS led the assault, firing at first against false targets – rocks and seals. In the meantime, *Antrim* had taken up post off the entrance of Cumberland Bay East, firing her 4.5in gun in support. Around 1700Z Sheridan radioed *Antrim* to appear in Cumberland Bay as a demonstration of force. This duly occurred and the Argentines agreed to surrender, which took place at Grytviken at 1715Z. White flags also appeared at King Edward Point. Leith had yet to surrender, but at 1815Z *Plymouth* and *Endurance* sailed for that location and at 1100Z Astiz radioed his desire to capitulate, which occurred the following morning, with the prisoners flown to *Endurance*. In all, without a single British fatality, South Georgia fell back into British hands.

On 27 April, M Company 42 Commando landed on the island as its garrison, with others from the company retained aboard *Endurance* to guard the **prisoners**, which numbered 151 naval personnel and marines and thirty-nine civilians. Engineers crippled the *Santa Fe* with an explosive device, leaving the vessel to settle on the floor of the harbour. One Argentine sailor, part of the skeleton crew ordered to move the vessel from the jetty, was shot and killed by a Royal Marine who suspected him of trying to scuttle the submarine; this constituted the only fatality of Operation Paraquet.

Having cross-decked the prisoners from *Endurance*, on 2 May *Tidespring* left South Georgia with the prisoners and made for Ascension, from whence the Argentines, after interrogation, were repatriated on 14 May via Montevideo. On the 25th the remaining members of M Company rejoined *Endurance* at Grytviken.

Astiz, held on *Endurance* and later flown to the UK to be held on allegations of human rights crimes committed in Argentina, was repatriated on 10 June, notwithstanding the requests by French and Swedish authorities for him to stand trial for the deaths of some of their nationals in the 'Dirty War'.

Spartan, HMS

Six **submarines** served in the South Atlantic, of which *Spartan* numbered among two of the nuclear-powered Swiftsure class, the other being *Splendid*. Upon intelligence received in London of an imminent invasion of the Falklands, *Spartan* was ordered immediately to embark for the South Atlantic; accordingly, she departed from Gibraltar on 1 April and arrived in Falklands waters on the 12th. As with all British submarines in the conflict, her role remains secret. *Spartan* arrived in Devonport on 24 July.

Commander:	Commander J.B. Taylor
Builders:	Vickers (Barrow)
Launched:	7 December 1978
Commissioned:	22 September 1979
Displacement (tons):	4,200 Full load, Surface 4,500 Submerged
Dimensions: length × beam; feet (metres):	272 × 33.0 (82.9 × 10.1)
Draught:	8.2m
Propulsion:	1 nuclear reactor = 2 geared steam turbines / 20,000shp = approximately 25 knots submerged
Armament:	5 × 21in (53cm) bow torpedo tubes; Mark 8 and 21in Tigerfish torpedoes
Complement:	12 officers and 85 ratings

Special Air Service (SAS)

Commanded by Lieutenant Colonel Mike Rose and based at Stirling Lines in Hereford, 22 SAS Regiment sent two squadrons to the South Atlantic, D and G, with each squadron consisting of about eighty men divided between four troops, each commanded by a captain and trained in a specialised function: Mobility, Mountain, Boat and Air. Operating clandestinely, the SAS only recruit from within the armed forces, with selection an extremely challenging business physically, psychologically and intellectually. Members of the SAS possess a high degree of fitness, marksmanship, integrity, intelligence and initiative. They become highly proficient in handling specialised weapons, encoding and sometimes in acquiring foreign languages.

The SAS always operates in secret, generally in small teams of four, for prolonged periods in the field under very demanding circumstances. Although it maintains a high degree of secrecy around its training and operations, the regiment came to public prominence during the Iranian Embassy siege in London in 1980, which highlighted the counter-terrorist role it plays, together with others such as in handling hijackings and hostage rescue.

With long experience around the world and in Northern Ireland, the SAS operated somewhat distinctly from the rest of the Army, since it possessed its own communications network that connected it to its headquarters at Hereford, and thence to SAS director Brigadier Peter de la Billière, based at the Ministry of Defence in Whitehall.

Men of the SAS often remained hidden but close to Argentine positions, often in dreadful weather, for up to twenty-six days. Some of the most active positions for insertion included **Stanley**, **Darwin**, **Goose Green**, **Port Howard**, **Fox Bay** and **Bluff Cove**. A patrol from D Squadron spent more than three weeks on **Beagle Ridge** to the north of Stanley. In general, patrols tended to involve a two-night approach march, three days in the target area and two days march to the extraction point.

SAS amidst tumultuous conditions on Fortuna Glacier, South Georgia. (AirSeaLand Photos)

Deployment of the SAS began when D Squadron reached **Ascension** on 5 April via a **VC10** carrying 5,000lb of palleted equipment, proceeding to operations on **South Georgia**. There, Mountain Troop experienced grave trouble with extreme weather conditions on Fortuna Glacier, from which they were extracted on 22 April, with the loss of two **Wessex**. The first insertion of an SAS patrol on East Falkland took place on the evening of 1 May, flown in by a **Sea King** HC4 of 846 Naval Air Squadron, with a patrol from G Squadron tasked with gathering intelligence on Argentine positions. By 3 May, eight SAS patrols of four men each had been inserted by helicopter at various points in the islands. Most initial SAS insertions, however, took place from small surface vessels, but with the arrival of the submarine *Onyx* in theatre on 31 May, teams could approach the coast more clandestinely – probably undetected altogether. G Squadron supplied several patrols, which were helicoptered ashore to patrol ahead of the 21 May landings in **San Carlos Water**. An observation post was also established overlooking Stanley to monitor helicopter activity.

On 10 May, **Woodward** requested an SAS raid on **Pebble Island**. The SAS believed the preparation would take three weeks, but Woodward insisted on the mission being carried out in five days owing to the lack of **helicopters** after the 15th. This was agreed and D Squadron was tasked with destroying the aircraft on the ground. Accordingly, on the night of 14–15 May, forty-five men of D Squadron and their **naval gunfire support** team were dropped by four Sea Kings to rendezvous with an earlier inserted reconnaissance team, and at about 0730Z raided the airstrip on Pebble Island, disabling or destroying all eleven aircraft on the ground – six Pucaras, four Turbo Mentors and a Skyvan – before withdrawing with only two men wounded.

When B Squadron arrived at Ascension its commander proposed a raid against Argentine air and naval bases in Patagonia in an effort to reduce the effectiveness of Argentine air attacks over the Falklands. Potential targets included Military Air

Base Rio Grande, from which Super Etendards had flown for their attack against the *Sheffield* on 4 May, and the Hotel Santa Cruz, an accommodation facility for pilots of Mirage, Skyhawk and KC-130 tankers flown out of the Rio Gallegos Military Air Base. The final plan involved a raid against Rio Grande. At 1315Z on 18 May six men from B Squadron left *Invincible* aboard a 846 Naval Air Squadron (NAS) Sea King HC4 (ZA290), specially adapted for an extended flight, under the command of Lieutenant Richard Hutchings. When the helicopter arrived undetected over the designated landing point, the troop commander insisted that it was the wrong location, despite repeated confirmation from Hutchings. The men were consequently landed at the wrong location. On instruction, Hutchings and two air crew ditched the helicopter on a beach near Agua Fresco, about 11 miles west of Punta Arenas, at the extreme southern end of the mainland, in neutral Chilean territory. The SAS team aborted the mission without approaching the airfield and set fire to the Sea King before going into hiding in the hills for several days, finally turning themselves over to Chilean authorities, who repatriated the SAS and air crew.

Tragedy occurred on 19 May while troops from D and G Squadrons were being transferred by an 846 NAS Sea King (ZA294) from *Hermes* to *Intrepid*. At 2215Z, while the helicopter was circling *Intrepid* waiting to land, the engines suddenly cut out and the machine plunged into the sea, turned over and rapidly sank, with twenty-one men drowned (nineteen SAS, plus one attached Royal Signaller and one RAF flight lieutenant, both attached as a forward air control team). The two pilots escaped through the cockpit window and seven others were plucked from their dinghy by a Sea King from *Hermes* and a boat sent from *Brilliant*. Some attributed the accident to a bird strike, but the cause has never been definitively ascertained.

At nightfall on 20 May, four PNG-equipped Sea King HC4s moved forty troopers of D Company to a position north of **Darwin** on the Goose Green isthmus for Operation Tornado in an operation to divert Argentine attention from the main force landings further north.

On the day of the landings in San Carlos Water, 21 May, in order to divert Argentine attention away from the nearby landings and to convince Task Force Mercedes at Goose Green that a regiment was attacking it, D Squadron was tasked with creating noise and providing a demonstration of firepower, but without closely engaging the Argentines. Accordingly, they fired upon the 12th Infantry Regiment Recce Platoon at the northern end of the Darwin–Goose Green isthmus in a diversionary operation from a position overlooking Darwin. Their intelligence gathering that day suggested the presence of only a single company of Argentine infantry – a gross miscalculation that could have compromised the subsequent success of 2 **Para** at Goose Green. A member of Air Troop shot down a Pucara based at Goose Green with a **Stinger** missile. A pair of Pucaras later attacked their position, but these were driven off by **Sea Harriers**. The SAS patrol then withdrew to **Sussex Mountain** and were extracted by three **Scout** helicopters. *Ardent* sat in Grantham Sound, part of Falkland Sound,

12.5 miles away, and fired shells on to the airfield from around 1130Z in support of this operation.

As a result of SAS reconnaissance of an encampment of Argentine Army **helicopters** just north of **Mount Kent, Harriers** attacked the position just before dawn on 21 May, destroying and damaging several machines on the ground.

Major Delves and three troopers from D Squadron recced Mount Kent on the night of 24–25 May, awaiting the arrival of the rest of the squadron. This plan came to naught when helicopters were required to rescue survivors from the attack on *Coventry*. The following night, 26–27 May, D Squadron was moved by Sea Kings in rain and poor visibility to the wrong insertion point miles from Mount Kent and had to be extracted hours later. The following night, 27–28 May, D Squadron reached the correct point east of Mount Kent, tasked to secure a landing zone for **42 Commando**, which was expected to arrive by helicopter the following night.

Just after dawn on 28 May, on Mount Kent, D Squadron encountered twenty-nine Argentine commandos, with Air Troop fighting a patrol on the eastern slopes. The British suffered two wounded. A second encounter took place on the 29th against another Argentine patrol about the time that K Company 42 Commando arrived by helicopter.

On 1 June, three PNG-equipped Sea Kings flew an SAS team on to Mount Vernet near Estancia House, only 14 miles west of Stanley.

On 10 June, Argentine Special Forces on **West Falkland** intercepted a Mountain Troop patrol directing naval gunfire on to Port Howard, killing Captain John Hamilton at Many Branch Point. The last SAS operation of the war took place on 14 June in the Cortley Hill area of Stanley, where a combined diversionary attack and attempt to destroy a fuel depot by men of D Squadron failed, with three wounded.

Special Boat Squadron (SBS)

Operating clandestinely, the SBS (now known as the Special Boat Service) is expert at recceing beaches in advance of amphibious landings, a task that includes checking gradients and beach composition to aid in planning amphibious landings, underwater swimming, parachuting into the sea to swim ashore and landing from two-man canoes, rigid or inflatables launched from submarines or small coastal craft. In advance of landings by conventional forces, the SBS gathers intelligence on enemy troop strength, disposition and movements. Specifically, SBS played a key role in bringing back information vital for the critical task of choosing beaches suitable for the main amphibious landings.

All such skills require an extremely high level of physical fitness and stamina. The men of the SBS are also experts in signalling, map and chart reading, explosives and other skills. Only a very small proportion of candidates pass selection.

To carry out their various tasks in the South Atlantic, the two squadrons present, 2 and 6 SBS, usually worked in teams of three or four, landing under cover of darkness initially from **frigates** and trawlers, but from the end of May a more surreptitious method was followed with the aid of the submarine *Onyx*. Insertion by sea was greatly aided by the long coastline of the Falklands and its numerous secluded coves, although difficult weather conditions sometimes hampered operations. Air insertion was performed by naval **helicopters**.

2 SBS served in the operation to recapture **South Georgia**, although they were plagued by problems with their **Geminis**. On East Falkland, SBS patrols recced **Berkeley Sound**, San Salvador Water and **San Carlos Water** to determine the feasibility of a landing. In general, patrols tended to involve a two-night approach march, three days in the target area and two days' march to the extraction point. Once San Carlos Water was confirmed as the objective, SBS patrols recced the four assault beaches at **Ajax Bay**, Bonners Bay, **San Carlos** and **Port San Carlos**. One such patrol operating near Port San Carlos identified the presence of a small Argentine observing force, Combat Team Eagle, at **Fanning Head** on 14 May, confirming a presence already detected by signals intelligence. All patrols were withdrawn by the 18th, apart from one watching Ajax Bay. Meanwhile, G Squadron monitored activity on **West Falkland** at **Port Howard** and **Fox Bay**.

At about 0600Z on 21 May, just prior to the landings in San Carlos Water, thirty-five men from 3 SBS equipped with night-vision equipment landed on Fanning Head from *Antrim* to neutralise the Argentine patrol identified there earlier.

On the assault beaches the SBS was meant to use torch signals in Morse to communicate with the landing force: Alpha: 'Beach safe'; Bravo: 'Be careful'; Charlie: 'Enemy on beach'; no light: 'Serious problem' or 'enemy on beach'. In the event, the SBS believed the landings would take place on the 24th, so no signal was shone and the troops came ashore to their astonishment.

After the landings, other deployments followed: on 22 May, *Plymouth*'s **Wasp** inserted SBS teams at locations in West Falkland; a team from the ship was landed near **Teal Inlet** on 24 May. On 29 May, a **Lynx** flown from *Avenger* (although borrowed from *Ambuscade*) inserted teams at Volunteer Bay just north of Berkeley Sound; on 1 June, an SBS sergeant was killed when his patrol was dropped in the **Mount Kent** area and mistakenly ambushed by an SAS patrol; and on 6 June, a Lynx inserted an SBS team on to Sea Lion Island in Choiseul Sound.

To prepare for the move of **5 Infantry Brigade** to **Bluff Cove** in early June, Commodore Michael Clapp, Commander **Amphibious Task Group**, ordered the SBS and a diving team to recce and choose landing beaches at **Fitzroy** and Bluff Cove. They reported to Clapp and Brigadier **Wilson** no obstacles at Bluff Cove on the afternoon of 5 June, making them viable for **landing craft** operations.

On the evening of 7 June, *Avenger* entered Falkland Sound and dropped an SBS patrol on Sea Lion Island to search for a suspected **radar** station. Four days later, a **Wessex** attack on the town hall in **Stanley** (in the event it struck the police station) came about as a consequence of SBS reconnaissance that discovered senior Argentine officers met there on a daily basis.

Splendid, HMS

Six **submarines** served in the South Atlantic, of which *Splendid* numbered among two of the Swiftsure class, the other being *Spartan*. Nuclear powered, she sailed from Faslane on 1 April and arrived off the Falklands in mid-April. Her movements during the campaign remain secret, but she likely patrolled off the Argentine coast to shadow the carrier *25 de Mayo*. *Splendid* arrived in Devonport on 12 June.

Commander:	Commander R.C. Lane-Nott
Builders:	Vickers (Barrow)
Launched:	5 October 1979
Commissioned:	21 March 1981
Displacement (tons):	4,200 Full load, Surface 4,500 Submerged
Dimensions: length × beam; feet (metres):	272 × 33.0 (82.9 × 10.1)
Draught: 8.2m	
Propulsion:	1 nuclear reactor = 2 geared steam turbines 20,000shp = approximately 25 knots submerged
Armament:	5 × 21in (533mm) bow torpedo tubes; Mark 8 and 21in Tigerfish torpedoes
Complement:	12 officers and 85 ratings

Springtrain, Exercise

Flying his flag in the destroyer *Antrim*, Admiral **Woodward**, Flag Officer First Flotilla, was at the time of the Argentine invasion of the Falklands conducting this naval exercise off Gibraltar involving four other **destroyers**, *Coventry*, *Glamorgan*, *Glasgow* and *Sheffield*, the **frigates** *Arrow*, *Brilliant* and *Plymouth*, and the **Royal Fleet Auxiliary** vessel *Tidespring*. Springtrain fortuitously placed a number of warships already at operational readiness – and slightly closer to the coming theatre of operations.

Stanley

Officially known as Port Stanley, the capital of the Falkland Islands, home to about 1,000 of the territory's 1,800 inhabitants, the principal objective of the Argentine invasion of 2 April and of British repossession of the Islands.

    The Argentines organised the build-up for their invasion of the Falklands during the period of Anglo–Argentine negotiations following the landing on **South Georgia** that began on 19 March. With talks failing to make headway, the junta initiated Operation Rosario, dispatching ships south, their destination unknown to British intelligence, but by the 31st observers in London assumed that in light

Aerial view of Stanley with ships of the Task Force in the harbour. (AirSeaLand Photos)

of events on South Georgia an invasion was imminent and warned the islands' governor, Rex Hunt, who on the evening of 1 April announced by radio the likelihood of invasion occurring the following day. The garrison of the islands consisted of a mere sixty-nine **Royal Marines** of **Naval Party 8901** under Major Mike Norman, who, anticipating that the main landing would take place near Stanley airfield with a subsequent advance on the town, deployed his men into four delaying sections along the Stanley road. His main force was concentrated at Government House, with the twenty-three men of the Falkland Islands Defence Force manning observation posts.

The Argentines landed from ship and helicopter at several sites in the early hours of 2 April, with many heading for **Moody Brook Barracks**, which the Royal Marines had wisely abandoned. The main landing took place at Yorke Bay at 1000Z, their objective Government House on the western fringe of the town. There, the defenders were already under attack from the small force but holding firm. The Argentines soon brought up armoured vehicles and more troops arrived at the airfield by helicopter. Those Royal Marines detachments outside Government House, finding themselves unable to resist the assault, fell back to the main position, with one section managing to disable an Amtrac vehicle with its anti-tank weapons.

By dawn Argentine forces had surrounded Government House and kept it under constant small arms fire, with Amtracs approaching in support. Unable to resist such overwhelming numbers and firepower, Governor Hunt ordered the defending troops to surrender, which duly took place at 1325Z, by which time they had inflicted several casualties on their attackers while suffering none themselves.

Stanley figured strongly in British strategic plans for repossessing the Falklands. During the course of their journey to **Ascension**, Commodore Michael Clapp, Commander Amphibious Task Group, and Brigadier Julian **Thompson** chose three possible beaches on which to effect a landing, one of which included **Berkeley Sound**, a few miles north of Stanley. Although distant **San Carlos Water** was chosen, the capture of Stanley was always considered the main effort of ground operations given its importance as the Argentines' centre of gravity. In light of the decision to approach Stanley from the west, the British would face two rings of Argentine defences there: the outer consisting of **Mount Harriet**, **Two Sisters**, and **Mount Longdon**, and the inner ring of **Mount Tumbledown**, **Mount William** and **Wireless Ridge**. The fall of these positions would leave the Argentines hemmed in at Stanley and unlikely to offer further resistance. Admiral Woodward had hoped for 3 Commando Brigade to attack Stanley on the night of 5–6 June, with several vessels in support: the destroyers *Cardiff* and *Yarmouth* and the **frigates** *Active* and *Arrow*, but this proved too ambitious a timetable. Instead, the attacks on the outer ring took place on 11–12 June, and against the inner on the 13–14th, with General Menéndez surrendering the capital and all forces on both West and East Falkland on the 14th.

On an intermittent basis, Stanley airfield became the target of naval gunfire, beginning on 1 May, when from a position off Cape Pembroke *Glamorgan*, *Alacrity* and *Arrow* briefly shelled Stanley airfield. On the night of 11–12 June, naval gunfire rendered all but half a dozen Hueys unable to fly.

Stanley also figured very heavily in the air campaign, with a long series of attacks carried out against it, specifically the airport.

In the **Black Buck raids**, British aircraft attacked Stanley airport several times, beginning on the first day of the air campaign, 1 May. Notwithstanding this onslaught, within days the Argentines had filled in the craters produced in the raid and restored the runway to operational use, so that on 6 May a C-130H Hercules bearing supplies constituted the first transport aircraft to arrive (and return to Argentina with wounded troops) since the Black Buck 1 raid five days before. To mitigate further damage, the Argentines transferred six Pucaras based there to **Pebble Island**.

On the same day, nine **Sea Harriers** from 800 Naval Air Squadron (NAS) led by Lieutenant Commander Andy Auld approached the airport, four from the north carrying three 1,000lb airburst bombs to target Argentine AAA positions. Having dropped their loads, a second group of five attacked from the north-west at low level, dropping cluster bombs on static aircraft, airfield facilities and the runway. Two 1,000lb retard bombs hit the runway, adding to the damage already inflicted earlier that day by the **Vulcan** raid. Several civilian aircraft were also damaged, including the governor's plane. In all, fifteen 1,000lb bombs and 12 cluster bomb units were dropped on Stanley airport by Sea Harriers on 1 May.

On 9 May, two Sea Harriers took off to execute a medium-level raid against the airport, but finding visibility obscured by cloud they declined to drop their bombs for fear of hitting civilians.

On the morning of 12 May, the aircraft of 800 NAS conducted three raids beginning at 1155Z against the airport, with all sorties flown at medium altitude to minimise the risk from the Roland missiles used in its defence. None of the bombs struck their intended targets.

Cloud cover and mist prevented further attacks for a few days, but with improved weather in the early hours of 15 May, Sea Harriers of 800 NAS resumed their raids against the airport, some conducted in the morning from high altitude with disappointing results, and another in the afternoon by means of high altitude toss-bombing, which proved more effective. Often Sea Harriers simply chose targets of opportunity rather than concentrating on the airport, confusing the Argentines as to their next target.

Sea Harriers of 801 NAS flew several **combat air patrols** on the morning of 18 May, bombing Stanley airfield from high altitude in these instances.

On the evening of 23 May, four Sea Harriers of 800 NAS flew from *Hermes*, approximately 90 miles north-east of Stanley, raiding the airfield on the basis of intelligence that the Argentines were preparing it with arrester gears to accommodate jets. One Sea Harrier unaccountably crashed into the sea, but the others dropped their loads in the teeth of significant anti-aircraft fire.

On 24 May, four **Harrier** GR3s supported by two Sea Harriers raided Stanley airfield with 1,000lb air-burst VT-fused bombs deployed against anti-aircraft and surface-to-air missile sites as well as parachute-retarded bombs targeted against the runway itself, all in the face of considerable ground fire. Three of the twelve bombs dropped hit the runway, but none inflicted serious damage since they bounced before exploding. It was clear by this point that low-level retard bombs offered little prospect of putting the runway out of action until the new laser-guided bombs (LGBs) arrived. Fortuitously, the first batch of bomb conversion kits (altering 'dumb' to 'smart' bombs) were airdropped to *Hermes* the same day by a **Hercules** operating from Ascension. With a trained forward air controller and laser-marking equipment the potential now opened for much more accurate targeting, although the first trial would not occur until the day before the Argentine surrender.

At 1415Z on the 25th, two Sea Harriers took off from *Hermes*, followed shortly thereafter by four Harrier GR3s, all of which toss-bombed the airfield, but to little effect. At 1782Z two Harriers left *Hermes* on another raid conducted from 20,000ft, releasing six bombs, only half of which struck their target. Another mission followed in which three aircraft – one Harrier and two Sea Harriers – took off at 1927Z, releasing their loads over the airport but, again, with little damage inflicted.

Reports of jets being sited at the airport and the presence of arrester gear on the runway prompted speculation that the Super Etendards that had attacked *Atlantic Conveyor* earlier in the day might conceivably land at Stanley rather than back on the mainland. Accordingly, three Sea Harriers left *Hermes* at 2155Z and toss-bombed the airfield, outcome unknown.

On the 26th, a single Harrier left *Hermes* at 1659Z to toss-bomb Stanley airport, with one bomb failing to release owing to a technical problem; low cloud rendered any assessment of the raid impossible. Another toss-bomb attack against the runway occurred at 1200Z on the 27th involving two Harriers dropping six delayed-action 1,000lb bombs.

Despite high winds, poor visibility and heavy seas affecting the **aircraft carriers**, Sea Harriers flew more than a dozen **combat air patrol** sorties in the course of 28 May, although none were possible in support of **2 Para's** attack at **Goose Green**. However, four Sea Harriers dropped 1,000 bombs on Stanley airfield, albeit with little effect.

Several raids were flown against Stanley airfield on 29 May: at 1208Z, two Sea Harriers toss-bombed their target; at 1430Z two more Sea Harriers took off, followed at 1555Z by another pair with the same objective; and two further Sea Harriers, each with three 1,000lb VT-fused bombs, attacked the airport later that afternoon.

A raid conducted against Stanley airfield by two Harriers on 30 May, beginning at 1435Z, was notable as the first instance of these aircraft deploying the Paveway LGB during the war. However, these new weapons did not live up to their name in the absence of a forward air controller on the ground capable of marking the target. Conventional weapons continued in use, however: four Sea Harriers toss-bombed Stanley airport after taking off from *Hermes* at 1717Z on 30 May.

The following day at 1130Z, three Harriers of 1 Squadron carrying a combination of 1,000lb bombs, 2in rocket pods and LGBs attacked the airport, the second time in which the laser rangefinder failed to provide accuracy. Later the same day two Harriers and two Sea Harriers took off from *Hermes* at 1452Z and attacked the airfield with bombs and rockets, but with no serious damage inflicted to the MB-339As present there.

Perhaps the most unusual helicopter attack against the town took place in the early morning of 11 June, when on the basis of **Special Boat Squadron** reconnaissance that reported a daily meeting in the town hall by senior Argentine officers, a **Wessex** HU5 of 845 NAS flying from **Teal Inlet** fired two **AS.12 anti-ship missiles** at the target from a distance of about 3 miles to the north-west. The first missed the town hall and hit the second floor of the police station next door, used as an Argentine Army intelligence HQ; the second fell into the sea after the control wire became caught on high ground short of the target.

In light of a Pucara attack on British artillery on 10 June, another toss-bombing raid was conducted on Stanley airport the following day involving four Sea Harriers of 800 NAS launched from *Hermes* around 1100Z. Twelve 1,000lb VT-fused bombs in total were dropped on the airfield, of which eleven exploded on target. An LGB attack by Harrier GR3s meant to take place later the same day (11 June) was aborted when the laser target marker operated by a **Special Air Service** team on the ground suffered from a weak battery.

While at least two reconnaissance reports indicated the presence of swept-wing aircraft at Stanley airport, it does not appear that any Argentine jet aircraft ever used the airfield there apart from MB339-As, and while the incessant attacks on the airport certainly proved a nuisance to the Argentines and may have unsettled the garrison in and around it, they never rendered the airfield non-operational. Indeed, an Argentine Air Force C-130 Hercules transport continued to fly resupply missions to Stanley on virtually a daily basis, carrying troops and supplies into East Falkland and the wounded out, with five such flights occurring on the 13th, the penultimate day of the war. All told, between 1 May and 13 June the Argentines managed to evade the air blockade and deliver more than 400 tons of supplies and more than 500 personnel, withdrawing about 300 personnel back home during return journeys.

St Edmund, MV

A roll-on/roll-off vehicle ferry taken up from trade on 12 May from British Rail Sealink UK. Used as a troop transport, she carried Naval Party 2060 under Lieutenant Commander A.M. Scott RN. *St Edmund* departed Devonport on 19 May but did not reach the Falklands until 15 June – the day after the end of hostilities. Still, she remained of practical use well into the post-war period, returning about 300 Argentine **prisoners of war** to their country on 30 June. With much work to be done in the Falklands in the months after war's end, she did not arrive at Southampton until 25 February 1983.

Commander:	Captain M.J. Stockman	
Built:	1974	
Tonnage:	8,987 Gross Register	1,830 Deadweight
Dimensions: length × beam; feet (metres):	427 × 74 (130 × 22.6)	
Propulsion:	2 sets of diesel engines	20,400bhp = 21 knots
Helicopter platform – no embarked aircraft		

Stena Inspector, MV

A diesel-electric offshore support vessel chartered from Stena Caribbean on 25 May, she did not depart from Charleston, South Carolina, until 6 June, and arrived at **Ascension** on 21 June, a week after the cessation of hostilities. She served off the Falklands from early July and did not return to the UK until November 1983.

Commander:	Captain D. Ede	
Launched:	1980	
Tonnage:	6,061 Gross Register	4,835 Deadweight
Dimensions: length × beam; feet (metres):	367.5 × 90.5 (112.2 × 27.6)	
Propulsion:	5 diesel engines, 4 electric motors	18,000bhp = 16 knots
Helicopter platform – no embarked aircraft		

Stena Seaspread, MV

A diesel-electric offshore support vessel requisitioned from Stena Atlantic on 8 April, she departed Portsmouth on the 16th, reached **Ascension** on the 28th and **South Georgia** on 11 May. Technicians from *Stena Seaspread* repaired the gaping hole made by a Skyhawk bomb in the flight deck of *Broadsword*, inflicted on 25 May. *Argonaut* had hoped to have repair work conducted at sea at the end of May by *Stena Seaspread*, but the frigate's damage proved too extensive and she departed for the UK. *Stena Seaspread* arrived in Portsmouth on 18 August.

Commander:	Captain N. Williams	
Launched:	1980	
Tonnage:	6,061 Gross Register	4,835 Deadweight
Dimensions: length × beam; feet (metres):	367.5 × 90.5 (112.2 × 27.6)	
Propulsion:	5 diesel engines, 4 electric motors	18,000bhp = 16 knots
Helicopter platform – no embarked aircraft		

Steveley Bay

During the course of their journey to **Ascension**, Commodore Michael Clapp, Commander **Amphibious Task Group**, and Brigadier **Thompson** chose three possible beaches on which to effect a landing, one of which was Steveley Bay on **West Falkland**. This was soon discounted since resources could not be found to construct an airfield on the island and, in any event, landing on West Falkland would necessitate another amphibious landing on East Falkland, by which time the element of surprise would have been lost.

Stinger

A man-portable, shoulder-mounted surface-to-air missile, at least one of which the **Special Air Service** (SAS) acquired while on a recent training course in the United States. On 21 May a forward SAS patrol near **San Carlos** employed this weapon and scored a hit on a Pucara that had just left the airstrip at **Goose Green**. The pilot ejected and evaded capture. The only trained operator of this weapon, Staff Sergeant P. O'Connor, had died two days earlier during the **Sea King** accident, leaving the Stinger in the hands of an untrained colleague, whose insufficient acquaintance with the weapon accounted for his lack of further success in spite of five more launches conducted later the same day.

Strategy

In military terms, restoring the Falklands to British rule represented an exceedingly daunting task. The islands lie approximately 8,000 miles (c. 7,200 nautical miles, 13,000km) from the United Kingdom and consist of the two main islands of **West Falkland** and East Falkland, with another 100 smaller islands covering between them just over 4,600 square miles, or two-thirds the area of Wales, with a population according to the 1980 census of 1,813. The landscape and climate resembles that of the western isles of Scotland and the main islands consist largely of boggy, undulating moorland and windswept rocky outcrops, almost bereft of trees. Extremely isolated, the Falklands form the only major island group in the South Atlantic and lie 300 miles east of the Strait of Magellan, with a climate suitably inclement. The temperature varies between 49°F (9°C) in January – which, of course, represents the height of summer in the Southern Hemisphere – and 36°F (2°C) in July, which conversely marks the depth of winter. From a military perspective, such a distinctive, changeable and, depending on the season, harsh climate requires troops to be well protected. Troops improperly equipped, clothed, fed or unaccustomed to operating in these unforgiving conditions could not be expected to function in an effective manner.

Stanley, the capital and only town in this overseas territory, sits on the east coast of East Falkland and represented the ultimate objective of British forces. Its 1,000 residents accounted for more than half the entire population of the islands, with the other 800 living in widely scattered settlements in the 'camp', unconnected by road, although in some cases airstrips offered limited access. Retaking the Falklands appeared to planners in London to depend partly on early success against the small Argentine garrison on **South Georgia**, a 100-mile-long island lying 900 miles east south-east of the Falklands. Retaking the island would not only boost morale even before the main landings took place in the Falklands themselves, but would provide a safe haven for troopships – particularly those rapidly acquired from civilian use, like the luxury liner *Queen Elizabeth 2*. Once safely ensconced in the waters around Grytviken, men and supplies could be transferred by cross–decking to military vessels with at least limited air cover provided by the carriers and escort by warship.

The British had by necessity to operate along a lengthy chain of command, with the Secretary of State for Defence, John Nott, reporting to his staff in London, led by the Chief of the Defence Staff (CDS), Admiral of the Fleet Sir Terence Lewin and other service heads. The **Task Force** commanders, under the Commander-in-Chief Fleet, Admiral Sir John **Fieldhouse**, worked at Northwood, Middlesex, near London. Fieldhouse would control military and naval affairs in the South Atlantic via the various commanders *in situ*: Rear Admiral Sandy **Woodward**, commander of the **Carrier Battle Group**, Commodore Michael Clapp, commander of the **Amphibious Task Group**, and Brigadier Julian **Thompson** RM, commander of the Landing Force Task Group and **3 Commando Brigade**. Major General Jeremy **Moore** would, in due course, arrive with **5 Infantry Brigade** and assume the role of Commander, Land Forces.

Recapturing the islands, which by the end of April boasted a garrison of 13,000 Argentines, would require a strategy based on stages. The principal military objectives involved imposing a sea blockade around the Falklands; retaking South Georgia to make use of it as a secure base and transit area; establishing air and naval supremacy around the Falklands; and, lastly, defeating the Argentine garrison on the Falklands and reoccupying the islands. All this required use of **Ascension** Island, which stood approximately halfway between Britain and the Falklands – about 4,000 miles (6,500km). With its American-built runway at Wideawake Airfield, Ascension could accommodate all aircraft, especially those carrying vital supplies for the **Task Force**; serve as an intermediate base for stores and fuel; and permit cross-decking and the reloading of supplies already embarked on the island.

Whatever strategy the British formulated, time was of the essence. The UN could call a ceasefire and place Britain in an awkward diplomatic position if she refused to comply. Even if diplomatic obstacles and all the logistical problems associated with the prosecution of a campaign 8,000 miles away could be overcome, autumnal conditions in the South Atlantic would imminently turn for the worse. With the approach of winter, and with well over a month before the Task Force could reach the islands and carry out a successful landing, the temperature would have dropped and precipitation increased. Even if ground forces could operate, their progress would be hindered by heavy seas, conditions rendering all but impossible the launching of sorties from the swaying decks of **aircraft carriers**, the cross-decking of troops and supplies between vessels pitching amid the swells. This would eventually disrupt or sever general resupply – not to mention cause serious problems for airborne anti-submarine surveillance and the ability to launch defensive sorties to protect vital maritime assets.

To compound these already formidable problems, given the Argentines' superior numbers, firepower and defensive posture, executing an amphibious landing depended heavily on the ability of the Task Force to come ashore unopposed while its supporting craft established a secure and sheltered anchorage. The size of the expeditionary force would also require an area large enough to enable an oversized brigade to establish a strong bridgehead. Heavy **casualties** – at least at such an early stage in the campaign – could not be tolerated given the uncertain nature of the British public's appetite for a costly war conducted for a distant and remote territory whose occupation by Argentina, however unpalatable, constituted no threat to British security at home. In any event, a contested landing would without doubt slow the break-out and subsequent advance on Stanley, while the troops (hardened though they were) would be condemned to operate in the extremely inhospitable conditions of a rapidly approaching Antarctic winter. In short, the campaign had by necessity to be short, sharp and decisive, with a high tempo maintained throughout and success achieved with minimal casualties – daunting requirements for a nation that had not conducted a large-scale expeditionary operation since the Suez Crisis of 1956.

By its nature the Falklands campaign was to be primarily a naval operation, but careful integration of naval, land and air assets would be vital to success. However, even if British naval and air assets could establish a dominant presence around and over the Falklands, repossession of the islands still depended ultimately on success on land.

With respect to ground forces, the UK was fortunate that the timing of the Argentine invasion fell at a point when two brigades – 3 Commando Brigade and 5 Infantry Brigade – intended for rapid deployment were both available, while the rest of UK forces were committed to NATO or Northern Ireland, leaving only one battalion, the 1st Battalion Queen's Own Highlanders, in reserve for possible South Atlantic service. As a **Royal Marines** formation, 3 Commando Brigade understood the language, ethos and procedures of the **Royal Navy**. It was understood that, at more than 10,000 men, the Argentine occupation force would inevitably outnumber those British forces deployable to the Falklands; hence, it was recognised that both brigades would have to be dispatched. Fortunately, the Royal Marines were well trained in winter warfare, precisely what was required in the very cold and wet climate of the Falklands at that time of the year. The **Parachute Regiment** had less experience of training in extreme cold, but its fitness and endurance would stand it in better stead than any other unit in the Army.

A conference attended by all Task Force commanders aboard the aircraft carrier *Hermes* on 17 April led to tense exchanges between Woodward on the one hand, and Thompson and Clapp on the other, with neither of the latter two being aware in advance that Northwood had tasked Woodward to evaluate the possibility of building an airstrip on West Falkland capable of deploying air defence aircraft there as a means of enhancing Britain's hand in negotiations with Argentina over the future of the islands. Thompson and Clapp articulated the many problems associated with such a proposal: the likelihood of constant air attacks by land-based Argentine aircraft; the vulnerabilities faced by the aircraft carriers, which, if only likely to be able to provide a small element of air cover over East Falkland once deployed, would now be expected to furnish the same capability over West Falkland – considerably closer to Argentina itself – while subject to attack themselves. Nor, they argued, did 3 Commando Brigade possess the materials, manpower or engineering specialists to construct such an airfield – an enterprise certain to require months to complete. Finally, a landing on West Falkland would still require a second amphibious assault across Falkland Sound – a wholly unsound strategy given the opportunity it allowed for the Argentines to strengthen their defences in anticipation of this inevitable second descent. Accordingly, Thompson and Clapp comprehensively quashed the idea in favour of establishing a beachhead on East Falkland.

During the course of their journey to Ascension, Thompson and Clapp chose three possible sites at which to effect a landing: **Steveley Bay** on West Falkland; **San Carlos Water** on East Falkland, and **Berkeley Sound**, a few miles north of Stanley. Eventually they settled on San Carlos Water.

British strategy, as far as the air campaign was concerned, was meant to open dramatically with a **Vulcan** strike to neutralise Stanley airfield, followed by further strikes after dawn by **Sea Harriers** to deny the Argentines use of the runway to their Mirage, Super Etendards and Skyhawks. A naval bombardment and further air strikes would follow, on that day and on successive days, both against Stanley and **Goose Green**.

Air operations around the Falklands themselves – that is, excluding operations around South Georgia and the cross-decking and other tasks performed at Ascension) occurred every day between 1 May and the Argentine surrender on 14 June, with six days of particularly high rates of activity: 1 May (i.e. the Black Buck 1 raid on Stanley airfield), 21, 23, 24, 25 May (operations in San Carlos Water and Falkland Sound) and 8 June (the attack against *Sir Galahad* and *Sir Tristram* near **Fitzroy**).

The British opened the campaign dramatically on 1 May, with a Vulcan raid against Stanley airfield followed by Sea Harriers on the same target and against Goose Green, so demonstrating to the Argentines that UK forces were serious in their resolve to repossess the islands.

For much of the campaign adverse weather conditions hampered operations, such that, for instance, a ten-day period of regular poor weather – storms, low cloud, fog, poor or limited visibility – between 5 and 14 May grounded many aircraft on both sides. However, there were still some attacks against British warships and British air raids conducted against Stanley airport and other targets.

By obliging the Argentine Navy to withdraw from Falklands waters as a result of the loss of the cruiser *General Belgrano* on 2 May and striking Stanley airfield with the Vulcan raids, British strategy sought to confine and isolate the Argentine garrison on the Falklands, since major shipping could no longer supply their troops or confront Royal Navy warships and the more vulnerable supply vessels of the Task Force. Constant bombardment of the airfield at Stanley prevented the Argentines from using it as a main operating base for their fighter aircraft and thus condemned them to fly the 400 miles from the mainland with sufficient fuel only for a few minutes' loiter time over the western end of East Falkland, thus severely restricting their tactical effectiveness.

All such air and naval activity established the prerequisites for launching an amphibious landing on 21 May, with Argentine air attacks on the beachhead at San

Carlos Water blunted within a week of that event. With thousands of troops and tons of stores and equipment now safely ashore, Argentine defeat appeared a realistic prospect – although by no means a foregone conclusion.

On the other hand, with the loss of *Atlantic Conveyor* on 25 May with its ten **helicopters** aboard, British strategy had to be altered accordingly, since some of the troops would now have to move east on foot. From the 26th, the break-out from San Carlos Water could now only depend on thirty-two available helicopters, only half of which were designed for transport. In short, **logistics** remained key to success.

Thompson and Clapp agreed that a northern approach to Stanley was far preferable to a southern one, since an advance along the **Darwin** to Stanley track carried a number of disadvantages, including a coastline punctuated with inlets capable of concealing Argentine patrol boats and constituting an area extremely difficult to navigate, particularly at night. The strategy for ground operations envisioned a break-out from San Carlos along a northern route eastwards towards **Douglas**, **Teal Inlet** and **Mount Kent**, followed by assaults against the Argentine elevated defensive positions around Stanley and entry into the capital itself. Ultimately, this developed into a two-pronged offensive once Goose Green was captured, with a southern route opened that then formed a pincer movement with the northern approach.

As a consequence, Thompson favoured using 5 Infantry Brigade to secure San Carlos Water and the **Darwin** isthmus, thus enabling 3 Commando Brigade to advance east from the beachhead once sufficient supplies had been landed. 3 Commando Brigade would then proceed to occupy the high ground from Long Island Mount through **Mount Kent** to **Mount Challenger** as a preparatory move before launching a series of night assaults on the Argentine outer defence zone. **45 Commando** would then seize **Two Sisters**; **42 Commando** would take **Mount Harriet**; and **3 Para** would take **Mount Longdon**. In the event that sufficient darkness remained to offer cover and that combat effectiveness remained, the momentum of the offensive would be maintained, with 3 Para taking **Wireless Ridge**, 45 Commando attacking **Mount Tumbledown**, 42 Commando standing in immediate reserve and **40 Commando** and **2 Para** serving as brigade reserve. This would complete the clearance of both the outer and inner defensive zones, leaving only flat ground west of Stanley and remaining Argentine forces isolated and demoralised.

On his arrival at 3 Commando Brigade HQ at **San Carlos** on 30 May, Moore assumed command of land forces from Thompson and, with the arrival of 5 Infantry Brigade imminent, announced a modification of Thompson's original plan. 3 Commando Brigade would continue its advance along its northerly axis, while 5 Infantry Brigade would take a southerly route, the two brigades to execute a three-phase plan. In Phase One 3 Commando Brigade would strike the outer defensive zone; in Phase Two, 5 Infantry Brigade would assault Mount Tumbledown and **Mount William** from the south; and in Phase Three 3 Commando Brigade, with 5 Infantry Brigade in support, would advance on Stanley. All elements were to maintain the momentum, denying the Argentines the opportunity to regroup. Moore intended the offensive to begin on the night of 6 June.

As such, on 2 June, on orders from Brigadier Wilson, who acted without prior approval from Moore, the single remaining **Chinook** moved 2 Para to the **Fitzroy/Bluff Cove** area, thereby unilaterally opening up a southern flank in the advance towards Stanley. Wilson then persuaded Moore of the advantages of this alteration to strategy and requested immediate support.

With respect to moving 5 Infantry Brigade forward, Woodward and Fieldhouse suggested it could move on foot to Teal Inlet, rather than via the southern route to Fitzroy/Bluff Cove. In the end, Moore and Clapp concluded that a sea move from San Carlos to the **Port Pleasant** sector was the only viable option. Wilson and Clapp chose Fitzroy.

Thompson argued for the offensive to assume a broad front, involving the seizure of Mount Longdon, which derived its strategic significance from its dominating position over the ground both north and south of Stanley harbour. Wilson advocated a narrow front operating along the Fitzroy to Stanley track south of Mount Harriet, to be followed up by a divisional move against Stanley Common. This plan suited his geographical position, with his brigade operating within the relatively narrow confines between the southern coast of East Falkland to the south and Wickham Heights to the north. Discussions over these issues were under way aboard *Fearless* but ceased when news arrived on 8 June of the attack on Port Pleasant, the heavy casualties sustained at which delayed the final advance by two days as a result of the need to reorganise troops to make up for losses in men and stores.

In the end, both brigades would be involved in a three-phase attack. In Phase One, 3 Commando Brigade would seize Mount Harriet, Two Sisters and Mount Longdon; in Phase Two, 5 Infantry Brigade would attack Mount Tumbledown and Mount William; and in Phase Three, elements of 5 Infantry Brigade would secure **Sapper Hill**. The first phase of attack was to begin on the night of 10–11 June, but had to be delayed by Moore until the following night because Wilson's formation was not ready, and the shortage of artillery ammunition, amongst other logistical problems.

The success of the five ground engagements of 11–14 June fully justified British strategy, leading to Argentine surrender on the 14th.

Stromness, RFA

A Ness class stores support ship, five such vessels of the **Royal Fleet Auxiliary** served in the South Atlantic, the others being *Regent, Resource, Fort Austin* and *Fort Grange*.

In reserve when the conflict began, *Stromness* left Portsmouth on 7 April with most of **45 Commando** and rations to maintain 7,500 men for thirty days. She reached **Ascension** ten days later and arrived off the Falklands on 16 May.

On the morning of 21 May she lay due west of the opening of **San Carlos Water**, where she disembarked 45 Commando into their **landing craft** in Falkland Sound on the morning of 21 May. She was withdrawn that evening for protection against air attack, returning on the 23rd, when she unloaded further supplies and troops. Some of her cargo included 11,000 aluminium planks for a prefabricated vertical take-off and landing pad to accommodate **Harriers** and **Sea Harriers** landing near **Port San Carlos**, as well as rubber fuel bladders and other equipment. The following day *Stromness* narrowly escaped the bombs of several waves of Argentine air attacks.

At **South Georgia** she embarked approximately 400 men from **5 Infantry Brigade**, together with their stores and ammunition, and set out back to the Falklands on 27 May. Her service in the campaign ended on her arrival back in Portsmouth on 19 July.

Commander:	Captain J.B. Dickinson	
Builders:	Swan Hunter	
Launched:	16 September 1966	
Commissioned:	21 March 1967	
Tonnage:	9,010 Light Displacement	16,800 Full Load
	7,780 Deadweight	12,360 Gross Register
Dimensions: length × beam; feet (metres):	524 × 72 (159.8 × 22)	
Propulsion:	1 diesel engine	11,520bhp = 17 knots
Armament:	Improvised – GPMGs and rifles	
Aircraft:	1 × **Scout** AH1	

STUFT

See Ships Taken Up From Trade

Submarines

Submarines formed part of the **Task Force**, with the designation CTG 324.3. Six served in total: the patrol submarine *Onyx* and five fleet submarines: *Conqueror*, *Courageous*, *Valiant*, *Spartan* and *Splendid*. These were normally deployed in the North Atlantic and elsewhere in an anti-submarine role, but for the Falklands War they reverted to a traditional anti-warship role.

Submarines gathered intelligence, patrolled the waters off Argentina, the Falklands and **South Georgia** and acted as a deterrent against Argentine naval activity, both surface and sub-surface. Although unseen and few in numbers, British submarines performed a disproportionately important role in the war, keeping the Argentine Navy guessing as to the strength of the submarine presence in the South Atlantic.

S

The nuclear-powered HMS *Splendid*, one of six British submarines to serve in the South Atlantic. (AirSeaLand Photos)

Secrecy concerning the movements of **Royal Navy** submarines makes determining the nature of their activities in South Atlantic waters problematic, but at least one ballistic missile submarine was probably in theatre, with its nuclear reactor enabling it to remain submerged for a considerable time.

Among the fleet submarines, *Valiant* operated with steam-driven turbines powered by a pressurised water-cooled nuclear reactor. With six forward tubes, she fired 21 in Mark 24 Tigerfish torpedoes, operating by wire guidance for part of their course and an active/passive homing device closer to the target. At a depth of down to 330ft (100m) she could run at almost 45 knots and fire at surface or submerged targets at up to 18 miles. She had a maximum speed of about 28 knots when submerged and could remain under water for several months. *Valiant* had a complement of fourteen officers and ninety-five ratings, and weighed 3,410lb. She maintained her own supply of fresh water and could produce a limited amount of oxygen via electrolysis. All submarines carried approximately fifteen weeks' supply of food, enabling them to remain at sea for extended periods.

Conqueror and *Courageous* were built to a more recent design than *Valiant*, and although similar in size they achieved greater speed. They carried five bow tubes instead of six forward tubes. Other Fleet submarines of improved design and performance included the Swiftsure class such as *Splendid* and *Spartan*. Carrying a smaller complement than older classes, they could patrol submerged for longer periods without land-based support. Improvements over their predecessors included a purification plant, a distilling plant, laundry facilities and superior air conditioning.

The American UGM-84 Harpoon, designed as an anti-ship weapon, was newly available during the war. Compressed air launched it through 21in torpedo tubes, but upon reaching the surface a booster rocket carried it up to 60 miles to its target.

Fleet submarines normally seek and destroy their counterparts and surface vessels, but in the absence of Argentine naval activity they carried out important patrolling missions and, together with surface vessels, imposed the Maritime Exclusion Zone established on 12 April, and later the **Total Exclusion Zone**. At least one submarine is likely to have maintained a vigil off the approaches to **Stanley** harbour. By the end of May, four submarines were on station ensuring that all Argentine warships remained within the limit of home waters – within 12 miles of the South American coast – while gathering information on merchant shipping activity in the vicinity.

After the loss of the *Sante Fe* in the **South Georgia** operation, the Argentines' submarine strength was reduced to just one, the Salta class *San Luis*, which although it sailed for the Falklands in mid-April, was found to be so easily detected by sonar owing to the excessive noise generated by her engines and plagued by her torpedo fire control system that, unbeknown to the British, she was withdrawn from operations, leaving their opponents to carry on the necessary, though ultimately fruitless, search for submarines for the duration of the conflict.

Support Oilers (RFA)

These five vessels, constituting modified commercial tankers chartered by the **Royal Fleet Auxiliary**, normally transported ship and aviation fuel between terminals and depots, but were capable of replenishing fleet tankers and directly refuelling other vessels. They consisted of *Appleleaf, Bayleaf, Brambleleaf, Pearleaf* and *Plumleaf*.

Support Oilers (STUFT)

Twelve support oilers were taken up from trade: *Anco Charger, Balder London, British Avon, British Dart, British Esk, British Tamar, British Tay, British Test, British Trent, British Wye, Eburna* and *G A Walker*, though the last did not arrive at **Stanley** until after the surrender.

Surface-to-Air Missiles

See Seacat; Sea Dart; Seaslug; Sea Wolf

Survey Vessels

Three of these served on Operation **Corporate**, all employed as ambulance ships: *Hecla, Herald* and *Hydra*.

Sussex Mountain

Located just south of the head of **San Carlos Water** – the site of the major anchorages and three of the four landing beaches – it stands about 900ft high in a cluster of other mountains sometimes bearing the name collectively. In order to forestall the Argentines from occupying this point, which overlooked the whole of the eastern arm of San Carlos Water, Brigadier **Thompson** changed the order of landing so that 2 **Para** could be in a position to come ashore closest to this feature, at Blue Beach One at **San Carlos**, and occupy it by nightfall on 21 May. **45 Commando**, which landed at **Red Beach** in **Ajax Bay**, followed up the northern slopes of Sussex Mountain behind 2 Para.

The Paras found the water table too high to enable them to dig trenches, obliging them to construct sangars. This proved the case for the remainder of the campaign: the boggy terrain on East Falkland and its high water table did not lend itself to trench-digging, as a consequence of which many troops built up by constructing sangars of rock and peat above ground. From atop Sussex Mountain they witnessed the air attacks against the ships in **'Bomb Alley'** before finally moving off towards **Goose Green** at sunrise on 26 May.

Sutton, Operation

Code name for the amphibious landings in **San Carlos Water** over the course of 21 May. *Antrim* and *Ardent* were detached from the **Amphibious Task Group** as the lead vessels in the approach to San Carlos Water, *Ardent* entering Falkland Sound from the north. *Antrim* followed two hours later and landed a **Special Boat Squadron** team on **Fanning Head** before assuming charge of air operations over the area. The approach benefited from excellent weather conditions: fog, low cloud and high winds, which kept Argentine aircraft grounded and allowed the Amphibious Task Group to proceed without opposition. At the same time, two **Sea King** HAS5s performed sonar sweeps to detect any presence by the submarine *San Luis* around the northern approaches of the sound.

Before sunrise on the 21st, the ships of the Amphibious Task Group and their close escorts (the destroyer *Antrim*; the **frigates** *Ardent, Argonaut, Brilliant, Broadsword, Plymouth* and *Yarmouth*; LSLs *Fearless* and *Intrepid*; RFAs *Sir Galahad, Sir Geraint, Sir Lancelot, Sir Percival, Sir Tristram, Fort Austin* and *Stromness*; and three **Ships Taken Up From Trade**: *Norland, Europic Ferry* and *Canberra*) entered Falkland Sound, followed by the troop transports, with *Canberra* entering San Carlos Water first, followed by *Norland, Stromness* and the **Landing Ships Logistic**. Escorting **frigates** and **destroyers** remained on guard in Falkland Sound in defence of these vessels against an Argentine assault from the air, with *Plymouth* the lone warship in San Carlos Water itself. *Fearless* and *Intrepid*, the two assault ships, duly launched their **landing**

Paras prepare for transfer into landing craft. (AirSeaLand Photos)

craft – eight from each – to take aboard the troops waiting in the transports for conveyance to the respective designated beaches, an operation that began at 0530Z. **40 Commando, Royal Marines,** were accordingly moved to **San Carlos, 2 Para** and **45 Commando** landed at **Ajax Bay** and **3 Para** went ashore at **Port San Carlos**.

Antrim was hit by a bomb around 1330Z but the device failed to explode. *Argonaut* was seriously damaged at about the same time by Skyhawks, two of whose 1,000lb bombs struck her, failing to explode but causing crippling damage, including fires and heavy flooding.

Ardent, struck multiple times by Skyhawk bombs, was abandoned after she began to list from flooding. Fires aft eventually reached the magazine, causing the ship to explode and sink on the evening of the 22nd off North West Island. Twenty-two men had been killed and more than thirty were wounded, the survivors being moved to *Canberra* by *Yarmouth.* Thus, on the first day of the landings the **Task Force** lost *Ardent,* with *Antrim* and *Argonaut* severely damaged. All the troops put ashore arrived unharmed, and by the end of the day almost 1,000 tons of stores and more than 3,000 troops stood on dry land, establishing a beachhead 4 miles long, thus qualifying Sutton as a remarkably successful achievement. The air and surface defence screen established in Falkland Sound had performed very well in protecting the Amphibious

Task Group, from which no amphibious vessels had been damaged. Fortunately for the British, the Argentines concentrated their efforts on warships instead of the defenceless troop transports, whose loss might have been catastrophic for Operation **Corporate** as a whole.

Several days' build-up of supplies at the beachhead were required before a break-out could be launched, during which time the troops dug themselves in, prepared for the expected counter-attack, certainly by air and possibly by land.

Sea Harriers not only engaged Argentine aircraft through the course of the day, shooting down ten of the thirteen aircraft lost, but maintained nearly constant **combat air patrols** around both ends of Falkland Sound and over West Falkland in an effort to prevent Argentine jets from menacing the ships in the sound.

By the end of the first day of the landings the **Sea Kings** of 846 Naval Air Squadron had flown an average of nine and a half hours, with seven of its helicopters moving tens of thousands of tons of stores and more than 500 troops, involving 288 sorties.

As the very success of the campaign depended on the landings on 21 May establishing a secure foothold in San Carlos Water, this may well be considered the most critical day of the conflict, for a successful repulse by the Argentines would probably have compromised Operation Corporate entirely.

Losses of aircrew during the first day of the landings numbered just three, including a **Gazelle** shot down by small arms fire from the Port San Carlos area. Sergeant Edward Candlish helped his wounded pilot, Sergeant Andrew Evans, ashore, but the latter died of his wounds within minutes. A second Gazelle was brought down over Clam Creek, the pilot shot in the head and chest and the aircrewman dying when the helicopter crashed into a hillside.

Swan Inlet House

Situated on the coast midway between **Goose Green** and **Fitzroy**, this isolated residence became a transit point for the airlift of **2 Para** eastwards. Initially opposed to the plan to move the battalion to the Fitzroy/**Bluff Cove** area by helicopter after the victory at Goose Green, Brigadier **Wilson** changed his mind and consented to Major John Crosland's (Officer Commanding B Company) plan to move in stages, with Swan Inlet House as an intermediate stop. Accordingly, on the morning of 2 June, five **Scouts** of 656 Squadron, two fitted with SS-11 anti-ship missiles and the other three providing support and carrying four Paras each, approached Swan Inlet and fired four missiles, only one of which hit its target. The advanced party of Paras found the settlement uninhabited, but Crosland discovered the telephone line was still working. He then simply telephoned Bluff Cove settlement and learned from Ron Binney, the settlement manager, that there were no Argentines at Fitzroy or Bluff Cove, so ensuring the safe reception of the rest of the battalion, carried by aircraft in stages.

Tab

Army acronym for 'tactical advance to battle' – a loaded march. Many units 'tabbed' in the Falklands, but that conducted by 3 Para from **Port San Carlos** to Estancia House is best associated with this term. As part of the break-out from the beachhead planned by Brigadier **Thompson**, 3 Para left Port San Carlos on 27 May by a more direct route than **45 Commando** during its **yomp**, reaching, after a respite to allow those suffering from the toll, **Teal Inlet**, a tiny settlement on Port Salvador Bay, at 0230Z on the 29th. The following day, with two **helicopters** now available to resupply the battalion and convey some of its mortars and other support weapons forward, 3 Para proceeded at 1430Z to Estancia House, where it arrived at 2240Z and from where it occupied Mounts Estancia and Vernet on 1 June. This effort entailed a march of 50 miles in six days across extremely difficult ground in wintry conditions and is rightly considered a feat of enormous physical and mental proportions, not least owing to the prodigious weight carried by the Paras – at least 100lb each and in many cases well in excess of this.

Task Force

The Task Force dispatched on Operation **Corporate** comprised various groups and components, each departing the UK at different times, and is thus collectively known by this term of convenience. However, the major components are easily identifiable.

The **Antrim Group** sailed on 2 April and consisted of the County class **destroyers** *Antrim* and *Glamorgan*, the Type 42 destroyers *Coventry*, *Glasgow* and *Sheffield*, the frigates *Arrow*, *Brilliant* and *Plymouth*, and the Royal Fleet Auxiliary (RFA) fleet tanker *Tidespring*.

The **Carrier Battle Group** departed from Portsmouth on 5 April, including *Hermes* and *Invincible*, with the RFA support tanker *Pearleaf* carrying heavy fuel oil for *Hermes*. On the same day the frigates *Alacrity* and *Antelope* left Devonport, together with the RFA fleet tanker *Olmeda*, while the RFA replenishment ship *Resource*, containing naval stores, left Rosyth to rendezvous with the carriers. A few days later *Antelope* joined the ships conveying **3 Commando Brigade**, with *Yarmouth* and *Broadsword* replacing *Antelope* after they sailed from Gibraltar on the 8th.

Other single-vessel or small group departures following these two substantial contingents included the sailing of the destroyers *Ardent* and *Argonaut* from Devonport on 19 April, together with the support tanker *Plumleaf* and replenishment ship *Regent*.

On 10 May the **Bristol Group**, eight vessels in all, comprised the last of the major components of the Task Force to leave UK shores for the South Atlantic. The Carrier Battle Group and the **Amphibious Task Group** – the latter formed from various elements while travelling south – both underwent changes to their respective orders of battle before reaching the **Total Exclusion Zone**. By 20 May, when the Task Force divided into these two constituent parts, the Carrier Battle Group consisted of

T

Sea Harriers and Sea King helicopters aboard HMS *Hermes*. (AirSeaLand Photos)

the two **aircraft carriers**, *Hermes* and *Invincible*, escorted by the destroyers *Coventry*, *Glamorgan* and *Glasgow*, the frigates *Alacrity* and *Arrow*, and various **Royal Fleet Auxiliaries** and **Ships Taken Up From Trade** (STUFT). The Amphibious Task Group and its escorts consisted of the destroyer *Antrim*; the frigates *Ardent*, *Argonaut*, *Brilliant*, *Broadsword*, *Plymouth* and *Yarmouth*; the two **Landing Ships Logistic**, *Fearless* and *Intrepid*; seven Royal Fleet Auxiliaries – *Sir Galahad*, *Sir Geraint*, *Sir Lancelot*, *Sir Percivale*, *Sir Tristram*, *Fort Austin* and *Stromness* – and three STUFT: *Norland*, *Europic Ferry* and *Canberra*.

All told, the Task Force consisted of thirty-five ships and six submarines of the **Royal Navy**, twenty-two RFAs, forty-nine STUFT commissioned for Royal Navy service (of which forty-three deployed before the end of the fighting), and two vessels provided by the **Royal Maritime Auxiliary Service**.

Teal Inlet

A small settlement along the north coast of East Falkland, first recced on the night of 24 May by a six-man **Special Boat Squadron** team. Six days later, **45 Commando** reached Teal in the course of its **yomp** from **Port San Carlos** to **Mount Kent**.

In order to ease the logistical problem associated with supplying **3 Commando Brigade** all the way from **San Carlos Water,** once that formation moved east towards Stanley, Teal was designated as the Brigade Forward Maintenance Area. Accordingly, on the night of 31 May, with Mount Kent now in the possession of **42 Commando** and **Top Malo House** cleared by the **Mountain and Arctic Warfare Cadre,** HQ 3 Commando Brigade moved forward from **San Carlos** to Teal in **BV 202Es,** under escort by **CVR(T)s** from the **Blues and Royals.** HQ M&AWC was also located at Teal. To support the advance along the northern route, 845 and 847 Naval Air Squadrons established a joint forward operating base at Teal Inlet on 4 June. Over the previous few days, **Sea Kings** had flown in guns, ammunition and stores, with two batteries of artillery and a **Rapier** battery arriving on the 5th.

Thompson, Brigadier Julian, CB OBE RM

The commander of **Landing Force Group** on Operation **Corporate,** his force consisted of **3 Commando Brigade,** which he had led since January 1981, and several smaller units from the Army and **Royal Air Force.**

Joining the **Royal Marines** in 1952, Thompson served in the Near East, Aden, and at home, then the Far East, after which he was promoted to Brigade Major of 3 Commando Brigade. He led **40 Commando** for more than two years from 1975, including a tour in Northern Ireland, after which he was made Colonel General Staff on the staff of HQ Commando Forces in Plymouth. He was appointed commander of 3 Commando Brigade in 1981.

Thompson established his HQ at Hamoaze House in Devonport, near Plymouth and held a briefing for his staff and unit commanders on 4 April. He had three fundamentally important tasks: landing his troops; establishing a beachhead; and defeating Argentine ground forces. He was pleased to learn from Admiral **Fieldhouse** during a meeting aboard HMS *Hermes* off **Ascension** on 17 April of the decision to include **2 Para** in 3 Commando Brigade, bringing the total up to five battalions/ commandos, the maximum he wished to command in battle.

Major General **Moore** flew to Ascension to confer with Thompson and Commodore Michael Clapp, Commander **Amphibious Task Group,** who on 29 April jointly presented various options to him on locations for an amphibious landing. In turn, Moore presented them to Fieldhouse, and possibly later to the Chiefs of Staff. On 12 May, Thompson and Clapp learned that their joint plans had been approved. Accordingly, Thompson issued his orders aboard *Fearless* on the 13th.

He and his HQ staff moved by **Sea King** to **Teal Inlet** on 31 May and later to the lower slopes of **Mount Kent.** On 8 June, while aboard HMS *Fearless* with Brigadier **Wilson,** CO 5 Infantry Brigade, and Major General Moore, Thompson argued for a strategy involving a broad front attack against **Stanley** involving his brigade, as opposed to Wilson's narrow strike along the **Fitzroy**–Stanley track to the south.

T

Brigadier Julian Thompson, commander of 3 Commando Brigade. (AirSeaLand Photos)

The catastrophe befalling the **Welsh Guards** near **Fitzroy** rendered Thompson's the favoured option and on 10 June he issued orders for a three-phase attack, with contingencies of exploitation further east if Argentine resistance collapsed.

3 Commando Brigade

Based in Plymouth and commanded by Brigadier Julian **Thompson** RM, 3 Commando Brigade consisted of highly trained, highly motivated units, mostly Royal Marines, and was the country's only amphibious force. It formed a vital part of the UK contribution to the NATO alliance by virtue of its winter training intended for operations on the northern flank, i.e. north Norway.

At the outbreak of hostilities, some men were still returning from their annual three-month winter warfare exercise in Norway, and **40 Commando** had recently exercised with both *Hermes* and *Invincible* along the British coastline in February and March. Most of **45 Commando** had just completed a training period at home, but with one company in Brunei on jungle training. 3 Commando Brigade was most comfortable with amphibious operations rather than the all-arms scenarios associated with formations composed entirely of Army units, but the journey to the South Atlantic would take several weeks, and the components of the brigade would have time to acquaint themselves with each other's methods of warfare.

The brigade was continuously on seven days' notice to move, but with the outbreak of hostilities on 2 April this was reduced to three. HQ immediately moved to Hamoaze House in Devonport near Plymouth and began the process of placing all three commandos on alert, locating available shipping, packing stores for either air or sea movement, recalling those personnel already on Easter leave, and formulating plans for embarkation and service in the South Atlantic. With extraordinary efficiency, most of 3 Commando Brigade, supplemented on 3 April by **3 Para** and later many supporting units, embarked at Southampton, Portsmouth and Devonport in a range of vessels, mainly *Canberra* and *Stromness*, between 7 and 9 April, with a strength of 3,500 men, approximately 50,000 tons of stores and sixty vehicles, with Brigade HQ, Commodore Amphibious Warfare, Commodore Michael Clapp, and his staff together in *Fearless*, Thompson and his staff joining by helicopter from Portland.

3 Commando Brigade consisted of a number of substantial elements plus many smaller attachments. These were: Headquarters and Signals Squadron RM, the Commando Logistic Regiment RM, 59 Independent Field Squadron **Royal Engineers**, 29 Commando Light Regiment **Royal Artillery** (6 × 105mm guns), and four basic infantry formations: 40, **42** and 45 Commando RM, and 3 Para. To these

Men of one of the two Parachute battalions of 3 Commando Brigade. (AirSeaLand Photos)

would soon be added **2 Para**, formerly of **5 Infantry Brigade**, making a total of about 4,350 men. It also included an Air Defence Troop, equipped with twelve **Blowpipe** surface-to-air missiles, and 1st Raiding Squadron RM, which brought with it rigid raiding craft and was trained to establish Forward Operating Bases (FOB) and to camouflage and conceal both itself and its means of transport.

The brigade also contained an organic air arm, 3 Commando Brigade Air Squadron (3 CBAS), divided between Plymouth and Arbroath in Scotland, with ten **Gazelle** AH1s and nine **Scout AH1s**, both light **helicopters**. Four of the latter were fitted with **SS-11 anti-ship missiles**. All twenty-two aircrew consisted of Royal Marines, with the pilots drawn mostly from the same corps but a handful from the **Royal Navy** and the Army.

On D-Day, 21 May, HQ 3 Commando Brigade landed at Blue Beach Two near the settlement of **San Carlos**, while the brigade's various components landed at their respective objectives. The break-out began when 42 Commando moved by helicopter to **Mount Kent** in stages beginning on the 29th, while 45 Commando and 3 Para moved on foot beginning on 27 May owing to the lack of helicopters resulting from the loss of *Atlantic Conveyor* on 25 May. 40 Commando remained at the beachhead to protect the BMA from any potential Argentine attack launched from **West Falkland**.

On the 28th, 2 Para attacked **Darwin** and **Goose Green**, while the following day support helicopters moved some elements of the brigade forward to **Teal Inlet** as part of the northern advance route to **Stanley**. This included four **Rapier** fire units of 'T' Battery, 12 Air Defence Regiment, which was to provide local air defence at Teal until the next move east. On 31 May, with most of the brigade having left **San Carlos Water**, **Sea Kings** moved the brigade staff forward to Teal Inlet. 2 Para stood in reserve for the attacks on **Mount Longdon** and **Two Sisters**. Commando HQ accordingly shifted to Teal Inlet, moving to a position on the west side of **Mount Kent** on 7 June.

After the disaster befalling the **Welsh Guards** at **Fitzroy** on 8 June, Major General **Moore** decided to adopt Thompson's **strategy** for a broad front, northern approach to Stanley, employing 3 Commando Brigade in a three-phase attack; a plan Thompson had finalised by the following day. 3 Para was to capture Mount Longdon and exploit to **Wireless Ridge** if possible; 45 Commando was to attack Two Sisters and exploit to **Mount Tumbledown** and **Mount William** if possible; and 42 Commando, with elements of the Welsh Guards in reserve, was to seize **Mount Harriet** and, if necessary, support 45 Commando if it was able to exploit to Mount Tumbledown after taking Two Sisters.

With the overwhelming success achieved at Longdon, Harriet and Two Sisters on the night of 11–12 June, 3 Commando Brigade had cleared the outer defence ring of its entrenched defenders and faced only Wireless Ridge, seized by 2 Para on 13–14 June. Mount Tumbledown would fall to the responsibility of the **Scots**

Guards in **5 Infantry Brigade**. 3 Commando Brigade remained in the Stanley area following the surrender.

Total casualties for 3 Commando Brigade during the campaign amounted to sixty-eight killed in action, 183 wounded in action, 122 injured (e.g. broken limbs sustained on patrol) in action and twenty-five out of action due to illness.

3 Para

See Parachute Regiment

Tidepool, RFA

A Tide class **Royal Fleet Auxiliary** fleet oiler, she had actually been sold to the Chilean Navy when the conflict began and on 16 April was hastily recalled from the Pacific, sailed through the Panama Canal, took on fuel at Curacao and on 27 April arrived at **Ascension**, where she acquired stores and a helicopter. She arrived off the Falklands on 18 May.

Tidepool did not take part in the amphibious landings in **San Carlos Water** on 21 May but remained there to replenish other vessels, usually under cover of darkness. She was finally handed over to Chile in mid-August.

Commander:	Captain J.W. Gaffrey	
Builders:	Hawthorn Leslie	
Launched:	11 December 1962	
Commissioned:	28 June 1963	
Tonnage:	8,530 Light Displacement	25,930 Full Load
	18,900 Deadweight	14,130 Gross Register
Dimensions: length × beam; feet (metres):	583 × 71 (177.6 × 21.6)	
Draught:	9.8m	
Propulsion:	1 set geared steam turbines	15,000shp = 17 knots (service speed)
Capacity:	17,400 tons FFO; 700 tons diesel oil	
Armament:	Improvised – machine guns and rifles	
Aircraft:	2 × **Wessex** HU5	

Tidespring, RFA

A Tide class fleet tanker and part of the **Antrim Group** of vessels dispatched south from Exercise **Springtrain** on 2 April to retake **South Georgia**. Leaving Gibraltar, she arrived at **Ascension** on 12 April and reached South Georgia on the 21st, playing an important role in the operation to recapture the island. Approximately 150 Argentine

prisoners captured on South Georgia were transported by *Tidespring* to Ascension, reaching the island on 12 May. She transferred to the **Bristol Group** by 21 May and sat in **San Carlos Water** replenishing other vessels, usually at night when she was less vulnerable to air attack. *Tidespring* finished her service in the conflict on arrival at Portsmouth on 22 July.

Commander:	Captain S. Redmond	
Builders:	Hawthorn Leslie	
Launched:	3 May 1962	
Commissioned:	18 January 1963	
Tonnage:	8,530 Light Displacement	25,930 Full Load
	18,900 Deadweight	14,130 Gross Register
Dimensions: length × beam; feet (metres):	583 × 71 (177.6 × 21.6)	
Draught:	9.8m	
Propulsion:	1 set geared steam turbines	15,000shp = 17 knots (service speed)
Fuel capacity:	17,400 tons FFO; 700 tons diesel oil	
Armament:	Improvised – machine guns and rifles	
Aircraft:	2 × **Wessex** HU5	

Top Malo House

An isolated, two-storey timber former residence, including an outhouse and a privy, overlooking a small corral near the Mullow Stream, about 5 miles south of **Teal Inlet**. On 28 May, a section of Argentine commandos was dropped by helicopter nearby and established an observation post near the summit, but deteriorating weather conditions at dusk on 30 May obliged them to take refuge in the abandoned Top Malo House.

Unbeknown to the Argentines, patrols from the **Mountain and Arctic Warfare Cadre** (M&AWC) had been sent to the area around **Mount Kent**, ahead of the arrival of larger formations. On 30 May, a patrol under Lieutenant Fraser Haddow observed the Argentine presence at Top Malo House. Captain Rod Boswell RM brought reinforcements of nineteen men of the M&AWC, which arrived in **Sea King** HC4 ZA291 on 31 May to a position about ¾ mile from the house. It launched an attack at 1300Z, beginning with 66mm rockets, which set the building on fire and temporarily stunned the occupants before they fled from the building and returned fire, eventually forcing them to take cover in dead ground. Some surrendered when called to do so, others carried on the fight until, after fifteen minutes, the remainder capitulated, leaving the Argentines with virtually no advanced positions with which to observe the imminent advance of **3 Commando Brigade**.

Tor Caledonia, MV

A roll-on/roll-off vehicle ferry requisitioned from Tor Line on 18 May and furnished with Naval Party 2020 under Lieutenant Commander J.G. Devine RN. She departed Southampton on 20 May and reached **Ascension** on the 31st. Arriving off the Falklands on 12 June, just two days before the fighting ceased, *Tor Caledonia* played an important part in resupplying the islands and the reconstruction effort. She arrived at Portsmouth on 19 August.

Commander:	Captain A. Scott	
Built:	1977	
Tonnage:	5,056 Gross Register	9,882 Deadweight
Dimensions: length × beam; feet (metres):	534 × 69 (162.8 × 21)	
Propulsion:	2 diesel engines	12,000bhp = 18.5 knots
Helicopter platform – no embarked aircraft		

Total Exclusion Zone (TEZ)

The Chiefs of Staff first discussed the possibility of imposing an Exclusion Zone around the Falklands on 5 April. Formally established as a Maritime Exclusion Zone on the 12th, it declared that all Argentine warships entering or discovered within the area would be treated as hostile and subject to attack. Civilian vessels and aircraft found in the area would be considered to be supplying Argentine forces or warships. With respect to the vessels of other nations, the **Royal Navy** would take what action was deemed necessary to ensure these did not supply the Argentines. British forces would not use more force than was deemed necessary and unarmed merchant vessels or aircraft would only be attacked as a last resort after proper warnings had been issued but to which no heed had been taken. The Maritime Exclusion Zone was converted to the Total Exclusion Zone, to include aircraft of all nations, on 28 April.

The TEZ formed a circle of 200 nautical miles from latitude 51 degrees 40 minutes South and longitude 59 degrees 30 minutes West, which represented the approximate centre of the Falklands. This area was deemed adequate to provide sufficient space for a signal to be issued to a merchant vessel to heave to and reverse course, or to pursue it if it refused to stop. By providing warning of the risks faced by Argentine vessels, the UK government believed the imposition of the TEZ constituted enough disincentive for Argentine units bound for the islands, and might thus contribute to cutting off supplies to the garrison on the islands.

On 7 May Britain extended the general war zone, making liable to attack any Argentine vessel that strayed outside the 12-mile coastal limit representing home waters. As such, **submarines** patrolling offshore were liable to sink vessels presumed to be hostile. Argentines reciprocated by declaring the whole of the South Atlantic a war zone, later confirmed when they attacked British vessels outside the TEZ.

Most of the vessels of the **Task Force** remained on the edge of the TEZ on 1 May, but they re-entered it on 20 May in order to assume positions for the amphibious landings in **San Carlos Water** to take place the following day.

Tugs

Four ocean-going tugs served in the conflict: *Typhoon*, belonging to the **Royal Maritime Auxiliary Service** (RMAS), and three requisitioned vessels, *Salvageman*, *Irishman* and *Yorkshireman*. In the closing days of the war, the tugs extracted **Special Air Service** and **Special Boat Squadron** patrols scattered across the islands. Three of them helped to dispose of the captured Argentine submarine *Sante Fe* by towing it out to sea.

2 Para

See Parachute Regiment

Two Sisters

Eminences immediately west of **Stanley**, they formed the objective of **45 Commando** on the night of 11–12 June. With the break-out from the beachhead at **San Carlos Water** beginning on 27 May, the northern approach to Stanley had begun in earnest, and included 45 Commando, whose **yomp** brought it close to **Mount Kent** and in a position to strike the outer Argentine defensive ring just west of Stanley.

After Major General **Moore** issued instructions on 9 June for a three-phase attack against the capital, the following day Brigadier **Thompson** gave orders for an attack on Two Sisters and the same day two **Harriers** conducted **photographic reconnaissance** of the position.

The feature consisted of two peaks each of about 1,000ft in elevation, extending more than a mile in length from west to east and notable for its five jagged ridges, which formed a ragged spine. Climbing it required particular determination, for the wet rocks and scree slowed progress considerably. This formidable defensive position was held by approximately 200 men of C Company, 4th Infantry Regiment, plus two additional sections. B Company, 6th Infantry Regiment stood in support, including heavy machine guns and 120mm mortars.

The commanding officer of 45 Commando, Lieutenant Colonel Andrew Whitehead, laid plans involving an attack in two phases. X Company, leaving the start line at 0100Z on the 12th, was to seize within two hours the ridge known as 'Long Toenail', which lay just south-west of the principal rocky formation, before offering covering fire for the main attack coming from the north-west around

Murrell Bridge. This plan would also enable the unit to offer covering fire over **Goat Ridge**, which acted as the boundary between 45 and **42 Commando,** and prevent the Argentines from occupying that low-lying feature. With 'Long Toenail' secured by X Company, Z Company was then to capture the western peak of Two Sisters, followed by Y Company passing through to seize the eastern eminence known as 'Summer Days'. While the **Royal Marines** would approach in silence, support was available if necessary from the guns of the destroyer *Glamorgan* and the frigate *Yarmouth,* artillery and the 81mm mortars attached to 45 Commando itself.

On 11 June, Whitehead's unit, minus X Company, left its position behind **Mount Kent** and, proceeding on a northerly route, arrived at the main start line known as 'Pub Garden' according to schedule. At the same time, X Company, moving between Mount Kent and **Mount Challenger**, arrived at the start line more than two hours late owing to problems encountered during the approach march; specifically, the excessive weight of their equipment – including MILAN anti-tank launchers and their 30lb ammunition, which represented an immense burden when carried over broken ground. Instead of the expected three hours to reach their start line, Captain Ian Gardiner's company took six – so confirming Clausewitz's dictum that 'friction' sometimes inconveniently imposes itself on operations, unravelling even the most carefully laid plans. Still, the situation proved salvageable, since Whitehead remained calm and ordered them to proceed when ready.

At 0300Z, X Company began its move over open country towards 'Long Toenail', but halfway up Gardiner and his men were met with bursts of heavy machine-gun fire and were obliged temporarily to withdraw. With MILANs and mortar fire directed against these positions, supported by artillery, 2 Troop managed to reach the summit, only to be thrown back by artillery fire before again pushing on, finally to overwhelm the machine gun positions and secure the feature.

Around 0400Z, while X Company was engaged in its struggle for 'Long Toenail', Z Company, with Y Company on its right, advanced silently uphill from the start line while the Argentines remained concentrated against X Company's attack. Once the defenders sent up a flare to illuminate the sky, 8 Troop of Z Company opened fire, causing such a furious response from the Argentines – including heavy artillery and mortar fire – that the company lost four men killed and a lieutenant ordered a charge against the summit to bring an end to resistance, while at the same time 7 Troop engaged in a heavy exchange of fire while held up by stiff resistance.

On Z Company's right flank, meanwhile, Y Company swung in to develop a parallel attack, in so doing silencing some of the machine guns blocking Z Company's advance. This enabled 8 Troop to proceed further towards the summit with covering fire from 7 Troop, and in due course the two companies cleared the Argentine positions on both the northern and southern sides of the feature. The western section of 'Summer Days' thus fell to Z Company 2½ hours after it left the start line, while Y Company passed between the peaks of Two Sisters and proceeded towards the north-eastern summit amid a shower of small arms fire. After deploying anti-tank weapons and further hard fighting with its rifles, 45 Commando prevailed and occupied its final objective by 0818Z. As it began to dig in and reorganise, shellfire fell upon its position as Whitehead prepared to move against **Mount Tumbledown**. Thompson considered this unwise and ordered the unit to remain in place, for **5 Infantry Brigade** was already poised to take part in the advance on Stanley, with the task of seizing Tumbledown allocated to the **Scots Guards**.

The fall of Two Sisters represented a serious blow to the Argentine main defences, yet 45 Commando lost only three killed along with one sapper from the **Royal Engineers** – all from artillery and mortar fire – during the phase when Y and Z Companies were pinned down, plus ten wounded. The Royal Marines took fifty-four **prisoners**, of whom fifty were wounded, and killed about ten of the defenders. The remaining Argentines fled eastwards, probably into Stanley. The attackers had received excellent support from the **Royal Artillery**, who fired about 1,500 rounds.

Typhoon, RMAS

The only **Royal Maritime Auxiliary Service** (RMAS) ocean-going tug in theatre, although there were three other requisitioned tugs present: *Salvageman*, *Irishman* and *Yorkshireman*. She departed Portland on 4 April, reaching **Ascension** on the 20th. She served at **South Georgia** from 27 May for several weeks, performing excellent work transferring troops and stores between vessels of **5 Infantry Brigade**, and later helped refloat the stricken Argentine submarine *Sante Fe*, which had been abandoned after being crippled by **helicopters** on 25 April. *Typhoon* arrived in Portsmouth on 24 September.

Commander:	Captain J.N. Morris	
Launched:	14 October 1958	
Commissioned:	1960	
Displacement:	800 Standard	1,380 Full Load
Dimensions: length × beam; feet (metres):	200 × 40 (60.5 × 12.3)	
Propulsion:	2 diesel engines (1 propeller)	2,750bhp = 17 knots

Uganda, SS

In peacetime an educational steam cruise liner belonging to P&O, she was docked at Alexandria on the Egyptian coast when the Ministry of Defence (MoD) requisitioned her on 10 April while she was carrying more than 1,000 passengers, mostly schoolchildren. Upon reaching Naples en route to Gibraltar, an MoD survey team, a surgeon and engineers began the process of planning her conversion to a hospital ship, a transformation that began in earnest when *Uganda* reached the Royal Naval Dockyard at Gibraltar on 16 April and was completed within an astonishing three days. In that time she was fitted with a casualty receiving area, operating theatre and a main ward. Special means were devised for moving **casualties** on stretchers without recourse to gangways and ladders, and the ship boasted a dispensary, X-ray facilities, operating theatre and wards for burn victims and other intensive care requirements. All told, the ship could accommodate more than 100 medium dependency and intensive care patients, and dozens more less critical cases. Her medical team numbered 135 doctors and nurses.

Uganda departed from Gibraltar on 19 April, reached **Ascension** on the 28th, and arrived off the Falklands on 11 May to occupy her post in the **Red Cross Box**, an area about 30 miles north of the islands where she and her Argentine counterpart could operate without molestation. Although she had no embarked helicopter, before

The hospital ship SS *Uganda*. (AirSeaLand Photos)

she left the UK she had a landing platform fitted on her stern to receive patients from shore- and ship-based **helicopters**. Her first patients arrived on 12 May, after the attack on HMS *Sheffield*. Once fit to be moved, they would be transported by one of the three ambulance ships *Herald*, *Hecla* and *Hydra*, to Montevideo, the capital of Uruguay, to be flown by **VC10** C1s to the UK, via Ascension, for further treatment. Wounded Argentines in British care were either given over to their own hospital ship or transported by sea to Montevideo for repatriation.

For easy identification, *Uganda* bore large white and red crosses – one on each side of her funnel and two each on her port and starboard sides, respectively. In conformance with the Geneva Convention, she carried no cryptographic facilities and no armament.

Uganda did not take part in the amphibious landings in **San Carlos Water** on 21 May. Instead, casualties sustained that day were airlifted to *Canberra* for medical treatment. On 29 May she sailed into Grantham Sound, part of Falkland Sound, little more than a mile from the main casualty clearing station at **Ajax Bay**.

When she received the badly burned victims of the *Sir Galahad* and *Sir Tristram* attacks of 8 June, her officers' mess was turned into another ward to accommodate the large numbers of patients. The following day, **Wessex** and **Sea King** flew wounded involved in the tragedy from Ajax Bay to *Uganda*. Two days later, in company with *Hydra*, she entered Grantham Sound in Falkland Sound to take aboard casualties from the actions at **Mount Longdon**, **Mount Harriet** and **Two Sisters**, her new location enabling the wounded to travel only the very short distance up San Carlos Water from Ajax Bay instead of to the Red Cross Box. *Uganda* took aboard as many as 150 casualties a day during the period of most intense fighting between 11 and 14 June, with no distinction made between British and Argentine wounded, which in total exceeded 700 in-patients, of which 150 were Argentines. Her medical staff performed more than 500 operations. *Uganda* conveyed the Gurkhas back to the UK, leaving the Falklands on 18 July and arriving at Southampton on 9 August.

Commander:	Captain J.G. Clark	
Launched:	1952	
Naval Party 1830:	Commander A.B. Gough RN	
Tonnage:	16,907 Gross Register	5,705 Deadweight
Dimensions: length × beam; feet (metres):	540 × 71 (164.6 × 21.8)	
Propulsion:	2 sets geared steam turbines	12,300shp = 17 knots
Helicopter platform – no embarked aircraft		

Valiant, HMS

Six **submarines** served in the South Atlantic, of which *Valiant* numbered among three of the Valiant class, all nuclear powered, the others being **Conqueror** and **Courageous**. She departed Faslane on 3 May and arrived off the Falklands in mid-May. Her South Atlantic service ended on her arrival back in Faslane on 29 July.

Commander:	Commander T.M. Le Marchand	
Launched:	3 December 1963	
Commissioned:	18 July 1966	
Displacement (tons):	3,500 Standard	4,000 Full Load, Surface 4,900 Submerged
Dimensions: length × beam; feet (metres):	285 × 33.0 (86.9 × 10.1)	
Propulsion:	1 nuclear reactor = geared steam turbines	20,000shp = approximately 25 knots submerged
Armament:	6 × 21in (533mm) bow torpedo tubes; Mark 8 and 21in Tigerfish torpedoes	

VC10 C1

The mighty Vickers VC10 C1 transport aircraft carried a payload of up to 20 tons and could complete a return flight between Britain and **Ascension** in a single day by rotating its crew.

Its principal responsibility lay in the aeromedical role, flying British wounded out of theatre from Montevideo back to the UK via **Ascension**, as well as Argentine wounded and **prisoners** such as the first batch of 137 captured at **South Georgia**, which arrived in Montevideo on 13 May. In the course of the conflict these heavy-lift aircraft, marked with a red cross, conveyed 570 patients. They also ferried men, stores and equipment to Ascension with onward transport by sea to the **Total Exclusion Zone**. Several flights left RAF Brize Norton in Oxfordshire each day, with a stop at Banjul in Gambia or Dakar in Senegal.

The first mission carried out by the thirteen VC10s of 10 Squadron occurred on 3 April when an aircraft collected Falklands Governor Rex Hunt and the **Royal Marines** of **Naval Party 8901** from Montevideo after the Argentines had released them from their short captivity. On 21 April a VC10 repatriated the British personnel captured at South Georgia, consisting of twenty-two Royal Marines from the *Endurance* and thirteen scientists of the British Antarctic Survey team.

On 27 May, two VC10s flew survivors from *Sheffield* from Wideawake Airfield to Brize Norton. The last repatriation flight of the war took place on the penultimate day, 13 June, leaving Montevideo and arriving in the UK, via Ascension, on the 14th with sixty-one wounded aboard.

Victor K2

The extraordinary distances involved in the conflict, particularly travel between **Ascension** and the Falklands, rendered the British Aerospace (Handley Page) Victor K2 tanker a critical asset to the RAF's ability to provide both **Harriers** and **Sea Harriers** with in-flight refuelling for long-range operations.

Normally based at RAF Marham in Norfolk, only two squadrons of Victors served this need in 1982, a shortage exacerbated by the few aircraft capable of receiving air-to-air refuelling when war broke out. If the Victor crews were well-acquainted with air-to-air refuelling – together with most of the Harrier GR3 pilots – this did not apply to the **Vulcan** crews, for whom this became a newly acquired skill.

The first Victor tankers arrived at Ascension on 18 April, five that day and another four the following. On the 20th, in the aircraft's first mission during the conflict, four Victors departed from Wideawake to fly a reconnaissance mission over **South Georgia**, a destination 3,850 miles' distant and, ironically, requiring in-flight refuelling from another Victor. By the end of the month, six more Victors had arrived at Wideawake to support the Vulcans, as well as the Sea Harriers and Harriers.

Hercules and **Nimrods**, hitherto without in-flight refuelling probes, duly underwent modification and their crews received training, thereby extending their range and time in the air very substantially and in turn contributing to the many extraordinarily long sorties flown during the war. In support, ground crews provided a superb level of maintenance of these ageing machines, so that during the course of sixty-seven missions flown involving 375 sorties, aircraft failed to operate in just three instances.

Victors operating from Marham and Dakar refuelled the three **Phantom** FGR2s flown out of RAF Coningsby that in late May replaced the Harrier GR3s initially assigned to air defence duties on Ascension. They also flew long-range maritime reconnaissance sorties, using cameras fitted in their noses.

Eleven out of the fourteen Victors at Ascension on 1 May were employed during the Black Buck 1 raid from Ascension, thereby stretching their capacity almost to the limit. By mid-May the number of Victors at Wideawake peaked at seventeen. On 1 June, two Harrier GR3s flew an eight-hour twenty-minute mission from Ascension to the aircraft carrier *Hermes*, a distance of 3,900 miles, refuelled several times by four Victors. Neither pilot had ever landed on the deck of an aircraft carrier before. A similar mission was flown a week later.

Vulcan B2

Based at RAF Waddington in Lincolnshire and designed to carry nuclear rather than conventional weapons to deter aggression by Soviet ground forces in Europe, the British Aerospace (Avro) Vulcan B2 bomber carried a crew of six: pilot, co-pilot, radar/navigator, navigator/plotter, air engineer and air-to-air refuelling instructor. It could fly 610mph at 40,000ft.

Nearing retirement after twenty-five years' service with the **Royal Air Force** when war in the South Atlantic broke out, even then their deployment seemed unlikely with operations 8,000 miles' distant and only the runway on **Ascension** between them and the Falklands. Moreover, until the first **Black Buck raid** on 1 May – five would be successfully flown – the aircraft had never flown operationally.

With their normal range with a full bomb load below 5,000 nautical miles, preparations for the unprecedentedly long air strikes against **Stanley** airport demanded the rapid refitting of in-flight refuelling equipment and alterations to six aircraft, enabling the Vulcans to carry ECM pods. Herculean efforts before and during the raids rendered the Vulcan – by 1982 a generation old – capable of delivering twenty-one 1,000lb bombs nearly 4,000 miles: no mean feat. Later they would be further modified to carry two or four Shrike radiation-homing missiles designed to strike **radar** installations.

As they were so close to retirement, the Vulcans contained no new radar or satellite navigation systems; this was rectified by the fitting of a new inertial system that enabled the aircraft to fly for long distances beyond land. RAF technicians also fitted new electronic counter-measures equipment to jam enemy radar. With all these and other modifications, both pilots and engineers required practice, and with conventional bombs fitted the five selected crews from 44, 50 and 101 Squadrons, and a final one from the newly defunct 9 Squadron, tested their aircraft and weapons before deployment.

With the aid of two in-flight refuellings, on 29 April the first two Vulcans reached Ascension, leaving on the first Black Buck mission against Stanley the following day. Five successful Black Buck missions were flown, mostly with disproportionately mediocre results given the resources dedicated to each sortie. A Shrike missile fired on two separate attacks resulted in partial success, with shortcomings of the weapons apparent with the absence of in-built memory, which denied it accurate guidance if the radar ceased to operate in the process of launching.

During the Black Buck missions the Vulcans carried approximately 6,000lb in excess of the maximum load normally allowed for take-off. After each Black Buck raid the Vulcans were flown back to RAF Waddington, to return to Wideawake for each successive mission.

V

Wasp HAS1

Only eight Westland Wasp HAS1 **helicopters** served in the South Atlantic owing to their replacement in most cases by the **Lynx HAS2**. Their primary function was in the anti-submarine warfare role, deploying Mark 44/46 lightweight torpedoes, or armed with the wire-guided **SS-12 anti-ship missile** deployed against vessels and surfaced submarines. Several of the Leander and Rothesay class **frigates** had embarked Wasps, including two on *Endurance*, one each on three frigates and one each on the three **ambulance vessels**.

Endurance's Wasp served well in the recapture of **South Georgia**, including her deployment of AS.12 missiles to disable the submarine *Santa Fe*.

Welsh Falcon, Exercise

A two-week exercise organised by Colonel Christopher Dunphie for **5 Infantry Brigade** at Sennybridge and the Brecon Beacons in mid-Wales, deemed necessary in light of the recent reorganisation of the brigade that saw the transfer out of both Parachute battalions to 3 Commando Brigade and their replacement by a battalion each from the **Welsh Guards** and **Scots Guards**. Consequently, none of these units were accustomed to training together and time was required to prepare and re-equip them for the coming campaign.

The first week consisted of basic military skills and the second included a simulated landing with barracks serving as ships, lorrys in the place of **landing craft**, and twenty-four RAF Puma **helicopters**. The 1st Green Howards, together with RAF **Harriers** and Jaguars, acted as the enemy. It was particularly hot during the exercise, which began on 21 April and ended on the 29th. With rolling hills, boggy ground, a high level of precipitation and mist, the Beacons proved well suited as a training ground for service in the South Atlantic, with time devoted to physical fitness, weapon handling and section, platoon, company and battalion attacks.

Welsh Guards

The 1st Battalion Welsh Guards, commanded by Lieutenant Colonel Johnny Rickett since March 1980, formed part of London District under Major General Sir Desmond Langley. At the outbreak of conflict the battalion was involved in public (ceremonial) duties but soon transferred to **5 Infantry Brigade** to compensate for the shifting of **2 Para** and **3 Para** to **3 Commando Brigade**.

Recent service saw 1 Welsh Guards in Germany and Ulster, and on exercise in Kenya during the winter of 1981–82. Based at Pirbright, near Aldershot, the battalion was warned of possible service in the South Atlantic on 4 April, two days after the Argentine invasion. Together with other elements of 5 Infantry Brigade, including

2 **Scots Guards**, the Welsh Guards took part in Exercise **Welsh Falcon** at the end of April to improve their fitness, tactics and fieldcraft, for the battalion was not trained for 'out-of-area' operations.

The Welsh Guards, together with the Scots Guards, embarked from Southampton aboard the *Queen Elizabeth 2* on 12 May and transferred, via the trawlers *Farnella*, *Cordella* and *Pict*, to *Canberra* at **South Georgia** on the 27th.

With misty conditions helping to mask them from possible air attack, the battalion came ashore on one of the **Blue Beaches** in **San Carlos Water** on 2 June from **landing craft**, about 3 miles south of **San Carlos** settlement. As part of Brigadier **Wilson's** plan for a southern approach to **Stanley** with his brigade, he tasked the Welsh Guards with defending **Bluff Cove**.

Rickett persuaded Wilson to allow the battalion to move overland to Bluff Cove via **Sussex Mountain** and **Darwin**, which was agreed. The Recce Platoon was lifted forward by **Scout helicopters** as the 'eyes and ears' of the battalion. Snocats would be provided if possible to convey mortars, machine guns, ammunition and bergens, but when the Snocats failed to materialise, the battalion set off, with their mortars, MILANs and ammunition on a light tractor and farm trailer, but with the machine guns man-packed. Snocats arrived soon thereafter, but were deemed inadequate for lack of space and were low on fuel. The tractor meanwhile bogged down in the mud several times, leaving the battalion with the options to continue without their bergens and heavy weapons or return to San Carlos and wait for another method of transport, since it could not continue without its support weapons. The troops duly returned to San Carlos and hoped to be moved forward the next day, but were told that the move would now be conducted by water. Ordered by Commodore Clapp, Commander **Amphibious Task Group**, on 5 June to embark aboard *Intrepid* for Bluff Cove, the Guardsmen returned to their trenches when this was countermanded.

They embarked again on the evening of 7 June aboard *Fearless* and were off Elephant Island around 0200Z on the 8th where they were meant to cross-deck into two LCUs from *Intrepid* coming from Bluff Cove, with the other half of the battalion to go aboard two LCUs from *Fearless*, the whole to proceed to **Fitzroy**. In the event, the *Intrepid* LSUs missed the rendezvous, so half the Welsh Guards proceeded in the two *Fearless* landing craft to Bluff Cove, where Wilson's orders were that they dig in north-east of that settlement on either side of the track from Stanley. Thus, the first move of the battalion involved Battalion and Tac HQs, Number 2 Company and the Recce, Anti-Tank and Machine Gun Platoons, together with other supporting elements such as 1 Troop, 9 Parachute Squadron, **Royal Engineers** with responsibility for repairing Fitzroy bridge. After a 19-mile, four-hour journey, escorted part of the time by *Avenger*, the two companies arrived at the Bluff Cove jetty, thereafter establishing themselves in positions to the north-east astride the road to Stanley, then under construction. Patrols made contact a few hours later with Argentines south and east of **Mount Harriet**.

The rest of the battalion was to arrive the following day, 8 June, consisting of the Prince of Wales Company and 3 Company, plus supporting units of 4 Field Troop Royal Engineers and a detachment from the Royal Signals. Accordingly, on the evening on the 7th they boarded *Sir Galahad* and reached Fitzroy at about 1150Z on the morning of 8 June, to find their arrival unexpected by Major Ewen Southby-Tailyour and Captain Green of *Sir Tristram*, which was engaged in unloading stores. Southby-Tailyour's urgent recommendation that the men be immediately disembarked was rejected by the two company commanders, who wanted to spare the men the march to their ultimate destination, Bluff Cove. Southby-Tailyour offered to transport them after dark by LSU. When the company commanders insisted on no delay in being taken to Bluff Cove aboard *Sir Galahad*, Southby-Tailyour informed them of the extreme danger of doing so in daylight and demanded the alternative of immediate landing and movement on foot via Fitzroy Bridge, a journey of approximately 7 miles.

Under the impression that the presence aboard *Sir Galahad* of 4 Field Troop RE indicated that the bridge at Fitzroy had yet to be repaired and that the march would in fact total 14 miles via Ridge Camp, the company commanders again refused. The bridge repairs were, in fact, already under way. Southby-Tailyour urged disembarkation, using landing craft and the one available **Mexeflote**, then engaged in unloading *Sir Tristram*. The company commanders observed that regulations forbade the movement of troops and ammunition in the same mode of transport, upon which Southby-Tailyour replied that during war peacetime restrictions did not apply and repeated the view that the Guardsmen stood in mortal danger from air attack. References to the fact that majors in the **Royal Marines** carried the equivalent Army rank of lieutenant colonel – thus rendering Southby-Tailyour the senior officer present – did not receive due recognition from the Welsh Guards majors, who refused to follow the direct order of an officer whom they deemed of equal rank to themselves. Southby-Tailyour accordingly returned to shore.

The Welsh Guards company commanders eventually changed their minds, and ordered the men ashore by LCU, the first of which appeared at 1530Z. However, at about 1700Z, *Sir Galahad* was struck by Skyhawks, causing extensive damage to the ship and heavy casualties. Some of the Guardsmen were evacuated by LCU, others by helicopter or lifeboats. The wounded were first laid out on the beach for treatment and then transferred to Fitzroy Community Centre before being triaged and sent on for further treatment where necessary. The Welsh Guards suffered thirty-nine killed and many more wounded, mostly burns.

With half the battalion out of action, it was not capable of leading an attack, even with reinforcements. Accordingly, elements of the Welsh Guards were ordered to act in reserve of the **42 Commando** attack against Mount Harriet. To bring the Welsh Guards up to four-company strength to compensate for the two companies decimated aboard *Sir Galahad*, A and C Companies from **40 Commando** joined it.

As part of 5 Infantry Brigade's plan of attack, after the Scots Guards and **Gurkha Rifles** captured **Mount Tumbledown** and **Mount William**, respectively, the two companies of Welsh Guards – at the time acting as brigade reserve – were to seize **Sapper Hill**, so aiding the Gurkhas' exploitation on to Stanley Common. When on the 10th a company of Gurkhas advanced to **Mount Challenger** as a prelude to an attack on Mount William, they and the Welsh Guards nearly exchanged fire owing to poor radio communications and a failure to co-ordinate their respective movements. One company of the Welsh Guards was delayed for about four hours in a minefield in its attempt to reach Sapper Hill on the 14th, but it was flown in with A and C Companies of 40 Commando, meeting minimal resistance.

The Welsh Guards, together with the Scots Guards, left the Falklands aboard *Norland* on 19 July and arrived at Ascension, from where they flew to RAF Brize Norton on the 29th. Total casualties for the Welsh Guards up to 23 June amounted to thirty-nine killed, twenty-eight wounded, eight injured and one out of action due to illness.

Wessex HAS3/HU5

Although its avionics limited its operational capacity in rough weather or at night, the Westland Wessex HU5 proved itself a hard-working, reliable helicopter, standing up well against the harsh conditions of the South Atlantic in a variety of roles: anti-submarine, troop and logistic support, and communications.

Capable of carrying up to twelve fully armed men, an underslung Land Rover, or 3,500lb of stores, forty of these machines served in the campaign, of which six went down with the *Atlantic Conveyor* and two crashed during the operations to repossess **South Georgia**, where they inserted a **Special Air Service** patrol and later lost two machines trying to extract them. A variation of the HU5, the anti-submarine warfare HAS3, also took part in operations, one aboard *Antrim*, which featured prominently in operations at **South Georgia**, and a second that was destroyed on 12 June on the deck of *Glamorgan* by an **Exocet** missile.

Lieutenant T. Hughes and Chief Petty Officer W.R. Tutty, flying Wessex HU5 XT480 of 847 Naval Air Squadron (NAS), particularly distinguished themselves when on 8 June they assisted a dinghy filled with survivors from *Sir Tristram* drifting back towards the ship's burning stern. By positioning his Wessex between the ship and the dinghy and using the downdraft from his rotor blades, Hughes pushed the boat towards the shore and gave inspiration to other pilots to follow suit in support of other stricken parties.

West Falkland

The smaller of the two main islands, approximately 2,038 square miles, as opposed to East Falkland, which covers about 2,580 square miles. West Falkland is separated from its eastern counterpart by Falkland Sound, with a few isolated communities but most of its inhabitants centred around the settlements of **Port Howard** and **Fox Bay**.

At the strategy meeting held with Admiral **Fieldhouse**, Brigadier **Thompson**, Commodore Clapp and others aboard HMS *Hermes* off **Ascension** on 17 April, Admiral **Woodward** proposed the establishment of a beachhead and construction of an airstrip on West Falkland. **Steveley Bay** on West Falkland figured among the three possible beaches for a landing considered by Clapp and Thompson during the journey to Ascension. In light of Major General **Moore's** directive of 12 May to dominate the Argentines morally and physically, Thompson rejected the idea of a landing on West Falkland since it would involve a second amphibious effort and was fraught with many other problems. West Falkland in this context is perhaps best associated with **Pebble Island**, just to the north, the focus of a **Special Air Service** raid against the airstrip there on the night of 14–15 May.

At first light on 23 May, four **Harriers** attacked the airstrip at Dunnose Head in the belief that it was being used by transport aircraft resupplying flights from the mainland. Four cluster bomb units and six 1,000lb retarded bombs struck their target, although one bomb was inadvertently dropped on the settlement, damaging a number of buildings and injuring two local residents. In fact, the airstrip was not in use by the Argentines.

The island was the scene of many Special Forces insertions by PNG-equipped **helicopters**, which observed Argentine forces and monitored possible attempts at resupply and reinforcement of the garrison there.

On 15 June, the day after General Menéndez capitulated in **Stanley**, B Company **40 Commando** arrived in Port Howard to accept the surrender of the 5th Infantry Regiment, while a **Lynx** from *Avenger* landed a small party at Fox Bay to disarm the 8th Infantry Regiment.

Wideawake Airfield

See Ascension

Wilson, Brigadier Matthew John Anthony 'Tony' OBE

Commanding Officer, **5 Infantry Brigade**, Wilson led the southern thrust across East Falkland, while **3 Commando Brigade** under Brigadier **Thompson** advanced along the northern route to **Stanley**.

Wilson was born on 2 October 1935 into a military family with long connections to the King's Own Yorkshire Light Infantry, into which he was commissioned after leaving Sandhurst in 1956. He later served in Aden, Borneo, Malaya, Northern Ireland and Hong Kong, appointed an MBE in 1971, earning an MC in 1972 for distinguishing himself as a company commander in Ulster, and receiving an OBE the following year. He joined the General Staff in 1989 and was promoted to brigadier on appointment as commander of **5 Infantry Brigade** in the South Atlantic. He travelled south aboard *Queen Elizabeth 2* with Major General **Moore**, Commander, Land Forces Falkland Islands.

Understanding his strategic concept, marred by the disaster to befall the **Welsh Guards** near **Fitzroy**, is perhaps instructive in light of the varied assessments later made of his role in the conflict. On 2 June, without consulting with Moore, Wilson unilaterally opened a southern approach towards Stanley when he dispatched **2 Para** by helicopter to the **Bluff Cove**/Fitzroy area. Faced with a *fait accompli*, Moore accepted this development and agreed immediately to support it.

Wilson's plan now involved the Welsh Guards defending Bluff Cove; the **Scots Guards** to replace D Company, **2 Para** east of Bluff Cove Inlet; and 2 Para concentrating at Fitzroy as Brigade Reserve. 5 Infantry Brigade would then be in a position to move through 3 Commando Brigade in the advance on Stanley to commence on 6 June. In this scenario he initially planned for the Welsh Guards to proceed on foot from **San Carlos**, but when their physical fitness proved wanting for such a task they proceeded by sea.

In the event, the **Scots Guards** arrived at Bluff Cove on 7 June by LCU. Then, with his Tac HQ, Wilson flew from San Carlos to Fitzroy and established his Brigade HQ in a sheep-shearing shed, there agreeing to the suggestion of Lieutenant Colonel Chaundler, CO 2 Para, that the Scots Guards remain at Bluff Cove and that 2 Para return to Fitzroy via the **landing craft** that had brought the Scots Guards.

At a strategy conference aboard *Fearless* on 8 June involving Wilson, Thompson and Moore, Wilson pressed for the southern thrust against Stanley involving his own brigade on a narrow front, as opposed to Thompson's broad front option. As the decimation of the Welsh Guards at **Port Pleasant** that day rendered this approach questionable, leaving as it did only two of the brigade's three battalions fully operational, Moore adopted the broad front approach, although in the event only the Scots Guards saw serious action, at **Mount Tumbledown**.

Unaccountably, Wilson was the only senior officer in the campaign not to receive recognition in the form of honours for his service on Operation **Corporate**, but whether this may be attributed to the disaster suffered by his brigade at Port Pleasant remains speculative. He retired from the Army in January 1983 and took up writing and charity work.

Wimpey Seahorse, MV

One of several dozen **Ships Taken Up From Trade** (STUFT), *Wimpey Seahorse* served in offshore support, but was later employed as a mooring vessel, carrying Naval Party 2000. She departed Devonport on 16 May and reached **Ascension** on the 29th. She served for part of the war at **South Georgia** before arriving back in Falklands waters on 22 July. Her South Atlantic service ended upon her reaching Portsmouth on 4 September.

Commander:	Captain M.J. Slack	
Launched:	1982	
Tonnage:	1,600 Gross Register	2,085 Deadweight
Dimensions: length × beam; feet (metres):	227 × 52 (69.3 × 16)	
Propulsion:	4 diesel engines	11,200 bhp = 15.5 knots

Wireless Ridge

The last elevated feature of the Argentine inner defensive ring just west of **Stanley** and 2 miles north-east of **Mount Tumbledown**, and the scene of a major engagement on 13–14 June, Wireless Ridge was the objective for **2 Para**, the only major unit already to have fought in a principal engagement, at **Goose Green**. Wireless Ridge, in fact, consisted of two separate pieces of high ground, which Lieutenant Colonel David Chaundler, Lieutenant Colonel Jones's successor, decided to attack from the north. Whereas 2 Para had received relatively little fire support at Goose Green, quite the reverse prevailed at Wireless Ridge, with support from two batteries of artillery through the course of the night, other guns available from the **Royal Artillery**, if needed, as well as the firepower of the **frigate** *Ambuscade*, plus additional mortars supplied by **3 Para** and those attached to 2 Para itself. Finally, two **Scorpions** and two **Scimitars** of the **Blues and Royals** were available, capable of offering close support since the ground offered no steep sides. Opposing 2 Para were A and G Companies, 7th Regiment, plus the remnants of B Company that had fought 3 Para on **Mount Longdon**. The defenders had at their disposal snipers, heavy machine guns, mortars and artillery.

Chaundler divided his plan into four phases to include preparatory artillery fire. In the first phase, D Company was to assault 'Rough Diamond', an occupied position slightly to the north of the main objective and north-east of Mount Longdon. In the second phase, A and B Companies were to capture the 250ft 'Apple Pie' position, also north of the main feature. Once 'Rough Diamond' had fallen, D Company would move in the course of phase three to seize the southern section of Wireless Ridge, nicknamed 'Blueberry Pie', from west to east, supported by fire provided by A and B Companies. In the fourth and final phase, C Company would march east before taking the westernmost contour, which rose a mere 100ft above the valley.

Having concluded its march from Furze Bush Pass on the evening of 13 June, 2 Para prepared to assault Wireless Ridge as supporting fire opened on 'Rough Diamond' at 0115Z on the 14th. Half an hour later, D Company left the start line, supported by the Scimitars and Scorpions. On reaching 'Rough Diamond', D Company discovered the defenders, minus a few killed, had withdrawn under the weight of incoming fire, but while the Paras sought to consolidate this newly occupied ground, they themselves became the target of an artillery barrage from 155mm guns. At this point, to the east, A and B Companies began their advance from the start line, suffering in the process one soldier killed by artillery fire. The two companies approached 'Apple Pie' and prepared to engage the defenders, when the Argentines, bowing to the pressure of the combination of artillery, mortar and machine-gun fire directed against their position, withdrew, enabling C Company to occupy Ring Contour 100 rapidly without meeting any resistance.

Moving on from 'Rough Diamond', D Company then proceeded to the western end of Wireless Ridge and prepared to assault across the length of the feature at the same time as the light tanks of the Blues and Royals, situated on 'Apple Pie' with A and B Companies, offered supporting fire, together with the Paras' MILANs and machine guns. D Company succeeded in seizing the first half of the ridge with little effort, but the defenders offered stubborn resistance over the remaining half, with the Paras obliged to clear one bunker after the next. Their advance never faltered, however, and eventually the defence collapsed, leaving D Company in possession of the 300ft ridge. The victors then began to dig in and, as in the wake of other operations conducted that day, the Argentines bombarded their lost position with shellfire through the night. At the same time, 2 Para, perceiving the Argentines regrouping in the area of **Moody Brook** under the cover of darkness, prepared for a possible counter-attack.

As anticipated, at daybreak a small force of Argentines assaulted D Company's position, only to be repulsed by the defenders and their supporting fire from mortars and the 105mm guns of the Royal Artillery. As the sun rose higher, the Argentines fled in the direction of Stanley as 2 Para, having lost two men killed by friendly artillery fire and another through Argentine small arms, urged **Thompson** to allow them to follow up their victory and advance east. Argentine losses may have numbered as high as 100, plus seventeen prisoners.

Woodward, Rear Admiral John Forster 'Sandy', RN

Born on 1 May 1932 at Penzance and educated at Stubbington House School and the Royal Naval College, Dartmouth, Woodward served time in the Home Fleet before training as a submariner in 1954, serving in *Sanguine*, *Porpoise*, and *Valiant*. He passed the submarine command course in 1960 and gained command of the **submarines** *Tireless* and *Grampus*.

He later served as second-in-command of *Valiant* before promotion as her commander. At the end of 1969 he commanded *Warspite* and was promoted to captain in 1972, and Captain of Submarine Training two years later. In 1976 Woodward returned to general service in order to command the Type 42 guided missile destroyer *Sheffield*. He served as Director of Naval Plans from 1978 to 1981, opposing the Strategic Defence Review (also known as the Nott Review) that recommended drastic cuts in the **Royal Navy**, including the loss of many **destroyers** and **frigates**, one of the fleet's **aircraft carriers**, two **amphibious assault**

ships and the ice patrol vessel *Endurance*, all of which would actually serve in the Falklands War.

As Flag Officer First Flotilla, at the end of March 1982 Woodward led Exercise **Springtrain** off Gibraltar with five destroyers. Woodward initially travelled south aboard the destroyer *Glamorgan*, leading the initial **Task Force**, but he transferred his flagship to the aircraft carrier *Hermes* in mid-April.

At a **strategy** meeting held with Admiral **Fieldhouse**, Brigadier **Thompson**, Commodore Clapp and others aboard *Hermes* off **Ascension** on 17 April, Woodward proposed the establishment of a beachhead and construction of an airstrip on **West Falkland** – a plan strongly opposed on grounds that it would require a second amphibious landing on to East Falkland without the benefit of surprise.

As a submariner, Woodward naturally felt most at home making decisions concerning naval affairs; at this he showed himself adept, whereas his grasp of land warfare left something to be desired. In light of a possible land-based Exocet threat from Argentine positions on the Falklands, Woodward ordered a 25-mile exclusion zone south of **Stanley** into which British ships were not to sail. The seaworthiness of his ships after so many weeks at sea ranked high among Woodward's many concerns, as well as the safety of the fleet from air attack, as a consequence of which he generally deployed his carriers and supporting vessels well east of Stanley, safe from attack. Always conscious that deteriorating weather strongly dictated the timing of the campaign, he felt **3 Commando Brigade** spent too much time in the bridgehead at **San Carlos Water** rather than executing the required break-out towards Stanley, ignorant though he was that Thompson could not move without first ensuring the adequate build-up of food, ammunition and other stores.

After the war Woodward served as Flag Officer Submarines and Commander Submarines Eastern Atlantic in 1983–84. His final appointment was as Commander-in-Chief Naval Home Command from 1987 to 1989. He died on 4 August 2013.

Yarmouth, HMS

One of fifteen **frigates** to serve in the South Atlantic, and one of two Type 12s (Rothesay class), her sister ship being HMS *Plymouth*. *Yarmouth* departed Gibraltar on 8 April and arrived at **Ascension** eight days later.

Reaching Falklands waters on 1 May, *Yarmouth*, together with *Brilliant* and three **Sea Kings**, was tasked with investigating the possible presence of an Argentine submarine off the north coast of East Falkland, although in the event nothing was found.

After *Sheffield* was hit by an **Exocet** missile on 4 May, *Yarmouth* mistakenly believed its sonar was tracking the sound of moving torpedoes, prompting her to put her helicopter aloft to drop depth charges while the ship's mortar fired nine rounds. In fact, no Argentine submarine was present.

On 8 May, *Yarmouth* reached the stricken *Sheffield* to the south-east of East Falkland and took the vessel under tow with the prospect of salvaging her. On D-Day, 21 May, *Yarmouth* lay off **Fanning Head**. After *Ardent* was mortally damaged in **San Carlos Water** on that day and had to be abandoned, *Yarmouth* transferred her survivors to *Canberra*, including more than thirty wounded, and later took *Ardent* under tow. The stricken ship, however, exploded and sank off North West Island on the following evening.

Yarmouth was meant to support **3 Commando Brigade's** attack on **Stanley**, which Admiral **Woodward** hoped would take place during the night of 5–6 June. However, after Major General **Moore** postponed this by several days, *Yarmouth*, together with *Cardiff*, remained to ambush Argentine aircraft en route to Stanley.

On 8 June off Lively Island, *Yarmouth* was called to assist the *Monsunen*, whose propeller had snagged with a tow-line meant for the crippled and abandoned LCU Foxtrot Four. *Yarmouth's* divers duly freed the propeller.

On the evening of 11–12 June *Yarmouth* lay on the southern gunline together with *Avenger* and *Glamorgan*, bombarding various positions in support of the ground operations then under way. Together with *Ambuscade*, she fired on **Wireless Ridge** on the night of 13–14 June in support of **2 Para's** attack, as well as against **Mount Tumbledown**, the focus of the **Scots Guards'** attention. *Yarmouth* completed her service in the war upon reaching Rosyth on 28 July.

Commander:	Captain A. Morton	
Builders:	John Brown	
Launched:	23 March 1959	
Commissioned:	26 March 1960	
Displacement (tons):	2,380 Standard	2,800 Full load
Dimensions: length × beam; feet (metres):	370 × 41 (112.8 × 12.5)	
Draught:	5.3m	

Y

Propulsion:	2 sets geared steam turbines	30,000shp = 28 knots
Armament:	2 × 4.5in Mark 6 guns	
	2 × 20mm AA guns	
	1 × **Seacat** system (GWS 20)	
	1 × Limbo ASW Mortar Mark 10	
Aircraft:	1 × **Wasp** HAS1	

Yomp

Royal Marines acronym for 'your own marching pace', the counterpart to the Army **Tab** (tactical advance to battle) and coined in reference to the epic loaded march carried out by **45 Commando**, conducted simultaneously with the march carried out by **3 Para** along a slightly different route after the loss of **helicopters** aboard *Atlantic Conveyor* on 25 May, obliged these units to advance east on foot. With each man carrying at least 100lb, and many carrying 120lb or more, especially those with mortars, machine guns, or anti-tank weapons. 45 Commando left **Port San Carlos** after first light on 27 May, moving over soft boggy peat and large clumps of tussock grass, nicknamed 'babies' heads', slowing progress and in many instances

Royal Marines conducting their famous yomp. (AirSeaLand Photos)

causing ankle or knee injuries. The commando passed New House that night after a 12-mile trek and reached **Douglas** settlement, a further 8 miles, early the next day. They arrived at **Teal Inlet** by 0030Z on 31 May. The distance from Douglas to Teal amounted to 25 miles, covered in thirty-six hours over wet and rough terrain, and resulted in twenty-six leg and foot injuries, requiring the evacuation of six men. With still no helicopters available, 'Four-Five' carried on, leaving Teal Inlet on the 3rd and establishing a patrol base just west of **Mount Kent** by 1700Z on 4 June, completing their epic journey. 'Yomp' and 'yomping' soon entered ordinary British vocabulary after journalists with the **Task Force** introduced them in their press releases.

Yorkshireman, MT

An ocean-going motor tug requisitioned from the United Towing Company on 7 April, *Yorkshireman* numbered among the several dozen **Ships Taken Up From Trade** to serve in the campaign. *Salvageman* and *Irishman* were also requisitioned from the same shipping firm. She departed Portsmouth on 13 April and reached **Ascension** on the 27th. Her service off the Falklands began on 24 May, but *Yorkshireman*'s service did not end until she reached Hull on 23 July 1983.

Commander:	Captain P. Rimmer
Launched:	1978
Tonnage:	686 Gross Register
Dimensions: length × beam; feet (metres):	138 × 38 (42 × 11.6)
Propulsion:	2 diesel engines = 13 knots

Y

APPENDIX A
FURTHER READING

Adkin, Mark. *Goose Green: A Battle is Fought to Be Won*. Phoenix, 2007.

Anderson, Duncan. *The Falklands War 1982*. Osprey Publishing, 2002.

Arthur, Max, ed. *Above All, Courage: Personal Stories from the Falklands War*. Phoenix, 2007.

Attrill, Mark. *Harrier: Inside and Out*. The Crowood Press, 2002.

Aulich, James, ed. *Framing the Falklands War: Nationhood, Culture and Identity*. Open University Press, 1991.

Badsey, Stephen, Havers, Rob and Grove, Mark, eds. *The Falklands Conflict Twenty Years On*. Routledge, 2004.

Banks, Tony. *Storming the Falklands: My War and After*. Abacus, 2012.

Barrington, James. *Falklands: Voyage to War*. Endeavour Press, 2012.

Beaver, Paul. *The British Aircraft Carrier*. Patrick Stephens Ltd, 1982.

Beaver, Paul. *Encyclopedia of the Fleet Air Arm Since 1945*. Patrick Stephens Ltd, 1987.

Beaver, Paul. *Modern Combat Ships 2: Invincible Class*. Ian Allan, 1984.

Benson, Harry. *Scram!: The Gripping First-Hand Account of the Helicopter War in the Falklands*. Preface Publishing, 2012.

Bicheno, Hugh. *Razor's Edge: The Unofficial History of the Falklands War*. Weidenfeld & Nicolson, 2007.

Bilton, Michael and Kosminsky, Peter, eds. *Speaking Out: Untold Stories from the Falklands War*. André Deutsch, 1989.

Bishop, Patrick and Witherow, John. *The Winter War: The Falklands*. Quartet Books, 1982.

Blackman, Tony. *Vulcan Boys: From the Cold War to the Falklands: True Tales of the Iconic Delta V Bomber*. Grubb Street, 2014.

Blakeways, Denys. *The Falklands War*. Sidgwick & Jackson, 1992.

Bound, Graham. *Fortress Falklands: Life under Siege in Britain's Last Outpost*. Pen & Sword Military, 2012.

Bowman, Martin. *Lockheed C-130 Hercules*. Crowood Press, 1999.

Boyce, D. George. *The Falklands War*. Macmillan, 2005.

Bramley, Vince. *Forward into Hell*. John Blake Publishing, 2011.

Bramley, Vince. *Two Sides of Hell*. John Blake Publishing, 2009.

Bransby, Guy. *Her Majesty's Interrogator: Falklands*. Pen & Sword Books, 1995.

Braybrook, Ray. *Battle of the Falklands (3): Air Forces*. Osprey Publishing, 1982.

Braybrook, Ray. *Harrier and Sea Harrier*. Osprey Publishing, 1984.

Brookes, Andrew. *Vulcan Units of the Cold War*. Osprey Publishing, 2009.

Brown, David. *The Royal Navy and the Falklands War*. Leo Cooper, 1987.

Burden, Rodney, et al. *Falklands: The Air War*. Weidenfeld & Nicolson, 1986.

Burns, Jimmy. *The Land that Lost its Heroes: How Argentina Lost the Falklands War*. Bloomsbury, 2012.

Carr, Jean. *Another Story: Women and the Falklands War*. Hamish Hamilton, 1984.

Carrington, Peter. *Reflect on Things Past: The Memoirs of Lord Carrington*. William Collins, 1988.

Chant, Chris. *Air War in the Falklands 1982*. Osprey Publishing, 2001.

Childs, Nick. *The Age of Invincible: The Ship that Defined the Modern Royal Navy*. Pen & Sword Maritime, 2009.

Clapp, Michael and Southby-Tailyour, Ewen. *Amphibious Assault Falklands: The Battle of San Carlos Water*. Pen & Sword Maritime, 2007.

Coates, Tim, ed. *War in the Falklands, 1982*. Uncovered Editions. 2001.

Colbeck, Graham. *With 3 Para in the Falklands*. Greenhill Books, 2002.

Cooksey, Jon. *Falklands Hero: Ian McKay – The Last VC of the 20th Century*. Pen & Sword Military, 2007.

Cooksey, Jon. *3 Para Mount Longdon: The Bloodiest Battle*. Pen & Sword Military, 2004.

Cordesman, Anthony and Wagner, Abraham. *The Lessons of Modern War. Volume III: The Afghan and Falklands Conflicts*. Westview Press, 1991.

Craig, Christopher. *Call for Fire: Sea Combat in the Falklands and the Gulf War*. John Murray, 1995.

Cummings, Colin. *Lost to Service: A Summary of Accidents to RAF Aircraft and Losses of Personnel, 1959 to 1996*. Nimbus, 1998.

Curtis, Mike. *CQB: Close Quarter Battle*. Transworld Publishers, 1998.

Danchev, Alex. *International Perspectives on the Falklands Conflict*. St. Martin's Press, 1992.

Davies, Peter and Thornborough, Anthony. *The Harrier Story*. Arms and Armour Press, 1996.

Devereux, Steve. *Terminal Velocity: His True Account of Front-line Action in the Falklands War and Beyond*. Smith Gryphon, 1997.

Dillon, G.M. *The Falklands, Politics and War*. Palgrave Macmillan, 1989.

Dyson, Tony. *HMS Hermes, 1959–1984*. Maritime Books, 1984.

Edwards, Sidney. *My Secret Falklands War*. Book Guild Publishing, 2014.

Ely, Nigel. *Fighting for Queen and Country: One Man's True Story of Blood and Violence in the Paras and the SAS*. Thistle Publishing, 2015.

English, Adrian. *Battle for the Falklands (2): Naval Forces*. Osprey Publishing, 1982.

Eyles-Thomas, Mark. *Sod That for a Game of Soldiers*. Kenton Publishing, 2007.

Finlan, Alistair. *The Royal Navy in the Falklands Conflict and the Gulf War*. Routledge, 2004.

Fitzgerald, Warren. *All in the Same Boat: The Untold Story of the British Ferry Crew who Helped Win the Falklands War*. John Blake, 2016.

Fitz-Gibbon, Spencer. *Not Mentioned in Despatches: The History and Mythology of the Battle of Goose Green*. James Clarke and Company, 2001.

Fowler, Will. *Battle for the Falklands (1): Land Forces*. Osprey Publishing, 1982.

Fowler, Will. *Royal Marine Commando, 1952–82: From Korea to the Falklands*. Osprey Publishing, 2009.

Franks, Lord. *Falkland Islands Review: Report of a Committee of Privy Councillors. Command Paper 8787*. HMSO, 1983.

Freedman, Sir Lawrence. *The Official History of the Falklands Campaign. Volume I: The Origins of the Falklands War*. Abingdon: Routledge, 2007.

Freedman, Lawrence. *The Official History of the Falklands Campaign. Volume II: War and Diplomacy*. Routledge, 2004.

Freedman, Lawrence and Gamba-Stonehouse, Virginia. *Signals of War*. Faber & Faber, 1991.

Freeman, Richard. *A Close Run Thing: The Navy and the Falklands War*. Endeavour Press, 2012.

Fremont-Barnes, Gregory. *The Falklands 1982: Ground Operations in the South Atlantic.* Osprey Publishing, 2012.

Fremont-Barnes, Gregory. *Goose Green 1982.* The History Press, 2013.

Frost, John. *2 Para Falklands: The Battalion at War.* Sphere, 1988.

Gardiner, Ian. *The Yompers: With 45 Commando in the Falklands War.* Pen & Sword, 2012.

Geddes, John. *Spearhead Assault: Blood, Guts and Glory on the Falklands Frontlines.* Arrow, 2008.

Geraghty, Tony. *Who Dares Wins: The Story of the SAS, 1950–1992.* Little, Brown, 1992.

Godden, John. *Harrier: Ski-jump to Victory.* Brassey's 1983.

Hampshire, Edward. *British Guided Missile Destroyers.* Osprey Publishing, 2016.

Hart Dyke, David. *Four Weeks in May: The Loss of HMS Coventry.* Atlantic Books, 2007.

Hastings, Max and Jenkins, Simon. *Battle for the Falklands.* Pan, 2012.

Higgitt, Mark. *Through Fire and Water: HMS Ardent – The Forgotten Frigate of the Falklands War.* Mainstream Publishing, 2000.

Hilton, Christopher. *Ordinary Heroes: Untold Stories from the Falklands Campaign.* The History Press, 2012.

Hobbs, David. *British Aircraft Carriers.* Seaforth Publishing, 2013.

Hobbs, David. *The British Carrier Strike Fleet After 1945.* Seaforth Publishing, 2015.

Hobson, Chris, with Noble, Andrew. *Falklands Air War.* Midland Publishing, 2008.

Hunt, Rex. *My Falklands Days.* Politico's Publishing, 2002.

Hutchings, Richard. *Special Forces Pilot: A Flying Memoir of the Falklands War.* Pen & Sword, 2009.

Inskip, Ian. *Ordeal by Exocet: HMS Glamorgan and the Falklands War 1982.* Frontline Books, 2012.

Jane's Fighting Ships, 1982–83. Jones & Bartlett Publishers, 1982.

Jennings, Christian and Weale, Adrian. *Green-Eyed Boys: 3 Para and the Battle for Mount Longdon.* HarperCollins, 1996.

Johansen, Alan. *A Great White Whale of a Time During the Falklands War: Memoirs of a Night Steward on board the SS Canberra 1982.* Johansen and Johansen Publications, 2015.

Johnson-Allen, John. *They Couldn't Have Done it Without Us: The Merchant Navy in the Falklands War.* Seafarer Books, 2011.

Jolly, Rick. *Doctor For Friend and Foe.* Conway Maritime Press, 2012.

Kemp, Anthony. *The SAS: The Savage Wars of Peace.* John Murray, 1994.

Kemp, Paul. *The Admiralty Regrets: British Warship Losses of the 20th Century.* Sutton, 1999.

Kinzer Stewart, Nora. *Mates and Muchachos: Unit Cohesion in the Falklands / Malvinas War.* Brassey's, 2002.

Kitson, Linda. *The Falklands War: A Visual Diary.* M. Beazeley and the Imperial War Museum, 1982.

Koburger, Charles. *Sea Power in the Falklands.* Praeger, 1983.

Laming, Tim. *Vulcan Story.* Arms and Armour Press, 1993.

Lippiett, John. *Modern Combat Ships 5: Type 21.* Ian Allan Publishing, 1990.

Lippiett, John. *War & Peas: Intimate Letters from the Falklands War 1982.* Maritime Books, 2007.

Lofthouse, Robert. *A Cold Night in June: Falklands Battle of Mount Longdon.* SDS Publishing, 2013.

Lukowiak, Ken. *A Soldier's Song: True Stories from the Falklands*. Weidenfeld & Nicolson, 2007.

Mackay, Francis with Cooksey, Jon. *Pebble Island: The Falklands War 1982*. Pen & Sword Military, 2007.

Maltby, Sarah. *Remembering the Falklands War: Media, Memory and Identity*. Palgrave Macmillan, 2016.

Marriott, Leo. *Modern Combat Ships 3: Type 42*. Ian Allan, 1985.

Marriot, Leo. *Modern Combat Ships 4: Type 22*. Ian Allan, 1984.

Marriott, Leo. *Royal Navy Aircraft Carriers, 1945–1990*. Littlehampton Book Services, 1985.

Marston, Bob. *Harrier Boys. Volume One: Cold War Through the Falklands, 1969–1990*. Grub Street Publishing, 2015.

McCart, Neil. *County Class Guided Missile Destroyers*. Maritime Books, 2014.

McCart, Neil. *Harrier Carriers. Vol. 1: HMS Invincible*. Fan Publications, 2004.

McManners, Hugh. *Falklands Commando*. Collins, 2014.

McManners, Hugh. *Forgotten Voices of the Falklands: The Real Story of the Falklands War*. Ebury Press, 2008.

McNally, Tony. *Still Watching Men Burn: Fighting the PTSD War*. Tony McNally, 2016.

McNally, Tony. *Watching Men Burn: A Soldier's Story*. Monday Books, 2010.

McQueen, Bob. *Island Base: Ascension in the Falklands War*. Whittles Publishing, 2008.

Meyer, C.J. *Modern Combat Ships 1: Leander Class*. Littlehampton Book Services, 1984.

Middlebrook, Martin. *Argentine Fight for the Falklands*. Pen & Sword Military, 2009.

Middlebrook, Martin. *The Falklands War 1982*. Pen & Sword Military, 2012.

Milburn, I.H. *Falklands War: Get Stuft*. Lulu.com, 2012.

Ministry of Defence. *The Falklands Campaign: The Lessons. Command Paper 8758*. HMSO, 1982.

Ministry of Defence. *Fourth Report from the Defence Committee, Session 1986–87: Implementing the Lessons of the Falklands Campaign, House of Commons Paper 345-I – Report and Appendices, Together with the Proceedings of the Committee*. HMSO, 1987.

Ministry of Defence. *Fourth Report from the Defence Committee, Session 1986–87: Implementing the Lessons of the Falklands Campaign, House of Commons Paper 345-II – Minutes and Evidence and Appendices*. HMSO, 1987.

Monaghan, David. *The Falklands War: Myth and Countermyth*. Palgrave Macmillan, 1998.

Morgan, David. *Hostile Skies: The Battle for the Falklands*. Weidenfeld & Nicolson, 2007.

Morrison, David and Tumber, Howard. *Journalists at War: Dynamics of News Reporting During the Falklands Conflict*. Sage Publications, 1988.

Oakley, Derek. *The Falklands Military Machine*. Spellmount, 2002.

O'Connell, James. *Three Days in June: 3 Para Mount Longdon*. James O'Connell, 2014.

Parker, John. *SBS: The Inside Story of the Special Boat Service*. Headline, 2004.

Parry, Chris. *Down South: A Falklands War Diary*. Penguin, 2012.

Parsons, Michael. *The Falklands War*. Sutton Publishing, 2000.

Perkins, Roger. *Operation Paraquat: The Battle for South Georgia*. Picton Publishing, 1986.

Prebble, Stuart. *Secrets of the Conqueror: The Untold Story of Britain's Most Famous Submarine*. Faber & Faber, 2013.

Preston, Antony. *Sea Combat off the Falklands*. Willow Books, 1982.

Price, Alfred. *Harrier at War*. Ian Allan, 1984.

Privratsky, Kenneth. *Logistics in the Falklands War*. Pen & Sword Military, 2014.

Pugh, Nicci. *White Ship, Red Cross: A Nursing Memoir of the Falklands War*. Melrose Books, 2012.

Ramsey, Gordon. *The Falklands Then and Now*. After the Battle, 2009.

Reynolds, David. *Task Force: The Illustrated History of the Falklands War*. Sutton Publishing, 2002.

Rivas, Santiago. *Wings of the Malvinas: The Argentine Air War over the Falklands*. Hikoki Publications, 2012.

Ross, P.J. *HMS Invincible: The Falklands Deployment*. Royal Navy, 1983.

Rossiter, Mike. *Sink the Belgrano: The Dramatic Hunt for the Argentine Warship*. Bantam Press, 2007.

Seear, Mike. *Return to Tumbledown: The Falklands-Malvinas War Revisited*. Critical, Cultural and Communications Press, 2012.

Seear, Mike. *With the Gurkhas in the Falklands: A War Journal*. Pen & Sword Books, 2002.

Shackleton, Lord. *Falkland Islands Economic Study 1982. Command Paper 8653*. HMSO, 1982.

Smith, Gordon. *Battles of the Falklands War*. Ian Allan Publishing, 1989.

Southby-Tailyour, Ewen. *Exocet Falklands: The Untold Story of Special Forces Operations*. Pen & Sword Maritime, 2014.

Southby-Tailyour, Ewen. *Reasons in Writing: A Commando's View of the Falklands War*. Leo Cooper, 2003.

Strange, Ian. *The Falkland Islands*. David & Charles, 1983.

Sunday Express. War in the Falklands: The Campaign in Pictures. Weidenfeld & Nicolson, 1982.

Thatcher, Margaret. *The Downing Street Years*. HarperCollins, 1993.

Thompson, Julian. *3 Commando Brigade in the South Atlantic 1982: No Picnic*. Pen & Sword Military, 2007.

Thomsen, George. *Too Few Too Far: The True Story of a Royal Marine Commando*. Amberley Publishing, 2012.

Thorp, D.J. *The Silent Listener: Britain's Electronic Surveillance – Falklands 1982*. The History Press, 2012.

Underwood, Geoffrey, ed. *Our Falklands War: The Men of the Task Force Tell Their Story*. Maritime Books, 1983.

Van der Bijl, Nick. *Argentine Forces in the Falklands*. Osprey Publishing, 2012.

Van der Bijl, Nick. *5th Infantry Brigade in the Falklands War*. Pen & Sword Books, 2002.

Van der Bijl, Nick. *Nine Battles to Stanley*. Barnsley: Leo Cooper, 1999.

Van der Bijl, Nick. *Victory in the Falklands*. Barnsley: Pen & Sword Military, 2007.

Vaux, Nick. *March to the South Atlantic: 42 Commando Royal Marines in the Falklands War*. Pen & Sword Maritime, 2007.

Vaux, Nick. *Take that Hill! Royal Marines in the Falklands War*. Brassey's, 1987.

Villar, Roger. *Merchant Ships at War: The Falklands Experience*. Conway Maritime Press, 1984.

Vine, Andrew. *A Very Strange Way to Go to War: The Canberra in the Falklands*. Aurum Press, 2012.

Ward, Sharkey. *Sea Harrier over the Falklands: A Maverick at War*. Weidenfeld & Nicolson, 2007.

Washington, Linda. *Ten Years On: The British Army in the Falklands War*. National Army Museum, 1992.

Way, Peter, ed. *The Falklands Way: The Day to Day Record from Invasion to Victory*, Marshall Cavendish, 1983.

West, Nigel. *The Secret War for the Falklands: The SAS. MI6 and the War Whitehall Nearly Lost*. Warner Books, 1998.

White, Rowland. *Vulcan 607: The Epic Story of the Most Remarkable British Air Attack Since the Second World War*. Corgi, 2007.

Wilsey, John. *H Jones VC: The Life and Death of an Unusual Hero*. Arrow, 2003.

Winton, John. *Signals from the Falklands: The Navy in the Falklands Conflict – An Anthology of Personal Experience*. Leo Cooper, 1995.

Woodward, Sandy. *One Hundred Days: The Memoirs of the Falklands Battle Group Commander*. HarperPress, 2012.

Yates, David. *Bomb Alley, Falkland Islands 1982: Aboard HMS Antrim at War*. Pen & Sword Maritime, 2006.

APPENDIX B

LIST OF SHIPS AND SUBMARINES IN THEATRE

Note: Only vessels that reached or were already serving in the Total Exclusion Zone by 14 June are listed.

Royal Navy Ships and Submarines

Active, HMS	*Cardiff*, HMS	*Hydra*, HMS
Alacrity, HMS	*Conqueror*, HMS	*Intrepid*, HMS
Ambuscade, HMS	*Courageous*, HMS	*Invincible*, HMS
Andromeda, HMS	*Coventry*, HMS	*Leeds Castle*, HMS
Antelope, HMS	*Dumbarton Castle*, HMS	*Minerva*, HMS
Antrim, HMS	*Endurance*, HMS	*Onyx*, HMS
Ardent, HMS	*Exeter*, HMS	*Penelope*, HMS
Argonaut, HMS	*Fearless*, HMS	*Plymouth*, HMS
Arrow, HMS	*Glamorgan*, HMS	*Sheffield*, HMS
Avenger, HMS	*Glasgow*, HMS	*Spartan*, HMS
Brilliant, HMS	*Hecla*, HMS	*Splendid*, HMS
Bristol, HMS	*Herald*, HMS	*Valiant*, HMS
Broadsword, HMS	*Hermes*, HMS	*Yarmouth*, HMS

Royal Fleet Auxiliaries

Appleleaf, RFA	*Blue Rover*, RFA	*Engadine*, RFA
Bayleaf, RFA	*Brambleleaf*, RFA	*Fort Austin*, RFA

Fort Grange, RFA
Olmeda, RFA
Olna, RFA
Pearleaf, RFA
Plumleaf, RFA
Regent, RFA

Resource, RFA
Sir Bedivere, RFA
Sir Galahad, RFA
Sir Geraint, RFA
Sir Lancelot, RFA
Sir Percivale, RFA

Sir Tristram, RFA
Stromness, RFA
Tidepool, RFA
Tidespring, RFA

Royal Maritime Auxiliary Service Ships

Goosander, RMAS
Typhoon, RMAS

Ships Taken Up From Trade

Alvega, MV
Anco Charger, MV
Astronomer, MV
Atlantic Causeway, SS
Atlantic Conveyor, SS
Avelona Star, MV
Balder London, MV
Baltic Ferry, MV
British Avon, MV
British Dart, MV
British Enterprise III, MV
British Esk, MV
British Tamar, MV
British Tay, MV

British Test, MV
British Trent, MV
British Wye, MV
Canberra, SS
Contender Bezant, MV
Eburna, MV
Elk, MV
Europic Ferry, MV
Fort Toronto, MV
Geestport, MV
Iris, CS
Irishman, MV
Lycaon, MV
Nordic Ferry, MV

Norland, MV
Queen Elizabeth 2, RMS
St Edmund, MV
Salvageman, MT
Saxonia, MV
Scottish Eagle, MV
Stena Inspector, MV
Stena Seaspread, MV
Tor Caledonia, MV
Uganda, SS
Wimpey Seahorse, MV
Yorkshireman, MT

Ships Taken Up From Trade for Royal Navy Service

Cordella, HMS
Farnella, HMS

Junella, HMS
Northella, HMS

Pict, HMS

APPENDIX C

AIR ORDER OF BATTLE

Fleet Air Arm (Royal Navy)

Only those units directly involved in the Falklands conflict are included. The number of aircraft indicated represents the total number that served with each unit during the conflict and deployed with the Task Force or to Ascension Island.

737 NAS
HMS *Antrim* and HMS *Glamorgan*
2 × Wessex HAS3

800 NAS
HMS *Hermes*
16 × Sea Harrier FRS1

801 NAS
HMS *Invincible*
12 × Sea Harrier FRS1

809 NAS
HMS *Hermes* and HMS *Invincible*
8 × Sea Harrier FRS1
The squadron was integrated with 800
NAS and 801 NAS

815 NAS
HMS *Alacrity*, HMS *Ambuscade*, HMS
Andromeda, HMS *Antelope*, HMS *Ardent*,
HMS *Argonaut*, HMS *Arrow*, HMS
Avenger, HMS *Brilliant*, HMS *Broadsword*,
HMS *Cardiff*, HMS *Coventry*, HMS
Exeter, HMS *Glasgow*, HMS *Minerva*,
HMS *Penelope* and HMS *Sheffield*
24 × Lynx HAS2

820 NAS
HMS *Invincible*
11 × Sea King HAS5

824 NAS
RFA *Fort Grange* and RFA *Olmeda*
5 × Sea King HAS2A

825 NAS
SS *Atlantic Causeway*, RMS *Queen
Elizabeth 2* and Falklands FOBs
10 × Sea King HAS2A

826 NAS
HMS *Hermes*
11 × Sea King HAS5

829 Squadron
HMS *Active*, HMS *Endurance*, HMS *Hecla*,
HMS *Herald*, HMS *Hydra*, HMS *Plymouth*
and HMS *Yarmouth*
11 × Wasp HAS1

845 NAS
RFA *Fort Austin*, RFA *Resource*, RFA
Tidepool, RFA *Tidespring* and Falklands
FOBs

846 NAS
HMS *Fearless*, HMS *Intrepid*, SS *Canberra*,
MV *Elk*, MV *Norland* and Falklands
FOBs
14 × Sea King HC4

847 NAS
RFA *Engadine*, SS *Atlantic Causeway* and
Falklands FOBs
27 × Wessex HU5

848 NAS
RFA *Olna*, RFA *Regent* and SS *Atlantic
Conveyor*
11 × Wessex HU5

Royal Marines

3 Commando Brigade Air Squadron
HMS *Fearless*, RFA *Sir Galahad*, RFA *Sir Geraint*, RFA *Sir Lancelot*, RFA *Sir Percivale*, RFA *Sir Tristram*, MV *Baltic Ferry*, MV *Europic Ferry*, MV *Nordic Ferry* and Falklands FOBs
10 × Gazelle AH1, 9 × Scout AH1

Army Air Corps

656 Squadron
MV *Baltic Ferry*, MV *Europic Ferry*, MV *Nordic Ferry* and Falklands FOBs
6 × Gazelle AH1, 7 × Scout AH1

Royal Air Force

The Vulcans of 54 and 101 Squadrons were based at RAF Waddington in Lincolnshire and flown to and from Ascension for specific missions. Squadrons composed of other types of aircraft were maintained in theatre.

1 (F) Squadron
HMS *Hermes*
10 × Harrier GR3

18 Squadron
SS *Atlantic Conveyor* and Falklands FOBs
5 × Chinook HC1

24/30/47/70 Squadrons
Wideawake Airfield
Unknown number of Hercules C1/C3

29 Squadron
Wideawake Airfield
3 × Phantom FGR2

42 Squadron
Wideawake Airfield
2 × Nimrod MR1

44/50/101 Squadrons detachment
Wideawake Airfield
4 × Vulcan B2

55 Squadron
Wideawake Airfield
10 × Victor K2

57 Squadron
Wideawake Airfield
10 × Victor K2

120/201/206 Squadrons
Wideawake Airfield
8 × Nimrod MR2

202 Squadron
Wideawake Airfield
1 × Sea King HAR3
2 Wing (HQ) Unit RAF Regiment
15 Field Squadron RAF Regiment
63 Squadron RAF Regiment
1 ACC Radar
Tactical Communications Wing
Tactical Supply Wing
UK Mobile Air Movements Squadron
Ordnance Demolition Unit
Mobile Met Unit
Mobile Catering Support Unit
HQ 38 Group TACP (MAOT)

APPENDIX D

NUMERICAL SUMMARY

British Aircraft Deployed to the South Atlantic and Ascension Island, 2 April to 14 June

Royal Navy		**Army Air Corps**	
Lynx HAS2	24	Gazelle AH1	6
Sea Harrier FRS1	28	Scout AH1	8
Sea King HAS2/2A	16	**Royal Air Force**	
Sea King HAS5	20	Chinook HC1	11
Sea King HC4	14	Harrier GR3	16
Wasp HAS1	11	Nimrod MR1	2
Wessex HAS3	2	Nimrod MR2	8
Wessex HU5	54	Phantom FGR2	3
Royal Marines		Sea King HAR3	1
Gazelle AH1	11	Victor K2	20
Scout AH1	7	Vulcan B2	4
		OVERALL TOTAL	**266**

APPENDIX E

BRITISH AIRCRAFT LOSSES, 2 APRIL TO 14 JUNE

Royal Navy		**Army Air Corps**	
Lynx HAS2	3	Gazelle AH1	1
Sea Harrier FRS1	6	**Royal Air Force**	
Sea King HAS5	2	Chinook HC1	3
Sea King HC4	3	Harrier GR3	4
Wessex HAS3	1		
Wessex HU5	8	**OVERALL TOTAL**	**34**
Royal Marines			
Gazelle AH1	2		
Scout AH1	1		

APPENDIX F

CHRONOLOGY OF BRITISH AIRCRAFT LOSSES

22 April   'C' Flight 845 NAS Wessex HU5s XT464 and XT473. Crashed on Fortuna Glacier, South Georgia, in bad weather.

23 April   846 NAS Sea King HC4 ZA311. Crashed in South Atlantic in bad weather.

4 May   800 NAS Sea Harrier FRS1 XZ450. Shot down at Goose Green by AAA.

6 May   801 NAS Sea Harrier FRS1s XZ452 and XZ453. Missing (probably collided) during CAP south-east of East Falkland.

12 May   826 NAS Sea King HAS5 ZA132. Crashed in sea east of the Falklands due to engine failure.

18 May   826 NAS Sea King HAS5 XZ573. Crashed in sea east of the Falklands due to altimeter failure.

19 May   846 NAS Sea King HC4 ZA290. Force-landed near Punta Arenas, Chile; destroyed by its crew while on a special operation.
846 NAS Sea King HC4 ZA294. Crashed in sea east of the Falklands, probably due to a bird strike.

21 May   'C' Flight 3 CBAS Gazelle AH1s XX402 and XX411. Shot down near Port San Carlos by small arms fire.
1 Squadron Harrier GR3 XZ972. Shot down near Port Howard by Blowpipe.
815 NAS Lynx HAS2 XZ251. Lost when *Ardent* bombed and sunk in Falkland Sound.

23 May   800 NAS Sea Harrier FRS1 ZA192. Crashed into sea after take-off at night from *Hermes*.

25 May   815 NAS Lynx HAS2 XZ242. Lost when *Coventry* was bombed and sunk north of Pebble Island.
815 NAS Lynx HAS2 XZ700, 'D' Flight 848 Squadron Wessex HU5s XS480, XS495, XS499, XS512, XT476 and XT483; 18 Squadron Chinook HC1s ZA706, ZA716 and ZA719. Lost when *Atlantic Conveyor* was hit and sunk by an Exocet missile north-east of the Falklands.

27 May   1 Squadron Harrier GR3 XZ988. Shot down near Goose Green by AAA.

28 May   'B' Flt 3 CBAS Scout AH1 XT629. Shot down near Goose Green by Pucara.

29 May   801 NAS Sea Harrier FRS1 ZA174. Fell into sea from deck of *Invincible* during rough weather.

30 May   1 Squadron Harrier GR3 XZ963. Damaged near Stanley by small arms fire and abandoned off Falklands.

1 June   801 NAS Sea Harrier FRS1 XZ456. Shot down at sea off Stanley by Roland.

6 June   Army Air Corps Gazelle AH1 XX377. Shot down near Mount Pleasant Peak by Sea Dart fired by *Cardiff*.

8 June   1 Squadron Harrier GR3 XZ989. Crashed on landing at Port San Carlos FOB due to engine failure.

12 June   737 NAS Wessex HAS3 XM837. Destroyed by Exocet missile that hit the hangar of *Glamorgan* off Stanley.

APPENDIX G
GROUND FORCES ORDER OF BATTLE

3 Commando Brigade

HQ 3 Commando brigade (Brigadier Julian Thompson RM)
29 Commando Regiment Royal Artillery
29 Battery, 4 Regiment, Royal Artillery
59 Independent Commando Squadron Royal Engineers
40 Commando RM
42 Commando RM
45 Commando RM
2nd Battalion, the Parachute Regiment plus attached units
3rd Battalion, the Parachute Regiment plus attached units
9 Parachute Squadron Royal Engineers
Commando Logistics Regiment RM
3 Commando Brigade HQ and Signals Squadron RM
2 Medium Reconnaissance Troops, B Squadron, the Blues and Royals
T Battery, 12 Air Defence Regiment
Air Defence Troop
1 × Raiding Squadron RM
43 Air Defence Battery, 32 Guided Weapons Regiment, Royal Artillery
Mountain and Arctic Warfare Cadre RM
2, 3 & 6 Section Special Boat Squadron RM
D & G Squadrons, 22nd Special Air Service Regiment
3 × Tactical Air Control Parties
4th Assault Squadron RM
Air Maintenance Group
Rear Link Detachment, 30 Signals Regiment
3 × Mexeflote Detachments, 17 Port Regiment
5 × Landing Ship Logistics Detachments, 17 Port Regiment
3 × Surgical Support Teams
Postal Courier Communications Unit Detachment of 1 PC Regiment
Detachment RAF Special Forces
Detachment 47 Air Despatch Squadron Royal Corps of Transport
Detachment 49 Explosive Ordnance Disposal Squadron, 33 Engineer Regiment
Y Troop Detachment (Communications)
Commando Forces Band (Stretcher-bearers)

5 Infantry Brigade

HQ 5 Infantry Brigade and Signal Squadron (Brigadier Anthony Wilson)
2nd Battalion Scots Guards
1st Battalion Welsh Guards

1/7th Duke of Edinburgh's Own Gurkha Rifles
97 Battery, 4th Regiment, Royal Artillery
HQ 4 Field Regiment, Royal Artillery
21 Air Defence Battery, Royal Artillery
656 Squadron Army Air Corps
16 Field Ambulance, Royal Army Medical Corps
81 Ordnance Company, Royal Corps of Ordnance
5 Infantry Brigade Provost Unit, Royal Military Police
Forward Air Control Party

Other Army Units
49 Field Regiment, Royal Artillery
137 Battery, 40 Regiment, Royal Artillery
16th Air Defence, Royal Artillery
148 Commando Battery
11 Field Squadron, Royal Engineers
33 Engineer Regiment
Military Works Force, Royal Engineers
14th Signals Regiment
202 Signals Squadron
602 Signals Troop (Special Communications)
10 Field Ambulance, Royal Army Medical Corps
2 Field Hospital, Royal Army Medical Corps
Joint Helicopter Handling Support Unit (407 Troop, Royal Corps of Transport)
29 Transport and Movement Regiment, Royal Corps of Transport
91 Ordnance Company, Royal Army Ordnance Corps
421 EOD Company, Royal Army Ordnance
Blowpipe Troop, 43 Air Defence Battery
32 Guided Weapons Regiment, Royal Artillery
9 Parachute Squadron, Royal Engineers
407 Troop, Royal Corps of Transport
16 Field Ambulance, Royal Army Medical Corps
81 Ordnance Company, Royal Army Ordnance Corps
10 Field Workshop, Royal Electrical and Mechanical Engineers
5 Infantry Brigade Platoon of 160 Provost Company, Royal Military Police
8 Field Cash Office, Royal Army Pay Corps
81 Intelligence Section
601 Tactical Air Control Party
602 Tactical Air Control Party

INDEX OF ENTRIES